FOUNDATIONS OF SPORT MANAGEMENT

Other Titles in the Sport Management Library

Case Studies in Sport Marketing

Developing Successful Sport Marketing Plans, 2nd Edition

Developing Successful Sport Sponsorship Plans, 2nd Edition

Economics of Sport

Ethics & Morality in Sport Management

Financing Sport, 2nd Edition

Fundamentals of Sport Marketing, 2nd Edition

Media Relations in Sport

Sport Facility Management: Organizing Events and Mitigating Risks

Sport Governance in the Global Community

Sport Management Field Experiences

FOUNDATIONS OF SPORT MANAGEMENT

Andy Gillentine, PhD
UNIVERSITY OF MIAMI

R. Brian Crow, EdD
SLIPPERY ROCK UNIVERSITY

Editors

Fitness Information Technology
A Division of the International Center
for Performance Excellence
262 Coliseum, WVU-PE, PO Box 6116
Morgantown, WV 26506-6116

Library of Congress Card Catalog Number: 2005927597

ISBN: 1-885693-61-3

Production Editor: Corey Madsen
Typesetter: Jamie Merlavage
Proofreader: Jessica McDonald
Cover Design: Jamie Merlavage
Indexer: Corey Madsen
Printed by Sheridan Books
Cover photo ©2005, SportsChrome Inc. All rights reserved.

10   9   8   7   6   5   4   3   2

Fitness Information Technology
A Division of the International Center for Performance Excellence
262 Coliseum, WVU-PE, PO Box 6116
Morgantown, WV 26506-6116
304.293.6888 phone
304.293.6658 fax
Email: icpe@mail.wvu.edu
Website: www.fitinfotech.com

Table of Contents

Acknowledgments

The completion of a project such as this is the result of the efforts and sacrifices of many people. I would like to recognize the chapter authors for their work and passion for this project; the faculty and staff of the University of Miami for their constant and unwavering support during this project; and to the many students who served as the inspiration for the development of this text.

I also want to thank Corey Madsen, editor at Fitness Information Technology, for his patience, persistence, and understanding for a new book author during the development and publication of this text.

Finally, I wish to acknowledge my wife Glenna, for her patience and support for the duration of this project. Thanks for being a great sounding board for good ideas and bad ones and loving me enough to tell which ones were which and when to quit talking and get back to work.

AG

To my colleagues and friends at Slippery Rock University, especially Robin Ammon and Catriona Higgs, whose support, guidance, and friendship have been instrumental in my development. To Kirsty, whose Level-5 friendship has been inspiring. To my students at Slippery Rock University—thanks for keeping me focused. A special thank you to my co-editor Dr. Andy Gillentine, whose leadership on this project has kept us on task and on time. Let's do this again soon.

RBC

Dedication

This book is dedicated to my father Frank Gillentine, who embodied the meaning of hard work, ethical behavior, love of family, and an understanding of all that sport has to offer. I appreciate and miss you every day.

AG

To Samuel and Hannah. You are the light of my world.

RBC

Guest Foreword

My theory is that sport management was invented 50,000 years ago when Neanderthals battled mammoths with stones and spears.

Men, women, and children would gather around and watch. Sometimes the Neanderthals won and sometimes the mammoths won. It was an exciting spectacle with tons of body contact.

I imagine that one day a slightly more evolved Neanderthal, who was sitting out the season with a torn knee ligament and had lots of time to think, got a brilliant idea:

"Hey, maybe we should charge admission."

Next thing you know, the Neanderthals were organizing teams and hiring coaches and setting up vendors ("Yo, raw meat! Get yer raw meat here!") and selling merchandise and promoting the events in the media.

The Mammoth Games probably weren't huge moneymakers, but player salaries back then were a fraction of what they are today, so the overhead was less.

Since those times, there have been brief periods where sport management has tapped into the public's fascination with athletes—the Olympians in ancient Greece, the gladiators in Rome, those knucklehead jousters in Europe.

But it's only been within the last few decades that sports have crossed the threshold into Big Business.

I first became aware that something big was happening when I was a sports editor back in the 1980s. I was fresh out of journalism school and working for *The Maui News*. (Yeah, I know. Tough gig. I covered Hawaiian canoe races, surfing contests, the NFL Pro Bowl, tennis tournaments. Once, after a match in Lahaina, I asked John McEnroe a really stupid question and his answer was "That's a really stupid question.")

A perfect storm was brewing in sports. There were brilliant athletes such as Joe Montana, Magic Johnson, Larry Bird, and Wayne Gretzky. ESPN was born. Monday Night Football was in its glory days. Marketing geniuses turned player endorsements into multimillion dollar deals and team brands into a merchandising bonanza.

It all converged and suddenly it wasn't enough to just say, "OK, everyone get out there and kill a mammoth—and have fun!"

Sport management ascended into the Big Leagues.

Everyone got real serious about business, but you know what? Somehow we forgot about the game.

Player egos soared along with their salaries. Ticket prices doubled, tripled, quadrupled. Bench-clearing brawls, once an annoying quirk of hockey, spread to baseball, basketball, and football. Even fans lost their playfulness and found ever more blatant ways to disrupt games.

I started the "In the Bleachers" cartoon in 1985 for two reasons. First, I needed the money. Journalists don't get lucrative shoe endorsement deals. And second, I wanted to create a sports feature that would deliver this message to a world gone crazy over sports:

Lighten up. It's just a game.

If after reading *Foundations of Sport Management* you decide that this is the career for you, please do yourself a favor. Every now and then, walk out of your office and look down onto the field or the court or the rink or the mammoth arena. Take a deep breath. Look around. Think back to when you were a kid and the games were just games.

Then go back into your office and crunch numbers and sign contracts and deal with the media and fire the peanut vendor.

You'll have a lot more fun.

Steve Moore
"In the Bleachers" creator

Foreword

While there has been considerable discussion about the growth in the number of sport management programs since 1980, what is more impressive to me is the growth of the knowledge base and academic resources available in the field. When I first came to the University of Louisville as an assistant professor in the mid-1990s, I was assigned five different courses to teach. Among those five courses, there was a textbook available for only one, and that textbook was only a few months old. In other words, if I had the same schedule a year earlier, I would have been 0 for 5. At that point, the possibility that those of us teaching sport management would be able to choose a book that was best for our course and our students seemed a distant dream; if there was one textbook in the area, we were generally thrilled to have it and quickly adopted it.

In recent years, this has changed. The field has produced a much larger number of textbooks and more books for each course topic. *Foundations of Sport Management* is the newest option for those given the task of teaching undergraduate introduction to sport management courses at their institution. It is also a valuable resource for those who are simply looking to find out more about the field of sport management.

I commend the books editors, Dr. Andy Gillentine and Dr. Brian Crow, for adding to the available options. I believe they have done an excellent job of focusing on the fundamentals of a good sport management textbook. They used the Sport Management Program Review Council's standards as a guide and were sure to include the traditional sport management topic areas (e.g., sport marketing, sport finance, sport economics, sport governance, management and leadership in sport). They provide a solid introduction to each of the topic areas, which will prepare students for further study in any sport management program. The authors blend theoretical foundations and practical implications together throughout the book and provide students with some of the most recent examples.

However, the editors have also taken their own approach to providing the fundamentals. They clearly wanted to make a book that was enjoyable for undergraduate students to read and easy for instructors to use. Their focus from the very beginning was to present the material in a way that would make students excited about the field and get them to want to learn more, without being unrealistic about the challenges of working in the sport industry. They then targeted a group of authors who they believed could present the material in this way. The editors clearly focused on identifying emerging leaders in our discipline who are effective at inducing passion for the field. I believe that the approach taken by Dr. Gillentine, Dr. Crow, and their hand-picked authors will be appealing to those who are teaching undergraduate introduction to sport management courses and many will find this book is good for "their course and their students." It will also be a valuable resource to many who are teaching in this field.

I am honored to have been asked to write the foreword to this book, and I truly appreciate the contributions of those involved with the book to the field of sport management.

Daniel F. Mahony
Assistant University Provost
Professor of Sport Administration
University of Louisville

Preface

For the Educator

The dramatic growth of the sport industry over the last 25 years has given many individuals the initiative to seek a career in this dynamic industry. In order to prepare these future sport administrators, it is important that educators continue to monitor and adjust educational programs and professional preparation needs. This text is designed to provide an initial introduction to the sport industry to those students interested in a career in sport. In order to have an opportunity to succeed in this industry, it is important that the future administrator moves beyond water cooler or ESPN SportsCenter discussions and recognize the multiple and often complex components of the sport industry.

This text is written in a contemporary manner to enhance comprehension and to minimize the shock factor for those examining the sport industry for the first time. The contents of the text were designed to address the core competencies identified by the North American Society of Sport Management and the National Association of Sport and Physical Education. It is the goal of the editors to briefly introduce each of the core competencies and instill a sense of excitement in the student regarding each subject. We hope that the reader will leave each chapter with a feeling of "That's cool! I'd like to know more about this!"

Each chapter is designed to both inform and entertain the student. Cartoons from the popular comic strip "In the Bleachers" by Steve Moore have been used to make the text more enjoyable for students than the ordinary type-filled pages they might have come to expect from regular college textbooks, and to perhaps match, if only in some small way, some of the passion and excitement they might feel for the subjects of sport and sport management. Additionally, supportive quotes from a variety of sources are used to introduce areas of importance. Key words are highlighted in each chapter to help emphasize main points and important terminology. Review questions are supplied at the conclusion of each chapter to help the student master the material provided.

It is our hope that instructors will appreciate the availability of PowerPoint presentation for each chapter. The slides are designed to allow for simple modification by individual instructors. A comprehensive test bank has also been made available for instructors and consists of a wide variety of objective questions.

Too often textbooks fail to identify their targeted audience and consequently try to be everything for everyone, from the casual reader to the Ph.D. student. The authors of this text have chosen to target undergraduate students, and this book is written to address that specific audience. The intent of this text is not to teach individual subjects in their entirely, but simply to introduce them and generate interest and understanding in continued study of the sport industry. Each of the selected chapter authors was selected as a recognized expert in their area and represents the next generation of sport industry authorities.

For the Student

You are about to embark on the study of one of the most dynamic, exciting, and visible industries in the world today. Throughout your academic career, you will be exposed to a variety of topics, career options, and issues to research; embrace them, and become passionate about your study of sport management. Oftentimes in sport, there are hundreds of applicants for a single job—what will make your resume stand out? As you read this, think of the classmates in your Introduction to Sport Management class. What makes you different? You can distinguish yourself by understanding and applying the principles found in this text, along with gaining practical experience in a variety of sport settings. Best wishes as you embark on your academic study of the sport industry.

Chapter One

Introduction to the Sport Industry

Andy Gillentine and R. Brian Crow

Learning Objectives

Upon completion of this chapter, the reader should be able to

- Understand the growth of the sport industry;

- Describe the growth of the academic study of sport;

- Identify the myths surrounding the sport industry;

- Discuss the unique features of the sport industry; and

- Elaborate on the challenges of selecting a career in the sport industry.

Cost of an average college degree in sport management	$ 42,000

Number of weeks you will work nights and weekends in this industry	52

Percentage of friends who will ask for free tickets	100%

Seeing your stadium full of cheering fans despite a poor record	*Priceless*

Welcome to the Sport Industry!

©Media Focus LLC

Introduction

The sport industry today represents the 4th largest growth industry in the United States and the 11th fastest growing industry in the world (Pitts & Stotlar, 2002; Sports Business Journal, 2003). This accelerated growth has fueled the desire of many people to pursue a career in the sport industry. Thousands of students each year, in the U.S. and abroad, enter academic programs specializing in the study of sport management to prepare for a future in sport.

In addition to the rapid growth of the sport industry, the nature of sport business has changed as well. Sport is now a major component of the entertainment industry, competing for the discretionary income of fans world-

> "SPORT IS NOT SIMPLY ANOTHER BIG BUSINESS. IT IS ONE OF THE FASTEST GROWING INDUSTRIES IN THE U.S., AND IT IS INTERTWINED WITH VIRTU-ALLY EVERY ASPECT OF THE ECON-OMY—FROM THE MEDIA AND APPAREL TO FOOD AND ADVERTISING . . . SPORTS IS EVERYWHERE, ACCOMPANIED BY THE SOUND OF A CASH REGISTER RINGING INCESSANTLY."
>
> MICHAEL OZANIAN

wide. Gone are the days of collecting gate receipts in "cigar boxes" (Gillentine, 2004). Sport is now a multi-billion-dollar industry and growing. This increases the need for sound administrative and business practices and for individuals specifically educated for the unique nature of the sport industry.

Why a Career in Sport?

Before launching into a college degree program and professional career in sport, individuals should fully understand the commitment and dedication required for success in this field. In order to evaluate their current status, it is important to answer the most basic of Socratic questions, *"Why?"*

Probably the most common answer to this question is *"I love sports!"* While it is important to have a passion for your work, a love of sports is probably not enough to ensure a happy and productive career in the sport industry. Upon entering the sport profession, this "love of sport" becomes a job and, like all jobs, will have its good moments and bad. If your motivation also includes "getting to watch lots of games," your time and money may be better spent purchasing a 52-inch Plasma TV. When you choose sport as a career, you will be preparing for the upcoming event while others are tailgating in the parking lot; most likely you will be working during game time, in addition to several hours after the event. Your passion has now become your occupation. Helping others enjoy watching the event while you earn your paycheck is the reality.

Another common answer is *"I hope to rub elbows with the rich and famous."* While you may have greater access to well known athletes and coaches, don't be misled in thinking they will be your new lunch buddies. Frequently entry-level sport managers find themselves disappointed after meeting the "star player" of their new employer. According to David Sampson, President of Florida Marlins, "Quite often you will find these guys are immature, overpaid, and over indulged, just because they can throw hard" (Sampson, 2004).

Others enter the sport industry with dollar signs in their eyes. The sport media is full of stories chronicling the astronomical salaries and monies generated in the sport industry. While it is true that a lucrative living can be made in the sport business, the reality is few in sport administration receive those salaries. The vast fortunes of the owners of today's professional sport franchises were typically made outside of the sport industry. Don't be disappointed, though; a comfortable living can be made in sport management . . . but individuals must be prepared and patient to work toward that level of compensation (see Chapter 14 & 15).

Opportunities in Sport: Myth and Reality

The sport industry is subject to a high level of public scrutiny. Daily fans evaluate every move made not only by the players on the field, but also by the executives directing the organization. This constant evaluation, however, does not ensure the credibility of those making the evaluation. Therefore many "myths" regarding the sport industry flourish (additional myths are also discussed in various chapters). Many of these myths focus on the potential for a career in the sport industry. Most of these myths are based on antiquated ideas and/or dated information, while others merit

closer analysis because they also infuse accurate information but are presented in a questionable context. Listed below are some of the most frequently cited myths, compiled from a variety of sources regarding seeking a career in the sport industry.

1) Opportunities are limited and the field is saturated with applicants.

It seems almost paradoxical to state that sport is the 4th fastest growing industry and in the next breath state that opportunities are limited. While obviously there are not an unlimited number of jobs available in the sport industry, there are, in fact, jobs available. In order to be successful in the sport industry, individuals must be mobile. Opportunities in sport are found in locations ranging from New York City to Waco, Texas, to Seattle, Washington, and all points in between. Individuals wishing to enter the sport industry must be willing to "go where the jobs are." Often people are too myopic in their vision of where they are willing to work, and therefore limit their access to jobs. With regard to over-saturation of the job market, most administrators will agree there are never enough qualified applicants for positions, while there are always too many unqualified ones. It is important for individuals to appropriately prepare and position themselves to become attractive to potential employers.

2) Short-term opportunities are not worthwhile.

One of the quickest and most effective ways to enter the sport industry is through internships (see Chapter 14). Quite often these positions are designed to be seasonal or short-term. They do, however, provide the individual with the experience necessary to apply for better full-time opportunities as they arise. Often individuals will fill multiple short-term internships in order to gain valuable experience and to begin networking in the sport industry. Do not be discouraged from accepting positions that initially

Photo by Don Whitaker, courtesy of ©stock.xchng iv

indicated a specific beginning and ending date. View these opportunities as a chance to gain new skill and to showcase your abilities.

3) Opportunities for minorities are limited.

While the number of minorities holding high-ranking sport industry positions is verifiably low, these numbers are changing (Lapchick, 2004). As more and more minorities decide to pursue a managerial career in the sport industry and prepare themselves for that career, we will see a marked change in the demographic make-up of sport managers. The process is and will be slower than any of us desire, but the sport industry has always been willing to allow individuals the opportunity to pursue this career option, and it is often more willing than the rest of society to judge a person on their successes rather than on their race, ethnicity, or gender. Becoming successful in a management position in the sport industry requires the same skills athletes must have to succeed: dedication, commitment, and a willingness to work harder than your competitors. (Further exploration of this topic will be found in Chapter 2.)

Despite the continued existence of these myths, the sport industry does offer many exciting, challenging, and rewarding positions for those deciding to pursue this career path. Managerial challenges in the sport industry may be compared to completing a crossword puzzle. You can clearly see the problem that needs to be solved; there is at least one clue to help identify the best possible answer; the answer's position in relationship to the entire situation is evident; and once the answer is found, immediate gratification is mentally and visually present.

The Evolution of Sport Management Education

"MEN DO NOT QUIT PLAYING BECAUSE THEY GROW OLD; THEY GROW OLD BECAUSE THEY QUIT PLAYING."

OLIVER WENDELL HOLMES

Projections that by the end of the 20th century the GNP for the sport industry would consume more than $121 billion proved to be entirely too conservative (Rosner, 1989; Meek, 1997; Pitts, 2001). Actual estimates indicate the figure during that time period well exceeded $200 billion (SBJ, 2003; Pitts & Stotlar, 2002). As employment opportunities in the sports industry have grown, the need for training of sport professionals has received much attention. Universities have quickly tried to develop sport management curricula at the graduate and undergraduate levels to fill the need for professionals trained specifically in sport management/administration. The number of universities offering sport management curriculums has increased from 1 to approximately 200 in the past 40 years (Stier, 2003).

As the interest and participation in sport have grown to all-time highs, so has the need for professional preparation of sport managers and administrators. Large numbers of undergraduates and sport professionals are rapidly returning to the campus to take discipline-specific courses to improve the current or potential employment opportunities (Parkhouse, 1996). The impetus for the development of a sport administration academic program developed when Walter O'Malley (of the Brooklyn Dodgers) urged University of Miami (FL) educator James Mason to imagine the effectiveness of individuals specifically trained to deal with the business of the growing sport industry (Mason, Higgins, & Owens, 1981).

> "I ask the question, where would one go to find a person who by virtue of education had been trained to administer a marina, race track, ski resort, auditorium, stadium, theatre, convention or exhibit hall, a public camp complex, or a person to fill an executive position at a team or league level in junior athletics such as a Little League baseball, football, scouting, CYO, and youth activities, etc . . . A course that would enable a graduate to read architectural and engineering plans; or having to do with specifications and contract letting, the functions of a purchasing agent in plant operations. There would be problems of ticket selling and accounting, concessions, sale of advertising in programs, and publications, outdoor and indoor displays and related items . . ." (Mason et al., 1981, p. 44)

From this modest and carefully orchestrated beginning, sport management and sport administration programs have grown rapidly throughout the United States and the world. While the University of Miami may claim to be the "birthplace of sport management education," the curriculum proposed by Mason in 1957 was considered "ahead of its time" and was not implemented by the Coral Gables institution (Sawyer, 1993). Mason started the first graduate program in Sport Administration at Ohio University in 1966. Ironically, Biscayne College, now known as St. Thomas University, located only 15 miles from the University of Miami campus, became the first university to establish an undergraduate program in sport administration (Masterlexis, Barr, & Humms, 2005). The state of Florida remains a leader in sport management education with no fewer than 18 colleges and universities offering academic programs (SportsBusiness Journal, 2004). The Miami-Dade public schools have even established a special academic program for high school students wishing to pursue a career in the sport industry (One Community One Goal Annual Report, 2004).

The expansion of academic programs was not confined to only undergraduate and master's degree programs. Results of a study completed in 1996 showed that no fewer than 22 universities offered doctorate programs with at least an emphasis area in sport administration and/or sport management (Gillentine & Crow, 1996). Despite this finding, sport administration/management academic programs struggle to find enough discipline-specific trained professionals to fill their faculty needs (Mahony, Mondello, Hums, & Judd, 2004).

The rapid development of sport management graduate programs occurred through the independent efforts of various universities throughout the country. The lack of coordination between schools caused a fragmentation in the development of programs. Each university or department was free to establish its own

---

Table 1.1 NASSM/NASPE Core competencies for undergraduate programs

1. **Socio-Cultural Dimensions in Sport** – Enables the student to recognize that sport is a microcosm of society and is influenced by cultural traditions, social values, and psychosocial experiences.

2. **Management Leadership and Organization in Sport** – Enables the student to define and understand the concepts of management and leadership in sport.

3. **Ethics in Sport Management** – Students should be able to recognize and identify moral issues related to sport in its intrinsic and extrinsic dimensions.

4. **Marketing in Sport** – The student will be able to apply fundamental marketing concepts to the sport industry.

5. **Communication in Sport** – Students will become familiar with the principles of interpersonal communication, mass communication, and interaction with the public as they relate to the sport industry.

6. **Budget and Finance in Sport** – The student will understand why budget and finance ins sport is a critical component of all sport related industries.

7. **Legal Aspects of Sport** – The student will become familiar with the legal concept in those areas that they are likely to encounter in the sport workplace.

8. **Economics in Sport** – The student will obtain an understanding of economic principles and their application in the sport industry.

9. **Governance in Sport** – The student will be familiar with various governing agencies in sport and examine their authority, organizational structure, and function.

10. **Field Experiences in Sport Management** – The student will benefit from a culminating in-depth practical experience, bridging the gap between classroom learning and practical application in the sport industry.

(NASPE/NASSM, 1993)

priorities and areas of emphasis (NASPE/NASSM, 1993). The sport management/administration programs were established and housed in different departments (general business, physical education, management, etc.) according to university preference (Bridges & Roquemore, 1992).

The Sport Management Arts and Science Society (SMARTS), a group organized at the University of Massachusetts, Amherst, first examined this curricular fragmentation (Masteralexis et al., 2005). From the initial explorations of the SMARTS organization, greater emphasis was placed on the academic credibility of graduate sport management programs. The recognized need for a standardized review of sport management curricula and programs prompted the formation of the North American Society of Sport Management (Parkhouse, 1996).

The National Association for Sport and Physical Education (NASPE) organized a Sport Management Task Force in 1986 to begin the development of standardized core competencies. The NASPE task force formed a partnership with the North American Society for Sport

Management (NASSM) to further explore and develop the standardized core requirements for sport management programs. The recommended standards established by the joint task force identify minimum competencies that should exist in undergraduate and graduate sport management programs. Standards were also established identifying the minimum number of course offerings and faculty needed to offer a program. The Sport Management Program Review Council (SMPRC) was created through the NASPE/NASSM task force to help universities "attain and maintain excellence in undergraduate and graduate education for sport management" (NASPE/ NASSM, 1993). The SMPRC reviews programs volunteering for the approval process through use of the identified criteria and evaluates the program curriculum by area and as a whole.

The development of minimum program requirements and the move toward standardization are the first steps to establish credible sport administration and sport management curriculums. The failure to properly train and prepare managers and administrators is the number one cause of management failure today. Over ninety-eight percent of managers are placed in positions for which they have not been properly trained (Bridges et al., 1992). To help ensure that sports professionals do not follow the same pattern of failure, it is imperative to continue developing quality sport management programs. Currently only 28.6 percent of approximately 220 sport management programs have received approval from the SMPRC (see Figure 1.1). In order for the sport industry to maintain consistent educational and preparation standards, it is important that universities recognize and implement the recommended standards, ultimately leading to program approval.

What's the Deal with the Name?

The rapid development of sport management academic programs also created another point of confusion within the industry . . . the name. Individuals examining sport management academic programs will find them listed under a variety of different titles. The most common names for academic programs are either sport(s) management or sport(s) administration. While most professionals agree that the particular name of the program is much less important than program course

Figure 1.1 SMPRC Approved Sport Management Programs as of spring 2005

Undergraduate	33
Graduate	26
Doctoral	4

©Media Focus LLC

content, it is important to understand why there are differences in *sport* and *sports, management* and **administration**. The early academic programs in sport were frequently housed in departments of physical education. Therefore, the programs were referred to as *sports* management or *sports* administration. The term "*sports*" typically refers to separate sports activities such as football, baseball, etc. The implication, then, is that *sports* management would therefore encompass only the management of these sports activities. *Sport*, on the other hand, offers a more universal description of the variety of activities and occurrences in the sport industry as a whole. These activities may include planning, organizing, and controlling sport programs (discussed in Chapter 4). Parks and Quarterman (2002) offer a clarifying analogy by surmising that the difference between sport and sports is similar to the difference between religion and religions. While religions refer to the different beliefs and denominations (i.e., Catholic, Baptist, Jewish, Muslim, etc.), religion is a broader term that encompasses leadership, belief, operation, and function.

The variance between the use of administration or management also traces it origins to its original home department. The term *administration* was typically associated with those programs and individuals working in the public sector, such as high school or university athletic directors. Since many early programs were housed in physical education departments, the use of this term seemed most logical. The term *management* was typically associated those organizations and individuals working in the private sector. As graduates of those early programs often saw a larger job market available in educational settings, many programs adopted the term *administration* in their name. Regardless of the name, the true test of an academic degree lies in the program content.

Unique Aspects of the Sport Industry

The need for discipline-specific academic preparation for the sport industry is magnified by the uniqueness of several primary features included in the discipline. While at an elementary level these features are similar to skills needed in other business ventures, closer analysis clearly identifies how this industry differs from others. Mullin (1980) first identified three unique features of sport management: marketing, finance, and career paths. Parks et al. (2002) suggest that the social influence of sport was an additional unique feature of this industry. In addition to these unique features, we believe that the customer base (fans) and the venues also separate the sport industry from other business enterprises.

Marketing

The marketing aspects of sport offer a great many challenges to the sport professional. Not only does the sport marketer have to clearly identify who the customer is, it is also necessary to recognize where the customer will consume the product. Unlike many products, the same sport product may be consumed in multiple ways simultaneously. Additionally, the sport product is commonly produced and consumed at the same time, offering the marketer little room for adjustment. The specifics of the unique features of sport marketing are covered in Chapter 7.

Finance

A brief overview of sport finance will quickly indicate the unique components of this industry. Few industries generate the multiple sources of revenue that the sport product does. In many instances, more revenue is generated for these alternate revenue streams than from the core product itself. The sport product also differs from other industries in that multiple forms of business enterprise (corporations, partnerships, sole proprietorships, and non-profits) exist within the same environment. Additional detailed explanations of these varied financial and economic differences will be offered in Chapter 6.

Career Paths

As the sport industry continues to mature and evolve, new positions and job descriptions will emerge. There are few areas of career emphasis that are not currently available through the various branches of the sport industry. In addition to the emergence of new positions in the sport industry, the current trend toward diversification of the sport industry workforce will continue. The move toward diversification will generate additional positions for underrepresented groups throughout the sport industry. Future changes in technology will only serve to launch new positions within the industry.

Social Influence of Sport

In order to view the social impact of sport, one only needs to attend a sporting event and observe the myriad of emotions and actions of the crowd. Not only will they support their chosen team, they will suffer with them if they are not successful. Fans demonstrate their emotional and psychological attachment to the event; they will also show their involvement through the purchase of ancillary items from the sport product. From the playing fields to the water cooler, sport is pervasive throughout our country. In 2004, the U.S. was blanketed with a sea of yellow wristbands, indicating support for Lance Armstrong and others who had battled cancer. What started as a small show of support soon became a national phenomenon. These social implications of sport will be discussed in greater detail in Chapter 2.

Customer Base (Fans)

Fans (customers) are yet another consideration that adds to the unique aspects of the sport industry. Rarely is such an intense sense of loyalty found in other industries. Sport fans also often exhibit intense levels of identification with the sport product, which makes them feel psychologically connected to a team (Wann, Merrill, Russell, & Pease, 2001). This connection is not deterred by poor seasons or regional location, which allows for expansion of the sport product. Fans also add to the uniqueness of the sport product in that they can influence potential revenue streams of the sport organization in a variety of ways outside of consumption of the core product. Team names and logos are present on almost any product imaginable and purchased by fans. While loyal customers may have strong feelings regarding a particular consumer good, rarely do you find them painted in corporate colors cheering for their favorite detergent!

Sport Venues

Lastly, the venues in which sport events take place further separate sport from most industries. Most often an industry operates in a single setting that typically offers a quite controlled environment. The sport industry, however, produces and displays its product in a variety of settings that are subject to a variety of external influences. The sport product may also be consumed in a variety of venues at the same time. This consumption can take place at the stadium or arena, the consumer's home, a sports bar or restaurant, on a radio, or even via the internet. While the sport manager may not be able to control these environments, he/she must recognize the impact they may have on the sport product. The sport manager must also recognize the potential impact that the venue has on customer satisfaction with the sport product.

Summary

The sport industry is a dynamic, exciting, and visible field for career opportunities and academic study. Ultimately, your mastery of the field will provide you with the opportunity to advance beyond entry-level work to a rewarding career. As you look back at the information in this chapter regarding the growth of sport and the study of sport management, think of ways you can improve upon the body of knowledge contained herein. You represent the future of the sport industry, and therefore are responsible for knowing the history and fundamentals of the field, as well as building upon it for the future.

Discussion Activities

1. What are some of the myths surrounding employment in the sport industry? Why do they continue to exist?

2. Identify and discuss the unique aspects of the sport industry.

3. What professional opportunities are available in the sport industry?

4. Explain the differences between sport and sports, and management and administration.

References

Boucher, R. L. (1998). Toward achieving a focal point for sport management: A binocular view. *Journal of Sport Management, 12*, 76-85.

Bridges, J. B., & Roquemore, L. L. (1992). *Management for athletic/sport administration*. Decatur, GA: EMS.

Cuneen, J., & Sidwell, J. (1998, Winter). Evaluating and selecting sport management undergraduate programs. *The Journal of College Admissions*, 6-13.

Gillentine, A. (2004). "Moving mountains" encouraging a paradigm shift in sport administration/management. Paper presented at the Annual Convention of the Florida Alliance of

Health, Physical Education, Recreation, & Dance. Oct. 13. Orlando, FL.

Gillentine, A. (2000). The evolution of sport administration/management graduate programs. *MAHPERD Journal.* 4(1), 7-10.

Gillentine, A., & Crow, B. (1997). *Sport management doctoral programs.* Paper presented at the Annual Convention of the Southern District Alliance of Health, Physical Education, Recreation, & Dance. Feb. 13. Biloxi, MS.

Lapchick, R. (2004). *2003 racial & gender report card.* The Institute for Diversity and Ethics in Sport. Orland, FL.

Mahony, D., Mondello, M., Hums, M., & Judd, M. (2004). Are sport management doctoral programs meeting the needs of the faculty job market? Observations for today and the future (Perspectives). *Journal of Sport Management, 18,* 91-110.

Mason, J. G., Higgins, C., & Owen, J. (1981). Sport administration education 15 years later. *Athletic Purchasing and Facilities,* 44-45.

Masterlexis, L. P., Barr, C. A., & Hums, M. A. (2005). *Principles and practice of sport management* (2nd ed.). Sadbury, MA: Jones & Bartlett.

Meek, A. (1997). An estimate of the size and supported economic activity of the sports industry in the United States. *Sport Marketing Quarterly, 6*(4), 15-21.

Mullin, B. J. (1987) Sport management: The nature and utility of the concept. *Arena Review, 4*(3), 1-11.

NASPE-NASSM Joint Task Force on Sport Management Curriculum and Accreditation. (1993). Standards for curriculum and voluntary accreditation of sport management education programs. *Journal of Sport Management, 7*(2), 159-170.

OneCommunityOneGoal (2004, June). *Industry Focus Academies Annual Report.* Miami, FL: Dade County Public Schools.

Ozanian, M. K. (1995, 14 Februrary). Following the money. *Financial World,* p. 5.

Parkhouse, B. L. (2005). The management of sport: Its foundation and application (4th ed.). New York: McGraw-Hill.

Parks, J., & Quarterman, J. (2002). *Contemporary sport management.* Champaign, IL: Human Kinetics.

Pitts, B. (2001). Sport management at the millennium: A defining moment. *Journal of Sport Management, 15*(1), 1-9.

Pitts, B. G., & Stotlar, D. K. (2002). *Fundamentals of sport marketing.* Morgantown, WV: Fitness Information Technology.

Pitts, B. G., Fielding, L. W., & Miller. L. K. (1994) Industry segmentation theory and the sport industry. *Sport Marketing Quarterly, 3*(1), 15-24.

Rosner, W. (1989). The world plays catch-up: Sport in the 90s. *Sports Inc., 2,* 6-9.

Sampson, D. (2004, 14 January). Personal correspondence. Sunrise, FL.

Sawyer, T. H. (1993). Sport management: Where should it be housed? *Journal of Physical Education, Recreations, & Dance, 64*(9), 4-5.

Street & Smith's SportBusiness Journal (2004). Sport business programs, 7(30), 17-30.

Street & Smith's SportBusiness Journal (2003). By the numbers 2003, 5(36), 148-154.

Street & Smith's SportBusiness Journal (2004). By the numbers 2004, 6(36), 10–14, 84, 127.

Stier, W. (2001). The current status of sport management and athletic (sport) administration programs in the 21st century. *International Journal of Sport Management, 2*(1), 66-79.

Wann, D., Merrill, J., Russell, G., & Pease, D. (2001). *Sport fans.* New York: Routledge.

Suggested Readings

Brassie, P. S. (1989, November/December). A student buyer's guide to sport management programs. *Journal of Physical Education, Recreation, & Dance, 60*(9), 25-28.

Danylchuk, K. L., & Judd, M. (1996) Journal of sport management: Readership survey. *Journal of Sport Management, 10,* 188-196.

Hardy, S. (1987) Graduate curriculums in sport management: The need for a business orientation. *Quest, 39,* 207-216.

Olafson, G. A. (1995) Sport management research: Ordered change. *Journal of Sport Management, 9,* 338-345.

Slack, T. (1996). From the locker room to the boardroom: Changing the domain of sport management. *Journal of Sport Management, 10,* 97-105.

Stier, W. (1993). Alternate career paths in physical education: Sport management. Washington, DC: Eric Digest – Clearing House on Teaching and Teacher Education.

Weese, W. J. (1995). If we're not serving practitioners, then we've not serving sport management. *Journal of Sport Management, 9,* 237-243

Weese, W. S. (2002). Opportunities and Headaches: Dichotomous Perspectives on the current and future hiring realities in the Sport management Academy. *Journal of Sport Management, 16,* 1-17.

Zakrajsek, D. B. (1993). Sport management: Random thoughts of one administrator. *Journal of Sport Management, 7,* 1-6.

Chapter Two

Why Sport Management Matters

Catriona Higgs and Betsy McKinley

"Don't cry, Billy. It was just a practice game.
When the regular season starts, *then*
it's life or death."

Learning Objectives

Upon completion of this chapter, the reader should be able to

■ Describe the reasons why sport managers should study sport;

■ Identify current myths in sport;

■ Know what we can learn from studying sport;

■ Understand the relationship between society and sport;

■ Discuss why diversity is such an important topic for sport managers;

■ Outline the major laws that prohibit discrimination in the workplace; and

■ Describe the major methods utilized in socio-cultural studies to understand sport behavior.

Introduction

Sport is estimated to be a $213 billion enterprise. The phenomenal global impact has resulted in the academic study of sport from a variety of different perspectives. Sports are popular and public activities with a close relationship to society. Together with the financial impact of sport on society, there is a need to analyze the political and cultural importance of sport. **Sport sociologists** focus on many of these issues including the analysis of sport as an industry, the political and cultural implications of sport, sport and globalization, the relationship between gender, class and economics, deviance in sport, and the social organization of sport. Carefully examining **sociological analysis** of sport competition and participation enables us to learn more about human social organization in the sport setting.

> "SPORT RECAPITULATES SOCIETY AND WHEN YOU LOOK AT SPORT, WHAT YOU'RE REALLY DOING IS LOOKING IN A MIRROR AND AT SOME POINT YOU HAVE TO REALIZE THAT THAT SAYS SOMETHING VERY IMPORTANT ABOUT US ALL."
>
> HARRY EDWARDS

In many sport management classes, the primary focus of learning for students is, of course, on management. While many students are interested in sport and have a good working knowledge of trivia, statistics, and teams, few students understand the complexities of sport as a **social institution** and phenomenon. We all think we know a great deal about these activities, but we often readily buy into the myths that are perpetuated by those involved in the management and organization of sport. It is important to separate the truth from the falsehoods so that we can gain a clear idea of the role of sport in our lives. Students will gain a great deal from an analysis of sport from a socio-cultural perspective that is both applicable to their future roles as sport managers and to their own knowledge base in sport.

Why should we study this subject and why is it important that we dispel the myths surrounding this activity? Understanding the answers to those questions will en-

able you ultimately to become a better consumer of sport and a better sport manager.

> "THE SADDEST DAY OF THE YEAR IS THE DAY BASEBALL SEASON ENDS."
>
> TOMMY LASORDA

Why Should We Study Sport?

Undoubtedly, why we should study sport is an important question for any student and appears to be easily answered by the following examples:

- **Sport is omnipresent.** It is all around us and affects our lives in a myriad of different ways. It is an important part of our lives and thus merits our attention. We all know of people whose lives revolve around their favorite team or athlete. These individuals (fans) often know more about sport trivia than what is happening economically or politically in the U.S. or the world. Why would someone be so interested in what appears to be a trivial and unimportant part of society? The answer is fairly simple—sport is a fascinating and multi dimensional activity. In many ways, it is far more interesting than many other aspects of our lives. Why do we know so much about sport? It's similar to learning the words of a song—the tune appeals to us and we commit it to memory. We love sport and most of us want to know and learn more about it.

- **Sport coverage has increased dramatically over the past decade.** It would be impossible to pick up a newspaper or switch on the radio or television and not see some form of sports coverage. Television in particular has been responsible for bringing sport to the masses. Network and cable stations utilize sport to attract viewers and advertise other television programs. The Super Bowl and other major sporting events attract millions of viewers each year and command millions of dollars in advertising revenues.

- **Many of the role models adopted by our children are athletes.** Players such as Mia, Kobe, Serena, Michael, and Shaq are instantly recognizable and have an impact on the way our children act, dress, and think. Similar to other media figures, sports stars are entertainers and may provide a distraction from reality. The media coverage afforded to these sport stars is unparalleled. As a public, we appear unable to get enough of watching our favorite sports stars both on and off the court/field.

"Football is like life: it requires perseverance, self-denial, hard work, sacrifice, dedication, and respect for authority."

Vince Lombardi

Myths in American Sport

Myths are stories that often become our realities. As sport managers, we are assailed by a number of myths that appear to be real. In effect, the media has largely shaped our feelings and attitudes about sport. An overwhelming number of people get their information from watching television rather than reading a book. We do not reflect upon sport programs or sport information, we experience them. As such we fall victim to the ways in which the media shapes our perceptions of sport. In effect, the information often presented to us is highly subjective. An analysis of the socio-cultural aspects of sport reveals the following myths:

- College sports programs generate huge profits for their universities.

- **Title IX** has resulted in complete equity for men's and women's education-based athletic programs.

- **Title VII** has resulted in complete employment equity for men and women outside the education setting.

- Sport gambling is a victimless activity.

- Sport is the only way for many children to build self-esteem.

- Sport is apolitical.

- Communities benefit economically and psychologically from supporting a professional sport franchise, thereby justifying expensive public subsidies.

- Drug abuse is not a problem in sports.

- Sport is one of the few places in society where African Americans get equitable treatment.

"Sports do not build character . . . they reveal it."

John Wooden

What Can We Learn from Studying Sport?

Sport is an important element of American life that is so pervasive we are all affected by it. Studying sport from a social perspective will help us understand the **culture** of our society and help dispel some of the myths that have been purported. Imagine that a Martian spaceship landed in America on the day that a major sports event was being covered. What could those visitors learn about our society from watching that sports event and our reactions to it? If the event was the Super Bowl, perhaps the Martians could conclude that we as Americans love activities that are fast-paced, exciting, and aggressive. In addition, the signage around the stadium may help the alien conclude that there are major connections between sports and the business world. In watching the advertisements shown during the breaks in competition, they may also understand how economics play an important part in defining what sport is in this country. In

short, we study sport from a social perspective to learn more about our culture.

Culture represents the norms and values of individuals and groups within society. Sport in America mirrors what is occurring in the rest of our society. Politics, economics, inequities, social relationships, and deviance in society can all be viewed through an analysis of sport. Sport, in essence, is a microcosm of American culture. Thus, the more we understand about sport, the more we can reflect on what is happening in the rest of society.

Frameworks for Understanding the Relationship Between Sport and Society

"INDIVIDUAL COMMITMENT TO A GROUP EFFORT—THAT IS WHAT MAKES A TEAM WORK, A COMPANY WORK, A SOCIETY WORK, A CIVILIZATION WORK."

VINCE LOMBARDI

Not everyone agrees about what is important in studying sport and society. The method of analyzing sport from a cultural perspective has resulted in the development of a sub-discipline called **sport sociology**. Sports sociologists are interested in how humans relate to each other in the sport context, how values affect these relationships, and how humans organize sport activities (Coakley, 2004). Sport sociology is a science and derives most of its methods and theories from its parent subject: sociology. Sport sociology is often a difficult and complex area to analyze because social phenomena in the sports world are complex, subtle, and elusive. Sport is a *dynamic* activity that is constantly evolving and changing. Sport sociologists conduct research into the development of sport, patterns of culture, values, and sports organizations. Sport sociologists have many questions about what is important and what is not. To that end, cultural practices in sport are studied from a number of different perspectives. Understanding and applying these perspectives to a study of sport in the social context can be a valu-

able tool for students who wish to further their understanding of this area.

Theories are valuable ways to examine the effect of sport on society. Theories attempt to examine patterns and provide answers for why things happen in sport. The important thing to remember, however, is that no one theory can hope to explain all parts of the sport experience because of the inherent limitations of each one. Hopefully what these theories can offer us are methods by which we can answer questions related to the values of our culture and the relationship of these values to sport.

What Areas Do Sport Sociologists Investigate?

Sociologists study sport in a variety of different ways. The focus of analysis is not confined solely to elite athletic experiences (such as professional, Olympic, or intercollegiate participation); rather we are interested in all facets of involvement in sport and physical activity. Areas of consideration include, but are not limited to, the following:

- Sport and Social Values
- Socialization into Sport
- Youth Sport
- Sport and Education (interscholastic and intercollegiate)
- Sport and the Economy
- Sport and the Political System
- Violence in Sport
- Use of Performance-Enhancing Substances
- Gambling and Sport
- Sport and Religion
- Sport and the Mass Media
- Social Stratification
- Diversity Issues in Sport
- Future of Sport

Analyzing these areas permits us to look beyond statistics, teams, and trivia into a more meaningful exploration of the impact that sport has on our everyday lives. The analysis of sport from a longitudinal perspective (e.g., youth sport through interscholastic, intercollegiate, and professional participation) gives us an opportunity to review the major influences in our decision to engage in this practice and to explore the reasons for our continuance/non-continuance in this activity. Questions like the following can be answered by reviewing our own experiences:

- Why did we play the sports we played?

- How did we become interested in those particular activities as opposed to others?

- What was the role of our parents/ guardians in learning to love sports?

An investigation of the close relationship between the economy and sport reveals the multi-dimensional nature of this activity. To say that sport is *"big business"* is truly an understatement in the 21st century. Similarly, those who purport that politics have no impact on sport need to understand and appreciate how local and national governments affect sport participation and sport consumption.

A brief review of the political events surrounding the last 100 years of Olympic competition is enough to convince anyone that political interventions, particularly boycotts, are a fundamental part of international sport competition. Major problems in society (e.g., drugs, violence, gambling) can also be analyzed in the sports context. Understanding why these social problems exist in sport helps to explain the motivation of athletes to engage in these practices and the pressures that lead to these abuses. Why do athletes commit violent acts on and off the field? Why do athletes take performance-enhancing substances? Why do fans riot? Why do male athletes abuse women? All these questions can be answered from a sociological perspective.

Diversity and Sport

Perhaps the most important area for sport managers to appreciate and understand is that of **diversity**. In the 21st century, a focus on all discriminatory practices related to diversity in the workplace is critical. Functioning as an effective and efficient sport manager re-

"PREJUDICE IS A BURDEN WHICH CONFUSES THE PAST, THREATENS THE FUTURE, AND RENDERS THE PRESENT INACCESSIBLE."

MAYA ANGELOU

quires an understanding, true appreciation, and constant application of non-discriminatory practices. Diversity is more than just an analysis of **racism** and **sexism**. According to the U.S. Equal Employment Opportunity Commission (U.S. EEOC), federal laws including Title VII of the Civil Rights Act of 1964, the Americans with Disabilities Act (ADA) and the Age Discrimination in Employment Act (ADEA) specifically address the illegality of any employment-based **discrimination** with regard to race, color, religion, gender, national origin, disability, or age. Sexual harassment is also addressed.

Race/Color Discrimination

Although African Americans represent a large percentage of those who play professional sports, the opportunities for advancement to the administrative, front office, and coaching ranks are sadly limited for this minority group. Additionally, the contributions of Mexican Americans, Native Americans, and Asian Americans to sport have largely been ignored. Focusing on these issues is critical to our understanding of sport and to enhancing our role as sport managers in a diverse and complex society.

Title VII of the Civil Rights Act of 1964 covers federal, state, and local governments, employment agencies, labor organizations, and private employers of 15 or more people. The law states that it is unlawful to discriminate against any employee or applicant for a position based on his/her race or color (U.S. EEOC, 2002). The law prohibits discrimination in all phases of the hiring, employment, promotion, work compensation, and termination spectrum. Further, it is illegal to discriminate based on personally held or social stereotypes and assumptions about the competence, characteristics, or performance of any racial group. For example, the sport manager would be creating a hostile work environment by telling jokes that portray an individual or group in a negative light (either to the individual or behind his or her back). Such actions are illegal. Examples of stereotyping that may lead to a negative work environment also include the use of disparaging remarks and criticisms or negative statements made in relation to a person's race or color. Such actions are termed "verbal harassment." Race/color discrimination violations also include isolating one group from interaction with others in the work place (segregation) and requesting pre-employment information regarding race that may be used in excluding a job candidate from selection for employment.

Sex Discrimination

While sport is largely considered to be a meritocratic organization that does not discriminate according to sex, an analysis of stratification and diversity issues in sport can quickly reveal the realities. Sport has long been a male preserve, and females have been excluded from participating in sport-related activities. Federal laws prohibit such discrimination. In reference to the school and university setting, **Title IX** was passed in 1972 as part of the Educational Amendments Act and prohibits sex discrimination in education agencies that receive federal funding. Title IX has been effective in many ways in improving participation levels of females in sport associated with educational settings. The law, however, has not erased deep-rooted personal prejudice and discrimination against women athletes and administrators.

Title VII of the Civil Rights Act of 1964 prohibits sex discrimination in areas outside the education setting, such as in fitness centers, sport arenas, and other venues. Because sport is still organized and controlled primarily by white men, the "glass ceiling" that exists in the business world is certainly restrictive to women who wish to advance to upper management and front office positions in the sports world. Though the private sector has seen an increase in women in managerial positions from 29% in 1990 to over 36% in 2002, at the same time, women comprise 48% of the private sector workforce (U.S. EEOC, 2002). As a sport manager, it is imperative that management positions are equally representative of all facets of the public sector and do not reflect bias in hiring based on the sex of the applicant.

Sexual Harassment

Sexual harassment can be found in many forms in the workplace. **The Pregnancy Discrimination Act,** an amendment to Title VII of the Civil Rights Act of 1964, provides protection for pregnancy-based discrimination including pregnancy, childbirth, and pregnancy-related medical conditions. Further, pregnancy cannot be used as a reason to refuse to hire a woman. It is within the bounds of the law for an employer to request a doctor's statement regarding any work-related limitations due to pregnancy; however, an employer must hold open a position that was temporarily vacated due to pregnancy leave.

Title VII also protects men and women against workplace sexual harassment, including requests for sexual favors from those in a position of power (i.e., supervisors) or those serving as co-workers, workplace conditions that create a hostile or unwelcome environment for either gender, and same-sex harassment. EEOC statistics for fiscal year 2002 show 25,526 charges of sex-based discrimination. During the same time, 29,088 sex-discrimination charges were satisfied, resulting in recovery of monetary benefits of more than $94 million. Obviously, it is imperative that the sport manager understand and implement workplace practices that are free of all forms of sexual discrimination. Programs focusing on the prevention of sexual harassment include sensitivity training for all managers and employees, the establishment of a procedure for filing complaints, and quick resolution/action regarding every sexual harassment issue filed.

Religious Discrimination

It is illegal for employers or employees to discriminate based on religious beliefs in the workplace. This includes during the hiring process, during the creation

©Media Focus LLC

of work schedules, during the promotion process, or in establishing workplace rules. In fact, a manager is to make reasonable efforts to provide workplace flexibility regarding various religious convictions of workers, as long as those accommodations do not infringe on the beliefs or work environment of other employees. The manager must also take care to prohibit workplace religious harassment among employees and ensure that one person's religious beliefs do not result in negative workplace business interests for others in the facility. For example, the manager must take care to assure that additional business costs are not incurred as a result of their decisions regarding workers' religious convictions, and that one group of employees does not receive special considerations regarding salary, work schedule, or work materials to the detriment of other groups or individuals. While religious persecution has been practiced for hundreds of years, there has been an increase in discrimination regarding the employment of Muslims, Arabs, and Sikhs since the September 11, 2001, terrorist attacks.

Disability Discrimination

The Americans with Disabilities Act (ADA) of 1990 protects individuals with disabilities from being discriminated against in the workplace. The ADA delineates a person with disabilities as an individual who "has a physical or mental impairment that limits one or more major life activities, has a record of such an impairment, or is regarded as having such an impairment" (EEOC, 2002). As in previous areas of discrimination, the manager has the responsibility of accommodating schedules, modifying facilities, and adjusting policies and operating procedures for individuals with disabilities. Again, there is an undue hardship consideration wherein the accommodations enacted by the manager must not involve additional expense or hardship for the business owner, and the work or product produced by the facility must be of the same quality as expected from all employees.

Age Discrimination

Because many organizations have less than 20 employees, thus generally negating the position of a Human Resource officer for the company, it is critical for the sport manager to be aware of and implement non-discrimination in all areas of the workplace. This is true when working with individuals who are given less than satisfactory entry opportunities, job placement, work scheduling, and promotion/retention opportunities. **The Age Discrimination in Employment Act (ADEA) of 1967** was initially passed to protect workers age 40 and older from age discrimination in the above-mentioned areas. The ADEA was amended by the **Older Workers Benefit Protection Act of 1990 (OWBPA)** to include a focus on age discrimination and loss of workplace benefits. The OWBPA also provided for older worker protection in the area of protocol establishment that must be followed when employers are asked to waive their rights when filing settlement claims regarding age discrimination. This legislation is particularly critical to workers who have been affected by company mergers, acquisitions, and job displacement due to downsizing.

Methods Used in Socio-Cultural Studies to Understand Sport Behavior

Sport sociologists largely rely on the methods of the parent discipline (sociology) to research areas in sport. Sport sociology is a science, and as such the concentration of research in the area is geared towards the collection of accurate and verifiable evidence. **Surveys** (questionnaires) are valuable methods of learning about group and individual preferences and opinions. Sometimes the facts we need are not recorded by anyone and we have to ask people questions. For example, asking a fan what motivated them to attend a particular sports event can provide us with very valuable information regarding consumer (fan) behavior. A questionnaire can be completed by an individual in a fairly short period of time and may produce a large volume of data that can be analyzed quickly and efficiently. **Interviews** with fans, participants, and sport consumers are also widely used to explain various aspects of sports participation and consumption. Interviews can be more revealing than surveys, especially when open-ended responses are used to gather information. A close-ended (yes/no) response tells the researcher very little about the actual reasoning behind a decision. Asking questions such as "why" can be far more revealing, and some of the most interesting studies are ones that use this approach singularly (e.g., ethnographic studies). **Observational studies** also produce data that can help a sport sociologist understand aspects of sports participation. For example, subjects who are unaware they are being watched and their behavior recorded are acting naturally in their environment and are not being asked to recall past information or misrepresenting their experiences (as in an interview). There are many other methods of collecting data; however, the main responsibility of the researcher in this area is to accurately collect, record, analyze, and interpret the facts. In our search for the truth, we rely on scientific methods of data collection to accurately describe what really exists as precisely and objectively as possible.

"IN OUR LIVES WE WILL ENCOUNTER MANY CHALLENGES, AND TOMORROW WE FACE ONE TOGETHER. HOW WE ACCEPT THE CHALLENGE AND ATTACK THE CHALLENGE HEAD ON IS ONLY ABOUT US—NO ONE CAN TOUCH THAT. IF WE WIN OR LOSE THIS WEEKEND, IT WILL NOT MAKE A DIFFERENCE IN OUR LIVES. BUT WHY WE PLAY AND HOW WE PLAY WILL MAKE A DIFFERENCE IN OUR LIVES FOREVER."

BETH ANDERS

Summary

Examining sport from a socio-cultural perspective is obviously critical for those entering the sport management profession. Concepts related to sport and other social institutions are important for the sport manager to understand. The development of modern sport has been influenced by many factors that have affected our perceptions about this topic. In addition, the concepts of diversity discussed in this chapter are also critical from many perspectives. As a sport manager you will interact with individuals from different racial, ethnic, and religious backgrounds. A good sport manager is one who affirms diversity in the workplace and accepts all individuals for their contributions to the sport organization. Differences should be embraced and not feared, and individuals should be judged on their merit, not on the color of their skin or what they choose to believe. Confronting prejudice and discrimination in the workplace is a difficult thing to do, but as a manager it is important to realize that part of your

responsibility lies in challenging the barriers to employment diversity, thereby providing a safe and secure workplace for all employees. Strategies for managing diversity are important for achieving workplace equity; however, the first step in the process must be a review of one's own prejudices and an examination of why these prejudices exist. Only when we confront our own fears and discriminatory behaviors can we begin to effect change in others.

Discussion Activities

1. Does sport bring people together or tear them apart? What specific instances can you think of to support your view?

2. Go to the web site of a professional franchise or college athletic department and access the page that introduces their management team. Record the following:

   a) Number of male vs. female managers

   b) Types of managers by gender (e.g., Is the Athletic Director a man or woman? Is the Assistant Director of Marketing a man or a woman?)

   c) If pictures are provided—how many minority managers are there in this organization?

   Once you have collected this data, answer the following questions:

   a) Is there a disparity in gender of those associated with the franchise or sport organization?

   b) Are the administrative positions staffed by only men, only women, or a percentage of both?

   c) Are the administrative positions staffed only by Caucasian personnel, or are underrepresented groups evident in top management?

   d) Is the wording used by the franchise or sport organization inclusive or exclusive according to gender, race, or ability? Provide specific documentation of your findings.

3. Choose two of the myths outlined in this chapter. Using the web or other resources, provide two examples of specific information that help to refute each myth.

4. Analyze the content of a sports section of a local

or national newspaper. Record the following information:

a) The number of articles featuring male athletes

b) The number of articles featuring female athletes

c) The number of photographs featuring female athletes

d) The number of photographs featuring male athletes

e) The number of articles featuring minority athletes

f) The number of photographs featuring minority athletes

g) Answer the following questions: Who does the media choose to focus on with regard to sport? Which gender/races are most included? Which gender/races are most excluded?

5. Once Upon a Time. Many athletes are viewed as role models by children and youth. With a partner, write a fairy tale ("Once upon a time, there was a child who…), in which the child in the story emulates undesirable attributes of professional athletes (i.e., greed, drug abuse, gambling, poor sportsmanship, bullying). The negative attributes should not contribute positively to the growth or social interaction of the child in any way. Share your story with another pair in the class. Then, correct the two stories so that "all lived happily ever after!"

6. Shared Feelings. Create a list of words that describe you and your experiences. Include reference to gender, race, marital status, year in school, favorite food, hobby, religion, political affiliation, club membership, athletic team membership, sports you like to watch, sports you like to play, favorite dessert, pet ownership, favorite vehicle, socioeconomic status, favorite chain restaurant, favorite sports teams. Share this list with two other people, and compare your similarities and differences. What does this exercise tell you about yourself and those in your class, as related to this chapter?

References

Coakley, J. (2004). *Sports in Society: Issues and Controversies* (8th ed.). New York: McGraw-Hill.

Equal Employment Opportunity Commission. Retrieved September 23, 2004, from http://www.eeoc.gov/abouteeo/overview_practices.html.

Suggested Readings

Burstyn, V. (1999). *The Rites of Men: Manhood, Politics, and the Culture of Sport*. Toronto, ON: University of Toronto Press.

Cahn, S. (1995). *Coming on Strong: Gender and Sexuality in Twentieth-Century Women's Sport*. Boston, MA: Harvard University Press.

Waddington, I. (2000). *Sport, Health and Drugs: A Critical Sociological Perspective*. New York: Routledge.

Chapter Three

Communication and Media Relations in Sport

Andy Gillentine, R. Brian Crow, and Cheri Bradish

Chris Berman, age 6.

Learning Objectives

Upon completion of this chapter, the reader should be able to

■ Understand the important role of communication in the sport industry;

■ Identify the various components of effective communication;

■ Recognize the barriers to effective communication;

■ Discuss the importance of nonverbal communication; and

■ Appreciate the role of media relations in the sport organization.

Introduction

Sport organizations, like all other enterprises, strive to send a unique message to their many stakeholders. Think, for instance, of the Pittsburgh Steelers of the National Football League. The owner of the team (as well as league officials) is in constant communication with fans, sponsors, researchers, broadcasters, fantasy league players, schools, community groups, city officials, employees, volunteers, suppliers, vendors, licensees, and dozens of other individuals and organizations on a daily basis (Table 3.1). This information exchange occurs in a variety of ways: via phone calls, email, personal meetings, text messages, visits to a web page, written correspondence, visits to schools or hospitals, and other various methods of communication. The point is that sport organizations rely on communication to survive. A clear and consistent message is more likely to be understood by the recipient and responded to in a positive manner.

> "I KNOW YOU BELIEVE YOU UNDER-
> STAND WHAT YOU THINK I SAID, BUT
> I AM NOT SURE YOU REALIZE THAT
> WHAT YOU HEARD IS NOT WHAT I
> MEANT."
>
> RICHARD NIXON

Effective communication in sport is one of the most important and pervasive qualities and competencies a sport manager can possess. Communication can run the gamut from interpersonal and small group communication to public mass communication networks. The importance of developing communication skills necessary for success in the sport industry is heightened by the tremendous growth of electronic media. The expansion of media coverage of the sport industry will only continue to grow as innovative technologies offer sport managers new avenues through which to communicate. Therefore, it is essential that sport managers have a strong appreciation of the power of contemporary communication mediums, both as a means of connecting with key constituents and as an advantage that requires increasingly greater management skill and coordination.

Table 3.1 Sport Managers' Communication Demands

- Team Owners/Administration
- City Officials
- Coaches
- Vendors
- Competing Sport Organizations
- Sponsors
- Staff members
- Researchers
- The Media
- Game Officials
- Boosters
- Players
- Fans
- Parents
- Faculty

Modified from Anshel (1997)

Interpersonal and Small Group Communication

Sport mangers must constantly refine their communication skills in order to effectively deliver information to the diverse groups with which they may interact. From casual conversation with colleagues to formal meetings with financial sponsorship partners, the sport manager must be prepared to maximize the effectiveness of communication. The development of effective communication skills requires the sport manager to 1) acknowledge the importance of effective communication and 2) demonstrate a willingness to invest the time and effort to improve them.

Keys to Effective Communication

In order to become an effective communicator, the sport manager must understand that communication is a multi-faceted skill. The sport manager must recognize the multiple techniques for effective communication, evaluate the various methods through which communication can occur, and select the most appropriate action or actions. Effective **planning** is an often overlooked step in the communication process, compromising the usefulness of the information. After determining the most effective method(s) to utilize, the sport manager must effectively plan the content of the message, the timing for release of the information, and estimate the content, speed, and consequences of the recipient's feedback. Once the plan is in place, the sport manager must ensure the integrity of the information to be distributed. It is important that the **content** of the message is accurate and free from bias or inflammatory language. It is also important for the sport manager to establish his or her **credibility** with the intended audience. The credibility of the sender directly affects the perception of the receiver regarding the content of the message. Credibility is enhanced through an established reputation, a long history of truthful and accurate communication, and legitimacy. **Personal credibility** goes hand-in-hand with **message credibility**. Honest communication from the organization results in trust from the audience. Failure to be honest—for example, repeatedly denying trade rumors that ultimately prove to be true—will often damage the organization's and administrator's credibility. Never distribute information before it has been checked for accuracy. It is better to have a short delay in sending a message than to send one with inaccurate information.

Additionally, the sport manager must consider the *type of information* being transferred. *Complex* information may be potentially confusing and must be carefully presented, to avoid additional communication problems. Also, the **emotional content** of the message has to be considered. Often the information transmitted from the sport organization—for example, the trading of a star player or firing of a coach—contains emotionally charged content for recipients (i.e., fans, boosters, players). These messages must be delivered in the most positive manner possible. Also, specific words can be emotion laden. Words related to sex, religion, and politics may themselves evoke a response from recipients that may affect the delivery of the message.

Barriers to Effective Communication

Sport managers must also recognize that there are inherent **barriers to effective communication.** These barriers may be typically categorized into three distinct categories: 1) Linguistic barriers, 2) Psychological barriers, and 3) Environmental barriers. While it may be impossible for the sport administrator to completely eliminate these barriers, methods to minimize the potential impact of each should be considered during the communication planning process.

Barriers to Effective Communication

1) Linguistic barriers
2) Psychological barriers
3) Environmental barriers

The classic Abbot and Costello comedy routine *"Who's on first?"* depicts a conversation between two friends regarding the players on a baseball team. The ensuing miscommunication is a perfect example of a **linguistic** barrier to effective communication. Linguistics is defined as "the study of the nature, structure, and variation of language, including phonetics, phonology, morphology, syntax, semantics, sociolinguistics, and pragmatics" (*The American Heritage Dictionary of the English Language:* 4th ed., 2000).

While each of the above areas identifies an important component in the study of linguistics, perhaps the most important components are **semantics** and **sociolinguistics**. Semantics is defined as the meaning or the interpretation of a word and/or sentence. Individ-

---

Table 3.2 Guidelines for effective communication

- Plan for communication
- Be honest
- Establish consistent daily communication
- Encourage upward, downward, and lateral communication
- Respect other viewpoints
- Praise (in public) & criticize (in private) behavior, not the person
- Utilize humor
- Do not use sarcasm or embarrass others
- Never use stereotypes or prejudicial statements
- Avoid negative humor and obscene language

©iStockphoto.com

"Who's on first?"

Abbot & Costello's classic comedy routine may be heard at:

http://www.whos-on-first.com/

Table 3.3 Components of Linguistics

<u>Phonetics:</u> different sounds that are employed across all human languages

<u>Phonology:</u> patterns of a language's basic sounds

<u>Morphology:</u> the internal structure of words

<u>Syntax:</u> how words combine to form grammatical sentences

<u>Semantics:</u> the meaning or interpretation of words

<u>Sociolinguistics:</u> the effect of all aspects of society, including cultural norms, expectations, and context, on language

uals often define terms differently, which could impact the content of the message. The sport administrator must be cautious in the selection of terminology to ensure the proper interpretation of the message. This difference can lead to miscommunication or disagreement over a topic that both groups may actually agree on. Closely related to semantics and an area of great importance is sociolinguistics.

Sociolinguistics refers to the impact that differing social and/or cultural groups have on the meaning and interpretation of language. Very often words or phrases have a very different meaning from group to group. Social variables that could impact communication may include ethnicity, religion, economic status, and level of education (Wikipedia, 2004). Given the diverse audience the sport manager interacts with on a regular basis, it is critical these differences be noted. For example, certain language used by a rap music artist during a half-time performance might be interpreted differently by a 45-year-old man and his 15-year-old daughter.

The **environment** may also pose barriers to effective communication. The designated audience may not effectively receive verbal messages delivered in a crowded, noisy, or uncomfortable room. Distractions may impede a person's ability to hear and accurately interpret the message. The temperature and other weather conditions, such as high winds, rain, and snow, can promote levels of discomfort that may impede communication. While it is impossible for sport managers to control all of these environmental barriers, it is important to recognize them and to minimize their impact.

Additional environmental concerns can involve the physical structure of the facility. Aside from noise issues, inadequately furnished facilities may also create a level of discomfort, which might in turn impede effective communication. In an attempt to offset this problem, many administrators have turned to Feng Shui experts to help them design meeting spaces with comfortable seating to facilitate an effective communication environment (Broadhead, 2001).

Additional potential barriers to effective communication in the sport industry are **psychological** barriers. Psychological barriers are outside the scope of linguistic and environmental barriers, manifesting instead in the mind of the intended audience. While these barriers are among the most difficult to identify, the sport manager must recognize these potential barriers and take actions to offset or change them. Foremost among the psychological barriers is the **perception** of the information or sender. Perception is defined as the "recognition and interpretation of sensory stimuli based chiefly on memory" (*The American Heritage Dictionary of the English Language*, 4th ed., 2000). Individuals often rely on past experiences to positively or negatively interpret newly received information. While positive perceptions will most likely help the sport administrator, negative perceptions regarding the administrator, organization, or situation can damage the effectiveness of the message. Public perception and attitudes toward the organization must be continually monitored. If negative perceptions are ignored, innuendo, rumors, and other misinformation can be perceived as factual if immediate action to correct them is not taken.

The Communication Network

The establishment of an effective communication network also requires the recognition of the **flow of communication**. Sport managers must develop an information flow that moves downward, upward, and laterally.

Downward communication refers to information that is transmitted from the upper levels of management to the middle and lower levels of the organization. Frequently sport managers maintain communication systems that only allow for downward communication, eliminating the opportunity to receive valuable information and feedback from others in the organization.

The **upward** flow of information allows for upper management to receive information from subordinates, customers, suppliers, etc., that may be useful in correcting current operations and/or determining the future direction of the organization. Failure to develop an effective system to gather **feedback** from within the organization and its customers results in upper level management that is out-of-touch with its constituents.

Lateral communication refers to communication that flows between the various individuals or groups at the same or equivalent levels of management. This exchange of information is important to ensure that duplication of materials and information is not occurring within the organization. This type of communication can also be useful to help foster employee involvement and empowerment within the organization.

The communication network also includes identifying the medium through which the communication will be transmitted. These communication networks include *verbal communication, non-verbal communica-*

Table 3.4 Verbal Communication	
We hear half of what is said	50%
We listen to half of that	25%
We understand half of that	12.5%
We believe half of that	6.25%
And we remember half of that	3.125%
	Martens, 1987

tion, and mass media communication. Each of these communication mediums requires specific levels of understanding by the sport manager in order to maximize its effectiveness.

The most commonly used method of communication is verbal communication. Estimates indicate that 70% of a person's day is spent in at least one form of verbal communication (Sarthe, Olson, & Whitney, 1973). Verbal communication consists of speaking, listening, reading, and writing. In order to improve verbal communication, it is important for sport managers to consider multiple components of spoken communication. Aside from the credibility of content addressed earlier, sport managers need to consider articulation, tempo, and volume. These components are referred to as paralanguage, the features which accompany verbal communication but are not considered part of the language system.

Articulation refers to the ability to clearly enunciate words. Speakers may need to overcome national or regional accents that may impact the listener's understanding of the message. Speakers should also be aware of the correct pronunciations of words and terms used in delivery. Mumbling is another aspect of articulation that can impact the message. Speakers should strive to speak as clearly as possible and to carefully enunciate each word during a presentation. Although the speaker may initially feel awkward in this careful manner of speech, the reward is an audience that properly decodes the message.

Tempo refers to the speed at which we speak. Novice speakers often have a tendency to speak too rapidly in an important situation. This can be due to increases in adrenaline or general nervousness. No matter what the reason, effective communication requires speakers to speak slower than normal when addressing a group. Another aspect of tempo that should be avoided is a sing-song manner of speech, in which the pitch and timing of words follow a pattern that can be distracting to the listener.

Speakers should also be aware of the volume of their voice. In additional to always speaking slower than normal, speakers should also speak louder. A general rule of thumb is to speak in a manner such that someone in the back of the room can easily hear you. This should be a consideration when a addressing a large group. Often it is better to err on the side of caution and utilize a microphone than not be heard.

Another important aspect of verbal communication is listening. Research indicates that individuals spend nearly half of their daily verbal communication listening. The late Mark McCormack, founder of International Management Group (IMG), stated that the most important skill an administrator could have is effective listening. McCormick advocated active listening, a method through which the listener actively and physically participates with the speaker.

Table 3.5 Steps to Improve Listening

- Be prepared to listen
- Listen openly
- Concentrate on message
- Do not judge speaker
- Observe mannerisms and gestures of speaker
- Identify main concepts and points
- Eliminate distractions
- Be committed

adapted from Martens, 1987

Nonverbal Communication

Powerful nonverbal messages are transmitted through the mannerisms and physical actions of the sport manager. The way the speaker utilizes the space in which he/she is delivering the message, and the presentation of their physical attributes and appearance, sends ad-

ditional information to the recipient which may or may not reinforce the verbal message. Sport mangers must be aware of the importance of these nonverbal communication cues and take the appropriate actions to manage them effectively.

The study of how an individual communicates through the use of space is referred to as **proxemics**. This form of communication includes not only the amount of space between the receiver and the sender, but also how the speaker utilizes the environment. The appropriate use of space can have a dramatic impact on the effectiveness of communication. Often individuals are able to disengage from the speaker if specific personal space or physical barriers are present. It is important for a sport manager to effectively use the space available to deliver his/her message. Space may also provide the speaker with a "buffer zone" to increase his or her own level of comfort (Table 3.6).

Table 3.6 Hall's Proxemic (Distance) Model

Public Distance:	10' or more
Social/Consultive Distance:	4' - 10'
Personal/Casual Distance:	1 1/2' - 4'
Intimate Distance:	0" - 18"

Hall, 1959

The appearance and physical mannerisms of a speaker are referred to as **kinesics**. This may include the speaker's posture, gestures, facial expressions, and eye movement. It is important for a speaker to demonstrate good posture when speaking to an audience. Good posture—standing erect, shoulders back, head up—gives the image of a confident speaker, which may help with credibility issues mentioned earlier. The sport administrator may increase the effectiveness of the message through the use of effective eye and facial movements. Occasionally, speakers unintentionally send messages to listeners through inappropriate facial or eye movements. Presidential candidate Al Gore was publicly criticized for his facial and eye movements during the 2000 presidential debates. John Gruden of the Tampa Bay Buccaneers is often lampooned for his animated facial expressions. Speakers must carefully study their own appearance in order to make appropriate changes or modifications in both of these areas.

The use of physical gestures, including touching, can help the speaker in emphasizing important points of information and also in conveying the sincerity of the message. Simple gestures can send a variety of messages to the audience and it is important for speakers to review the gestures they commonly use or to identify ways to increase their use. In today's litigious society, sport managers need to exercise caution though when touching individuals. It should be recommended that the speaker know the recipient well before initiating any physical contact. Casual touching can increase the level of perceived familiarity with the speaker through appropriate use of space as mentioned earlier.

Mass Media Communication

"The Medium is the Message"

First penned by Marshall McLuhan, it has long been regarded that "the medium is the message." This indicates that in fact the means of interaction and communication often serve as the most pivotal means of the message in communication. This is true also of sport. There has been a longstanding relationship, even synergy, between sport and the medium of communication.

Sport Media

Sport media is a broad term encompassing many aspects of how sport consumers receive information. This information can be delivered directly by a team, league, or sport organization (via direct mail or the Internet) or through mass media (newspapers, radio, television, magazines, or the Internet). The growth of sport in the United States, both in participation and spectatorship, can be in part attributed to the increasingly complex role media plays in our lives. All the issues to be considered when dealing with sport and media are too numerous for one textbook chapter. However, several important topics will lead you to a greater understanding of the role media plays in our participation and consumption of sport.

Historical Perspectives

Print media

Organized sport in the United States has evolved tremendously in the past 150 years. Along with that evolution has come an increased thirst for information regarding those sports. Initially, the limited coverage of sport events, and even more limited advertising and promotion of those events, was through *newspapers*. These papers had narrow circulation and quite often not even one writer solely responsible for sport. Compare that to 2005, where some newspapers have several dozen sports writers. Sports writing improved dramatically after World War I, as the U.S. population became increasingly literate.

Sport, however, continued to grow in popularity, and many professional sport organizations, as well as the precursor to the NCAA, were formed around the turn of the 20th Century. Media coverage of sport continued to evolve as well, with *radio* becoming a major influence beginning in the 1920s. The first radio broadcast of a professional baseball game was in 1921, on KDKA radio in Pittsburgh. This new competition forced sportswriters to change their style of writing; since the game itself was on the radio, they had to provide in-depth, comprehensive information not available on the radio broadcast.

When television became a permanent fixture in the 1950s, sports writers had to change again, becoming investigative reporters and explaining how and why things happened instead of what happened. Today, newspapers devote 20-25% of their space to sports news (Nichols, Moynahan, Hall, & Taylor, 2002).

Radio

By the 1930s, nearly 300 million radios were being used in the United States. All 16 major league baseball teams broadcast their games live. Interestingly, play-by-play announcers did not travel with the team in those days; they would recreate the broadcast using Western Union tapes of the game (Nichols et al., 2002). Radio went from local broadcasts in its early days, to national network broadcasts in the middle of the 20th Century, back to broadcasts aimed at local audiences after World War II (Nichols et al., 2002). In 2005, national radio broadcasts are again becoming popular, with the advent of satellite radio competitors

Sirius Radio and XM Radio.

Television

The first televised sporting event was in 1939—a baseball game between Columbia and Princeton. The growth of professional sport and the growth of television as a viable medium run parallel. In the late 1940s and early 1950s, television in the US was fledgling, with only 190,000 TV sets in use in 1948. Sport—because the events already existed, and there were no sets to build and no actors to hire—became attractive programming.*

Sport was popular with television executives for several reasons: 1) It attracted a regular weekend audience, 2) it created cross-promotion, 3) it was popular with viewers, and 4) ownership of sports rights adds "credibility" to a network or cable outlet. Today there are more than 500 national and regional cable networks, and over 80% of homes subscribe to cable. ESPN, established in 1979, was the first 24-hour all sports network. Television rights fees are a significant source of revenue for professional and intercollegiate teams.

For a detailed discussion of TV rights fees, see www.sportsbusinessdaily.com.

Television specifically and media in general impact our sport consumption daily. For example, prior to 2000, it was rare to see a major college football game played on any day but Saturday or Thursday, or a professional game on any day but Sunday or Monday. But in 2004, ESPN proudly announced it would telecast live NCAA and NFL football over 19 straight days. College teams from less visible conferences such as the Sun Belt and Mid-American Conference grudgingly play on Tuesday, Wednesday, or Friday evening for two reasons: exposure and revenue.

Several issues related to televised sport are currently being debated. One involves the limited coverage of women's sports, which is somewhat of a catch-22. Perhaps the popularity of women's sports is narrow because it is rarely televised, and it is rarely televised because of its limited popularity. Another current issue is the impact of TiVo and Digital Video Recorders.

These devices allow viewers to manually edit live broadcasts and skip any portion they may not want to see (i.e., commercials). Since networks and cable broadcasters generate the majority of their income from advertisers, the impact of new technology remains to be seen.

*For a detailed discussion of sport and television, see http://www.museum. tv/archives/etv/S/htmlS/sportsandte/ sportsandte.htm.

Internet

A discussion of various forms of sport media would not be complete without mentioning the World Wide Web. Most sport management undergraduates cannot remember a time when streaming video, real-time information, and instantaneous communication via the Internet were not available. Those of us a few years older, however, remember with little fondness pre-Internet days. Today, every sport organization has an official website and hundreds, if not thousands, of unofficial sites created by loyal fans. Official sites specifically are a vast resource of information, as they include schedules, team news, player profiles, historical data, stadium information, and much more.

Every major news organization, media outlet, television and radio station, newspaper, and magazine has its own website, with material to supplement its mainstream offerings. Many web-only sport media organizations have been created as well, with the list too long to even count. Consumers must be wary, however, because at this point there are very few systems in place to check the veracity and accuracy of stories placed on the World Wide Web.

Sport will continue to grow along with new forms of media. In 2004, viewers of the NCAA Division I men's basketball tournament could answer various questions during the broadcast by sending Text Messages from their Cingular Wireless (NCAA sponsor) phones.

Sports Information

The current relationship between sport and the media has come a long way from the "good old days" when beat writers were on professional sport team payrolls and traveled with their team, in large part to share a public relations "goodwill" account with local and very loyal fans. Today, the relationship between sport and the media has become more tenuous, juxtaposing a more critical, yet accountable forum regarding professional sport organizations and athletes, while at the

Photo by Silvester Nuenenorl, courtesy of ©stock.xchng.iv

same time providing a multitude of enhanced outlets to promote and discuss these same sport products.

Historically, the formalization of "media relations" departments occurred similarly to the development of the sport industry during the 1950s. In response to the rise in interest of spectator sport, media outlets—specifically, local papers and radio outlets—increased their coverage and requests for information from sport organizations at both the professional and collegiate sport level. As these requests intensified, the need for full time sports information directors emerged and the official office of media relations was born. Today, this department works very closely within the greater public relations umbrella of the sport organization, which includes the growing area of community relations. Not only is this unit responsible for the ongoing dissemination of sports information outputs (Table 3.7), but it is also regarded as the first point of contact within the sport organization. It is essential that this department play a very proactive role, working closely with the management and marketing units of the organization, to craft a uniform message to their community.

Present Perspectives

Sports Journalism

Current insights with regard to sport and media point in particular to the role of sport journalists and sports journalism as having a major impact on the development of the sport industry. Specifically, these individuals, coupled with the increased scrutiny of star athletes and the enhanced style of investigative reporting, have created a magnifying glass approach to the sport media relationship. As such, increased scrutiny and management of sport media is warranted by sport managers. This elevated intensity and reliance on the

---

Table 3.7 Sports Information Outputs

The sports information or media relations director is responsible for delivering many outputs to their media outlets on a very regular and timely basis.

These include the following pieces:

Media Releases

Designed to positively position the sport organization and disseminate information about future developments or happenings within the organization.

Fact Sheets

Delivered in a more timely matter, these are designed to showcase future opportunities for the organization as well as highlight specific facets.

Pregame Notes

Similar in nature to fact sheets, these are produced prior to sporting events to profile key players and match-ups, as well as interesting and informative team notes.

Hometown Features

Geographically targeted to correspond to key targets, these are developed to highlight key individuals in their hometown region, while also positioning the organization in a positive light.

Media Guides

A very detailed analysis of all facets of the organization, including in-depth profiles of team members, an organization management overview, and information related to each competition (home and away).

Game Programs

For distribution at every home game, these are intended for both consumers and the media to profile the particular match-up and current happenings of the organization.

media is also most apparent in the television outlets, where the ratings game for sport programming has intensified. This is also similar to the impact of the Internet, where increased product extensions and sports information is communicated with sport fans and media alike.

Future Considerations

The future relationship between sport and the media will continue to provide examples of synergies and opportunities for grander levels of importance and influence for sport organizations and sport media outlets. The continued merging of sport and entertainment, including media integration, a number of leading media outlets, and national television companies, will further capitalize on utilizing sport and sport properties to enhance their program lineups. As well, new media will continue to emerge, such as digital media technology, which will generate a whole new genre of communicating with sport fans. A number of factors will contribute to this paradigm shift with regard to sport media, but will include global media convergence of professional sport outlets, sport property ownership by media conglomerates, and global sport markets.

The continued growth and expansion of Internet and wireless services will dramatically change communication strategies employed in the sport industry. The possibilities for interactive consumption of the sport product will expand potential exposure of such goods. These possibilities will present exciting challenges to sport administrators and serve as a continuum for the importance of effective sport communication.

Cases:

MONDAY NIGHT FOOTBALL

The introduction of the concept of ABC's "Monday Night Football" (MNF) in 1970 was a radical departure from traditional sport programming, which was typically understood and offered as a weekend leisure activity for sport consumers (Koppett, 2003). Advocated by then NFL Commissioner Pete Rozelle and pioneered by rising ABC sports division executive **Roone Arledge** (Gorman & Calhoun, 1994), packaging professional sport as a "prime time" television slot dramatically altered the means of distribution of a sport product to a greater, more captive sport audience, which had direct and important implications to sport media in particular, and permitted the ascent and popularity of professional sport in general. The effectiveness of this MNF programming change was a complete success for both the network and the league for many reasons.

Most obvious, the success of this partnership was reflected in the escalating rights for the League, which resulted in substantial dividends for each individual franchise (for example, in 1981, Rozelle negotiated a five-year contract worth $2 billion, netting each club $14 million annually) (Gorman & Calhoun, 1994). This signaled important considerations for a multitude of sport properties, effectively placing "media rights" at the forefront of revenue source.

Effectively, the introduction of MNF and its extensions transformed the consumption of sport for a specific audience from a passive experience to a complete entertainment offering aimed at a mass marketplace (Masteralexis, Barr, & Hums, 1998). This greater broadcast through television also permitted sport to be appreciated and consumed in much more depth, creating a whole greater legion of sport fans. The advent of changing technology also contributed to a successful synergy between the network and increased popularity of professional football, which continues today. This was compounded by the unique programming and never before seen innovations in broadcasting options (such as incorporation of enhanced camera angles, telephoto lenses, instant replay, and slow motion, all new to live programming) (Gorman & Calhoun, 1994). A platform of "celebrity" announcers, including the colorful personality of **Howard Cosell**, also contributed to this deepened appreciation of and loyalty for professional football, effectively personalizing the sport for a legion of fans. Joining these individuals, both on the field and in the press box, was also an increasing stream of other newsworthy "celebrity" guests, including musicians, actors, and politicians, which further added to the value and interest of the broadcast. The scheduling of teams also contributed to entertainment packaging, often pitting two natural rivalries (geographically, historically) and/or teams with "sport celebrity" (for successes on and off the field) interest in the Monday night slot, again promoting further interest in, and success of, prime time sport programming. The introduction of the half-time show, publicly broadcast, also signaled newfound interest in the sport, and as such, became an important offering for all spectator sport.

Further contributing to the success of MNF was the almost instant and unrecognized corporate support, through advertising and commercials, of professional sport properties. The network was able to effectively target major corporations through the identified, and very attractive, demographics of Monday night sport programming, and major corporations quickly became involved with the overall sport programming. With increased extensions to the game (such as timeouts), the television programming was able to incorporate further advertising time and corporate support. However, being the only prime time sport offering at the time, when advertising rates were at their peak, it proved a true benefit for both the NFL and the network (Gorman & Calhoun, 1994), and again, signaled important lessons for future sport media and programming considerations.

Profiles:

ROONE ARLEDGE

Roone Arledge is important to the enhancement of communications and media relations in sport, as a true pioneer of sport television. A member of ABC Sports since 1960, Arledge was an active advocate of sport packaged through television for the masses and was responsible for much of the innovation that contributes to the success of sport media today (Masteralexis, Barr, & Hums, 1998). With a vision to "take sport to the masses" through unique programming and television innovations (e.g., camera angles, sideline reporting, the broadcast booth), Arledge effectively personalized the sport experience and humanized the athlete competitors, packaging and delivering sport as entertainment and programming to the nation's growing fan base. In creating sport experiences like Monday Night Football, Arledge is also responsible for negotiating the rights for a number of other profitable sport programs, such as College Football, the Wide World of Sports, and the skillful negotiations to become the outlet of the Olympic Games, all of which deepened an appreciation for the growing sport offerings throughout America and the world. His contributions paved the way for a number of other sport property and network partnerships, catapulting many leagues to the "big time" through active and successful sport programming. In light of his sport division successes, Arledge went on to become President of ABC News in 1976, where he continued his innovation and unique television programming.

Profiles:

HOWARD COSELL

In the same way Roone Arledge is responsible for pioneering packaged sport entertainment to the masses, Howard Cosell is credited with leading the personalization of the sport experience through his cutting, "tell it like it is" sport reporting, which effectively made him a sport celebrity in his own right. Beginning as an attorney, Cosell began his career in sport representing many athletes and celebrities, including some smaller sport organizations, including the Little League of New York. These associations created opportunities for Cosell to become involved in broadcasting, hosting in 1953 a television sports program for children (Cosell, 1973). He then transitioned into professional boxing commentating, where he is well remembered for his support and advocacy of Muhammad Ali (He "floated like a butterfly and stung like a bee.") (Cosell, 1973). However, he rose to fame when, in the 1960s, Roone Arledge asked him to serve as the host for his soon-to-be successful creation, "Monday Night Football." As such, Cosell became an overnight celebrity sensation, known infamously for his outspoken character and critique of the sport landscape. Not only did he catapult himself to great fame, his character contributed to the rise and interest in MNF and also opened the door for the acceptance and success of several other sport broadcasting careers.

Summary

- Effective communication in sport is one of the most important and pervasive qualities and competencies a sport manager can possess.

- Effective communication requires sport managers to 1) acknowledge the importance of effective communication and 2) demonstrate a willingness to invest the time and effort to improve them.

- The keys to effective communication include effective planning of the message, the integrity of the message, and the credibility of the content.

- Sport managers must consider the type of information being transferred in the message. Messages that contain complex information need to be carefully planned before being issued. Messages that contain information or words that may have an emotional content should also be carefully reviewed before sending.

- Three major barriers to effective communication are: Linguistic barriers, Psychological barriers, and Environmental barriers.

- The sport manager must appreciate and understand the flow of communication throughout the organization. In an effective communication network, information flows downward, upward, and laterally.

- The major mediums through which communication typically transmitted include Verbal mediums, Nonverbal mediums, and Mass Media mediums.

- Sport media is a broad term encompassing many aspects of how sport consumers receive information.

- Mass media communication includes print media, newspapers, radio, television, and the Internet.

- Offices of sports information, both professional and collegiate, are important sources of information for the public and for the sport profession.

- The future relationship between sport and the media will continue to provide examples of synergies and opportunities for grander levels of importance and influence for sport organizations and sport media outlets.

Discussion Activities

1. Daily, there are a number of media and sport related issues occurring in the sport industry. Using current examples, consider how the media influences sport and how sport organizations interact with the media, from both a proactive and reactive perspective.

2. It has been said that the relationship between media and sport is a necessary "synergy," meaning each needs the other to survive in today's marketplace. Discuss.

3. Interpersonal and nonverbal communication are all important competencies central to the responsibilities and effectiveness of a sport manager and leader. Discuss how these characteristics are intertwined with the other important qualities of a contemporary sport leader.

4. From the chapter, it is noted that the developments of sport media have paralleled those of sport (as an industry and leisure activity). That being said, consider how future developments and expectations in the sport world will effect the delivery and needs of sport media to future sport consumers.

5. In the Cases section, Monday Night Football, Roone Arledge, and Howard Cosell are profiled as important pioneers and contributors to the development of sport media. What other specific outlets and/or individuals should also be considered as important to the development of this industry?

References

American Heritage Dictionary of the English Language (4ᵗʰ ed., 2000). Boston, MA: Houghton Mifflin.

Anshell, M. (1997). Sport psychology: From theory to practice (3ʳᵈ ed.). Menlo Park, CA: Benjamin/Cummings.

Broadhead, M. B. (2001). Feng Shui in the workplace. *Feng Shui Times.* Retrieved January 12, 2005, from www.FengShuiTimes.com.

Cosell, H. (1973). *Cosell.* New York: Simon & Schuster.

Gorman, J., & Calhoun, K. (1994). *The name of the game.* New York: John Wiley & Sons, Inc.

Hall, B. F. (2004, February). *On measuring the power of communications.* Raleigh, NC: Howard Merrill & Partners.

Hall, E. (1959). *The silent language.* Garden City, NY: Doubleday.

Koppett, L. (2003). *The rise and fall of the press box.* Toronto, ON: Sport Classic Books.

Martens, R. (1987). *Coaches guide to sport psychology.* Champaign, IL: Human Kinetics.

Masteralexis, L. P., Barr, C. A., & Hums, M. A. (1998). Principles and practices of sport management. Gaithersburg, MD: Aspen Publishers, Inc.

Nichols, W., Moynahan, P., Hall, A., & Taylor, J. (2002). *Media relations in sport.* Morgantown, WV: Fitness Information Technology.

Sarthe, S., Olson, R., & Whitney, C. (1973). *Let's talk.* Glenview, IL: Scott & Foreman.

Wikipedia (2005). *Wikipedia: The Free Encyclopedia.* Retrieved January 16, 2005, from www.wikipedia.com.

Suggested Readings

Cosell, H., & Whitfield, S. (1991). *What's wrong with sports.* New York: Simon & Schuster.

Cousens, L., Dickson, G., & O'Brien, D. (2004, June). *Beyond boundaries: A comparative investigation of change in the fields encompassing North American and Australian professional sport organizations.* Paper presented at the 2004 NASSM Conference. Atlanta, GA.

Helitzer, M. (1992). Taming the beast: Riding out a sports crisis. *Sport Marketing Quarterly, 1*(2), 33-42.

Key, M. R. (1975). *Paralanguage and kinesics (nonverbal communication).* Metuchen, NJ: The Scarecrow Press, Inc.

Mahony, D. F., & Moorman, A. M. (2000). The relationship between the attitudes of professional sport fans and their intentions to watch televised games. *Sport Marketing Quarterly, 9*(3), 131-139.

Smith, G. J., & Blackman, C. (1977). *Sport in the mass media.* Ottawa, ON: Canadian Association for Health, Physical Education and Recreation, University of Calgary Press.

Stoldt, C. G., Smetana, G. K., & Miller, L. (2000). Changes in the USA Today's sports coverage patterns during the National Basketball Association lockout: Implications for sport managers. *Sport Marketing Quarterly, 9*(3), 124-130.

Stotlar, D. K. (2000). Vertical integration in sport. *Journal of Sport Management, 14*(1), 1-7.

Turner, P. (1999). Television and internet convergence: Implications for sport broadcasting. *Sport Marketing Quarterly, 8*(2), 43-49.

Chapter Four

Management and Leadership in the Sport Industry

Jeremy S. Jordan and Aubrey Kent

"What part of 'bench clearing' don't you understand, Higley? Bench clearing means everyone runs onto the field and brawls! No exceptions!"

Learning Objectives

Upon completion of this chapter, the reader should be able to

■ Explain the four functions of management;

■ Differentiate between the three skills of management;

■ Identify the different types of decisions made by managers and how they go through the process of making decisions;

■ Discuss the ten managerial roles and how they are related; and

■ Compare and contrast leadership vs. management.

Introduction

"Management is a process of achieving organizational goals with and through other people within the constraints of limited resources" (Chelladurai, 2001, p. 94). Achieving goals is really at the heart of why we form organizations. Thus, management is critical to the success of organizations, whether through increasing the efficiency of operations or increasing the quality of products and services. Leadership is likewise looked to as a main driver of organizational success. If one watches the popular NBC television show "The Apprentice," it is easy to see that leadership skills are a highly attractive asset for any potential employee to have.

"MANAGEMENT IS DOING THINGS RIGHT; LEADERSHIP IS DOING THE RIGHT THINGS."

PETER DRUCKER

In order for an advantage to be gained by a company, its resources must be valuable, rare, and difficult to imitate or substitute (Barney, 1991). Developing leadership skills can make *you* a source of competitive advantage for organizations. As the sport industry endeavors to continue its growth, leaders with vision as well as competent managers will be in high demand. Leadership and management skills translate across contexts, in that you will be able to utilize them to your advantage whether you work in marketing, event management, or any of the many areas that the sport industry has to offer. In this chapter, we will explore the core functions, skills, and roles of management, as well as discuss leadership from its theoretical foundations to how you can develop your own skills.

The many facets of management are more easily understood if divided into the basic functions, skills, and roles that managers are expected to master.

Functions of Management

As mentioned in the introduction, managers can have a significant impact on the success of an organization. This fact has caused many researchers to study managers in an attempt to better understand what makes them successful in their roles at work. One result of these studies has been the identification of different functions that managers normally fulfill when successfully completing the demands of a particular position. These functions can be classified as 1) planning, 2) organizing, 3) directing, and 4) monitoring. Classification of managerial functions into these four areas helps us understand what managers do, and what you can expect when you assume a managerial position in a sport organization. However, because sport organizations are constantly evolving, these four functions do not represent a comprehensive list of responsibilities, but rather a starting point for understanding the complexities of management in sport. Furthermore, these four functions are not always sequential and many times managers must go back to a previous function to make the required adjustments.

Planning

The planning function of management involves the establishment of goals for the organization and its members, as well as the identification of the actions necessary to achieve those goals. Organizational goals tend to be general statements that help identify the direction of the sport organization. Because goals are broad in nature, they tend to be difficult to measure and thus have an aspect of subjectivity to them. For example, an athletic department may have the goal of increasing attendance at all home sporting events. While this goal helps identify an important issue for the athletic department, it does not identify what actions will be implemented in order to achieve the goal and what standards of measurement will be used to assess progress. Therefore, after a sport organization identifies selected goals, it is important to create measurable objectives that will lead to the successful achievement of established goals. Objectives tend to be more specific than goals and are also measurable so that evaluation can take place in order to determine if the objective is being met. A specific objective for the goal of increasing attendance at athletic contests could be to increase student attendance by 10% at all home basketball games. This objective is measurable and, if met, allows the athletic department to meet, in part, the established goal of increasing attendance. However, what is not known at this point is how the athletic department will go about increasing student attendance at home basketball games.

One way to solve this problem is to establish action plans (also called tactics or strategies) that identify specific actions that will be implemented in order to meet established objectives and goals. The athletic department may offer special promotional activities or giveaways for students who attend home basketball games. This is an action plan intended to achieve the objective of increased student attendance at basketball games, and thus the overall goal of increased attendance at home sporting events.

When establishing organizational goals, it is important to work within the constraints of the organization. These constraints are limitations placed on the organization that influence the creation of goals and subsequent organizational activities. Constraints can come from within the organization (internal) or from the environment in which the organization operates (external). A professional sport team that desires a new stadium within the next five years must consider internal and external constraints when going through the planning process. Internal constraints could be related to the amount of funding the team is able to put towards the new stadium. If the team has not been able to generate the type of revenue needed to completely pay for a new stadium, it must seek assistance with the portion of the cost it is unable to cover. This could mean that the sport team requests that some of the costs associated with the new stadium be paid with public funds (i.e., property, sales, and/or hospitality taxes). The willingness of local and state government to allocate public funds to help cover a portion of construction costs for the new stadium could represent an external constraint. If the public funds have been used for stadiums in the past or for other sport teams in the area, there may be reluctance on the part of government officials to allocate the necessary funds for the stadium. In addition, if the team has not recently been successful or does not have a large local fan base, getting public approval for the funding proposal may be difficult. Therefore, when executing the planning function of management, it is important to understand both the internal and external constraints placed on the organization. Failure to identify these constraints could result in the development of goals that are not likely to be achieved by the sport organization.

The planning function of management normally involves both long-term and short-term plans. Long-term plans, often called strategic plans, involve goals and objectives that are to be achieved in the future. An athletic department may have a strategic plan of building a new baseball stadium by the year 2010. This plan would have many components, but one major aspect would be raising the necessary funds through donations and sponsorships to pay for the stadium. The strategic plan may establish goals for how much money should be raised each of the next five years in order to start construction in 2009. In contrast to strategic plans, short-term plans tend to involve goals for the upcoming year and thus are more immediate in nature. In line with the previous example, the athletic department may have a kick-off campaign to introduce the plans for the new baseball stadium and have the objective of raising 5% of the estimated construction cost at this kick-off party. Once the sport organization has established its goals, objectives, and specific action plans, the next function of management that must be executed is organizing.

Organizing

The organizing function of management involves the identification of tasks that must be completed in order to achieve the goals identified in the planning process and the delegation of these tasks to different work groups or employees. Basically, management must decide what things need to be done and who will be responsible for completing these tasks. Not only does this process involve creating individual job responsibilities, but also grouping related tasks together so that they can be accomplished in an efficient manner. Often this grouping of job positions involves the creation of departments that are responsible for certain tasks and responsibilities. A professional sport organization may create a ticket department that is responsible for selling season tickets, mini-packs, and single-game tickets. Achievement of each task may require a slightly different action plan; however, linking them together in one department will allow individuals trained in ticket sales to work on each of the three assigned tasks. The manager's job then is to decide which employees are best qualified for certain tasks and who will be responsible for making sure these tasks are accomplished within a certain timeframe. This point identifies another aspect of organizing, and that is the development of an organizational chart. As mentioned previously, part of organizing is grouping job responsibilities and assigning these tasks to individuals who are part of a workgroup. This process is

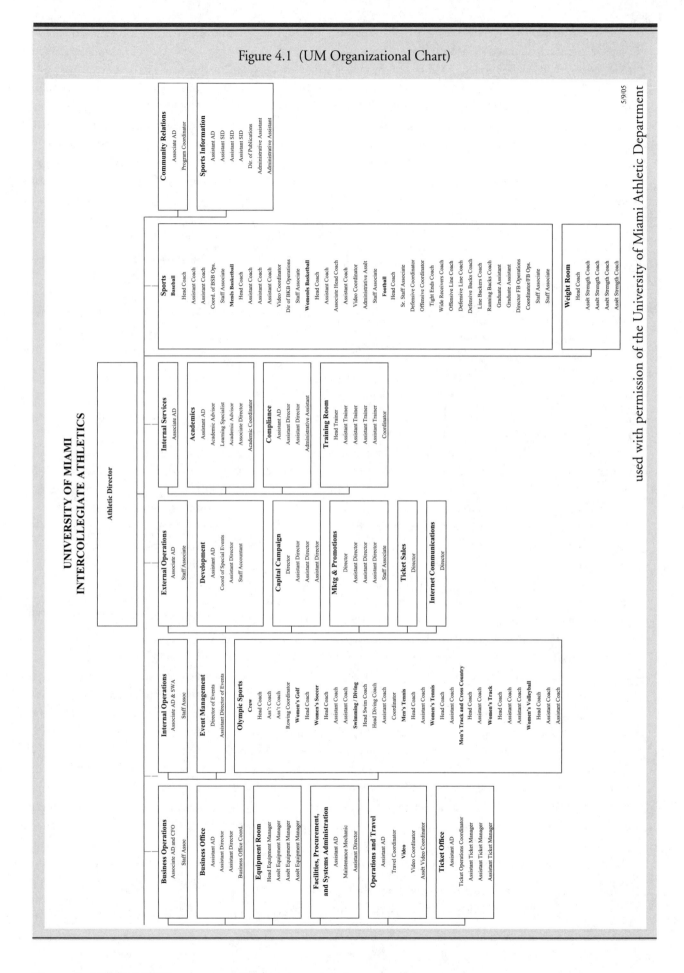

Figure 4.1 (UM Organizational Chart)

used with permission of the University of Miami Athletic Department

5/9/05

represented in graph form by developing a chart that identifies different departments in the organization and how these departments are linked. An additional aspect of organizational charts is the identification of management personnel who are responsible for the different departments. For example, Figure 4.1 identifies the organizational structure of an intercollegiate athletic marketing department.

Organizational charts should be developed for each individual department as well as the organization as a whole. According to Bridges and Roquemore (2004, p. 201), organizational charts should demonstrate the following:

1. Positions of responsibility (who is in charge of what)

2. Lines of authority (who has the power to do what)

3. Manager/employee relationships (levels of management)

4. Formal communication channels (who reports to whom)

5. Lines of responsibility (who is accountable for specific tasks)

6. Grouping of related work activities

Use of an organizational chart helps clarify how an organization is being organized and what responsibilities are being assigned to the different employees and work groups.

Directing

Once managers have completed the planning process and assigned work tasks to different members of the organization, they must motivate and direct employees to achieve established goals. A successful manager will direct employees to put forth their best efforts when implementing the action plans that have been created by the organization. The directing function of management tends to be one of the most difficult to fulfill because it involves direct interaction between management and employees. Each employee in an organization is likely to respond to managerial direction and motivation efforts differently. This means that a manager cannot use a "one best way" approach to all situations, nor when dealing with all employees. Therefore, a successful manager will be able to adapt their style to fit the requirements of a particular situa-

tion. Two main elements of the directing function are facilitating task accomplishment for employees and providing motivation for them to perform those tasks to the best of their ability.

Management personnel are responsible for providing support and direction to employees as they go about the process of completing work tasks. In most situations, the responsibility of management is to delegate appropriate tasks to employees and to make sure that these assigned tasks are completed in an efficient manner. This could mean that a manager must provide technical assistance on how to accomplish a task or evaluate the progress of an employee to make sure the task will be completed in a certain amount of time. The role of management then is to provide employees with the resources necessary to complete assigned tasks, train them in the skills required to complete these tasks, and provide assistance when employees experience difficulties in their work performance. When managers provide these elements of support for their employees, it likely leads to increased employee productivity and job satisfaction because employees are less likely to encounter "roadblocks" at work, which can lead to frustration (House, 1971). Therefore, in order for managers to successfully direct employees, they must have an understanding of the work that is needed within the organization and be able to facilitate the process by which it is completed.

Motivation

The second aspect of directing involves motivating employees to put forth maximum effort in the workplace. Being an effective motivator includes the ability to iden-

©iStockphoto.com

tify employee needs and desires and to provide processes that enable employees to achieve their goals in order to attain desired rewards. While this is sometimes a complicated process, successful managers will understand that effective motivation requires an appropriate balance of tangible, intangible, intrinsic, extrinsic, monetary, and non-monetary rewards. What this means is that different people will be motivated by different things in the workplace. For example, an external sales representative for the Chicago Cubs may be motivated by the possibility of receiving a $2,000 bonus if she meets her sales targets for the quarter. In contrast, a collegiate sports information director may be motivated by the satisfaction he receives from completing a media guide for the football team. In yet another setting, a marketing intern for Nike may be motivated because she was recognized as employee of the month in her department. The previous three examples illustrate how employees can be motivated in different ways, highlighting the need for managers to accurately discern employee needs and match their motivational strategies to them.

Monitoring

The final managerial function to be discussed is monitoring. This function involves the evaluation of employees, workgroups, or the organization as a whole on the progress that has been made towards achieving established goals and objectives. This means that periodically the work performance of employees and workgroups must be monitored to determine if changes need to be made, or if current performance levels are appropriate for the achievement of established objectives and goals. This process of control establishes a set of "checks and balances" for the organization but should not be viewed as a replacement for sound planning and organizing. The monitoring process involves three steps:

1. Developing standards that will be used to evaluate performance.

2. Conducting the evaluation by comparing actual performance to the desired performance identified by the standards.

3. Taking appropriate action to correct a situation when the desired standard of performance is not being met.

The development of performance standards generally takes place before the employee begins working on the assigned task. For example, when you enroll in a sport management course at your university, the instructor spends part of the first day explaining how your performance in class will be evaluated. If this was to occur at the end of the semester, after you had completed all the work, it would be impossible for you to make the necessary adjustments to improve your grade. The standards of evaluation that are developed must be clearly identified, explained, and should be easily measured. Finally, the standards that are developed should be directly related to the established objectives and goals associated with each particular task.

The next step in the monitoring process is to evaluate the performance of the organization, workgroup, or employee against the established standards. Important considerations in this process include which individuals will conduct the evaluation, how the evaluation process will occur, and when it will take place. Persons selected to conduct the evaluation should have knowledge of the task being performed and have the authority to make the necessary changes if actual performance does not match a particular standard. It is likely that the evaluation will involve both quantitative measures and qualitative measures. Quantitative measures involve evaluations of performance based on some type of easily measurable component. For example, if a professional baseball team had an objective to sell more season tickets than the previous year, the evaluation process would involve comparing the previous year's season ticket sales with the current year's. This evaluation involves the comparison of quantifiable outcomes (number of season tickets sold). Qualitative measures of work performance involve evaluations of work performance that are more difficult to assess accurately and objectively. For instance, employees might be evaluated on their contributions to group projects, attitude at work, or other behaviors that contribute to overall work performance. Additionally, qualitative work evaluations normally involve discussions with employees to determine their feelings about the work experience and the tasks they have been assigned.

After performance evaluations have been conducted, the manager is responsible for making necessary adjustments so that the desired standard can be achieved. This means the manager must determine why a particular performance standard is not being met by the employee's current work performance.

Figure 4.2 Factors affecting employee performance:

- Deficiencies in employee performance due to effort or motivation to perform the tasks

- Employee not having the necessary technical skills to successfully complete the task

- The performance standard is unrealistic and must be adjusted

- The employee, workgroup, or organization does not have the resources required to complete the task

- Poor planning or organizing

- Unclear task assignment

Once the manager has determined why the performance standard is not being met, the necessary changes must be made and, if required, a new performance standard must be established for the next evaluation period.

Generally, this function occurs in three phases: preliminary, concurrent, and feedback monitoring. Preliminary monitoring is a screening mechanism used by the manager in an attempt to prevent problems in performance before they occur. This involves establishing accurate job descriptions that detail the skills and qualifications necessary to successfully complete the tasks assigned to a particular position. Concurrent monitoring takes place during the process of completing assigned tasks. The manager makes periodic checks to determine the progress employees are making on completing assigned tasks. This is a proactive approach to monitoring, in that managers attempt to make appropriate changes in employee performance or task assignment prior to the project being completed. The final phase in the monitoring function occurs when the manager provides feedback to employees regarding their work performance after the project has been completed. This is done for two reasons. First, providing feedback based on evaluations of employee performance helps with employee development and generally improves future performance. This feedback should include specific information on what the employees did correctly, as well as areas that are in need of improvement. The second reason that

feedback is provided at the end of a project is so that formal performance appraisals can be conducted and used for administrative (reward) purposes. Often, these evaluations are documented and placed in employee files so that a record can be kept on each employee's performance and the feedback management provided regarding task performance.

Managerial Skills

Skills Needed by Sport Managers/ Administrators

- Technical skills
- Human skills
- Conceptual skills

Just as an employee develops the skills necessary to complete assigned tasks, managers must work on developing their skills in the workplace. Also, managers will have to use these skills at different times, and, in certain situations, a combination of the skills. This point reinforces the fact that being a manager is at times difficult, due to the complexities of the work environment. We will explore the skills of management by dividing them into three different categories: a) technical skills, b) human skills, and c) conceptual skills. Like any other activity that requires a certain level of proficiency, managers must work at becoming better at each of the aforementioned skills and seek opportunities to practice and refine these skills. The following is a brief description of each of the skills.

Technical skills involve knowledge of operations, activities, and processes necessary to accomplish organizational goals and objectives. You can think of technical skills as the "know how" in terms of what tasks employees are assigned. A ticket manager for a professional sport team must have thorough knowledge of the ticketing software used by employees when processing ticket orders. In addition to understanding the technical aspects of a task, managers must be able to educate and supervise employees on the task and be able to handle any difficulties that prevent employees from completing assigned responsibilities.

A second skill that is critical to being an effective manager is the ability to work with and supervise a variety of different employees. Thus, the **human skill** of management involves aspects of leading, communicating, motivating, and, in general, dealing with all aspects of employee relations on a daily basis. The difficult element of this skill is that each employee will be unique and thus respond to managerial influence in a different way. This means that a manager must understand what strategies to use when communicating, motivating, and supervising various employees in their work group.

A final skill required of managers is the ability to conceptualize how all the different parts of the organization fit together so that established goals and objectives can be achieved. The managerial term synergy describes this **conceptual skill**, in that a manager must be able to understand how the different departments of the organization are linked. Often you will hear someone say that it is important to understand the "big picture" when establishing a plan of action or organizing employees into work groups. This "big picture" approach requires the manager to imagine how things would best work together so that the organization can be efficient in its use of resources and effective in achieving goals.

One particular management skill that requires a mastery of all of the above-described categories is **decision making**. There is the distinct possibility that as you read this chapter you have already had to make a number of decisions today. These decisions could range from very simple, such as what to eat for breakfast, to difficult decisions such as choosing an academic major. When making a decision, whether simple or difficult, you must gather and evaluate necessary information so that your decision can be informed and based on relevant facts.

Decision-making is a **primary skill** that a manager will have to utilize when fulfilling the functions of management and executing the different skills necessary to direct employees towards the achievement of established goals and objectives. In fact, the ability to make correct decisions when confronted with organizational opportunities or challenges is one of the main factors that distinguish good managers from bad.

When making decisions, managers will be confronted with issues that are potential problems for the organization, as well as issues that represent opportunities for growth and advancement. Chelladurai (2001) defines a problem as "a situation that reduces or could reduce the effectiveness of the organization, or a situation that disrupts operations" (p. 201). For instance, an athletic director could be confronted with a problem if severe weather forces the cancellation of a home football game, creating the need to reschedule the game on a different date. Solving this problem involves not only rescheduling the game with the other school, but making sure that all groups involved (i.e., media, concessions, transportation, security, EMTs) can be present on the new date. While a problem has the potential to disrupt the operations of an organization, opportunities present issues or situations that could benefit the organization in terms of profitability, improved production or services, and growth (Chelladurai, 2001). Professional sport leagues will at times establish a new franchise in a market that does not have an existing team from that league. The creation of a new franchise allows the league to continue to grow and creates a new revenue stream based on the league entering a new market.

Decisions that managers have to make can also be classified as routine or complex. A routine decision is one that could involve clear decision criteria, be repetitive in nature, and involve the application of established rules or policies. An example of a routine decision could be how the National Basketball Association (NBA) decides the draft order for the upcoming amateur draft. Teams are placed in selection order based on their previous year's record, and for the top 13 spots a lottery is conducted to determine selection position. The process of deciding selection order is a routine decision in that it takes place every year and involves the application of specified rules created by the NBA. In contrast, complex decisions are those that have more complicated decision criteria, can be difficult to clearly define, and often involve no set policies or rules that can be used in the decision making process. After each NBA franchise learns which selection number it will have in the upcoming draft, it must then go through the process of deciding which player to select. There are no set rules or policies that dictate which player should be selected, and often the team cannot use the same decision criteria as the previous year because it has different player personnel needs, and the draft pool is comprised of a new group of players. This means that management must identify the needs of

Figure 4.3 Problem Solving Methodology

1. Define and clarify the problem or opportunity.

2. Identify the decision objectives.

3. List, categorize, and analyze all relevant information related to the decision.

4. Identify any issues that may present "roadblocks" to arriving at the correct decision.

5. Generate possible alternatives that solve the problem or capitalize on an opportunity.

6. Select the best two or three alternatives for consideration.

7. Make your decision by selecting the best alternative.

8. Implement the decision by activating policy or rule changes and necessary action steps.

9. Evaluate the effectiveness of the final decision after it has been implemented.

the team for the upcoming year and go through the process of evaluating players that demonstrate the potential to fulfill those needs.

Whether confronted with a complex or simple decision, managers will often use a systematic decision making approach to gather and analyze information. This process helps ensure that all relevant facts and information related to the decision will be considered, which increases the likelihood that the best decision will be made. While there are a number of different systematic decision making models that can be utilized by managers, Railey and Tschauner (1993) suggest a basic process that can be implemented by managers in a variety of settings.

Management personnel that utilize a systematic decision making process increase the likelihood that all relevant information will be evaluated and decision making within the organization will be consistent with the established goals and objectives.

In addition to using a systematic process when making decisions, managers must also understand the ramifications of the decisions they make. Managers use their conceptual skills so that they can determine the immediate and long-term effects of a decision. In addition, managers must consider how different groups or individuals will respond to decisions that are made. Hums, Moorman, and Wolf (as cited in Hums & MacLean, 2004) suggest that managers can develop increased understanding of their decisions and the ramifications they will have by applying the SLEEPE principle. Essentially this model allows managers to evaluate decisions from a number of different viewpoints with the goal being improved understanding of the impact of a particular decision. Following is a brief description of the different components of the SLEEPE model.

1. **Social** – How will society at large and the local community respond to the decision? Will there be the necessary support from different groups required to effectively put the decision into action? Will public perception of the organization change based on this decision, or is it in line with the mission of the organization?

2. **Legal** – Is the decision in line with organizational rules or policies? Does the decision being made violate any local, state, or federal laws? It is very likely that decisions which violate organizational rules or governmental laws will not be viewed in a positive manner.

3. **Economic** – How will this decision influence the economic situation of the organization? Are there the necessary resources required to carry out this decision? How will this decision affect the local economy?

4. **Ethical** – What are the ethical implications of the decision that is being made? Decisions that violate ethical principles of the organization or society as a whole are likely to meet with some resistance. Hums et al. identify this consideration as the most difficult and complex for managers of all the components of the SLEEPE model.

5. **Political** – The term political in the context of the SLEEPE model is not limited to elected officials, but rather includes all groups or individuals that have the ability to exert influence over an organization. If these groups or individuals are opposed to the decision being made, they may be less likely to support the organization in this or other endeavors.

6. **Educational** – This component applies to sport organizations that operate in the context of an educational setting (i.e., intercollegiate athletics). Decisions that are made must be evaluated in terms of whether they are in line with the overall mission of the educational institution.

Using the SLEEPE model when evaluating a decision can help managers understand how different groups will respond to a particular decision.

An additional consideration for managers in decision making is the inclusion of employees in the decision making process. Chalip (2001) identified that employees may provide assistance to management personnel in areas such as planning, generating ideas, problem solving, developing organizational polices/procedures, and governance. The benefits of including others in the decision making process include the following: a) the ability to gather and analyze a larger quantity of information relevant to the decision that must be made; b) increased likelihood of members having more comprehensive understanding of problem/opportunity being considered; c) improved member support of the final decision because they have been allowed to contribute in the decision making process; and d) less difficulty implementing the decision due to the fact that members have increased understanding and are supportive of the decision.

Despite these benefits, there are potential difficulties that also must be considered by managers when evaluating whether to include others in the decision making process. One difficulty is that group decision-making tends to take a longer period of time compared to the manager making the decision alone. A second challenge is that group members may not have the experience necessary to help in the decision making process. Complex decisions that must be made by managers require certain skills that often take time to develop and refine. An employee new to the organization may not have had the necessary experience in decision-making required for a particular dilemma. Finally, employees may not have access to or be able to understand information that must be gathered and analyzed when making a decision. In light of these benefits and challenges, a manager must be able to determine under what circumstances it would be best to include others in the decision making proces, and when it would be best to make the decision alone. One way that managers can make this determination is to answer the following three questions about a particular decision.

1. How important is the quality of the decision?

2. How much do others within the organization have to support and commit to the decision?

3. What is the timeframe for making a final decision? (Chalip, 2001)

As the quality required for a decision increases, so do the benefits associated with including others in the process. Remember, including employees in the decision making process increases the amount of information that is accumulated and also increases the quality of possible solutions. If the execution of a particular decision is going to require support from employees, it may be advantageous to allow group members to provide input, thus increasing the amount of ownership they have in the final decision. Finally, the amount of time available to make a decision will influence whether others can be included in the process or not.

A final consideration when discussing which decision style to use is the determination of which employees should be included in the decision making process. Chalip (2001) suggests that employees should be included in the decision making process when a) they have information that is relevant to the issues being considered, and b) the final decision will directly affect them or will require their support when being implemented. Also, in situations involving complex decisions or those that are somewhat risky in nature, managers should consider creating a group with individuals that have diverse viewpoints and opinions. This increases the possibility of analyzing a decision from different perspectives (i.e., SLEEPE model) and the creation of alternatives that are unique or represent a new approach to solving problems or taking advantage of an opportunity.

Managerial Roles

In addition to understanding the different functions of management and having the ability to implement the skills necessary to achieve organizational goals, managers must often fulfill particular roles within the organization. Mintzberg (1975) defined a managerial role as an "organized sets of behaviors identified with a position" (p. 54) and established that in most organizations a manager will occupy one of ten different roles at any particular time. These roles can be grouped into three different categories: interpersonal, informational, and decisional.

Interpersonal Roles

The formal position of the manager within the organization establishes three roles that require the manager to interact with employees. The first of these roles, **figurehead**, involves the manager fulfilling certain ceremonial functions as the result of being in charge of a certain department or the organization as a whole. An athletic director can fulfill this role by presenting an award to a team or individual student-athletes who have won championships in their respective sports. In this situation, the athletic director is not only representing the athletic department but the university as whole in recognizing the accomplishments of teams or individuals. The second role involves the manager being a **leader** to subordinates, directing them towards the achievement of assigned tasks. This role may require the manager to hire, train, supervise, motivate, and evaluate employees in the workplace. When discussing the leader role, Mintzberg states that "the influence of managers is most clearly seen in the leader role" (p. 55) and that, by their position, managers have significant power. However, their ability to use this power is largely dependent upon their capability to lead. The **liaison** role refers to the manager's ability to develop and cultivate relationships with individuals and groups in other departments or from different organizations. For instance, the general manager of a professional sports team will have to work with city and state government officials when seeking funding for a new stadium. In this situation, the general manager is the connection, or liaison, between government officials and the sport team. The type and quality of relationships that managers develop when fulfilling this role can have an impact on departmental or organizational success.

Informational Roles

A manager has access to many different sources of information based on the position occupied within the organization and the number of interpersonal contacts that occur in the workplace. After accessing information, managers must then process what was learned and distribute relevant pieces of information to different groups within the organization. Therefore, the manager can be viewed as an information center and, because of this, executes the roles of monitor, disseminator, and spokesperson. As **monitor**, the manager must search the internal and external environment for information that could affect the organization. In this role, the manager seeks information from liaisons, subordinates, superiors, different media sources, and the network of contacts that a manager develops over time. In addition, managers will rely on hearsay, gossip, and speculation at times, so that they can be up to date on events that are about to occur. Once the manager has accessed and processed the information, the decision must be made regarding which employees need to know the information. As **disseminator**, the manager screens information and passes it along to employees who otherwise would probably not have access to it. Furthermore, a manager acts a bridge between employees who must exchange information but are unable to easily access each other. Finally, as **spokesperson**, the manager communicates information to groups that are outside the organization. For example, in an attempt to be the host city for an upcoming Super Bowl, the management personnel from the convention and visitor's bureau will likely have to make a presentation to the NFL detailing the benefits of having the event in their city.

Decisional Roles

As mentioned previously, decision making is a primary skill of management that is used in many of the situations with which a manager will be confronted. Fulfillment of the aforementioned informational roles allows the manager to access the information necessary to make informed decisions. Therefore, the interpersonal and informational roles that a manager occupies, combined with his or her formal position in the organization, places the manager in four decisional roles: entrepreneur, disturbance handler, resource allocator, and negotiator.

Entrepreneur managers look for ways to improve their work group, adapt to internal and external changes, and direct the organization towards opportunities that initiate growth. This means that managers are often on the lookout for new and improved ways to deliver services, provide products, or become more efficient in the use of organizational resources. The ticket manager for a professional baseball team who updates existing ticketing software so that the organization will be better able to track and service season ticket holders would be fulfilling the managerial role of entrepreneur.

Disturbance handler managers are responsible for reacting to changes affecting the organization that are unexpected and beyond the immediate control of the manager. These are situations that if not dealt with, could cause significant hardship for the organization and its employees. Recently, management personnel for the NHL and the player's union (NHLPA) have had to deal with major changes due to the labor dispute between the NHL and its players. Managers on both sides function as disturbance handlers by reacting to the lockout, which has obviously altered the normal operations of NHL.

When managers distribute organizational resources to different employees or work groups, they are acting as **resource allocators**. Most organizations have a limited number of resources available and therefore allocating the appropriate amount of these resources throughout the organization becomes a very important task for managers. Some professional sport leagues (i.e., NBA and NFL) have a limit on how much money teams can pay to players in the form of salaries. The presence of these "salary caps" means management personnel for each of the teams must decide what salary will be paid to each player while making sure to stay within the guidelines of the salary cap restrictions.

The final decisional role identified by Mintzberg (1975) is manager as **negotiator**. In this role, managers are responsible for conferring with employees and work groups located within the organization, as well as those that are on the outside. In order to accomplish organizational goals and objectives, management must often negotiate with other groups with regard to resources or other factors that influence the operations of the organization. Returning to our NHL example, representatives from the league and player's association meet to negotiate the terms of a new contract between the league and players with the hope of ending the current "lockout."

A final consideration regarding managerial roles is that they are for the most part inseparable. This means that a manager must have the ability to fulfill each role if he

©Eyewire Images

or she is going to be successful at directing employees towards the accomplishment of established tasks. Additionally, these roles are often dependent upon each other. For example, an athletic director must be able to fill the liaison role when interacting with the NCAA so that she can have access to information regarding changes in policies that cover student-athlete recruitment. The A.D. must then process this information and, as disseminator, distribute this information to the appropriate employees in the department. Finally, as disturbance handler, the A.D. must deal with any conflict or problems that arise as the result of new recruiting policies.

Management vs. Leadership

One argument that is sure to arise in most introductory management classrooms is whether or not there is a difference between a manager and a leader. While there are fairly strong points to be made on both sides of this debate, consensus of management scholars seems to be forming around the idea that yes, indeed, there is a difference between the two. With that being said . . . what is it? One way to view the difference between management and leadership is to look at the core of their responsibility, with respect to the skills discussed above. Managers must have developed technical skills primarily, as well as some human skills. Leaders must have a command of all three skill sets and, in order to be truly successful, must have a mastery of the very complex human and conceptual skills especially.

For some, the manager is the person who is in charge of their daily activities at the workplace. This person is their immediate supervisor, and the person to whom they must be most attentive. For these same people, the person that they identify as the organization's leader might be someone whom they have never met. For example, a person working in an entry-level district sales position for the Nike Company might never meet Phil Knight face-to-face. So the question becomes, how can Phil Knight lead someone whom he has never met? Well, that brings us to the core of the distinction between managers and leaders, and also reminds us of the discussion about organization that we had earlier. Phil Knight (or any leader) is primarily responsible for setting the overall vision, mission, and organizational culture within which workers at Nike function. While people in management positions have much more direct contact with employees, they are functioning within the environment created and maintained by the leadership of the organization. A manager within the organization implements that vision by working with subordinates to achieve multiple goals.

At this point, it is important to note that, while different, there should be no value judgment placed on the management versus leadership debate. While describing the differences between the two, it might be easy to get the impression that leadership attributes are somehow superior and more desirable than management ones, but that is simply not the case. They both have an important role to play in an organizations' success, and one cannot prosper in any business without the other. They are not so much different as they are *complementary* to one another within an organization. Additionally, one person can display elements of one or the other at any given time, as they are not mutually exclusive concepts. In this vein, it is more useful to view management and leadership as distinct *processes*, but *not* as different types of people.

Leadership

Leadership is a phenomenon that has been present and of interest to society for almost as long as civilization has existed. A profound curiosity with leadership has led to a vast amount of research in the past century that has comprised a central part of the social science literature. In fact, many might say that the history of the world is traced through the history of great leaders. From Moses to Mohammed, to Joan of Arc to Napoleon, to Winston Churchill to Ghandi, to Nelson Mandela to Martin Luther King, we as humans record our history through the chronicling of great leaders. Researchers in the field of sport management have likewise been enamored with the concept of leadership, whether it concerns how coaches deal with their athletes, how Athletic Directors motivate their employees, or how people create successful sport companies.

As much as leadership has been studied, what it is and how it works has yet to clearly materialize. Within the academic community, a clear definition of leadership has remained elusive, and it has been noted that "there are almost as many definitions of leadership as there are persons who have attempted to define the concept" (Stogdill, 1974, p. 259). However, "most definitions of leadership reflect the assumption that it involves a process whereby intentional influence is exerted by one person over other people to guide, structure, and facilitate activities and relationships in a group or organization" (Yukl, 1998, p. 3). This general definition is our preferred definition of leadership because it contains the three elements that we deem critical for leadership to be understood. First, leadership is a complex process. Second, it is **relational**, in that if nobody is following, you aren't leading. Finally, it involves **induction**. That is, if your followers would have reached the same destination in your absence, you haven't truly led them.

Evolution of Leadership Theory

As noted earlier, research in the area of leadership has been extensive, and as different themes have evolved over time, the definitions of leadership have changed to reflect these themes. Leadership literature has largely focused on theoretical issues that have developed from early trait theories to behavioral theories, to more recent situational and contingency theories, and finally to the contemporary conceptualizations variously known as visionary, charismatic or transformational, and collectively termed 'the new leadership.' Also included in this evolution are specific applications of leadership theory appropriate for certain industrial contexts, among them the Multi-Dimensional Leadership model (MML), designed specifically for use in the sport domain.

Some of the earliest systematic attempts to conceptualize leadership were known as the **trait theories**. This approach focused on the characteristics, or attributes, that distinguished leaders from non-leaders. The traits under investigation included physical characteristics (e.g., height, appearance), personality traits (e.g., arrogance, self-esteem), and general ability traits (e.g., intelligence, insight, energy). Hundreds of trait studies were conducted in the early and mid-1900s, but it was ultimately realized that this line of research was not going to yield a consistent relationship to leadership effectiveness. It did, however, become clear to most that while particular traits were not predictors of leader success, certain characteristics would, in some situations, increase the likelihood of a leader emerging. In general, effective leaders appear to be more likely to have traits such as self-confidence, high energy, stress tolerance, integrity, and maturity than will unsuccessful or non-leaders (Yukl, 1998).

As the limitations of the trait theories became evident, many researchers shifted the focus of their studies towards specific behaviors exhibited by leaders. The **behavioral approach** emphasized what leaders and managers actually did on the job, as opposed to their personal characteristics. The behavior leadership theorists focused not only on what leaders do, but also on how often and at what intensity they do certain things to distinguish themselves as leaders. The perceptions of followers to this leader behavior would then, in turn, influence them to act in the manner that they saw fit.

Descriptive research into the leaders' decision making, monitoring practices, and motivating and problem solving processes is characteristic of the behaviorist approach (Yukl & Van Fleet, 1992). The major contribution of the behavioral line of research came from the Ohio State University in the 1950s, which classified leader behaviors into two independent categories: 1) task-oriented behaviors (initiating structure) and 2) people-oriented behaviors (consideration).

From these classifications, certain leader behaviors came to be associated with prescribed follower and organizational outcomes. However, the reliability of such associations was suspect. After a point it became clear that these broadly defined categories were too abstract to provide the basis for understanding the true complexity of leadership and the role requirements of leaders. As Yukl and Van Fleet (1992) stated, "As we found in the trait research, the behavior research suffers from a tendency to look for simple answers to complex questions" (p. 160). As such, the behaviorist view of leadership spurred the emergence of the consideration of time and circumstance alongside leadership traits and

behaviors. The results of this development in leadership thinking came to be more commonly known as the situational leadership theories.

The **situational approach** to the study of leadership attempted to build upon the foundation that was laid by the study of traits and behaviors. Situational leadership studies (also referred to as 'contingency theories') resulted in an understanding that the traits and behaviors identified previously would only be successful to the degree to which any particular situation allowed. Intervening, or moderating, factors were now being brought into the picture by researchers when assessing the overall impact, or appropriateness, of leader behavior. Among the theories that gained recognition in this era were Fiedler's Contingency Model (1967), House's Path-Goal Theory (1971), and Hersey and Blanchard's Situational Leadership Theory (1977).

These models and theories focused on how different moderating variables could affect the outcomes of certain leader behaviors. While these theories provided some deeper insight into the nature of leadership and its effectiveness, many of them were too generally stated and were not empirically testable (Yukl, 1998). As with the behavioral theories, the **contingency approaches** also tended to oversimplify the process of leading by focusing on the 'one best way' to behave in certain situations. This lack of flexibility ultimately revealed that these theories had very little utility for improving the effectiveness of practicing managers. Despite their shortcomings, the contingency theories do make a positive contribution for improving the effectiveness of managers in a general sense.

Contemporary Theories

In the past two decades, leadership researchers developed a broader perspective of the leader-follower relationship as they examined the changes in the followers that came as a result of leader influence. This approach led to the **contemporary theories** of leadership that characterized the leader as charismatic, inspirational, visionary, and/or transformational. Bryman (1992) collectively termed these contemporary approaches 'the new leadership' paradigm. Visionary leadership researchers focused on the effectiveness of leaders who were able to extrapolate future goals and successes from the mundane day-to-day activities that consume a leader's time and energy. These leaders are purported to make this a shared vision with others in the group or organization through the leader's heightened communication skills (Bennis & Nanus, 1985).

Charismatic Leadership

Charismatic leadership theorists have focused on leaders from the perspective that they were perceived to have certain exceptional qualities that allowed for greater influence over followers in particular situations. German sociologist Max Weber, often cited as the ultimate authority on charisma, saw charismatic leadership as a combination of certain magical qualities that a person would possess that were inaccessible to other, non-charismatic people (Weber, 1947). It is these unique qualities and attributes that compel followers to devote themselves to the leader.

House (1977) was a major contributor to the area of charismatic leadership. He suggested that the personal characteristics of a leader that make up charisma are a high level of self-confidence and a need to influence others, coupled with a dominant personality and a strong conviction in the integrity of their own beliefs. Charismatic leaders have been described as role models for their followers, who build their image so as to create an impression of success and competence. They express ideological goals that serve as ideals for the organization. They are good communicators who can motivate followers to strive towards set goals. In summary, charismatic leaders are believed to be those who have abilities and characteristics that allow them to identify closely with their followers, are able to see clearly into what they want the future to be like, and are able to chart a clear path towards fulfilling that vision.

Conger and Kanungo (1987) introduced Attribution Theory of charismatic leadership, which asserted that follower attributions were responsible for a leader's perceived charisma. This theory suggested that followers attributed charisma to those leaders who acted in an unconventional and sometimes risky fashion, and to those who made self-sacrifices and were confident in their vision, no matter the personal cost. This theory also argued that *facilitating conditions* were needed in order for charisma to be attributed to the leader. These conditions might include having a sense of urgency surrounding a particular situation, having a great deal of follower dissatisfaction with the status quo, or having a group of followers who receive satisfaction from their ability to please and/or imitate the leader.

Transformational Leadership

Charisma is an important component in transformational leadership, another aspect of the 'new leadership' paradigm, but is not the only important element. Bass (1985), defined charisma as "a necessary ingredient of transformational leadership, but by itself is not sufficient to account for the transformational process" (p. 31). Combining charismatic and visionary qualities with the ability to persuasively communicate that vision to followers is what constitutes the major components of a transformational leader. Transformational leadership theory has received the most attention among researchers investigating 'new leadership' paradigms. This theory focuses on the leader-follower relationship and examines how this relationship can be beneficial to both parties—to the group and to the organization as a whole (Bass, 1990; Bass & Avolio, 1994). This theory has two parts: transformational leadership and transactional leadership.

Transformational leaders are those people who "seek to raise the consciousness of followers by appealing to higher ideals and moral values such as liberty, justice, equality, peace, and humanitarianism, not to baser emotions such as fear, greed, jealousy, or hatred" (Yukl, 1989, p. 210). These leaders have been purported to heighten follower expectations and thereby instill in them a greater desire to put forth the effort needed to achieve. Transformational leaders are able to make the followers feel a part of the changing environment by making them feel included and supported, thereby instilling in them higher self-esteem, a willingness to change and put aside self-interest, and to commit themselves to the leader's vision (Bass & Avolio, 1994).

As described by Bass and Avolio (1994), transformational leadership theory has four major components labeled "the Four Is": (a) Idealized influence, (b) Inspirational motivation, (c) Intellectual stimulation and, (d) Individualized consideration.

Idealized influence refers to the position of role model that the transformational leader assumes in the eyes of his or her followers. This characteristic closely mirrors the term charisma used by other leadership theorists. This leader will be highly respected, admired, and trusted as a result of demonstrating high moral standards and ethical conduct. The leader will put the followers' feelings and needs above his or her own, which will lead to a heightened sense of commitment and a desire to emulate the leader and be leaders themselves.

Inspirational motivation refers to the concept that transformational leaders will inspire and motivate those around them, encouraging others to find challenge and personal meaning in their work, and will thereby foster enthusiasm throughout the organization. This component of transformational leadership involves the leader's ability to communicate clearly with followers, demonstrate commitment, and solve problems and achieve set goals.

Intellectual stimulation is the component of the theory that resides in the leader's ability to challenge followers to be more creative and innovative and to be supportive of follower efforts even when in error. Followers are encouraged in all instances to try new ideas and to question traditional techniques, assumptions, and problem solving methods. The intellectually stimulating leader also provides followers with the means to follow through on their initiatives. Through this process, followers are enabled to formulate their own methods of problem solving, which encourages them to take on positions of leadership in future situations.

Individualized consideration refers to the role of coach, or mentor, that the transformational leader assumes in the eyes of followers in an organization. Special consideration is given to the unique needs and desires of each individual as they interact with the leader. The leader stimulates followers to achieve higher levels of potential by creating new learning opportunities, increasing responsibility, and recognizing individual differences. The individually considerate leader is an effective listener who keeps open constant and effective lines of communication and attempts to be physically accessible to all followers.

The other element of transformational leadership theory is called *Transactional Leadership.* Transactional leaders seek to motivate people by appealing to their self-interests and by developing a relationship with their followers based on an exchange of effort for reward. This reciprocal relationship can exist comfortably, but the transactional leader would more aptly be classified as a manager (*see earlier discussion)*, as this re-

lationship rarely results in the followers performing beyond the status quo.

Figure 4.4 Yukl's (1998) Guidelines for Transformational Leadership

- Articulate a clear and appealing vision, and explain how the vision can be attained.

- Act confident and optimistic, and express that confidence in followers.

- Provide opportunities for early success, and celebrate these successes.

- Use dramatic, symbolic actions to emphasize key values.

- Lead by example.

- Empower people to achieve the vision.

It is important to note that transactional and transformational leadership are not mutually exclusive concepts. Leaders can display varying degrees of either behavior, depending on the situation. However, those leaders who consistently display more transformational behaviors have been shown to be considerably more effective within their organizations than those leaders who are consistently transactional (Bass & Avolio, 1994).

Multidimensional Model of Leadership (MML)

Chelladurai attempted to synthesize the earlier approaches to the study of leadership by developing the Multidimensional Model of Leadership (1978, 1993). This model of leadership incorporates the leader, follower, and situational context dimensions of leadership. According to the MML, situational characteristics (such as group size, structure, tasks, and goals, as well as technology, social norms, and expectations), leader characteristics (e.g., personality, ability, experience), and member characteristics (e.g., demographics, attitudes, ability) are antecedents of leader behavior. Leader behavior is further classified as being that which is required, preferred, or actual. Required leader behavior takes into account situational constraints on behavior (e.g., organizational goals, structure, technology, group task, social norms, external regulations, nature of the group). Preferred leader behavior incorporates the type of behavior that followers would like to see in their leader. Actual leadership behavior describes how a leader behaves in a given situation. It is the congruence of these three factors that in large part determines the levels of performance and satisfaction that are the consequences of leadership in the MML. More recently, elements of transformational leadership theory have been included in the MML to reflect the fact that these types of leaders will be able to significantly influence the environment within which they function. That is, they will be able to alter the situational and member characteristics in such a fashion that they can essentially create the facilitating conditions needed for them and their organization to succeed (Chelladurai, 2001).

Can You Be a Great Leader?

We have focused a lot on *what leadership is*, but not on *what leaders do*. It is the actions of leaders that will lead followers to form an opinion of that person, for better or worse. Therefore, we should address here the most important actions that you will take as a leader, and discuss how perceptions of your leadership style and effectiveness will be formed by your followers. There are three main criteria that people use when evaluating your quality as a leader. They will take note of 1) your use of power and influence, 2) how you communicate, and 3) how you make decisions. The decision making options that a leader has at his or her disposal were detailed earlier in the management skills section, but now we would like to discuss the other two criteria.

Sources of Power and Influence

If asked to boil leadership down to its core, we could say simply that it is the influence over followers. This influence process permeates organizations, and mastering it is a key to being an effective leader. As Yukl

Photo by Nick Manning, courtesy of ©stock.xchng iv

(1998) notes, "to understand what makes managers effective requires an analysis of the complex web of power relationships and influence processes found in all organizations" (p. 175). Further, it is your use of these power relationships that will contribute to the perception of your leadership style that others have of you. Managerial power can be defined as a person's potential to influence the contextual elements of an organization, as well as the attitudes and behaviors of others.

French and Raven (1959) identified five primary sources of power for leaders in organizations that were labeled *reward power* (ability to reward), *coercive power* (ability to punish), *legitimate power* (authority to make requests), *expert power* (special knowledge), and *referent power* (charisma). Another source of power in organizations derive from the political processes that are inherent within them. These political processes are, in fact, merely mechanisms by which an individual can increase his or her power within an organization. As outlined by Pfeffer (1981), *political power* refers to processes such as forming coalitions, keeping control over key decisions, co-optation (undermining expected opposition), and institutionalization (filtering information to artificially inflate ones importance).

Ultimately, the opinion that followers form of a leader and that leaders' success "depends greatly on the manner in which power is exercised. Effective leaders are likely to use power in a subtle, careful fashion that minimizes status differentials and avoids threats to the target person's self-esteem. In contrast, leaders who exercise power in an arrogant, manipulative, domineering manner are likely to engender resentment and resistance" (Yukl, 1998, p. 202).

Communication Styles

Most experts on organizations agree that the key process underlying effective organizational functioning is communication (see Chapter 3). This makes sense when you consider that the word 'organization' implies a coordinated effort by a group of people, and that communication is critical for coordination. Without effective communication, people in the organization would not know what to do and would not know what others were doing. The vast majority of a leaders' time is spent communicating with others, whether it is speaking or listening to others, emailing, writing personal notes, or reading material transmitted from others. As a leader, the communication patterns that you establish will be important in crafting your leadership image in the eyes of others.

Leaders communicate with others in many different ways. However, to be a good leader you must understand that *how* you communicate sends messages equally as strong as *what* you communicate. In the highly technological workplace of today, leaders have more communication options at their disposal than ever before. Communication options include any way that you choose to send messages to others, and they include face to face discussions, email, handwritten messages, memos posted on a bulletin board, newsletters, etc. Leaders must understand that virtually everything that they do will somehow communicate a message to those who surround them.

Most administrators have a consistent personal communication style that will help to define them as a leader. As you might expect, some methods are more effective than others. McCallister (1994) identified six main ways that people communicate:

- *The Noble* – tend not to filter what they are thinking and use few words to get their messages across.

- *The Socratic* – believe in carefully discussing things before making any decisions and enjoy the process of arguing their points in detail.

- *The Reflexive* – concerned with the interpersonal aspects of communicating, do not wish to offend others, and are therefore often great listeners.

- *The Magistrate* – style is a mix of Noble and Socratic; tell you exactly what they think, and may make their case in great detail; also tend to have an air of superiority about them because they tend to dominate discussion.

- *The Candidate* – a mix of the Socratic and Reflexive; tend to be warm and supportive while also being analytical and chatty; base their interactions on a great deal of information and do so in a very likable manner.

- *The Senator* – have developed both the Noble and Reflexive styles, but do not mix the two; rather, they move back and forth between them as needed.

Understanding which of these six styles best describes you will help you to accurately interpret your communication style from the 'receiver' point of view. It should be noted that most of us will often fluctuate among styles but will more consistently use just one. Also, each style has its own relative strengths and weaknesses and should not be thought of as superior or inferior to any other. The best advice for leaders is to understand your own predominant communication style, but then also endeavor to *match your communication style* with the situation and with those with whom you are trying to communicate.

Summary

- As the sport industry continues to grow and become more complex, the need for effective managers and leaders has increased. Critical to the success of sport organizations is individuals that can direct employees towards the accomplishment of established goals and objectives.

- The many facets of management are more easily understood if separated into the basic functions, skills, and roles that managers are expected to master. The functions of management include: a) planning (establishment of goals and objectives), b) organizing (delegation of tasks), c) directing (leading and motivating), and d) monitoring (evaluating performance).

- The skills needed to be an effective manager can be separated into three categories: a) technical (knowledge of operations), b) human (interpersonal skills), and c) conceptual skills ("big picture"). A manager will often use a combination of these functions and skills when fulfilling the ten managerial roles identified by Mintzberg.

- Decision making is a primary skill that managers will have to utilize when fulfilling the functions of management and executing the different skills necessary to direct employees towards the achievement of organizational goals and objectives.

- Decision making is a complex activity that involves dealing with problems and opportunities, decisions that are routine or complex, and whether to include others in the decision making process or make the decision in an autocratic manner.

- One issue that arises in most management courses is the difference between being a manager and being a leader. Managers tend to focus more on technical and human skills while leaders must have competency in all three skills. Furthermore, leaders may be required to deal with more "big picture" issues that affect the organization.

- Successful organizations must have people that are effective managers and leaders, and at times these roles are occupied by the same person. Therefore, it is helpful to consider management and leadership as distinct processes but not as different types of people.

- Study of leadership has evolved from initial examination of leader characteristics to the "new leadership paradigm," which examines the changes in follower attitudes and behaviors that result from the influence of the leader.

- Leadership theory can be separated into a) trait approach (focus on leader characteristics/attributes); b) behavioral approach (emphasis on leader actions/behaviors); c) situational approach (relationship between leader, member, and the situation); and contemporary theories (charismatic, transformational, and transactional leadership).

- The multidimensional model of leadership (MML) has attempted to combine the different approaches and theories into one explanation of effective leadership. This theory explores different antecedents that influence what a leader will do and combines this with the required, actual, and preferred leader behavior.

- The three criteria most often used to evaluate whether someone is an effective leader include: a) the leader's use of power and influence, b) ability to communicate, and c) how the leader makes decisions.

Discussion Activities

1. Of the four functions of management, directing is often identified as one of the more challenging responsibilities of being a manager. Discuss why directing employees can be difficult and what you can do to become better at this function.

2. Discuss how you would provide feedback to an employee who has not performed up to desired standards. What strategies could you use to improve performance and what could be done to make sure the employee does not become frustrated or discouraged?

3. The general manager of a professional football team must decide whether to release a veteran running back that has been with the team for ten years. This move is being considered because the team is currently over the projected salary cap. The running back has a high dollar contract, is at the end of his career, and will likely see limited playing time next season. However, this player is a fan favorite because of his dedication to the team and the community at large. Each year this player hosts numerous fundraising events that benefit different charitable groups in the area. Use the SLEEPE model of decision-making to identify the implications of releasing or not releasing the player from the football organization.

4. Explain how the Athletic Director at a NCAA Division I institution could fulfill the different managerial roles identified by Mintzberg. For example, as a resource allocator the Athletic Director must determine the budgets for individual teams and departments for the upcoming fiscal year.

5. Discuss what you think are some differences between management and leadership.

6. What are some reasons for including others in the decision-making process? As a manager, what challenges would you have to overcome when allowing employees to contribute to decision-making? Under what circumstances to you think it would be best for a manager to make decisions using an autocratic decision-making style?

7. In groups of 3 – 5 students, identify ten individuals you think exhibit good leadership qualities in sport. Which characteristics do they have in common? Which are different?

8. Develop a business plan for a new sport-related company, making sure to address the planning, organizing, controlling, and evaluating functions.

References

Barney, J. (1991). Firm resources and sustained competitive advantage. *Journal of Management, 17*(1), 99-120.

Bass, B. M. (1985). *Leadership and performance beyond expectations.* New York: The Free Press.

Bass, B. M. (1990). *Bass and Stogdill's handbook of leadership* (3rd ed.). New York: The Free Press.

Bass, B. M., & Avolio, B. J. (Eds.). (1994). *Improving organizational effectiveness through transformational leadership.* Thousand Oaks, CA: Sage Publications.

Bridges, F. J., & Roquemore, L. L. (2004). *Management for athletic/sport administration: Theory and practice* (4th ed.). Decatur, GA: ESM Books.

Bryman, A. (1992). *Charisma & leadership in organizations.* Newbury Park, CA: Sage Publications.

Chalip, L. (2001). Group decision making and problem solving. In B. L. Parkhouse (Ed.), *The management of sport: Its foundation and application* (pp. 93-110). Boston, MA: McGraw-Hill Higher Education.

Chelladurai, P. (1978). *A contingency model of leadership in athletics.* Unpublished doctoral dissertation. University of Waterloo, Waterloo, Canada.

Chelladurai, P. (1993). Leadership. In R. N. Singer, M. Murphey, & L. K. Tennant (Eds.), *Handbook of research on sport psychology*, pp. 647-671. New York: Macmillan.

Chelladurai, P. (2001). Managing *Organizations for Sport and Physical Activity: A Systems Perspective.* Holcomb Hathaway Publishers, Scottsdale, AZ.

Conger, J. A., & Kanungo, R. (1987). Towards a behavioral theory of charismatic leadership in organizational settings. *Academy of Management Review, 12*, 637-647.

French, J., & Raven, B. H. (1959). The bases of social power. In D. Cartwright (Ed.), *Studies of social power.* Ann Arbor, MI: Institute for Social Research, pp. 150-167.

House, R. J. (1971). A path-goal theory of leader effectiveness. *Administrative Science Quarterly, 16*, 321-339.

House, R. J. (1977). A 1976 theory of charismatic leadership effectiveness. In J. G. Hunt & L. L. Larson (Eds.). *Leadership: The cutting edge.* Carbondale, IL: Southern Illinois University Press.

Hums, M. A., & MacLean, J. C. (2004). *Governance and policy in sport organizations.* Scottsdale, AZ: Holcomb Hathaway.

McCallister, L. (1994). *I wish I'd said that! How to talk your way out of trouble and into success.* New York: Wiley Publishing.

Mintzberg, H. (1975). The manager's job: Folklore and fact. *Harvard Business Review, 53*, 49-61.

Pfeffer, J. (1981). *Power in organizations.* Marshfield, PA: Pittman.

Stogdill, R. M. (1974). *Handbook of Leadership: A survey of the literature.* New York: The Free Press.

Weber, M. (1947). *The Theory of Social and Economic Organization.* New York: The Free Press.

Yukl, G. A., & Van Fleet, D. D. (1992). Theory and research on leadership in organizations. In M. D. Dunnette & L. M. Hough (Eds.), *Handbook of Industrial and Organizational Psychology* (2nd ed.). Palo Alto, CA: Consulting Psychologists Press.

Yukl, G. A. (1989). *Leadership in organizations* (2nd ed.). Englewood Cliffs, NJ: Prentice Hall.

Yukl, G. A. (1998). *Leadership in organizations* (4th ed.). Englewood Cliffs, NJ: Prentice Hall.

Suggested Reading

Bass, B. M. (1960). *Leadership, psychology, and organizational behavior.* New York: Harper Publishing.

Bass, B. M. (1988). Evolving perspectives on charismatic leadership. In J. Conger et al. (Eds.), *Charismatic leadership: The illusive factor in organizational effectiveness.* San Francisco, CA: Jossey-Bass Publications.

Bennis, W., & Nanus, B. (1985). *Leaders: The Strategies for Taking Charge.* New York: Harper & Row.

Bennis, W. (1989). *Why Leaders Can't Lead: The Unconscious Conspiracy Continues.* San Francisco, CA: Jossey-Bass Publications.

Bennis, W. G., & Nanus, B. (1985). *Leaders: The strategies for taking charge.* New York: Harper & Row Publishers.

Burns, J. M. (1978). *Leadership.* New York: Harper & Row Publishers.

Conger, J. A. (1989). *The charismatic leader: Behind the mystique of exceptional leadership.* San Francisco, CA: Jossey-Bass Publishers.

Fiedler, F. E. (1967). *A theory of leadership effectiveness.* New York: McGraw-Hill.

Hersey, P., & Blanchard, K. H. (1977). *Management of organizational behavior: Utilizing human resources* (3rd ed.). Englewood Cliffs, NJ: Prentice-Hall.

Kelman, H. C. (1958). Compliance, identification, and internalization: Three processes of attitude change. *Journal of conflict resolution, 2*, 51-56.

Kerr, S., & Jermier, J. M. (1978). Substitutes for leadership: Their meaning and measurement. *Organizational behavior and human performance, 22*, 375-403.

Krzyzewski, M., & Phillips, D. T. (2000). *Leading with the Heart: Coach K's Successful Strategies for Basketball, Business, and Life.* New York: Warner Books, Inc.

Nanus, B. (1989). *The Leader's Edge: The seven keys to leadership in a turbulent world.* Chicago, IL: Contemporary Books.

Osborn, R. N., & Hunt, J. G. (1975). An adaptive-reactive theory of leadership: The role of macro variables in leadership research. In J. G. Hunt & L. L. Larson (Eds.), *Leadership frontiers.* Kent, OH: Kent State University.

Pfeffer, J. (1977). The ambiguity of leadership. *Academy of Management Review, 2*, 104-112.

Railey, J. H., & Tschauner, P. R. (1993). *Managing physical education, fitness and sports programs.* Mountain View, CA: Mayfield Publishing Company.

Summit, P., & Jenkins, S. (1998). *Reach for the Summit: The Definite Dozen for Succeeding in Whatever You Do.* New York: Random House.

Vroom, V. H., & Yetton, P. W. (1973). *Leadership and decision-making.* Pittsburgh, PA: University of Pittsburgh Press.

Chapter Five

Economic Impact: An Introduction to Economic Theory

Matthew T. Brown and David Matthew Zuefle

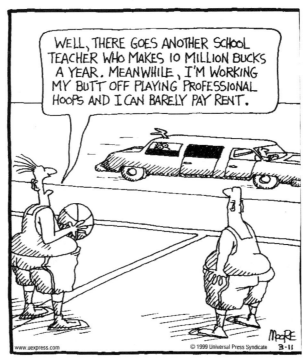

In another universe.

Learning Objectives

Upon completion of this chapter, the reader should be able to

- Appreciate economic theory in sport;

- Understand the laws of supply and demand;

- Analyze competitive balance in professional sport leagues;

- Understand the nuances of economic impact studies;

- Explain the realities and myths of economic impact studies; and

- Identify the abuses of economic impact studies.

Introduction

It is worth remembering that the social science of economics has long been jokingly referred to as the "dismal science," perhaps partially because of the pessimistic historical predictions made by early economists such as Thomas Malthus. Malthus became famous for suggesting—over 200 years ago—that unchecked world population growth would accelerate exponentially and would soon result in widespread famine and strife. Incidentally, most of Malthus's predications have failed to materialize due to what has been commonly seen as his failure to take new and emerging information into account. The lesson of Malthus should not be seen as a general criticism of the science of economics, but rather as a cautionary footnote to understanding the discipline's limitations.

> "IF IGNORANCE PAID DIVIDENDS, MOST AMERICANS COULD MAKE A FORTUNE OUT OF WHAT THEY DON'T KNOW ABOUT ECONOMICS."
>
> LUTHER H. HODGES

Economic questions most often involve dynamic, rather than static, analyses of collective human behavior—and these analyses are not limited to discrete mathematical formulae, but also should include insights from psychology, sociology, geography, political science, and other fields. The bottom line: economic questions, and the ways in which researchers attempt to address them, are complex and always changing. Studies attempting to gauge the economic impacts of sport development are no exception.

What is Economics?

Economics is the dynamic study of collective human behavior. Typically, economics involves the study of the market system. Why individuals have money, the determinants of the cost of products and the examination of the management of resources are all areas of study within economics. In sport, economists examine

- supply and demand within the sport industry;

- the market for sport broadcast rights;

- the relationship between team costs, profit and winning; and

- value of sports talent. (Fort, 2003)

Additionally, economists often examine the economic activity benefits accruing to a community hosting sporting events or building new stadiums or arenas. Sport managers may apply economic theory without realizing it. For example, when calculating price for games, a ticket manager may decide to use a variable pricing model. If she decides to charge $10.00 for general admission tickets on weekends and $7.00 for the same ticket Monday to Thursday, she is likely applying the economic principles of supply and demand. In this example, supply is fixed by the general admission seating capacity of the stadium. Demand likely is higher for the product on the weekend versus weekdays. With a static supply and a shift in demand on the weekends, the ticket manager can charge more for the same seat without negatively affecting attendance.

All in all, effective sport managers are ones with an understanding of key economic principles like opportunity and marginal costs, supply and demand, competitive balance, and economic impact. Managers with knowledge of these concepts will be able to anticipate the impact of financial decision-making on the sport enterprise.

Opportunity and Marginal Costs

A key belief of economists is that individuals and groups of people choose based on the costs and benefits of their actions. In Hamilton County, Ohio, the citizens approved a tax measure that ultimately led to close to $1 billion of public money being spent on two

new stadiums for the Cincinnati Reds (Great American Ballpark) and the Cincinnati Bengals (Paul Brown Stadium). Both stadiums have modern amenities, including the exclusive Fox Sports Net Club 4192 in Great American Ballpark (cincinnati.reds.mlb.com) and the 114 luxury suites and 7,600 club suites in Paul Brown Stadium (www.bengals.com).

Recently some critics have asked if there was or should have been a better use of taxpayer dollars. These missed chances are opportunity costs. The **opportunity cost** of a decision is what you must give up to have what you want. Those in Hamilton County wanted two new venues for their sport teams. They gave up $1 billion in public funds that may have been used to better the community infrastructure or improve public schools. In Washington D.C., the citizens are being asked by Major League Baseball to publicly fund a new stadium for the relocated Montreal Expos while the city lacks a public hospital. Their choice will be one of opportunity cost.

Opportunity costs involve either **explicit** or **implicit expenditures**. In Denver, if a fan decides to spend $75 to go to a Colorado Avalanche game, he then has $75 less to go to a Broncos game that week. This is an explicit expenditure, spending money on the Avalanche rather than the Broncos. If a friend in St. Louis invites you to a Rams game on Monday night and another friend invites you to a League Championship Series game between the Cardinals and Dodgers, you obviously cannot be in more than one place at once. Your choice is an implicit expenditure. The cost is the intangible benefits you would have received by going to the game you chose not to attend.

Opportunity costs also affect owners of sport properties. In the 1990s several profitable National Football League franchises moved. The Rams moved from Los Angeles to St. Louis, the Browns from Cleveland to Baltimore (where they became the Ravens), and the Raiders from Oakland to Los Angeles and then back to Oakland. While these franchises were making profits in their original locations, they were operating at an economic loss due to the new or renovated stadiums and revenue streams available elsewhere.

Sport managers, with an understanding of marginal costs, can predict human behavior through the examination of the benefits and costs of doing more. Another key rule of economic behavior is that people think about the marginal impact of their actions. **Marginal cost** is how much more an individual has to spend to get some more of what he or she wants, without worrying about what already has been spent. For the Texas Rangers, signing Alex Rodriguez to a $25 million per year contract drastically increased their payroll. The Rangers' marginal costs were not changed, however. Baseball teams like the Rangers sell tickets that allow people to see the players on their roster. The Rangers had to pay Rodriguez $25 million no matter how many people came to see him play in a given year.

The team raised ticket prices after signing Rodriguez, not necessarily because they had to, but because they could. Rodriguez's signing excited Ranger fans as he was, at the time, one of the best players in the game. With him on the team, Ranger fans were more willing to pay to see the Rangers play. This in turn makes them more willing to pay a higher price to see the team play.

Mark McGwire and his agent understood this concept when negotiating his contract with the St. Louis Cardinals. His presence on the team made the fans more willing to pay to see the team play, and seasonal attendance began to increase with McGwire on the roster. McGwire's agent negotiated a bonus for McGwire based on attendance. As a result, his salary increased by $1 for every fan in attendance above 2.8 million.

Supply and Demand

As a baseball fan earning $1,000 a month, you can afford to attend a certain number of games during the season based on the price of the team's tickets. If the team were to lower ticket prices suddenly in the middle of the year, you could then go to more games. This is the **Law of Demand**. The law states that when the price of an item declines, the demand for that item increases. When the price goes down enough, people like you can now afford to buy more of the product, which means you can attend additional games.

The relationship between price and the amount of product people wish to consume is called the demand curve. The demand curve slopes down because as price gets higher, the demand for a particular product decreases.

Supply is the quantity of a product that an owner is willing to offer or make available at a given price. The supply curve charts the relationship between the amounts of product a company or companies wish to sell and price.

Going back to the example discussed in the opening section of this chapter, a ticket manager determining price could plot the demand and supply curve for her product on one graph. The point where the supply curve and the demand curve overlap is the **equilibrium price**. Here is where the amount of product demanded (tickets) equals the amount of product supplied (number of seats in the ballpark). Notice the supply curve trends vertical. This is because the number of seats in the ballpark is fixed and does not change from game to game.

Changes in the demand curve also help explain why the ticket manager can charge $10 for tickets on the weekends and only $7 for those same seats on the weekdays. Figure 5.1 plots the supply curve for general admission seating at the ballpark. Again, the line trends vertical as the number of general admission seats is fixed. The demand curve for games Monday to Thursday (D_1) intersects the supply curve at $7.00. On weekends, the demand for those seats increases and the curve shifts to the right. The weekend curve (D_2) now intersects with the supply curve at $10. Because the demand for the product is greater on weekends, the ticket manager can charge more for seats because supply is fixed.

Competitive Balance

The National Football League (NFL) is likely the strongest league and sport property in North America. Most analysts attribute the league's strength to parity. In a given year, a last place team from the previous season has a realistic opportunity to compete for the Lombardi Trophy. The St. Louis Rams' rise from mediocrity to Super Bowl champion is the perfect example. In economic terms, the parity in the NFL is referred to as **competitive balance**.

The NFL is a league that shares a majority of its revenues—approximately 70%—between owners (Alesia, 2002). Additionally, the league's collective bargaining agreement limits the amount of money teams can spend on players (the salary cap). In Major League Baseball (MLB), where much less revenue is shared, where there is no salary cap, and where owners are willing to spend beyond the league's luxury tax threshold (e.g., the New York Yankees), **competitive imbalance** exists. Here certain teams consistently win more games over time than the rest of the teams in the league. As an example, the New York Yankees have won approximately one-in-

three World Series since 1920. When one team is located in a market where fans will pay more for wins, the more profitable team will win more over time. Therefore, as seen in Major League Baseball, profit variation harms competitive balance (Fort, 2003).

Competitive Advantage

Within the economic restrictions of the NFL, teams that are constantly successful understand competitive advantage. To operate within the framework of the NFL while signing better players than other teams in the league, it helps to have a thorough understanding of the collective bargaining agreement and league rules. As stated previously, NFL teams share approximately 70% of their revenues. The portion that is not shared primarily comes from amenities found in new stadiums like luxury and club seating (Brown et al., 2004). Owners can use their unshared revenue to create competitive advantage.

The NFL Collective Bargaining Agreement rules state that a signing bonus paid to a player is allocated over the time of the contract (up to seven years). So a player signing a 5-year $10 million contract with a $10 million signing bonus would be paid $12 million in year one and $2 million per year in years two through five. However, the salary counted against the team's cap would be $4 million per year (Brown et al., 2004). Teams with a new stadium filled with luxury seating have access to unshared revenue that can be used to pay large signing bonuses, which creates competitive advantage on the field.

Economic Impact

Economic impact, the focus of this chapter, is often used to justify the need to build these new stadiums with public taxpayer dollars.

What is Economic Impact?

In sport, **economic impact** is defined as the net economic change in a host community that results from spending attributed to a sport event or facility (Turco & Kelsey, 1992). This economic change has both tangible and intangible benefits. The tangible benefits can be seen in Figure 5.2.

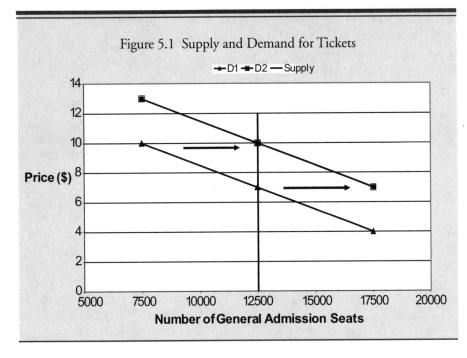

Figure 5.1 Supply and Demand for Tickets

As Figure 5.2 depicts, the community benefits when the city subsidizes a sporting event or facility if that subsidy leads to new visitors coming to the community. These visitors bring new money into the community, which then leads to job creation. Job creation lowers unemployment, and therefore the community as a whole benefits from its investment.

Economic impact studies measure the benefits a community receives. The study measures total economic loss or gain after accounting for costs (Agha, 2002). These studies were initially developed by cities to determine the economic impact individual business had on a community. Later they were adapted to measure spending based on a sporting event or a facility. In most communities, sport economic impact studies are conducted by the Chamber of Commerce or, in larger cities, the sports commission.

The first to apply economic impact studies to sport was the Indiana Sports Corporation (ISC). The ISC used their economic impact studies successfully to gain governmental support to build facilities and provide resources for sport in central Indiana. Some of the early events the ISC attracted included the 1982 Olympic Sport Fest and the 1987 Pan Am Games. The ISC's economic impact studies indicated that sporting activities in the state generated 60,000 new jobs and created 7,400 new businesses. The ISC was able to get funding from the state to support its activities because it could

prove that its activities created new jobs and brought new money to the region.

Types of Spending

Economic impact studies measure three types of spending: direct, indirect, and induced. **Direct spending** measures actual dollars spent in the local community on the event. This spending can be both on site and off site. On site spending includes items like concessions, tickets, parking, and merchandise. Off site spending is all other spending in the local community, like spending on hotels, for fuel, to shop, and to dine. The key to measuring direct spending is that it has to occur in the local economy as defined in the economic impact study.

Indirect and induced spending develops from direct spending (NASC, 2001). Direct spending creates secondary spending that circulates within the community (see Figure 5.3). This secondary spending includes indirect benefits like additional profits and incomes for local businesses and households. These local businesses then spend some of these dollars on goods and services that support additional local businesses. This is **indirect spending**.

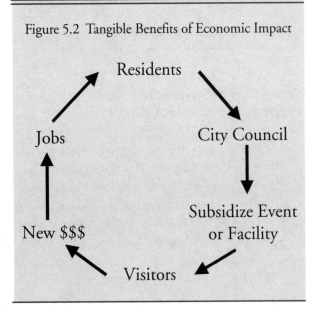

Figure 5.2 Tangible Benefits of Economic Impact

Residents

Jobs

City Council

Subsidize Event or Facility

New $$$

Visitors

At the same time, household wage earners receive additional income resulting from the increases in business spending. The wage earners spend some of their increased earnings on local goods and services. These expenditures are **induced spending**. Both indirect and induced are estimated using a regional multiplier.

The **regional multiplier** measures how many times money changes hands in the community before it leaves or leaks out of the region (see Figure 5.3). It is the value multiplied by direct spending to estimate total spending, or economic benefit. The multiplier estimates the secondary spending (indirect and induced) in a region. Figure 5.4 depicts the method by which a multiplier is calculated.

In Figure 5.4, the initial dollar is spent in the local economy. Of that initial dollar, $0.40 is respent in the local economy. Of the $0.40, $0.16 is respent. Then of the $0.16, $0.06 is respent and so on. By adding together the initial $1.00 of spending to the amount of money respent each round, you can calculate the multiplier for the region. For this example, when the initial round of spending is added to the five rounds of respending, the total spending generated in the community would be $1.66; therefore, the regional multiplier is 1.66.

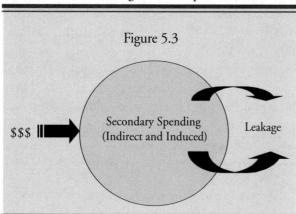

Figure 5.3

Steps to Completing an Economic Impact Study

To conduct an economic impact study, the first step is to define the local economy. For instance, when conducting an economic impact study on the American Legion State Baseball Tournament held in Athens, OH, researchers had to decide if the economy would be defined as the City of Athens, the area within the zip code of Athens, or Athens County. To define the economy, researchers must determine where a majority of impact will occur.

Second, the method for collecting data must be determined. In a basic economic impact study, direct spending is measured. Then the multiplier is applied to get total impact. To measure direct spending, data can be collected directly from participants and spectators or from indirect sources like hotels and restaurants. In some instances, it makes sense to use indirect sources. When hosting a conference tournament, the organizing committee knows where teams are staying. The committee can contact these hotels and obtain exact amounts spent by teams for the duration of the tournament.

In most instances, information will need to be collected directly from participants and spectators. Several data collection tools may be used, including self-administered questionnaires and logs or diaries. Most often, due to costs and efficiency of data collection, self-administered questionnaires are used.

Once the method of data collection is determined, the data must be collected. To accurately reflect the impact of an event, it is recommended that at least 350 surveys or diaries be collected. After the data collection, the results can be analyzed and direct spending determined.

Uses of Economic Impact in Sport

Economic impact studies are widely used in sport. As noted previously, the Indiana Sports Commission was the first to use economic impact studies to justify taxpayer subsidy. Other examples of the use in sport vary widely. In the National Football League (NFL), it is estimated by the Maryland Department of Business and Economic Development that the impact of the Baltimore Ravens was $202 million in gross expenditures and $96 million in personal income, with 2,772 full time jobs being created. An economic impact study on the Buffalo Bills indicated that the team's impact was $111.5 million annually. The Detroit Lions generated $127 in direct spending ("The fans," 2002).

For the Olympics, it was estimated that the economic impact for Atlanta in 1996 was $1.2 billion in direct spending, with the total impact over the short term being $5.1 billion (Humphreys & Plummer, 2004).

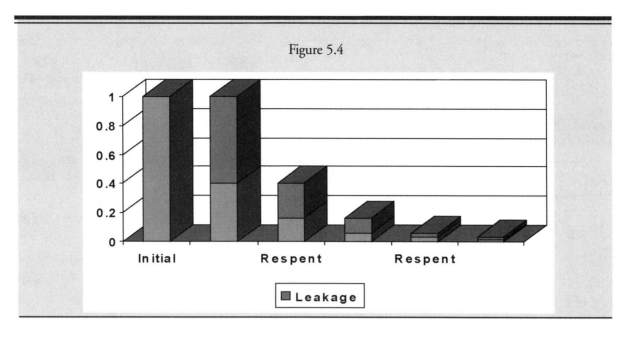

Figure 5.4

The impact for the 2002 Winter Olympics in Salt Lake was estimated to be $4.5 billion ("2002 Winter," 2003). In NASCAR, one study estimated that a new track would have an annual impact of $221 million (Trevison, 2004).

The Reality and Myth of Economic Impact in Sport

Rosentraub (1997) examined several sport economic impact studies. In an era where new stadiums were used to lure teams, these economic impact studies were used to justify the use of public funds to build the new sport venues. The Cleveland Browns moved to Baltimore when the owner was promised a new stadium built and paid for by taxpayers. The same was true for the Houston Oilers when they moved to Nashville. In hockey, the Winnipeg Jets moved to Phoenix and played for many years in the publicly funded America West Arena.

Rosentraub noted a problem with many of these studies, however. In several situations, studies were produced that gave the impression that for the right price one could get as large of an impact number as needed. For a team moving to a city, two studies could differ by over $100 million.

Economic Impact Study Abuses

While economic impact studies are valuable estimates that can aid in planning, development, and the public decision making process, they can also be misused—

sometimes through naïveté and unfamiliarity, and sometimes intentionally.

Professor John Crompton of Texas A&M University identified eleven sources of misapplication in a well-known 1995 article that appeared in *Journal of Sport Management*. Crompton's list includes such mistakes as failing to use the correct type of multiplier, failure to correctly calculate the multiplier itself, the inappropriate inclusion of local residents, "**time-switchers**," and "**casuals**" (types of visitors who were not drawn in by the event being studied), and the failure to consider opportunity costs. Along with these categories of mistakes, all of which could be committed unintentionally, Crompton also notes that some mistakes, such as the use of "fudged" multiplier coefficients, can be and are committed willfully (Crompton, 1995).

Crompton points out problems associated with multipliers that are not minor. Among these problems, one of the potentially most profound is that there is no one set of multipliers universally agreed upon and utilized by all researchers and critics. Commonly available commercial options include the RIMS II, IMPLAN, and REIM multipliers. Not only does the availability of competing multipliers contribute to the difficulty of making meaningful comparisons between studies, but it allows for the possibility of intentional misuse.

To illustrate this example, consider the case of a commercial firm with an interest in developing a downtown stadium complex in City A. The firm's best interests in this case would be promoted if an economic impact study demonstrated a large and sustainable return on the initial investment of City A in the project.

Thus, in theory, the firm—and perhaps its supporters within City A's government—could contract with a researcher who would calculate the total economic impact for City A using all common commercially available multipliers. If differences between the estimates existed, the researcher could then select the results that indicated the most favorable outcome for City A. The cost of buying several commercially calculated multipliers could be subsumed into the total project costs and would likely prove to be only a very small percentage of the total study's expense.

While this scenario is hypothetical, and an approach such as the one described in it could be seen as cynical at best and completely unethical at worst, it is clearly possible—and the forces that could promote this kind of questionable decision-making are present and powerful.

Intangible Benefits

Many American communities are in transition from more traditional economic bases of support, such as shipping and manufacturing, to new service-oriented industries, such as sport, entertainment, and tourism. And since all politicians must address issues related to employment and the economy, the ability to "create" jobs and wealth are often touted as reasons to support new initiatives and to vote for local tax and rezoning issues related to sport and tourism development.

Through new building, development, and policy changes, local government officials often hope not only to invigorate the private sector but to increase sport tourism-related revenues through the collection of sales taxes, lodging/hospitality taxes, user fees, and even fines from the visitors who come to their cities. In addition to these multiple streams of revenue, which are often seen as potentially lucrative, many believe that more subtle reasons exist for supporting sport tourism development.

Billy Payne, CEO for the Atlanta Committee for the Olympic Games (ACOG), was one notable proponent of the transformative power of major sport infrastructure development and the hosting of special events. Always a champion of this power, his belief appeared to remain unshaken eight years after the 1996 Atlanta Olympics when he noted that "the Games vaulted Atlanta into a very elite group of cities, on a global scale. Naturally, I think it was worth every minute and every dollar that we spent bringing them here and hosting the world . . ." (Yarbrough, 2004).

Not everyone shares Mr. Payne's exuberance, however. In considering the potential return from a proposed new stadium complex for Minneapolis (which has been promoted by Minnesota Governor Tim Pawlenty), financial experts such as Jeff Tollefson of Minnesota Venture Capital Association and Art Rolnick of the Federal Reserve Bank of Minneapolis expressed serious skepticism about the project's financial potential (Horwich, 2004).

Another expert, Mr. David Joy of American Express Financial Advisors, suggested that while the Minnesota stadium project might not be a good investment in terms of achieving a real financial return, it might be worthwhile from the perspective of promoting the community's "psychic income" (Horwich, 2004).

Psychic income, also sometimes referred to as "psychic capital," is increasingly referred to as a benefit of sport tourism development. This relatively new term refers to the real, yet intangible, qualities associated with community pride, prestige, and competitiveness that may be associated with major sport and event hosting.

National Association of Sports Commissions

The National Association of Sport Commissions (NASC) in 2000 attempted to address the aforementioned abuses of economic studies when they published guidelines for the computation of economic impact. The report stated, "The process of estimating the economic benefit of a sports event can become controversial" (NASC, 2000, p. 1). Because the bidding process on sports events is fairly competitive, event owners have learned how to market their events in an attractive way. Examples from one event, according to the NASC, had economic impact estimates from $7.5 million to zero. The need to clearly estimate the return on investment for a host community is critical for decision-making.

The main problem with economic impact studies is that experts disagree on how to conduct the studies. As a result, economists, using different but legitimate methodologies, can derive far different values of economic impact. Sport organizing committees, wanting to inflate the value of their work, are therefore able to "shop" for the methodology that will show the greatest return on investment (Crompton, 1995; Noll & Zimbalist, 1997). These authors stated that economic impact studies are frequently used to justify a position or to create the appearance of a greater public benefit. Organizing committees, however, need to be cautious. Often bid fees or guarantees promised to an event are partially based upon the economic impact of the event. By shopping for an economic impact study with an inflated estimate of the true economic impact of the event, organizing committees and host communities are artificially inflating the cost of bidding for and hosting the event (NASC, 2000).

One of the issues leading to differences in computation of economic impact is the calculation of visitor spending. Visitor spending is defined as the dollars left in a community by persons that came to the community because of the event (NASC, 2000). Upon examining this definition, one can see that spending by local residents (those who live within the community which hosts the event) is excluded. Only new dollars brought into the community as a result of visitor spending should be counted in an economic impact study. But as Hudson (2001) noted, economic impact studies often include spending by local residents. Thus, the true impact of the event on the local economy is inflated.

The purpose of the visit can also cause variations in the computation of economic impact. For example, an individual may be sent to a conference in Dallas, Texas. The purpose of her visit to Dallas was business—attending the conference. While in Dallas, if she learns that there is a Stars game and decides to go to the game, her money spent at the game would not be counted in the economic impact of that game. The

purpose of her trip to Dallas was to attend the conference, not to go to a hockey game. Even if the event has appeal to business visitors looking for entertainment, the spending by that business visitor only would be counted when calculating the economic impact of the conference, not the sporting event.

NASC Formula for Measuring Economic Impact

In reaction to the several known shortcomings and abuses common to economic impact studies, the National Association of Sports Commissions (NASC) sponsored a report on the subject. In this report, an overview of economic impacts, visitor spending, classification of visitors, and other important issues were discussed. Additionally, the NASC report reviewed the common formulas for calculating economic impact (EI) and proposed a methodology for two versions of a standardized formula.

The versions of the standardized formula were proposed as an attempt to remedy some of the common problems associated with economic impact studies, such as misrepresentation of data and the use of "fudged" multiplier values. Worksheets and tables to aid in the calculation of the standardized formulae were also developed. NASC recommended that communities and areas could utilize these tools in-house or in conjunction with outside professional consultants or academic institutions.

The recommended standard formula has three steps, with the first step being essential to all studies and the second two available for utilization to "increase the accuracy" of the EI estimate (NASC, 2001). This potential for choice of methods results in a bifurcation of possible applications that renders the standard formula into two de facto standard formulae.

In the first, and more basic, configuration of the formula, an estimate of Total Visitor Spending (TVS) is calculated by multiplying the Number of Out-of-Town Visitors (OTV) by Average Spending Per Day (ASD) and by the Number of Days (ND). This formula does not utilize a Regional Multiplier and can be represented as

$$TVS = OTV \times ASD \times ND$$

(Eq. 1)

The second formula configuration includes the other two recommended steps, which results in the calculation of a new base number (Direct Spending) and uti-

©iStockphoto.com

lizes a Regional Multiplier. Stepwise, the calculation of this formulation begins with the calculation of Direct Spending (DS) by adding Total Administrative Operations Spending to Total Visitor Spending. This step can be represented as

$$DS = TVS + TAS$$

(Eq. 2)

Once Direct Spending has been calculated, it can be multiplied by the Regional Multiplier (RM) to calculate the Total Economic Impact (TEI), or

$$TEI = DS \times RM$$

(Eq. 3)

Thus, the full version of the second formula can be represented as

$$TEI = RM [TAS + (OTV \times ASD \times ND)]$$

(Eq. 4)

The utilization of both the RIMS Type II Multiplier (available through the Bureau of Economic Analysis, U.S. Department of Commerce) and the IMPLAN Multiplier (available from the Minnesota Implan Group) are discussed in the NASC report and neither value is specified as preferable. A third value, the REIM Multiplier, developed by Regional Economic Models, Inc., is also among those commonly available, although it is not mentioned in the NASC Report.

While the NASC formula(e) was designed to help standardize calculations in economic impact studies, it seems that this method may have fallen short of the NASC's goal. The most apparent concern is that of the number of permutations of Economic Impact possible through the number of user choices built into the recommendation. The choice of using either the first formula configuration or the second formula configuration will result in an obvious difference in final result (Total Visitor Spending versus Total Economic Impact). Additionally, and perhaps more subtly, if three commonly available multiplier values are available, and a fourth choice of a self-generated or otherwise-selected value is possible, there are up to five different terminal values for economic impact that could be calculated through the NASC formula(e)—even if all of the same estimates for number of visitors, visitor spending, and length of visit are used.

In addition to differences resulting from simple variations in user choice, intentional misuse or manipula-

tion of the NASC standardized formula(e) is also clearly possible. One way this could be accomplished is by obtaining several multiplier estimates and then simply choosing the one with the largest value. There is nothing in the NASC recommendations that would prohibit this, nor is there any proviso that stops users from merely inventing a multiplier value that is much larger than any accepted and calculated values. In all such cases, users could exercise these different manipulations and still maintain that they were operating within all NASC recommendations.

Case Analysis Using NASC Methodology

An economic impact study was conducted at Ohio University football games during the 2003 season. The purpose of the study was to estimate the economic impact that these games had on the Athens, Ohio, community as a result of direct visitor spending within the community.

At each of the five home games during the 2003 season, a survey questionnaire was administered to a random sample of respondents. Information sought on the questionnaire included the amount of money spent (or estimated to be spent) during their time in Athens. The following categories of spending were included: groceries, convenience store, fast food, restaurants, lodging, game expenditures, retail shopping, fuel, bus/taxi/shuttle, rental car, entertainment, and other. An average of 431 surveys was collected from visitors during each of the five home games. Total visitor spending was then calculated.

From **Equation 1**, we get $TVS = OTV \times ASD \times ND$. Out of town visitor spending averaged $29.97 per person over the entire season. There was an average of 12,821 visitors to games in Athens in 2003. The number of days was equal to the number of games, five. Therefore,

$$TVS = 12,821 \times \$29.97 \times 5$$

$$TVS = \$1,921,226.85$$

Equation 2, $DS = TVS + TAS$, measures direct spending. As TVS = $1,921,226.85 (Eq. 1), we must now determine Total Administrative Spending (TAS). That season, the athletic department calculated that it spent approximately $90,000 on game operations. So, direct spending for the 2003 Ohio University football season was

$DS = \$1,921,226.85 + \$90,000$

$DS = \$2,011,226.85$

After calculating direct spending, total economic impact can be calculated (Eq. 3). As $TEI = DS \times RM$ and DS = \$2,011,226.85, and the regional multiplier for Athens is 2.0424, total economic impact is

$TEI = \$2,011,226.85 \times 2.0424$

$TEI = \$4,107,729.72$

Utilizing the full version of the formula (Eq. 4), the equation would take this form:

$TEI = RM \ [TAS + (OTV \times ASD \times ND)]$

$TEI = 2.0424[\$90,000 + (12,821 \times \$29.97 \times 5)]$

$TEI = \$4,107,729.72$

Utilizing the methodology put forth by the NASC, Equations 2-4 are used as a community option. The report stresses that Equation 1 is a simplified method of reporting economic impact; however, it truly does not measure the economic impact of an event because the secondary effects of visitor spending are ignored. Using only Equation 1 in this study would have led to a calculation of economic impact being \$1.9 million, or \$2.2 million less than the actual impact on the local economy if Equation 4 was used. By providing an option to use Equation 1 or Equation 4 (the stepwise combination of Equations 1-3), the NASC leaves room for confusion over what the true impact is. It is highly recommended that for all events Equation 4 be used.

It is also important to note that this formula really measures **economic benefit** rather than economic impact. As Crompton (1995) noted, the costs associated with hosting the event must be subtracted from the benefits gained. Agha (2002) noted that most economic impact studies are actually economic benefit studies, as they fail to make a distinction between economic benefit and economic impact. There is an important difference between economic benefit and impact. Economic benefit measures only the economic gain in the local economy. *Economic impact, then, is the total economic gain or loss after accounting for the event's costs.* True economic impact studies will account for losses in the local economy due to the studied event.

The NASC methodology actually measures economic benefit, as the costs associated with hosting the event are not subtracted from Total Economic Impact. Re-

call that Equation 4 states that Total Economic Impact equals the Regional Multiplier multiplied by Direct Spending. Local costs associated with hosting the event are not subtracted from the formula. These costs include items like vandalism, police and fire protection, and garbage collection. Equation 4 is not a true measure of economic impact and should be modified. So, prior to calculating Total Economic Impact (TEI), Economic Costs (EC) must be removed:

$TEI = RM \ [TAS + (OTV \times ASD \times ND)] - EC$
(Eq. 5)

With this equation, economic impact is accurately calculated as it determines net benefits to a community rather than gross benefits.

Conflicting Statements by Economists

It should come as no surprise that within the complex marketplace of ideas there exist conflicting statements by economists as to whether or not sport and sport tourism development projects are worthwhile.

There is certainly no shortage of experts who extol the virtues and benefits of these projects. Increasingly, though, many economists and other scholars are speaking out to challenge these assumptions. Among them, the aforementioned Art Rolnick has flatly stated that "if you want to try to make a case that we should invest public money in sport teams, it really shouldn't be based on what's good for this economy. You're going to lose that debate" (Horwich, 2004).

Still other researchers see questions about the value of sport-related projects as complicated and not lending themselves to easy answers. One doctoral dissertation on the subject noted that while "mounting evidence suggests that sports stadia have only marginal economic impacts upon the metropolitan economy," economic impact studies have reached these conclusions largely by utilizing the entire metropolitan area as the unit of analysis, rather than the districts and neighborhoods, or "microareas," which are most proximate to these development projects. This study suggests that merely changing the focus, or level of analysis, of these economic studies has far-reaching implications for understanding the value and impacts of sport-related projects (Chapin, 2001).

Economics Is a Social Science

While many researchers work hard to develop, standardize, and advocate appropriate methods for undertaking these studies, it may turn out that there is no one "best way" to design economic impact studies of sport-related developments, due to the tremendous diversity of project types and settings. However, if this is a truism, then it is one that imposes very real limitations on our ability to meaningfully compare results between studies, and to think of any study as much more than a "best guess" based on the available information.

With that in mind, the only true problem with these studies may be our failure, unintentional or otherwise, to realize and accept these limitations.

Summary

It should be quite apparent that measuring the economic impact of sport facilities, event operations, and team activities requires a solid understanding of economic theory. In this chapter you were exposed to the laws of supply and demand, opportunity costs, and how these theories are used in the sport industry.

There are many uses of economic impact studies in sport, and many ways in which the results are used. Teams and event organizers use these studies to justify public funding or support. Opponents of public funding can use the results to support their opposition. One must be wary of potential abuses of economic impact studies, and compare the results with previously gathered information.

The study of economic impact in sport is an art, not a science. It is, however, an essential part of the financial makeup of the sport industry.

Discussion Activities

1. Select a sport event and try to locate a related completed economic impact study. Look for inconsistencies, common errors, etc.

2. Examine the money you spent on the last vacation you took. Calculate how the money may have been re-spent, both in and out of that community.

References

2002 Winter Olympic games. (2003). Retrieved October 7, 2004, from http://olympicstudies.uab.es/eng/yellow/dir/et.html.

Agha, N. (2002). Choosing the optimal area of economic impact. *Sports Economics Perspectives, 1* (2), 1-17.

Alesia, M. (2002, October 21). Expert: Colts' claim is suspect. *The Indianapolis Star.* Retrieved October 21, 2002, from www.indystar.com.

Brown, M., Nagel, M., McEvoy, C., & Rascher, D. (2004, December). Revenue and wealth maximization in the National Football League: The impact of stadia. *Sport Marketing Quarterly, 13*(4), 227-235.

Chapin, T. S. (2001). Urban revitalization tools: Assessing the impacts of sports stadia at the microarea level. Thesis Abstract, University of Oregon, Eugene. Retrieved October 5, 2004, from SPORT Discus database.

Crompton, J. L. (1995, January). Economic impact analysis of sports facilities and events: Eleven sources of misapplication. *Journal of Sport Management, 9*(1), 14-25.

Fort, R. D. (2003). *Sports economics.* Upper Saddle River, NJ: Prentice Hall.

Horwich, J. (2004, April 7). *Financial experts see "psychic income," plenty of risk in stadium deal.* Transcript of Minnesota Public Radio. Retrieved September 30, 2004, from http://news.minnesota.publicradio.org/features/2004/04/08_horwichj_bizstadium.

Hudson, I. (2001, February). The use and misuse of economic impact analysis: The case of professional sports. *Journal of Sport and Social Issues, 25*(1), 20-24.

Humphreys, J. M., & Plumber, M. K. (2004). *The economic impact of hosting the 1996 Summer Olympics.* Retrieved October 3, 2004, from http://www.selig.uga.edu/forecast/olympics/OLYMTEXT.HTM.

Li, M., Hofacre, S,. & Mahony, D. (2001). *Economics of sport.* Morgantown, WV: Fitness Information Technology.

NASC (2000, October). *Economic impact study.* Cincinnati, OH: Author.

Noll, R. G., & Zimbalist, A. (1997). The economic impact of sports teams and facilities. In R. G. Noll & A. Zimbalist (Eds.), *Sports, jobs & taxes* (pp. 55-91). Washington, DC: Brookings Institute.

Rosentraub, M. S. (1997, April). The myth and reality of economic development from sports. *Real Estate Issues, 22*(1), 24-30.

The fans, taxpayers, and business alliance for NFL football in San Diego. (2002). Retrieved October 7, 2004, from http://www.ftballiance.org/stadiums/impact.php.

Trevision, J. (2004). Racetrack's potential economic effect difficult to gauge. *The Oregonian.* Retrieved October 7, 2004, from http://www.oregonlive.com/motorsports/oregonian/index.ssf?/base/sports/109395358759060.xml.

Turco, D. M., & Kelsey, C. W. (1992). *Conducting economic impact studies of recreation and special events.* Alexandria, VA: National Recreation and Park Association.

Yarbough, D. (2004). *Press Release, DickYarbrough.com.* Retrieved October 7, 2004, from http://dickyarbrough.com/pressrelease.htm.

Chapter Six

Sport Finance

Tom Regan and Matthew Bernthal

Learning Objectives

Upon completion of this chapter, the reader should be able to

■ Explore the relationship between accounting and finance;

■ Identify the elements of a balance sheet, income statement, and budgets;

■ Understand the relationship between the balance sheet, income statement, and the statement of cash flow;

■ Analyze the concept of time value of money;

■ Recognize the type of bonds that are used to fund public assembly facilities; and

■ Discuss how to analyze financial information.

Introduction

The financial aspects of the sport industry have grown exponentially in the last 20 years. A sport manager must be able to assess the operations of his or her team, league, conference, municipality, or other organization in order to make informed financial decisions. Consider the following recent developments in the sport industry:

- CBS Sports rights fees for the NCAA Men's Division I Basketball Championship reach over $6.1 billion for 11 years.

- Long-term stadium naming-rights deals generate over $200 million.

- Professional player salaries continue to escalate, in some cases reaching more than $20 million a year.

- Ticket prices continue to rise, threatening to make game attendance even more of a luxury.

- Sport facility construction continues at record pace.

Financial analysis of sport organizations is often very difficult due to their inconsistent structure. The **vertical integration** of current professional sport organizations make financial analysis very difficult to the casual observer. The degree to which a firm owns its suppliers and its buyers is referred to as vertical integration. Professional sports organizations want to be able to own the team, the media market, and related entertainment outlets. For example, Anaheim Sports—former owner of the Anaheim Angels and current owner of The Mighty Ducks of Anaheim—is owned by the Walt Disney Company, which encompasses ABC, ESPN, and other media outlets. The Tribune Company owns the Chicago Cubs and super station WGN and operates extensive television, radio, and newspaper outlets throughout the world. It is often difficult to find the sport-related financial statements within the filings of these multi-national corporations.

Sport organizations, not unlike individuals, are ultimately concerned with **cash flow,** or the amount of money earned relative to the amount of money paid. For example, consider purchasing a car. Your thoughts may include the following: How much cash do I have on hand? Do I have a car to trade? What is my payment going to be? How much should I borrow, if any? What does my income (cash inflow) need to be in

order to make my monthly payment? Should I even buy this car? Do I need it? What benefit is it going to provide? Can I get by with a less expensive car? What if I lose my job? This process is part of **personal financial management**.

> "UNLIKE ANY OTHER BUSINESS IN THE UNITED STATES, SPORTS MUST PRESERVE AN ILLUSION OF PERFECT INNOCENCE. THE MOUNTING OF THIS ILLUSION DEFINES THE PURPOSE AND ACCOUNTS FOR THE IMMENSE WEALTH OF AMERICAN SPORTS. IT IS THE CEREMONY OF INNOCENCE THAT THE FANS PAY TO SEE—NOT THE GAME OR THE MATCH OR THE BOUT . . ."
>
> LEWIS H. LAPHAM

Let's compare the above example to a sport finance situation. The Miami Heat acquired Shaquille O'Neal from the Los Angeles Lakers. He is under contract for $27.7 million for the 2004-05 season and $30.6 million in 2005-06. The Miami Heat intend to negotiate an extension, and O'Neal indicated he anticipates playing another five or six years. Therefore, as a manager, your thoughts might include the following: How much cash do we have on hand? Do we have players to trade? What is our payment going to be? How much should we borrow, if any? What does our income (cash inflow) need to be in order to pay him? Will season tickets and sponsorship increase? Do we need him? What benefit is he going to provide? Can we get by with a less expensive player? What if he gets hurt? This process is part of **business financial management**.

Importance of Finance in Sport

The goal of this chapter is to introduce basic concepts of business financial management in a sport environment. Sport finance utilizes the same business principles as any organization, except it usually involves players in professional sport as assets. Sport also is highly integrated in the public sector (city, county, state, and federal governments to a degree). The objective is to maximize profit through sound financial decisions.

Professional, college, and amateur sport organizations are borrowing money at record levels. New facilities are being built, remodeled, and expanded at a record pace. It is essential for these organizations to have adequate capital and profit to assure creditors that the assets are secure. Banks, mortgage companies, and insurance enterprises are diligent in lending money because they certainly do not want to repossess an arena or stadium. What would a bank or other financial lending institution do with a new stadium?

Accounting is a Partner to Sport Finance

Financial analysis requires useful information. A company's suppliers, creditors, and shareholders have an interest in analyzing a sport organization's financial performance. They need assurances that the sport enterprise has liquidity and solvency to meet short-term debts. Long-term creditors are concerned with projected profitability because they seek assurances that the company will be able to service its debt over several years. Public sport enterprises now must make financial decisions with the aspect of maximizing shareholder wealth. Sport stockholders, like public corporate shareholders, need to assess the potential cash flows and the inherent risks in order to estimate the future price of the common stock.

Analyzing financial performance begins with financial statements. The balance sheet, income statement, and the cash flow statement are the starting point for evaluating the current condition and financial future of the company. Further explanation and examples of the financial statements will occur later in the chapter. A few questions should arise when looking at financial statements:

1. Can the current debts be satisfied from the current liquidity (cash) position?

2. Is the company's long-term debt position overextended, or can the company borrow more money to alleviate liquidity problems?

3. What is the cash flow of the enterprise?

4. What is the debt to cash flow of the company?

5. Why is the sport enterprise more or less profitable than other comparable sport enterprises?

6. Is management aggressive or conservative concerning credit arrangements?

7. How does management's decision to enter the sport business compare to returns gained from non-sport related business enterprises?

Each of these questions requires information to be gathered in order to make sound decisions. The balance sheet and income statements are essential to initiate an analysis of any business enterprise. Sport managers must exercise caution when reviewing financial statements. Audited financial statements have been compiled by a third party and are independent of the company's accountants and financial officers. Internal financial statements are the product of the financial officers and have not had the scrutiny of an independent auditor. Answers to the questions will involve analysis from financial statements, ratio, trend analysis, and cash flow interpretation.

Data Gathering

How does one obtain financial statements for an enterprise that is not a public entity? Professional sport franchises will not provide you with a copy of the financial statements on request. Therefore, you may not be able to obtain the statements for comparison with other teams or franchises. Publicly traded companies will have audited financial statements for shareholders to review and for the potential investing public to access. Sounds great, but the reality is the sport related business will be part of a larger asset on the balance sheet, such as entertainment division or sport properties. It will not have the baseball or hockey team financial statements broken out for your review.

Gathering data is not a simple process. Public agencies are required by the Freedom of Information Act (FOIA) to provide data if requested. Following is a short synopsis of the law that will assist you in gathering data on public colleges and universities, teams that are publicly traded and other government agency involvement.

The **Freedom of Information Act**—FOIA—is a law enacted in 1966 that established citizens' statutory right to access government records and information upon request. The basic purpose of FOIA is to ensure an informed citizenry, vital to the functioning of a democratic society, needed to check against corruption and to hold the governors accountable to the governed. Basically, the public or any individual has the right to know or be informed about activities, decisions, and policies of U.S. federal agencies.

The financial statements and related summary material are part of the financial records. A record means any document, writing, photograph, sound or magnetic recording, drawing, computerized record (disks, database), electronic mail, policy, and company decision or other material from which information can be retrieved and/or copied. The balance sheet, income statement, statement of cash flows, and other specifically stated financial documents can be reviewed if not a confidential or privileged document.

Can you request such a document? Yes. Corporations, associations, public interest groups, private individuals, universities, and local, state, or foreign governments can all submit FOIA requests. The FOIA is a frequent vehicle for citizens to gain access to public records. You have the freedom to request these documents. Access the site www.aclue.org/library/foia.html to access letters and other legal information that will be helpful in data gathering.

Other sources for data gathering include a request to the Chief Financial Officer for access to the financial information or a written request to Board of Directors (if available). These requests will probably be unsuccessful. Financial data may have to be gathered from third parties, league contracts that are public (such as television and radio contracts), sponsorships, and revenue sharing. Next, a financial forecast will have to be completed to estimate revenue streams for the team and/or league. You will need attendance figures, ticket prices, merchandise and concessions sales estimates, parking data, luxury and club seating revenues, and other miscellaneous income.

Third party revenue and expense projections may also be available from regional newspapers, trade journals, and sport business journals. Financial World, Sport Business Journal, and the Sporting News routinely estimate net income and losses for teams, conferences, and leagues. The NCAA produces a document named "Revenues and Expenses of Intercollegiate Athletics Programs," an analysis of financial trends and relationships. The document is a very good basis for financial comparison of all NCAA division classifications.

©iStockphoto.com

Organizational Structure

Like any other business, sport has various organizational structures. The structure of the sport organization is vital to the financial analysis necessary to maximize profit. Sport companies exist in three major forms: sole proprietorship, partnership, and corporation. Each differs in legal, tax, and business management, and must be a concern when analysis occurs.

A **sole proprietorship** is a company owned by one person. In sport, many of the original professional franchises were sole proprietorships. This has changed due to the enormous capital necessary to finance the sport organization. A **partnership** is a company owned by two or more individuals who have entered into an agreement. A partnership agreement will determine how the partners share in the debt and profits of the company. Unless specifically stated in the agreement, all partners will share equally in debt and profit. A **corporation** is a company formed by an agreement between the state and the persons forming the company, with the state requiring legal documentation of the agreement. The agreement must be filed with the Secretary of State. A Corporation (called a C Corp) is a separately taxable entity. The profits and losses are taxed directly to the corporation. This can lead to double taxation on dividends that are paid out of corporate profits to the owners.

Special corporations exist in sport business. One special structure is called an **S Corporation**, which is simply a C Corporation (also known as a standard business corporation) that files IRS form 2553 to elect a special tax status with the IRS. The articles of incorporation that are filed with the state are the same, whether a corporation is a C Corporation or S Corporation. The main difference is a pass-through tax entity—this means that the income or loss generated by the business is reflected on the personal income tax return of the owners. Another special company is called a **Limited Liability Company,** or **LLC**, which is a business entity formed upon filing articles of organization with the proper state authorities and paying all fees. LLCs provide limited liability to their members and are taxed like a partnership, preventing double taxation. LLCs can be formed in every state. LLCs are now popular company structures in sport organizations.

Importance of Organizational Structure

The key to financial management is to structure the sport organization to maximize profit, limit liability, and provide opportunity for infusion of capital for growth. Each company has differences in tax issues, cash flow, and liability. Managing these companies requires knowledge of accounting, finance, and taxation issues. It should be noted that owners of corporations pay taxes twice. They pay taxes as the corporation and, as shareholders, they pay taxes on cash dividends they receive from the corporation.

Revenue Sources

Revenue sources for sport franchises have become increasingly diverse in recent years, with teams finding new and creative ways to generate income. Teams generate revenue through sources as standard as ticket sales and facility naming rights, and as creative as advertising on stadium/arena turnstiles or offering fans off-season trips with players and pre- and post-game fan entertainment opportunities. The escalating costs of operating profitable professional sport franchises, seen most visibly in dramatically escalating player salaries, have increased the importance of the generation and maintenance of a successful and consistent revenue stream. As standard practice, revenues of franchises are generated through numerous sources, including ticket sales, sponsorship, luxury suites, club seating, media revenue, licensing/merchandising, and concessions and parking. Indeed, a team's annual revenue is linked directly to its market value. For example, NFL franchises are commonly valued at three to

four times net revenue, while MLB teams are valued at between two to three times net revenue ("CEO Network Chat," 2003). The Washington Redskins, the NFL's most valuable franchise, generate over $200 million annually in revenue. The purpose of this section is to provide a brief illustrative example of the primary revenue sources for sport organizations. Each of the sources is briefly described below.

Ticket Revenue

Ticket revenue accounts for a significant portion of revenue for sport franchises, though the proportion that it contributes to total revenue varies by league. The NFL, for example, generates approximately two-thirds of its revenue from media rights and merchandising. Each of the NFL's teams receives an equal share of revenue from these two categories. Other leagues that are less media-rich, such as the NHL, and certainly the numerous minor leagues of professional sports, as well as colleges and universities, rely on ticket sales to generate a larger proportion of their revenue. Ticket revenue is distributed differently among the four major American pro sports leagues. Approximately two-thirds of each NFL team's ticket revenue goes to the home team, while the other third is put into a pool that is shared by all of the other teams. MLB teams also share ticket revenue, with 30 percent of this revenue shared among the teams in the league and 70 percent going to the home team. NHL and NBA teams, on the other hand, keep their ticket revenue, often called the "gate" ("CEO Network Chat," 2003).

The significance of the gate can be seen in the steadily increasing ticket prices in sport. The average NFL ticket in 2003 cost $52.95, the NBA $44.68, the NHL $43.57, and $18.69 for Major League Baseball. Further, many franchises have increasingly turned to **variable pricing** to increase ticket sales and revenue. Variable pricing refers to pricing different events at different levels according to fan demand. Many teams have raised ticket prices for games that have higher demand due to factors ranging from playing a rivalry team, the presence of a superstar on a visiting team, or when the game is played. For example, the New York Mets charge up to twice as much for tickets when the cross-town rival Yankees are visiting or when Barry Bonds is in town with the San Francisco Giants. The Pittsburgh Penguins have added $5 to weekend game prices as well as three high-profile opponents, generating an additional one million in ticket revenue (Fatsis, 2003). The University of Miami charges $45 for high-profile football games against Florida State and Virginia Tech and $35 for lesser-profile games that historically have more trouble selling out, such as the University of Connecticut and Florida A&M. The bottom line with this increasingly popular variable pricing is to increase revenue by catering to fluctuating fan demand. Teams boost their revenue by capitalizing on high demand games and offering lower prices on low demand games.

Sponsorship

Sponsorship can be broadly defined as a company or brand building equity through association with a specific event, team, athlete, or league (see Chapter 8). Sponsorship marketing represents an enormous revenue source for sport organizations, growing 613 percent over the past 16 years (Shank, 2002). Even relatively poorly performing teams can and do generate significant sponsorship revenue. For example, the Florida Panthers of the NHL generated approximately $10.5 million in sponsorship revenue in the 2003-2004 season ("NHL Franchise Switches Gears,"

Table 6.1 Naming Rights

Facility	City/School	Price (millions)	No. of Years	Tenants
Big-League Facilities				
Reliant Stadium	Houston	$300 million	30	Houston Texans, Houston Livestock Show & Rodeo, Houston Bowl
FedEx Field	Landover, MD	$205 million	27	Washington Redskins
American Airlines Center	Dallas	$195 million	30	Dallas Mavericks, Dallas Stars, Dallas Desperados (AFL)
Philips Arena	Atlanta	$185 million	20	Atlanta Hawks, Atlanta Thrashers
Minute Maid Park	Houston	$170 million	28	Houston Astros
Minor League Stadiums				
Raley Field	Sacramento	$15 million	20	Sacramento River Cats (PCL)
KeySpan Park	Brooklyn, NY	$10 million	20	Brooklyn Cyclones (NY-Penn)
PGE Park	Portland	$8.52 million	10	Portland Beavers (PCL), Portland Timbers (USL), Portland State U. football
Fifth Third Field	Dayton, OH	$6.5 million	20	Dayton Dragons (ML)
Fifth Third Field	Toledo, OH	$5.0 million	15	Toledo Mud Hens (IL)
Minor League Arenas				
Qwest Center of Omaha	Omaha, NE	$14 million	15	Creighton U. men's basktball, U. Nebraska-Omaha ice hockey
Wells Fargo Arena	Des Moines, IA	$11.5 million	20	To Be Determined
Verizon Wireless Arena	Manchester, NH	$11.4 million	15	AHL Manchester Monarchs
Allstate Arena	Rosemont, IL	$10 million	10	AFL Chicago Rush, AHL Chicago Wolves, DePaul U. men's basketball
Dunkin' Donuts Center	Providence, RI	$8.3 million	10	AHL Providence Bruins, Providence College men's basketball
NCAA Division I-A Football & Basketball Facilities				
Save Mart Center	Fresno State U.	$40 million	20	
Comcast Center	U. of Maryland	$20 million	25	
Jones SBC Stadium	Texas Tech U.	$20 million	20	
Value City Arena	Ohio State U.	$12.5 million	Indefinite	
Cox Arena at Aztec Bowl	San Diego State U.	$12 million	Indefinite	

Source: *Street & Smith's SportsBusiness Journal*, Vol. 6, Issue 36, pp. 10 – 14

2004). In 2000, IEG (International Events Group) estimated that $8.7 billion was spent by companies sponsoring special events, with $5.9 billion of this spent on the sponsorship of sport events ("Record Growth without Gold," 2000). Sponsorship revenue is expected to cover approximately 27.7 percent of the revenues from the 2004 Summer Olympics, making sponsorship second only to international broadcasting rights (37.5%) in overall revenue.

Sport organizations sell sponsorship in many forms, including but not limited to advertising (e.g., venue signage, programs), promotional opportunities tied to the sport property, the right to service the event or facility (e.g., Coors having exclusive beer service rights

Table 6.2 NFL Luxury Suites and Club Seats

Team	No. of Suites	Price Range	No. of Club Seats	Price Range
Arizona Cardinals	68	$50,000 - $85,000	5,000	$765 - $2,025
Atlanta Falcons	203	$26,000 - $148,000	4,604	$1,200 - $2,400
Baltimore Ravens	109	$100,000 - $250,000	7,900	$112.50 - $302.50*
Buffalo Bills	166	$26,880 - $94,250	8,800	$945 - $2,350
Carolina Panthers	159	$59,000 - $315,000	11,302	$975 - $2,975
Chicago Bears	133	$70,000 - $300,000	8,600	$195 - $315*
Cincinnati Bengals	114	$48,000 - $150,000	7,600	$1,020 - $2,050
Cleveland Browns	147	$40,000 - $150,000	8,754	$113 - $264
Dallas Cowboys	370	$30,000 - $125,000	-	NA
Denver Broncos	125	$85,000 - $135,000	8,800	$1,750 - $3,112
Detroit Lions	132	$70,000 - $250,000	8,464	$1,100 - $2,950
Green Bay Packers	166	$57,500 - $115,000	6,000	$1,750 - $2,500
Houston Texans	185	$55,000 - $225,000	8,300	$1,575 - $2,575
Indianapolis Colts	104	$42,000 - $250,000	5,000	1,490
Jacksonville Jaguars	90	$45,000 - $131,000	11,228	$1,925 - $2,160
Kansas City Chiefs	80	$42,825 - $128,100	2,400	$200*
Miami Dolphins	182	$55,000 - $600,000	10,184	$1,050 - $3,800
Minnesota Vikings	115	$60,000 - $170,000	-	NA
New England Patriots	80	$85,000 - $505,000	6,000	$3,750 -$ 6,000
New Orleans Saints	137	$52,500 - $105,000	13,995	$63 - $150*
New York Giants/Jets	118	$125,000 - $380,000	142	5,500
Oakland Raiders	143	$35,000 - $145,000	5,600	$800 - $2,200
Philadelphia Eagles	172	$70,000 - $300,000	8,115	$1,500 - $3,500
Pittsburgh Steelers	129	$44,000 - $120,000	6,600	$1,045 - $1,095
San Diego Chargers	112	$44,000 - $135,000	7,600	$1,160 - $2,330
San Francisco 49ers	93	$60,000 - $135,000	-	NA
Seattle Seahawks	84	$50,000 - $150,000	7,685	$1,500 - $2,800
St. Louis Rams	124	$75,000 - $140,000	6,500	$1,000 - $2,500
Tampa Bay Buccaneers	197	$45,000 - $150,000	12,000	$1,144 - $2,900
Tennessee Titans	175	$50,000 - $125,000	12,000	$800 - $2,550
Washington Redskins	234	DND	15,735	DND

*Denotes per game rates

NA: Not Applicable

DND: Did Not Disclose

Source: *Street & Smith's SportsBusiness Journal*, Vol. 6, Issue 36, p. 127

to Colorado Rockies events), and naming rights to event facilities. Examples of naming rights deals for big-league, minor league, and NCAA facilities, which provide an increasingly large portion of sponsorship revenue, are provided in Table 6.1.

Often, sponsorship revenue is limited only by a sport organization's creativity. For example, sports teams can sell signage alone in numerous categories, including on scoreboards, marquees, the playing surface itself, the facility concourse, turnstiles, game programs, media guides, team newsletters, and the backs of tickets, to name but a few. Further, teams can sell sponsorship of fantasy camps, school assemblies, coach's clinics, and the like. Sponsorship opportunities can range from the relatively small (e.g., $500 for the right to drop coupons from a small blimp hovering just over seats at a minor league baseball game or NCAA basketball game), to the seemingly astronomical, such as the $10 million per year for naming rights to Reliant Stadium in Houston, home of the Houston Texans. Sponsorship opportunities offered by sport organizations, and thus the revenue associated with this stream, has grown exponentially in recent years. Spending on North American Motorsports sponsorship alone, for example, was projected to reach $1.58 billion in 2004, over twice the amount spent on such sponsorship a decade earlier.

Luxury Suites and Club Seating

Luxury suites and club seating provide another major revenue source for sport franchises, and the percent of team revenue accounted for by this source has steadily increased over the past two decades. Luxury suites are special areas provided for premium seating and entertainment. Club seats provide the patron with special amenities such as wait staff, food and beverage service, and special parking privileges. Indeed, it is the revenue potential of luxury suites and, to a lesser extent, club seating that has been the major catalyst in the boom of new sport venue construction and the upgrading of existing venues. Table 6.2 provides an illustration of the revenue generating power of luxury suites and club seating for NFL teams. Franchises in other sports also capitalize on luxury suite and club seat revenue. The New York Knicks, for example, can earn more than $400,000 per season for each of their 89 luxury suites, while the Boston Red Sox take in $36,000 to $300,000 per season for each of Fenway Park's suites.

The Texas Rangers bring in $11 million in revenue each season with their 122 luxury suites at The Ballpark at Arlington.

Media Revenue

Media revenue is another major source of capital for pro sports leagues and franchises, and new media deals in recent years have increased the proportion of total league and franchise revenue accounted for by broadcasting rights. The importance of media revenue, particularly from television rights, as a source of capital cannot be overstated in today's sports business climate. Indeed, media revenue covers the vast majority of payroll expenses for some franchises with low payrolls, such as the NBA's Los Angeles Clippers. The NFL leads the four major pro leagues in broadcast rights, with ABC, Fox, CBS, and ESPN paying $17.6 billion, or $2.2 billion per season, to broadcast NFL contests from 1998 to 2005. This amount is nearly double the $1.1 billion per year fees broadcasters paid to the NFL for the contract period 1994 through 1997. The NBA is second to the NFL in broadcast rights revenue, taking in $4.6 billion ($766.7 million per season) from ABC/ESPN and AOL Time Warner for the 2002 through 2008 seasons. Media revenues also heavily support Major League Baseball, currently generating $558.5 million per year in broadcast rights revenue from Fox ($2.5 billion over the 2001 through 2006 seasons) and ESPN ($851 million over the 2000 through 2005 seasons). The New York Yankees organization is paid $40 million per year for its cable television contract. The NHL is currently without a television rights deal, as their latest contract expired after the 2004 season. However, over the 1999 through 2004 seasons, the NHL earned $600 million in television rights fees from ABC/ESPN, with each team receiving approximately $6 million annually from various national television contracts.

Other sports organizations also benefit healthily from media revenue. NASCAR, a sport whose popularity has grown rapidly over the last decade, has recently inked a new deal with Fox/NBC and Turner worth $2.4 billion, or $400 million per season. The PGA earns an average of $212.5 million per season for the rights of CBS, ABC, and NBC to broadcast their events. Collegiate sports also benefit from broadcast rights, with the NCAA earning $400 million from ABC through the sale of its Bowl Championship Series and an astronomical $6 billion from CBS for the rights to broadcast the NCAA Men's Basketball Tournament for 11 years, through the 2012-2013 season (Street & Smith's, 2004).

Licensing and Merchandising

Licensing and merchandising provide yet another source of revenue. Licensing is a contractual agreement whereby a company may use another company's intellectual property in exchange for a royalty or fee. Within the sport industry, this most often takes the form of selling the right to use team names and logos to companies (termed the licensee) or selling logoed apparel and other logoed merchandise. Generally, for this right, the licensee pays the sport organization (the licensor) 6 percent to 10 percent of gross sales of the licensed merchandise at wholesale, and this is termed royalty revenue for the licensor. Items beyond team names and logos can also be and are licensed. Facility names and designs, advertising slogans, mascots and their nicknames, and even terms or characteristics specifically associated with the sport organization can be licensed in order to generate revenue. As an example of the latter, the NFL secured the rights to the term "Dirty Bird" after it was popularized by the Atlanta Falcons during their Super Bowl season of 1998 (Irwin, Sutton, & McCarthy, 2002). The NFL secured the rights as opposed to the Falcons because the NFL collects licensing revenue for the entire League and distributes it evenly among the League's teams. Sharing of licensing revenue among teams is standard in some form among the four major American pro sport leagues, and each league has a form of a "properties" division that approves licenses and combats trademark infringement (i.e., counterfeiting).

Events also generate revenue from licensing. For example, the Kentucky Derby licenses its name and logo to grace products such as bobble head jockey dolls, steel Derby parking signs, model cars, calendars, mint julep glasses, beer mugs, and paper napkins. These account for a significant percentage of Derby merchandise sales, which amounted to nearly $8 million in 2004 (Olsen, 2004).

Licensing is big business. In 2003, sales of licensed products in total rose 4.3 percent from 2002 to reach $172.8 billion. While the largest contributor to this figure was Disney Consumer Products ($15 billion),

sports contributed significantly as well. The NFL sold $3.2 billion in licensed merchandise, while MLB and the NBA sold $3 billion each. The Collegiate Licensing Co., which as the nation's largest collegiate licensing and marketing organization handles licensing for more than 180 universities, conferences, the NCAA, bowl games, and the Heisman Trophy, sold more than $2.6 billion in licensed merchandise in 2003. NASCAR sold $2 billion in 2003, while the NHL sold $1.5 billion ("NHL Franchise Switches Gears," 2004). These figures represent retail sales of licensed merchandise, of course, and not revenue. When factoring in the fact that sport organizations generally earn 6 to 10 percent of wholesale sales (sales of licensees to retailers), more modest—yet nonetheless significant—figures are uncovered. NFL teams, for example, receive up to $5 million per season, while NHL teams receive an average of around $1 million per season ("CEO Network Chat," 2003). The sale of licensed apparel alone accounted for $4.21 billion in retail dollars in 2003 (see Table 6.3).

Table 6.3

RETAIL SALES OF SPORTS LICENSED APPAREL IN U.S. AND CANADA

YEAR	SALES (IN BILLIONS)	% +/-
2003	$4.21	18.6%
2002	$3.55	13.6%
2001	$3.125	-9.4%
2000	$3.45	-6.8%
1999	$3.70	-9.8%
1998	$4.10	NA

Sports Business Daily, published July 29, 2004

Concessions and Parking

Food and beverage sales account for an additional source of team and venue revenue, and sports teams have taken advantage of the increasing number and variety of concession items available to them to increase their concession revenue. This is the case even for the numerous teams that allow fans to bring food into the stadium, such as the Arizona Diamondbacks, Anaheim Angels, and Philadelphia Eagles. The vast majority of teams contract out their concession services, and, on average, teams retain 35% to 45% of concession sale dollars. However, with the litany of menu items available to sports fans today, this can mean significant money. Not only do today's fans enjoy the standard fare, such as hot dogs and burgers, seafood items such as crabcake sandwiches and salmon, various wraps, ethnic fare such as Mexican, Italian, and Chinese, and even vegetarian and vegan cuisine now tempt them. Fans also enjoy a much wider range of beverage selections in many venues, from a wide assortment of microbrew beers to premixed alcoholic beverages, such as Bacardi Breezers. Indeed, many of the newer sport venues have food courts that would rival those of the most upscale shopping malls. Odds are if you can find it at a restaurant, you can find it at a stadium or arena. Teams are also increasingly offering fans easier access to concessions to increase sales. For example, pre-paid cards are offered at many venues. These cards and merchandise debit cards that allow fans to use an express line devoted to users are increasingly preferred by customers. Estimates of per fan spending range from $8–$10 at basketball and hockey games, $10–$12 at baseball games, and $12–$15 at football games (Isidore, 2003). Indeed, for many minor league teams that have relatively low ticket prices and thus a smaller proportion of team revenue accounted for by ticket sales, concession sales can significantly impact profitability (Howard, 1998). Concessions are often accounted for in the same category as parking revenues, and when combined, can add significantly to a team's bottom line. For example, the NFL's Arizona Cardinals bring in approximately $1.75 million per season in concessions and parking.

Financial Statements

Financial information is only as good as the statements or detail gathered from the company. Standards are set in most countries to conform to a set of common practices in accounting. In the United States, these common standards are called **Generally Accepted Accounting Principles (GAAP)**. GAAP is a combination of authoritative standards (set by policy boards) and the accepted ways of doing accounting. Two private organizations, the American Institute of Certified Public Accountants (AICPA) and Financial Accounting Standards Board (FASB), in addition to the Security and Exchange Commission (SEC), an agency of the federal government, are the regulatory bodies that help determine GAAP.

Balance Sheet

A **balance sheet** is a snapshot of the financial condition of a business at a specific moment in time, usually at the close of an accounting period. A balance sheet comprises assets, liabilities, and owners' or stockholders' equity. Assets and liabilities are divided into short- and long-term obligations, including cash accounts such as checking, money market, or government securities. At any given time, assets must equal liabilities plus owners' equity (A = L + OE). An asset is anything the business owns that has monetary value. Liabilities are the claims of creditors against the assets of the business. Each time the company enters into a financial transaction, the snapshot of the company changes. The basic accounting equation is

Total assets = Total liabilities + shareholder equity

Income Statement

An income statement, otherwise known as a profit and loss statement, is a summary of a company's profit or loss during any one given period of time, such as a month, three months, or one year. The income statement records all revenues for a business during this given period, as well as the operating expenses for the business.[1]

Cash Flow Statement

The **cash flow statement** shows the sources and uses of cash for your business over a certain period of time. This period coincides with the reporting period of the income statement. For example, if a cash flow statement covers the 12 months ending on December 31, 2004, the associated income statement covers the same period. A cash flow statement shows you how your business performs on a cash basis. An income statement shows how your business performs on an accrual basis. In this respect, a cash flow statement generally supplements the information provided in an income statement.

Financial statement analysis requires understanding the strengths and weaknesses of the company. A student of sport finance should be able to understand where problems may occur and what questions need

Figure 6.1 Income Statement

Gross sales	Revenue from sales and services
Less: Cost of goods sold	Cost of goods sold to produce the sales
Gross profit	Gross income or gross earnings
Less: Operating expenses	Selling and administrative expenses
Earnings before interest and taxes (EBIT)	Net operating income
Less: Interest expenses	Interest paid on short and long term debt
Earnings before taxes	Income, or profit, before payment of tax
Less: Taxes	Federal, state, and local income taxes Earnings after taxes (net income or loss) Income, or profit (loss), after taxes

to be addressed. It is often more important to understand the weaknesses than to focus on the financial strengths of the enterprise.

Pro Forma Statements

Data often must be forecasted and **pro forma statements** generated to analyze a situation. *Pro forma* ("as if") financial statements have traditionally been statements based on hypothetical figures used as a means of assessing how assets might be managed under differing future scenarios. The company's financial statements are adjusted to reflect a projected or planned transaction. A "what-if" analysis is applied to consider future asset gains, revenue increases, and related financial activity due to changes that may occur.

A pro forma income statement is similar to a historical income statement, except it projects the future rather than tracks the past. Pro forma income statements are important tools for planning future business operations. If the projections predict a downturn in profitability, you can make operational changes, like increasing prices or decreasing costs, before these projections become reality.

For example, assume a college athletic director knows his or her football schedule for the next four seasons. With the number of home and away games known, he or she can accurately budget revenues and expenses for

these games. In addition, if the athletic department receives a fee from each student, it would be wise for the AD to stay abreast of enrollment projections in order to properly estimate revenue.

To create a pro forma statement, analyze an income statement from the current year. Consider how each item on that statement can or will be changed during the coming year. Ideally this should be done before year's end. You will need to estimate final sales and expenses for the current year to prepare a pro forma income statement for the coming year.

Budgets and Financial Analysis

Budgets affect all aspects of a company. Three types of budgets are commonly found in most companies. They are the **cash**, **revenue**, and **expense budgets**. Each budget has a specific purpose and assists the managers in decision making. Budgeting is about decision making and can provide useful information for important decisions, such as building a new arena, offering player salaries, increasing ticket prices, expanding club seats, moving the franchise, investing in additional marketing activities, etc. These decisions require all departments to work together and provide valuable information for decision-making.

Cash Budgets

Cash is essential in the sport business due to the seasonality of operations. Cash is often received during season ticket sales and major sponsorship deals. The management of the cash requires timing and planning to estimate cash inflows and outflows. The management of cash resources holds a central position in the area of short-term financing decisions. Results of investment decisions are estimated in cash terms and the value of a company. In other words, if we are going to expand our arena, how much cash do we have on hand to meet short-term payments, and if we need to borrow money, how much should we borrow?

Cash management is part of the wider task of the business manager, which covers not only the management of the company's cash in the normal course of business—making sure the company always has enough cash on hand to meet its bills and expenses and investing any surplus cash—but other things as well. Examples include arranging suitable mixes of short-, medium-, and long-term borrowing, and dealing with major fixed asset costs that may include new facilities, upgrades to stadiums, and/or signing bonuses for players and coaches.

A cash budget is focused on liquidity management. Liquidity means being able to receive cash within approximately ninety days from the sale of assets. These assets are usually current assets and easily transferable to cash. Sources of cash in sport may include but are not limited to the following:

- Ticket sales
- Concessions
- Parking
- Programs
- Club seats
- Luxury boxes
- Signage
- Television and radio sponsorships
- Borrowing money—line of credit
- Sale of assets
- Subsidy from a government agency
- Grants

Uses of cash include many of the major line items in the income statement related to expenses. Operating expenses are the major outflows of cash in a company. Following is a partial list of the major expenses that affect a cash budget.

- Operating expenses
- Payroll and payroll tax patterns
- Purchases of materials/supplies (seasonal factors)
- Debt service (principle, interest, and balloon payments)
- Income and other taxes (EBIT, property tax)
- Capital expenditures (down payment, retainage)
- Other (bonuses, interest expense, subsidy)

Other factors that are essential when starting a cash budget include an estimated beginning balance for cash, desired or required cash balance at the end of a period, and always the need to forecast borrowing and repaying debt.

Revenue Budgets

Revenue budgets are essential for decision-making. Company managers must be able to project future revenue for planning and management decisions. Revenue budgets in sport are usually straightforward. Revenue is recorded when earned. Whatever revenues your company earns during a certain period, you match the appropriate expenses that you incurred in earning those revenues during the same period.

For example, professional football season ticket renewals occur in February and March each year. Millions of dollars are received during these months in cash. However, the games are played in September, October, November, and December. You receive cash in February and March, but you earn the revenue when the games are played in the September through December timeframe. Revenue is matched against the expenditures related to the players, stadium, and fans.

Sources of revenue will include ticket sales, contributions, dividends, interest earned, sales of company assets, luxury box sales, sales of services, concessions, television, bowl games, playoff games, stadium rental, sponsorship, and promotional activities to name a few. Budgets must address a future decision, as demonstrated by the following question: Will our team make the playoffs or a BCS game? As this necessary question reveals, winning does matter and even influences the budgeting process for many organizations.

Expense Budgets

Expense budgets must closely identify with the revenue budgets due to the matching concept. Financial managers must be able to analyze expenses in relationship to the cash available to pay for the operational expenses incurred. Expenses are recorded when incurred. This means that professional athletes are paid when they play the game and not before, unless a special contractual arrangement exists.

Operational expenses have fixed and variable cost components. Financial managers must be aware of these expenses when making decisions on financial matters.

- **Expense** – any cost of doing business resulting from revenue-generating activities.

- **Operating expense** – expense arising in the normal course of running a business, such as an office electricity bill.

- **Variable expenses** – unavoidable periodic cost that does not have a constant value, such as electric, gas, and water bills.

- **Non-variable or fixed cost** – a cost that does not vary depending on production or sales levels, such as rent, property, insurance, or interest expense.

- **Semi-variable cost** – a cost that has a fixed cost component and a variable expense component.

- **Step cost or discretionary expense** – a recurring or non-recurring expense for goods and services that are either non-essential or more expensive than necessary; examples include entertainment expenses, wellness programs, and speakers.

Each expense item affects the cash outflow of a company, and this determines the need for proper cash management. Cash flow is essential in the sport business due to the nature of when the cash is received and when the expenses occur.

Budgets will help address the following issues: (1) The future is often uncertain. What problem or advantage will tomorrow bring? (2) The prices of good and services will increase (inflation). A dollar today will buy less in the future. (3) Will an investment today earn a positive return? Budgets are annual events with a three to five year projection for planning. That is why cash in hand is worth more than cash in the future.

©iStockphoto.com

Budgets and Financial Decision Making

Budgeting is a planning and controlling activity for the decision maker. Budget preparation prioritizes company future plans in a formalized process. A budget expresses these priorities and plans in financial terms. All departments of the company are involved in budgeting, even though many might believe otherwise. Astute employees can see the company vision by the money allocated to their department or area of interest. Accountability follows money; money is allocated during the budget process, and managers must be knowledgeable in accounting and finance in order to attain the company goals.

Sport Finance Essentials

The **time value of money** serves as the foundation for all other notions in finance. It impacts business finance, consumer finance, and government finance. Time value of money results from the concept of interest.

The introduction to simple interest and compound interest illustrates the use of time value of money tables, shows a matrix approach to solving time value of money problems, and introduces the concepts of intra year compounding, annuities due, and perpetuities. A simple introduction to working time value of money problems on a financial calculator is included, as well as additional resources to help understand time value of money. **Simple interest** is a topic that most people understand. Interest may be thought of as rent paid on borrowed money. Simple interest is calculated only on the beginning principle. For instance, if someone were to receive 6% interest on a beginning value of $100, the first year they would get .06 x $100, or $6 in interest. **Compound interest**, the preferred way to handle financial decisions, is another matter. It is good to receive compound interest, but not so good to pay compound interest. With compound interest, interest is calculated not only on the beginning interest, but also on any interest accumulated in the meantime. For instance, if someone were to receive 5% compound interest on a beginning value of $100, the first year they would get the same amount ($5) as if they were receiving simple interest. The second year, though, their interest would be calculated on the beginning amount in year 2, which would be $105— .05 x $105, or $5.25 in interest. Third year interest would be based on $110.25, and so on. Interest increases at a quicker rate due to the process of compounding.

Time Value of Money

The Time Value of Money concepts will be grouped into two areas: Future Value and Present Value. **Fu-** ture value describes the process of finding what an investment today will grow to in the future. **Present value** describes the process of determining what a cash flow to be received in the future is worth in today's dollars. The equations for present value, future value, present value of an annuity, and future value of an annuity are shown below.

Bonds and Other Investment Instruments

An essential element to any sport organization is the facility utilized to play the game and entertain the fans in the community. The financing of the public assembly facility is often the key to attract and retain the franchise. Following are the major financial instruments utilized in financing public facilities.

Public assembly facilities include large indoor and outdoor stadiums (50,000–100,000 seating capacity), arenas (12,000–30,000 seating capacity), and other entertainment-related multipurpose structures. These facilities become homes for professional, college, and minor league teams. Four types of instruments are typically used to finance public assembly facilities:

1. Municipal bonds

Table 6.4

PV = Present Value	FV = Future Value	CF = Cash flow
R = Interest rate	PMT = Payment	T = Time (years)

Annual Compounding

Present Value:

$$PV = \frac{CF_t}{(1+r)^t}$$

Future Value:

$$FV_t = CF_0(1+r)^t$$

Present Value of a Cash Flow Stream:

$$PV = \sum_{t=0}^{n} \frac{CF_t}{(1+r)^t}$$

Future Value of a Cash Flow Stream:

$$FV_n = \sum_{t=0}^{n} CF_t(1+r)^{n-t}$$

Present Value of an Annuity:

$$PVA = PMT\left[\frac{1-(1+r)^{-t}}{r}\right]$$

Future Value of an Annuity:

$$FVA_t = PMT\left[\frac{(1+r)^t-1}{r}\right]$$

2. General obligation bonds (GO bonds)

3. Revenue bonds

4. Certificates of participation

State and local governments issue bonds in the capital market to finance their capital spending programs for building arenas, stadiums, parking lots, and infrastructure upgrades. Infrastructure improvements often include roads, water/sewer, utility right of way, and other utility needs. Investors call these types of bonds **municipal bonds** or **munis**. Municipalities, subdivisions of states, issue the bonds; they are tax-exempt because the interest investors receive is exempt from federal taxation. Most states exempt state income tax as well on the interest earned from their bonds.

General obligation bonds (GO) are those bonds paid back through the taxing power of the issuing authority. These bonds are typically used to finance traditional capital projects such as highways, roads, and sewers. General obligation bonds are issued against the general full faith and credit of state and local governments. The issuing bodies (state, local, or regional government) generally require the use of **ad valorem taxes**. Ad valorem taxes are property taxes. This means taxes are levied according to the value of one's property; the more valuable the property, the higher the tax. The underlying theory of ad valorem taxation is that those owning the more valuable properties are wealthier; hence, this results in a lower cost of issuance and higher credit rating, which often reduces the bond size since a debt reserve fund is not always required. General obligation bonds are typically safe investments and a very dependable source of revenue for municipal budgeting.

Revenue bonds are paid back from revenues generated by the specific project (i.e., stadium). The specific bond is serviced by the cash flows from the project. They are special obligations in public financing that are payable solely from a particular source of funds that may include tax/surcharge revenues from hotel/motel, restaurant, liquor/beer sales, cigarettes, rental cars, and other sources. The "sin taxes" (i.e., alcohol and tobacco taxes) have become very popular. Following are some of the sources utilized to fund public assembly facilities utilizing revenue bonds: hotel tax, meal tax, liquor tax, sales tax, auto rental tax, property tax, tax increment financing districts, business license tax, utility tax, public and private grants, state appropriations, taxi tax, and team tax. The key is that no pledge of state, regional, or local ad valorem tax revenues is required; however, the typical revenue bond does carry a higher interest rate and requires a higher debt services coverage ratio, as well as debt services reserve.

Certificates of participation (COPs) are public financing instruments that require the governmental entity creating a corporation to buy/build a public assembly facility, such as an arena or convention and visitors' center. The corporation then issues certificates of participation to raise money to buy/build the public facility. The government leases back the building and the lease payments are supposed to pay back the bonds. All this happens without a public vote.

Certificates of participation seem like traditional bonds, but they are not backed by the full faith and credit of the government entity that issues the bonds. In a recession-hammered environment, certificates of participation and lease appropriation financing become popular with local governments looking to fund projects as real estate values decline, and with them property tax collections. These securities are not backed by the full faith and credit of a municipality. Therefore, they are a greater risk than a general obligation bond and rated lower.

Summary

Good financial planning is a roadmap to success. The revenues produced from facilities and sport events can be significant, but the expense side of the formula cannot be overlooked. Revenue minus expenses produces net income or net loss.

In this chapter, we discussed the rudiments of financial statements and a great many financial terms and concepts. We discussed the interrelationship between accounting and finance, and how each is a separate course of study in business schools. Accounting and finance work together to produce useful financial information to managers. This chapter identified the importance of organizational structure and the impact on financial statements. Organization structure is not just a management issue; it is a financial issue with tax implications.

A good financial roadmap will utilize financial statements and cash flow. The chapter discussed cash flow as it relates to sport organizations. Cash flow and budgeting are components of good financial decision making. Budgeting is a major part of decision making. The chapter identifies cash, revenue, and expense budgets and how timing (accrual) affects the budgeting process. During the budget process the time value of money (TVM) and investment of cash produces challenges to the manager to have cash available to pay bills, yet optimize the concept of TVM. The challenge for the manager is to balance cash on hand with good investments.

Sport finance is dependent on fan attendance. The fans produce the cash that transfers to net income or loss for the principals in sport organizations. Sport is a service industry, and sport finance is a key component of the business that assists managers by producing tangible information for decision making.

Discussion Activities

1. The authors identified many sources of revenue in professional and intercollegiate athletics. Using the sources provided, identify the main expense categories in college and professional sports.

2. Contact two organizations in the same sport and request their financial documents. Compare and contrast the information, and make a chart of current revenues, expenses, and overall financial position.

3. Using the Sports Business Daily (www.sportsbusinessdaily.com), conduct research into the broadcast rights fees of the four major professional leagues in North America. Why are they different? What are the similarities?

References

CEO network chat on the business of sports. (2003, February 10). *Forbes*. Retrieved August 29, 2004, from http://www.forbes.com/work/2003/02/10/cx_ml_0210sports chat.html.

Howard, D. (1998). Financial principles applied to sport management. In Masteralexis, L. P., Barr, C. A., & Hums, M. A. (Eds.), *Principles and practice of sport management*. (pp. 70-71). Gaithersburg, MD: Aspen Publishers Inc.

Irwin, R. L., Sutton, W. A., & McCarthy, L. M. (2002). *Sport promotion and sales management*. Champaign, IL: Human Kinetics, 261.

NHL franchise switches gears from team to venue, signs 22 new sponsors. (2004, June 28). *IEG Sponsorship Report, 23*(12), 7.

Olsen, A. (2004, April 26). Licensing a Champion. Retrieved September 10, 2004, from http://www.kentucky.com/mld/kentucky/business/8521135.htm?template=contentModules.

Record growth without gold. (2000, May). *Promo Industry Report*, A23.

Shank, M. D. (2002). *Sport marketing: A strategic perspective* (2nd ed.). Upper Saddle River, NJ: Pearson Education, Inc., 402.

Street & Smith's SportBusiness Journal (2004). By the numbers 2004, *6*(36), 10–14, 84, 127.

Suggested Reading

Fatsis, S. (2003, February). Hot ticket, higher prices. *The Wall Street Journal Classroom Edition*. Retrieved September 1, 2004, from http://www.wsjclassroomedition.com/archive/03feb/YMNY.htm.

Isidore, C. (2003, August 8). Life, Liberty and Hoagies. *CNN-money*. Retrieved September 1, 2004, from http://money.cnn.com/2003/08/08/commentary/column_sportsbiz/sportsbiz/.

Chapter Seven

Sport Marketing

John Clark

Immediately after the tournament, PGA officials pulled the plug on the "Bring Your 2-Year-Old, Get in Free" promotion.

Learning Objectives

Upon completion of this chapter, the reader should be able to

- Define marketing and its role in sport;

- Distinguish between marketing and promotions;

- Understand the need for market segmentation; and

- Identify the need for market research.

Introduction

Think about the last time you attended or watched a professional sporting event on television. In addition to the game, you likely saw signs of companies throughout the arena or stadium, cheerleaders or a dance team, or a mascot roaming the sidelines or stadium rows entertaining fans. You may have heard the public address announcer talking about special offers or upcoming events and noticed entertaining elements on the scoreboard. If you were at a professional baseball game and a hometown player hit a home run, there may have been a fireworks display. If you attended a baseball game in Milwaukee or Pittsburgh, in

"SPORT IS THE TOY DEPARTMENT OF
HUMAN LIFE."

HOWARD COSELL

the middle of the game you may have seen sausages or pierogis racing in the park. If you attended a National Basketball Association (NBA) game in Indianapolis, you may have seen Boomer, the Pacers mascot, repel from the rafters at the beginning of the game, or don a mask of the grim reaper and stand behind the opposing team's bench late in the game.

Photo by Andy Gillentine

Most activities seen or heard at a professional or collegiate sporting event are specifically designed to en-

hance our experience at that game. The same holds true for sporting events we watch on television or the Internet. Technological advances have allowed broadcast networks and production companies to enhance our viewing experience, making it easier to follow the action by providing the viewer with more information, increasing the number of cameras, and taking the viewer "into the action" with enhanced audio/visual capabilities. The end result, whether the game is viewed in person or from the comfort of our living room, is an elaborate strategy designed to keep the fans coming back. In essence, that is what sport marketing is all about—compelling customers to consume the sport product once, knowing that if they have a good time and are more than satisfied with their experience, they will keep coming back.

Sport Marketing Defined

Ask several industry experts what sport marketing is exactly, and several different answers will emerge depending on the area of the industry in which the respondent works. Any all-inclusive academic definition of sport marketing would certainly include something about each of the four Ps (product, price, promotion, and place) as they relate to the target consumers' behavior (often public relations is included as a 5th P). It is beyond the scope of this chapter to tackle such a daunting task as creating *the* perfect definition for sport marketing; therefore, we will use a two-part definition from Mullin, Hardy, and Sutton (2000):

> "Sport marketing consists of all activities designed to meet the needs and wants of sport consumers through exchange processes. Sport marketing has developed two major thrusts: the marketing of sport products and services directly to consumers of sport, and marketing of other consumer and industrial products or services through the use of sport promotions." (p. 9)

The latter portion of the definition—marketing other products or services through sport—refers to promotional licensing or sponsorship and will be dealt with extensively in the following chapter. As for the part of the definition that deals with the marketing of sport products and services, it bears exploring *why* the sport marketing specialty is needed. In other words, *how is sport marketing different than traditional marketing?*

Purpose of Marketing

An important caveat must be stated at this point. The primary purpose of marketing, both in the traditional and sport contexts, is ultimately to increase revenue for an organization. Certain marketing strategies may not lead to immediate sales (e.g., brand awareness strategies), but even these strategies have as their ultimate goal increased revenue. Aspiring sport marketers must remember that their efforts should pursue the objective of increasing revenue either in the short or long term.

Sport Consumers

In professional sport, all conceivable marketing strategies would not amount to a penny were it not for consumers. Both core and ancillary products in spectator and participatory sport rely on consumers for success. Sport is woven into the fabric of society—locally, regionally, nationally, and internationally. In the words of NBA Commissioner David Stern, as he watched the Houston Rockets and Sacramento Kings play a preseason game in China, "Fans are fans" (ESPN, 2004). As such, we learn to consume sport at a young age, both as participants and as spectators. For a sport marketer, two basic consumer characteristics exist that help differentiate types of sport consumers. These two characteristics are **involvement** and **commitment**. According to Mullin, Hardy, and Sutton (2000), involvement can be behavioral (the actual doing of a sport activity), cognitive (seeking out information and knowledge about a sport), and affective (the feelings and emotions a sport consumer has for a particular activity or team).

Commitment refers to the frequency, duration, and intensity of involvement in a sport, or the willingness to expend money, time, and energy in a pattern of sport involvement (Mullin et al., 2000, p. 57). Sport is rife with examples of both of these consumer characteristics. For example, fans of the Boston Red Sox continued to pack Fenway Park and drive the ratings for Red Sox games on the New England Sports Network despite enduring over eighty years without a World Series title—that is, until recently. It seemed as if each October brought heartbreak to the Red Sox nation, as when the team was ousted from the American League playoffs by their hated rivals, the New York Yankees, in the

year prior to their sweep of the World Series. Despite disappointments like this, each spring Red Sox fans would well up with optimism in anticipation of the upcoming season and the end of the Curse of the Bambino. Red Sox fans were highly committed to their franchise and were heavily involved with each up and down of the season. One could tune into a Boston sport radio talk show on any day between February and October to hear the Red Sox fans complain, suggest trades, disparage poor play, and of course, deride the Yankees. Researchers contend that highly committed and highly involved sport consumers are more loyal than casual consumers; therefore, the sport marketer who can foster these characteristics in a consumer base will derive the benefits of a loyal customer base.

Involved and committed customers are important tenets of relationship marketing—a theory gaining increasing popularity in the sport world. According to Gordon (1998), relationship marketing is

> the ongoing process of identifying and *creating new value* with individual customers and then *sharing the benefits* from this over a lifetime of association. It involves the understanding, focusing and management of ongoing collaboration between suppliers and selected customers for mutual value creation and sharing through interdependence and organizational alignment. (p. 9)

Howard Schultz, owner of the Starbucks Coffee empire and the NBA's Seattle Supersonics, along with Anaheim Angels' owner Arturo Moreno, are two excellent examples of professional sport managers who go to great lengths to ensure their customers are an integral part of the franchise by incorporating value-added strategies throughout the franchise operations. Both of these owners have created mechanisms to communicate directly with fans. More importantly, Schultz and Moreno have incorporated customer feedback into the franchises' operations to improve the overall consumer experiences. These men understand that each game attended by a customer is a vote of confidence for the franchise, as well as a product trial.

Fans spending their disposable income on the Sonics or Angels have certain levels of expectations about what their money will get them. Efficient, friendly service, comfortable seating in a clean facility, certain types of concessions, and an entertaining two to three hours are just some of these expectations. The key for a sport marketer to remember is that consumer expectations are unique to the individual, and whatever the consumer's individual perceptions may be, they are correct—at least for that individual consumer.

Consumer Expertise and Identity

One other important aspect of sport consumers is the familiarity that most consumers have with their chosen pastimes. Many consumers have actually participated with their favorite sport on some level—whether that level was during their formative years, in high school or college, or in some recreational capacity. Having played the game, consumers are better able to identify with the action on the field, court, or track. For example, Bill France, founder of NASCAR racing, was adamant that early racers drive stock cars available to the average person. Early racing fans actually witnessed drivers race the same model of car they would drive to church or to the grocery store.

Of course, this level of familiarity is a double-edged sword for a sport marketer. In Pittsburgh, Sunday afternoons during the football season find thousands of people second-guessing every move the Pittsburgh Steelers make—from play selection to player personnel issues. Of course Western Pennsylvania is a hotbed of high school football, so the level of familiarity with the sport makes it more likely that fans feel qualified to critique the Steelers organization. Whether the fans are actually qualified or not is irrelevant. It is each person's own perception that he or she is qualified that heightens the individual and collective levels of commitment and involvement with the team. So, when a team starts to lose, these fans will voice their opinions.

The Four Ps of Marketing

The following section explains the four Ps of marketing: Product, Price, Promotions, and Place. Each of these areas is common to every product or service, but in the sport industry, each requires the sport marketer to consider the unique aspects of sport when determining what marketing strategy to use.

The Sport Product

Imagine that immediately after class, you and your classmates go to the school gym to play basketball.

You play for one hour and then go on with the rest of your day. Exactly one week later, after the same class, you and your classmates go to the gym to play basketball again. Imagine the weather was exactly the same, everyone was wearing the same clothes, and you all had the exact same breakfast food as the week before. You did everything within your control to replicate the conditions of that basketball game you played one week earlier. Even with all the efforts to ensure the game would be the same—will it? In the words of the famous John Wayne movie character Jacob McCandles, "Not hardly." Each and every sporting activity or game is different from one consumptive episode to the next. This is part of sport's appeal, but this characteristic is problematic for the sport marketer because the core product is largely out of the marketer's control.

What if you had a job marketing Dial soap? To be more specific, say your job was to market the bath size, unscented bars of Dial soap. Due to production mechanisms and quality control programs, it is fairly certain that each bath size, unscented bar of Dial soap is the same as the next. The same cannot be said for a marketer of the Minnesota Vikings. One week, the Vikings may play flawless football, and the next, the Vikings' offense may turn the ball over seven times. The crux of the issue is that the sport product is inconsistent and is largely out of the sport marketer's control.

Sport Production and Consumption

The next important difference between the sport product and traditional products deals with *when* the sport product is produced. Go back to the earlier example of the class playing basketball. The ball, the gym, the baskets, and the clothes people wear were all "produced" at a time before the actual game; yet those things combined do not create the experience. It is the actual game form that makes the experience or product. Sport activities, similar to hotel rooms and plane flights, are produced in the same moment that they are consumed. Consequently, there is no inventory of the core product once the game is over. You cannot take empty seats and add them to the arena or stadium capacity at the next home game; likewise, no one will buy tickets to yesterday's game or flight. That is why there is such a great emphasis in the industry to presell the contest.

Core Product

If one were to list sport products, the first things to spring to mind would be spectator sporting events at all levels, participatory activities such as playing tennis or jogging, instructional lessons like karate or a session with a personal trainer, sporting goods (e.g., balls, golf clubs, equipment), and sport-related apparel (e.g., jerseys, hats). Most of these are usually considered part of sport's **core** product—the essential component to a sporting activity or event. These are all important aspects of the sport product, yet there are many more. Ticket stubs, programs, brochures, luxury suites, club seating, mascots, promotions, spirit squads, cheerleaders, broadcasts, and web pages are other components of the core product. In reality, a sport product can be anything related to a sport organization that has consumer demand, and in an industry where the ability to create new revenue streams is at a premium, sport marketers are always searching for new products to sell.

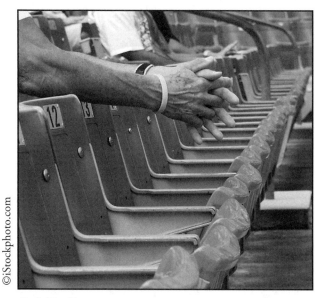
©iStockphoto.com

Pricing Sport

Potentially one of the most controversial issues facing a sport marketer is how to price an activity, event, or sponsorship. Compounding this problem, at least for spectator sport, is the previously mentioned fact about the inconsistent nature of the core product. For example, a Michigan–Ohio State football game will almost always be more attractive to a majority of the country than a Michigan–North Dakota game. Even so, sport marketers must devise a pricing strategy that appears fair to the paying public, while at the same time being careful not to set the price too low, thereby leaving the

proverbial money "on the table." In addition, a wrongly priced product could potentially lower the perceived value of the product. It was previously mentioned that perceptions by individual consumers, be they correct or incorrect, often dictate consumption patterns. Similarly, consumer perceptions about the cost of an event or activity relative to its value also dictate consumptive behavior. The benefits for a sporting event or activity range from health benefits to psychological benefits or sociological benefits. In the fall of 2004, Master Card International continued its "Priceless" themed ad campaign around the Major League Baseball (MLB) playoffs by running a commercial asking Boston Red Sox fans what it would be worth to them to see the Red Sox in a World Series. Fans' responses ranged from "My first born" to "My right arm." The spot ends with the Master Card catch phrase, "Seeing the Red Sox win the World Series—Priceless." Clearly for Red Sox fans, seeing their team in a World Series has a value far beyond any monetary figure.

Price vs. Total Cost

Conversely, the cost of a particular event or activity reaches beyond the actual dollar figure paid for a ticket or equipment rental. Also factored into the equation is the time it takes to travel to and from the activity or event, the cost of giving up something else to partake in the sporting activity or event, or the psychological or social cost of participating in an activity or event. In addition to these factors, a sport marketer also has to consider how frequently a particular activity or event is offered. NASCAR can charge more for a Nextel Cup race than a MLB franchise can charge for a regular season contest because the Nextel Cup race is only once a year, as opposed to the 81 home regular season dates for a MLB franchise. The National Football League (NFL) also enjoys the benefit of having a limited supply of home games when it comes to pricing strategy. The eight regular season home games in the NFL allow member franchises to charge, on average, higher ticket prices across the league, compared to their other professional league counterparts.

Additional Benefits

Another factor in pricing strategy is the amenities offered as part of the activity or event. Most professional sport franchises offer premium services and graduated benefits to season ticket holders, depending on how many games are in the season ticket package and where the seats are located. An NFL season ticket holder purchasing club seats will receive access to a special area in the stadium with premium food, more luxurious surroundings, special parking privileges, the ability to purchase discounted merchandise at the team store, invitations to special season ticket holder parties, and other benefits. Meanwhile, the NFL fan who purchases season tickets in the upper level of the stadium may only receive the discounted merchandise and parking privilege benefits. Naturally, the club seating ticket package will cost more, as there are consumers who value those types of benefits and have no problem paying extra for them.

Variable Pricing

A recent pricing trend in the spectator sport industry has seen franchises and athletic departments incorporate variable pricing strategies into their marketing efforts. Variable pricing refers to charging higher amounts for more desirable games and charging lesser amounts for the least desirable games. For example, assume the University of Wisconsin football team was to play Prairie View A & M one week and the University of Michigan the following week. The Badgers would be expected by their fans to beat Prairie View handily, which would impact the demand for tickets. On the other hand, the University of Michigan game, along with being a Big 10 match-up, would also be perceived as a "big game" by the Badger fans, which would drive demand for tickets. If the University of Wisconsin was to implement a variable pricing strategy, it would charge a lesser price for tickets to the Prairie View game than it would for the Michigan game.

Competition

A final consideration when determining a pricing strategy is the sport organization's competition in the marketplace. By setting a much higher price than the competition, a sport organization may create a perception of a high quality product; however, this could occur only if the core product and ancillary product components are of high quality as well. For instance, the Green Bay Packers, the only major professional sport franchise in their market, can set prices much higher than the University of Wisconsin-Green Bay

athletic program or local high school athletic programs, without experiencing any detrimental effect on attendance. This is due to the Packers' storied history of success and the affinity Wisconsin residents statewide have for the Packers franchise. In this case, the higher price is consistent with the image and value consumers place on the Packers.

On the other hand, in a market with many affordable entertainment options for consumers to choose from, a high price may have a negative impact on consumption levels, especially if there are not enough affluent consumers in the marketplace who value the core product offering. In this sense, a pricing strategy should consider the disposable income levels of both current and future primary consumer segments. To illustrate, consider the fans of the NBA. On average, NBA season ticket holders hold white-collar jobs and possess higher than average household income and education levels—in short, people who can afford to pay for tickets that may cost on average between $20 and $50. Yet, the NBA has many fans that are younger and live in urban areas with below average household income and education levels. From a long-term perspective, the NBA may have to develop alternative pricing strategies that will enable these customers to consume NBA basketball with more financial ease.

In conclusion, there is no universally accepted formula for pricing sport products. The shrewd sport marketer must consider all of the factors described above as well as conduct a thorough examination of the marketplace to ensure that the pricing strategy employed will generate sufficient levels of revenue without driving away large groups of consumers who are unwilling or unable to pay the price.

Promotions

While attending a minor league baseball game, fans, during the break between half innings, are likely to see some sort of contest involving fans on the playing field. This may have been a contest requiring contestants to place their forehead on a bat and spin around for several seconds before running to first base, or it may have required the contestants to throw a baseball through a target to win a prize. These contests are promotional contests. In general, the term promotion encompasses advertising, publicity efforts, personal selling, and sales promotion in all of their varied forms. Promotions can be categorized in two ways: **price promotions** and **non-price promotions**. To determine which type of promotion to use, sport marketers must first understand what she hopes to achieve through the use of promotions. Once these objectives are clear, then the appropriate promotional strategy can be employed.

Price Promotions

As their name implies, price promotions manipulate the actual cost of consuming a sport activity or event. Two-for-one ticket promotions are a popular promotional strategy used by many sport organizations on both the professional and amateur levels. Other popular price promotions involve coupons, a donation of canned goods in exchange for free or discounted tickets, children gaining free admission with the purchase of an adult ticket, and family packages in which a family of four receives four tickets and discounts at the concession stand for one packaged price. Price promotions are used to increase attendance and are most effective when a sport organization is in a market where

consumer demand for the core product is not strong or the customer base is price-sensitive. Used properly, price promotions can increase attendance for activities or events that would usually not have great appeal to the public.

However, a sport marketer must exercise caution when contemplating the use of price promotions. If discounted tickets or admission through the use of price promotions becomes the standard fare for the sport organization, the danger exists of cheapening the core product as perceived by consumers. For example, if a minor league hockey team has a buy-one-get-one-free price promotion for every Friday home game, consumers in that market may only consider attending a hockey game on a Friday, when they can get the tickets cheaper, as opposed to considering attending a hockey game on another night when the cost of admission is full price. Also, price promotions can anger full-paying season ticket holders who have already purchased their tickets and cannot take advantage of the discounted offer.

Table 7.1 Top 15 Promotional Giveaway Items and Their Impact on Attendance in MLB, NBA, & NHL teams

Giveaway	Change from Average (%)	Total Attendance	Additional Tickets Sold	Number of games
Jack-in-the-box	20.7	89,957	15,407	4
Travel Mug	19.8	156,828	25,939	6
Ring	14.3	142,653	17,863	4
Bobblehead	12.5	1,532,414	170,400	53
Stuffed Animal	11.3	127,344	12,920	4
Puzzle	10.8	172,369	16,805	5
Backpack	9.7	193,133	17,057	8
Notebook	9.1	304,391	25,292	8
Clock	8.9	98,085	8,035	4
Figure	8.3	659,520	50,460	22
Batting Helmet	7.2	187,479	12,590	5
Rally Towel	6.8	357,775	22,831	10
Cap	6.2	1,780,670	104,209	52
Ball / Puck	5.7	604,558	32,628	19
Wristband	4.9	138,778	6,441	4

This list does not include giveaways held by fewer than four teams, fan activities (ex. fireworks, concerts, etc.), or discounted ticket deals.

Source: *Street & Smith's SportsBusiness Journal*, October 18th-24th, 2004

Non-Price Promotions

The other type of promotions—non-price promotions—include all other activities designed to make the activity or event more attractive and enjoyable to consumers. Giveaways, fireworks, autograph signing sessions, and concerts are examples of non-price promotions used to increase interest and attendance at sporting events. Table 7.1 lists some of the more popular and successful non-price promotions used in professional sport.

From a sport marketing perspective, the question that must be answered is *how many people will we draw with this promotion and will the revenue generated from the additional people more than cover the cost of staging the promotion?* For instance, if team executives were to contract with Britney Spears to perform after a game, will the attendance spike not only cover the cost of paying Spears' appearance fee, but also cover the advertising that will promote the concert, the cost of paying staff for the extended time at the event, and any other costs that accompany staging the promotion? Ideally, a promotion like this example will not only break even financially, but generate a profit for the franchise as well. One way to improve the chance for financial success is to have a third party (sponsor) pay for some or all of the costs associated with the promotion (see below, and Chapter 8).

Of critical import to the sport marketer is the question of *when* to use this type of promotion. One school of thought suggests that larger non-price promotions (including historically successful giveaways like bobblehead dolls) should be used on a date that the sport organization is not expecting a very large crowd. If used at this time, the non-price promotion should provide the desired spike in attendance, creating at least some business on a date that was anticipated to have very little business. The conflicting viewpoint is that larger non-price promotions should be used on more desirable dates in an effort to reach the capacity of the stadium or arena. Proponents of this view would argue for placing the concert on a Saturday evening (usually a well-attended date for most spectator sport franchises) against a good opponent in hopes of having a sell-out crowd. Sport teams have experimented year-by-year with these types of non-price promotions with varying degrees of success. Each marketplace is different, which underscores the need for sport marketers to understand

their consumers so they might know what type of promotion will work at what time.

Fireworks and concerts are only one part of non-price promotions. The activities that occur during the down time in a game are also non-price promotions. Having a mascot shoot hot dogs into the crowd or deliver a pizza to a randomly chosen fan, or having sausages race around the ball park are also non-price promotions. These types of promotions add to the overall atmosphere and experience of attending a sporting event, especially for attendees who are only casual fans and are looking at the event more for its entertainment value. Moreover, these types of promotions are saleable. In other words, they can be built into a sponsorship package and generate revenue for the sport organization. The sausage race mentioned earlier is actually done by the Milwaukee Brewers franchise of MLB. This promotion has four people dressed up in over-sized sausage costumes race from the centerfield wall to home plate and is sponsored by Usinger's—a maker of bratwurst and other processed meats in Milwaukee.

Clever and memorable non-price promotions of this sort help a sponsoring company as much as the franchise, as attendees to the event link the promotion back to the sponsor, which will ideally remain with consumers until it is time for them to make a purchase from the sponsor's category of products/services. Minor league sport franchises are often the testing ground for novel promotions of this sort, which, if successful, often make their way to the major league level.

Place

In traditional marketing, place refers to distribution of the product as well as the "place" of consumption. In that sense, sport marketers also consider the final "P" both place and distribution, since the physical setting (i.e., stadium, arena, health club) is where the sport product is distributed. Place can be an important factor in the purchase decision for many sport consumers. A facility that is both physically and aesthetically appealing enhances the core product and improves the overall sport consumptive experience. The place also is a major factor in consumers' initial perception of a sport organization. For instance, if a consumer walks into a stadium or club and is met with rude workers, litter, and poorly marked directions, they are most likely to have a negative perception toward the sport organization. It takes twelve positives to cancel out one negative in a consumer's mind. If a sport organization does not cancel out the negatives, they may lose the consumer's business.

Today, newly constructed sport facilities are designed with amenities that provide additional revenue-generating streams for the sport organization, such as club seating, luxury suites, in-stadium retail stores, and a varied assortment of concessions and restaurants. Newer stadiums like the Pittsburgh Pirates' PNC Park and the Seattle Mariners' Safeco Field serve as attractions in-and-of themselves, which aids in driving attendance when the core, on-field product is perceived as substandard. The construction style is reminiscent of sport's Golden Age, evoking nostalgic emotions in older fans, while catering to fans' tastes for updated amenities. Even older facilities, with or without an update, can serve as attractions, drawing fans regardless of franchise performance. Wrigley Field in Chicago, Fenway Park in Boston, and Lambeau Field in Green Bay all are excellent examples of how a stadium exemplifies an experience and a franchise. Annually, thousands of fans visit these stadiums to experience the rich history associated with each one.

In sport, the amount of input a marketer has on the construction of a newer facility varies across the industry; however, every effort should be made in both new and existing facilities to accommodate fans and facilitate customer service. Such issues as the appropriate number and placement of restrooms, concession stands, customer service stations, and entrances should be thoroughly planned to anticipate the ideal customer experience. Merchandise kiosks, food stands selling locally flavored concessions, and in-stadium restaurants serve as another revenue-generating source for the sport organization, while offering more choices for the consumer base. Interactive zones are also commonplace in sport stadiums featuring activities for fans that tie entertaining activities with an organization's history to provide a richer experience for the consumer. Additionally, these areas serve as a mechanism to attract consumers with low involvement who may otherwise grow weary of just the core product. However you view it, the place in sport is an integral component of the marketing mix and should be managed if a sport organization desires to stand out from the competition.

The Role of Research in Sport Marketing

Earlier in this chapter, the involvement and commitment of sport consumers was discussed as a means of determining the best consumers of a sport organization. That discussion brings up the question, *How do you get that type of information?* Furthermore, in order to make calculated, strategic marketing decisions, a sport marketer requires additional information about the market, the competition, and the consumers. These issues can be addressed by incorporating a systematic marketing research agenda into the business practices of a sport organization. Market research is a topic with such sufficient depth that one semester of study barely touches all the issues involved in designing and analyzing research. Needless to say, a portion of a chapter can only introduce the aspiring sport marketer to the utility of research. Therefore, in this section, we will touch on consumer market research and its applicability for the sport marketer.

Sound market research helps the sport marketer understand who comprises the customer base, what characteristics are similar between customers, how they prefer consuming the sport product or service, when they are most likely to consume, and where the consumers reside. Once compiled, this information can be analyzed to divide the consumers into similar groups. This process is called **segmentation**. Segmentation is the process of dividing large, unlike groups of consumers into smaller, more defined groups of people who share similar characteristics (Mullin et al., 2000). The smaller groups of consumers allow a sport organization to communicate more effectively and efficiently because marketing communication messages can be constructed that appeal to the unique characteristics of the small groups. Two popular segmentation methods use **demographics** and **psychographics** to group consumers. Demographics describe consumers' state-of-being, including such factors as income level, education level, zip code, marital status, age, race, religious affiliation, occupation type, number of children in the home, and gender. Psychographics refers to consumers' state-of-mind, exploring the likes and dislikes of consumers and using the similarities to create the segments. Exhibit 7-1 at the end of this chapter displays a survey with both demographic and psychographic items from a minor league baseball franchise. Once collected, this information will allow the franchise to develop marketing strategies aimed at specific segments that appeal to the characteristics used in segmenting the consumers. For instance, if a sport organization conducts research and discovers a segment of its customer base is married with two children under the age of twelve, they may approach a local Chuck E. Cheese restaurant and develop a family package whereby consumers purchasing the package receive tickets to a game and discounted dinner at Chuck E. Cheese. This example brings up another important use of research: the ability to use the information to not only increase consumption levels of consumers, but to also sell corporate sponsorships.

When used correctly, market research helps the sport marketer make decisions that improve customer service, the type of merchandise or concessions sold, the number and type of promotions staged, as well as where marketing communications messages should be placed for maximum efficiency. Increasingly, sport organizations of all sizes and types are utilizing market research to improve their businesses, both from a revenue-generating and a customer service standpoint. As you progress through your academic career, you will be wise to learn as many market research techniques as you can, as they will be instrumental in your sport marketing career.

Summary

Any successful sport organization relies on its customers for stability and solvency. Sport marketing plays the primary role in acquiring and keeping customers. While the task may seem daunting at times, the great asset that many sport marketers enjoy is that they are marketing sport. As we have discovered, sport holds a special place in our society, where consumers' emotions are heightened and their involvement exceeds many other products or services. By utilizing sound market research to incorporate the proper mix of the marketing elements, sport marketers will be able to generate the revenue necessary to operate the organization, while creating fun and exciting experiences that will keep consumers returning game after game, season after season.

Discussion Activities

1. Describe how the 4 Ps of sport marketing can be inter-related by developing a marketing plan for a new minor league baseball team in your hometown.

2. Explain relationship marketing and provide an example of how marketers from your university's athletic department could do a better job creating a relationship with the student body.

3. Describe some of the main unique aspects of sport marketing and apply them to the sport with which you are most familiar.

References

ESPN SportsCenter Interview with NBA Commissioner David Stern. Aired October 17th, 2004.

Gordon, I. (1998). *Relationship Marketing*. New York: John Wiley & Sons.

Hagstrom, R. G. (1998). *The NASCAR Way*. New York: John Wiley & Sons.

Mullin, B., Hardy, S., & Sutton, W. A. (2000). *Sport Marketing* (2nd ed.). Champaign, IL: Human Kinetics.

Normann, R. (2000). *Service Management* (3rd ed.). New York: John Wiley & Sons.

Suggested Reading

D'Alessandro, D. F. (2002). *Brand Warfare*. New York: McGraw-Hill Education.

Earls, M. (2002). *Welcome to the Creative Age—Banana, Business and the Death of Marketing*. New York: John Wiley & Sons.

Grant, J. (2002). *After Image: Mind-Expanding Marketing*. London, UK: Profile Business.

Exhibit 7.1 *Attendee Survey of Lake County Captains*

Lake County Captains 2004 Fan Survey

Thank you for taking this survey about attendees of Lake County Captains games. Please carefully read each question, and mark the correct answer that is closest to your opinion about your experience at Captains' games. This is not a test. There are no correct or incorrect answers. Most questions simply ask for your opinion and the results will be anonymous. Work quickly and record you immediate thoughts. Some of the questions may seem similar to you, or may not be worded exactly the way you would like them to be. Even so, give your best estimate and continue working through the survey. It is important that you answer all the questions. Your best response is far more valuable than an incomplete response.

Below are some statements regarding how you feel about the Lake County Captains. Please read each statement, and then circle the appropriate number printed on the right to indicate your level of agreement or disagreement with the statement.

	Strongly Disagree					Strongly Agree	
The Captains stadium is a clean, comfortable facility.	1	2	3	4	5	6	7
There is ample parking around the Captains stadium.	1	2	3	4	5	6	7
The ushers are courteous and friendly.	1	2	3	4	5	6	7
It is enjoyable to visit the Captains stadium.	1	2	3	4	5	6	7
I enjoy going to the stadiums for Captains games.	1	2	3	4	5	6	7
To me, the Captains are the same as other franchises.	1	2	3	4	5	6	7
On most nights, the Captains provide quality entertainment.	1	2	3	4	5	6	7
Captain ticket-takers are courteous.	1	2	3	4	5	6	7
I consider myself a loyal customer of the Captains.	1	2	3	4	5	6	7
I enjoy the in-game promotions at Captains games.	1	2	3	4	5	6	7
There are many items to choose from at the concession stands.	1	2	3	4	5	6	7
I think the price of concession items is fair.	1	2	3	4	5	6	7
If I had to do it over again, I would not come to a Captains game.	1	2	3	4	5	6	7
I follow the Captains because they are my hometown team.	1	2	3	4	5	6	7
It is important for me to support the Captains as my hometown team.	1	2	3	4	5	6	7
The Captains are an important part of the community.	1	2	3	4	5	6	7
I come to Captains games because it is the best choice of entertainment for me.	1	2	3	4	5	6	7
The Captains provide a rallying point for the community.	1	2	3	4	5	6	7
The Captains do not have adequate in-game entertainment.	1	2	3	4	5	6	7
I am proud to attend Captains games.	1	2	3	4	5	6	7
I care about the long-term success of the Captains.	1	2	3	4	5	6	7
I am a loyal fan of the Captains.	1	2	3	4	5	6	7
I feel a sense of belonging at Captains games.	1	2	3	4	5	6	7

Please provide answers to the following questions about the Captains and other area entertainment options.

1. Approximately how many Captains games do you go to each season?_____

2. Please tell us how you hear about Captains games and promotions?

    A. Newspaper / Circulars   B. Radio

    C. Television   D. Internet website

    E. Word-of-Mouth   F. Pocket Schedule

    G. Other (please specify)

    _____

    _____

3. Your decision to attend today's game was made within the past:

    A. 24 hours

    B. 2-7 days

    C. 8-14 days

    D. 15-30 days

    E. 31+ days

4. How did you purchase/receive your ticket for today's event?

    A. Mail order

    B. Bought it today at the box office upon arriving

    C. Telephone order

    D. Ticket was given to me

    E. I have season tickets.

5. For the following organizations, please indicate how many times a year you attend:

    _____ Cleveland Indians games

    _____ Movies at a theater

    _____ Swimming at a public pool

    _____ Amusement Park

    _____ Eating out at a restaurant

    _____ Other Minor League Baseball games

    _____ Other Amateur baseball games

    _____ Plays / Symphony / Ballet

6. Please rank the following sport organizations according to your personal preference. Use #1 for your favorite organization, #2 for your second favorite organization, and so on.

    _____ Lake County Captains

    _____ Cleveland Indians

    _____ Cleveland Browns

    _____ Cleveland Cavaliers

    _____ Cleveland Barons

    _____ Cleveland Force

7. Are you at today's game as a member of a group?

    YES   NO

8. Are you a Captains' season ticket holder?

    YES   NO

Below are some more statements about the Captains. Please circle the number that best describes your opinion about each statement.

I feel the Captains franchise is…

Very Undependable	1	2	3	4	5	6	7	8	9	10	Very Dependable

Very Incompetent	1	2	3	4	5	6	7	8	9	10	Very Competent

Of Very Low Integrity	1	2	3	4	5	6	7	8	9	10	Of Very High Integrity

Very Unresponsive to Customers	1	2	3	4	5	6	7	8	9	10	Very Responsive to Customers

I feel the <u>EMPLOYEES</u> of the Captains are…

Very Undependable	1	2	3	4	5	6	7	8	9	10	Very Dependable
Very Incompetent	1	2	3	4	5	6	7	8	9	10	Very Competent
Of Very Low Integrity	1	2	3	4	5	6	7	8	9	10	Of Very High Integrity
Very Unresponsive to Customers	1	2	3	4	5	6	7	8	9	10	Very Responsive to Customers

For the prices you pay at a Captains game, would you say the experience at a Captains game is a…

Very Poor Deal	1	2	3	4	5	6	7	8	9	10	Very Good Deal

For the time you spend in order to get to the game, would you say attending a Captains game is…

Highly Unreasonable	1	2	3	4	5	6	7	8	9	10	Highly Reasonable

For the effort involved in coming to a Captains game, would you say attending a game is…

Not at all worthwhile	1	2	3	4	5	6	7	8	9	10	Very Worthwhile

How would you rate your overall experience at a Captains game?

Extremely Poor Value	1	2	3	4	5	6	7	8	9	10	Extremely Good Value

Please provide us with some demographic information about yourself.

1. Gender   A. Male   B. Female

2. Marital Status   A. Married   B. Single   C. Divorced   D. Widowed

3. How many children are living at home with you? _____

4. What is your Race?   A. African American   B. Asian
                             C. White   D. Hispanic
                             E. Other

5. What is the highest level of education you have completed?
                             A. High School Graduate   B. Trade School / Technical School Diploma
                             C. Some College   D. College Graduate
                             E. Graduate Degree

6. What is your annual household income level?
                             A. less than $25,000   B. $25,001 - $40,000
                             C. $40,001 - $60,000   D. $60,001 - $80,000
                             E. $80,001 - $100,000   F. $100,001 - $120,000
                             G. More than $120,000

7. What is your age?   A. 18-24   B. 25-34   C. 35-44
                        D. 45-54   E. 55-64   F. 65 or older

8. What is your occupation? _____

9. What is the zip code of your primary residence?_____

Thank you for completing the survey! Please use the space below to share any additional comments or opinions with the Lake County Captains.

Case Study

What does a one-year old minor league baseball franchise do to continue the success from its inaugural season into year two? How does it ensure that the fans continue to have a good experience and develop new revenue streams? The answer for the Lake County Captains, a Class A affiliate of the Cleveland Indians organization, is to use market research. The Captains organization plays games in a new stadium located in Eastlake, OH, just minutes from the parent club's home in downtown Cleveland; yet, the franchise routinely fills its stadium to near capacity. They do it with a mix of family entertainment off the field, and quality, developing players on the field. The first year of the franchise's existence was a success, but like any other business, the Captains management felt they needed to keep a pulse on their consumers' wants and needs pertaining to their experience, so the Captains could alter their marketing strategy to meet those changing wants and needs. How did they know what the customers wanted? They asked them.

Exhibit 7.1 shows the survey the Captains disseminated to their customers. Because they already had information about ticket package holders, the vast majority of respondents were individual game attendees. Standard demographic questions (age, income levels, education levels, number of children at home, etc.) were asked of respondents to allow Captains management to obtain a clearer picture of their non-ticket plan holding fan base. These demographic questions, along with select psychographic questions (e.g., How many times a year do you eat out at a restaurant?) help the franchise determine business categories that should be pursued for sponsorship opportunities or other strategic partnerships.

Finally, certain survey items ask the respondents to indicate their opinion of the franchise's performance on several different elements. These items allow the franchise to gauge customers' attitudes toward operational and procedural elements of the franchise. If a particular area turns up lacking (based on fan responses) the franchise management can then make changes designed to improve fans' experience at a Lake County Captains game.

As you can see, market research plays an important role in the operation of a minor league baseball organization, as well as any sport organization. From an organizational perspective, it is important to regularly plan to collect data from your customer base. Survey research is only one method. Focus groups, stadium intercepts and secret shoppers are other methods that allow a franchise to collect valuable information about their organization and fans. The important point to remember is that you cannot meet the wants and needs of your customer base if you don't know those wants and needs.

Chapter Eight

Sponsorship and Sales in the Sport Industry

Nancy Lough

"... There! Smell that? I *love* the aroma of a major league ballpark. Smells just like money!"

Learning Objectives

Upon completion of this chapter, the reader should be able to

- Define and describe the use of corporate sponsorship in sport;

- Describe how "fit" is determined between a sport property and potential sponsor;

- Discuss the product adoption process and relationship to sponsorship;

- Identify the three levels of branding and importance of brand equity;

- Identify two primary reasons sponsors defect and how activation and leveraging can prevent sponsor defection; and

- Describe methods of evaluating and measuring sponsorship effectiveness.

Introduction

Sport could not exist without the financial support provided by corporate sponsorship. This practice of seeking a cash and/or in-kind fee paid to the property (typically in sports, arts, entertainment, or causes) in return for access to the exploitable commercial potential associated with the sport property, was once thought to be the antithesis of all that was good about sport (Ukman, 1995). Yet, throughout the last decade, corporate investment in sponsorship became a key indicator of a sport property's legitimacy. Sponsorship can make a sport, as is the case with NASCAR. Lack of sponsorship can contribute to the dissolution of a sport entity, as was the indication from WUSA officials when the league ceased operations.

"A QUINTESSENTIAL NEED FOR ANY CORPORATION IS TO DIFFERENTIATE ITSELF FROM ITS COMPETITORS VIA A COMPETITIVE ADVANTAGE."

DAVID STOTLAR

Sponsorship

Sponsorship has many definitions and many potential benefits. The essence of any quality definition includes reference to a relationship between a business and a sport entity in which the business provides funding, resources, and/or services to the sport property in exchange for rights and privileges provided as a result of the association and/or affiliation with the sport entity. Pope (1998) provided the following definition:

> *Sponsorship is the provision of resources (e.g., money, people, equipment) by an organization (the sponsor) directly to an individual, authority or body (the sponsee), to enable the latter to pursue some activity in return for benefits contemplated in terms of the sponsor's promotion strategy, and which can be expressed in terms of corporate, marketing, or media objectives.*

Primary **benefits** sought by sponsors who invest in a sport relationship include generating brand awareness, image enhancement, improved trade relations, increased market-share, client acquisition, hospitality, product trials, and sales opportunities (Howard & Crompton, 2004; Stotlar, 2002; Gwinner & Eaton, 1999). Given the prospect for achievement of the aforementioned benefits, a sponsorship may appear to be an easy sell. Yet, the bottom line for the majority of businesses that invest in this type of communication vehicle is **return on investment** (Lough & Irwin, 2001).

"CORPORATION BOSSES ARE INCREASINGLY HAVING TO JUSTIFY THEIR MARKETING INVESTMENTS TO THEIR SHAREHOLDERS AND CAN NO LONGER JUST SAY BEING ASSOCIATED WITH THE OLYMPICS IS GOOD FOR A COMPANY - THEY WILL HAVE TO PROVE IT WITH HARD FACTS." (KEEPING THE OLYMPICS, 1997, P. 32)

Every business should have its own marketing plan that incorporates each of the Ps of sport marketing: product, price, place, and promotion. In order for a sport sponsorship to deliver a positive return on the investment made by the business, consideration must be made regarding the integration of the sponsor's **marketing objectives** and the benefits provided via the sport affiliation. For example, the AVP signed Nissan trucks to a deal in which the volleyball players were delivered to the beach volleyball court in Nissan trucks. This utilization of the truck (product) demonstrated the performance capabilities in sand (place), in front of beach sport fans that meet Nissan's **target market** criteria (can afford the price) and have some degree of involvement with the sport sponsored (promotion). When *Sports Business Journal* published an article regarding the AVP's new sponsorship (public relations), all of the Ps were addressed. This type of relationship illustrates the **symbiotic**, or win-win, nature of effective sponsorship in sport. Will Nissan sell more trucks as a result of this deal? Properly conducted research could indicate whether AVP fans will be more likely to consider Nissan in their next automobile purchase. An increase in sales would be one method to measure return on investment and sponsorship effectiveness.

Advertising ≠ Sponsorship

Advertising may appear to serve the same purpose as sponsorship. Yet upon analysis of the components of a sponsorship relationship, the limitations of advertising can be illuminated. In promotions such as advertising, one of the most common approaches is referred to as the **AIDA** concept. The goal of the AIDA (Awareness, Interest, Desire, and Action) approach is to move consumers along in the progression towards actual product purchase. Yet, this model stops short of acquiring the ensemble of benefits available via sponsorship. In advertising, little opportunity exists in a thirty second televised spot to gain access to a specific target market segment, and even less opportunity is available to create trust or enhance employee morale via an element such as hospitality. Still the most convincing argument for sponsorship versus advertising may be the potential for building loyalty and, thereby, **brand equity**. True fans of beach volleyball and the AVP tour may perceive the success of the tour as hinging on the success of the sponsors. In many cases, sport fans have become loyal consumers of the products and companies that support their sport. They understand that without sponsors, they might not be able to see their favorite athletes compete whether on television or in person.

Sponsorship Growth

Sponsorship prior to the late 1980s was typically simplistic in nature. Often the primary rationale for a company to sponsor a sport was the CEO's intent to "rub elbows" with elite athletes. However, the 1984 Olympic Games changed the landscape of sport sponsorship dramatically. After years of debt accruing to host cities for the Olympic Games, the Los Angeles Olympic Organizing Committee set out to prove that hosting this one-of-a-kind world class event could prove profitable for the city and others involved. A total of 32 companies agreed to pay between $4 million and $13 million in cash, goods, and services. At the previous Olympic Games in Montreal, 628 sponsors were involved for a total of $4.18 million. The result of the shift to category-specific sponsors and enhanced contributions was a net profit reported to be $222 million.

Today, corporate sponsors can be involved at various levels with the Olympic Games. For the example, the sponsorship fee to be one of the 11 TOP (The Olympic Partner Program) sponsors has been reported to be approximately $70 million for the 2008 Beijing Olympics. **TOP sponsors** sign up for a four-year contract that includes both the Summer and Winter Games. They are granted the right to Olympic affiliation in every participating country with worldwide **exclusivity** in their product category. Overall, sponsorship growth has been phenomenal following the example set by the 1984 Olympic Games success.

Additionally, recent corporate scandals have created an enhanced need for demonstration of responsibility in all facets of a company's financial matters. Accountability for sponsorship investment is more often required in today's business environment, including some validation of the potential for increasing company profitability as a direct result of the sport sponsorship. The process of **evaluation** and servicing has taken on a new level of importance with regard to the likelihood of **renewal**. Those sport entities that fail to evaluate and/or quantify for the sponsor the value received, will likely find a higher rate of **defection** (current sponsors that decide not to renew).

Competition in the sport marketplace has proliferated at a rate commensurate with the growth of sponsorship in the sport industry. More sport products exist today in the form of tours, leagues, special events, professional sport properties, and intercollegiate athletics, so one can quickly appreciate the need for more sophisticated approaches to sponsorship and selling within the sport industry. As the sport marketplace splinters, the opportunity to address specific target

Photo by Andy Gillentine

segments via lifestyle and affinity marketing opens the door for new and more creative sponsorship opportunities. Similarly, growing sophistication resulting from competition and marketplace fragmentation has necessitated the growth of inventory that may be offered to potential sponsors.

Sport Legitimatization

The 1999 Women's World Cup of soccer proved to be one of the most successful sport events ever held on U.S. soil. Yet, few realize the struggle event organizers experienced as they sought corporate involvement. Women's soccer had received needed exposure leading up to and following the 1996 Olympic Games. However, convincing corporate decision makers that investing in the Women's World Cup would provide substantial return on their investment was a hard sell. Few decision makers understood the value of associating with a women's sport property. Many companies who had committed to support the men's World Cup when the U.S. hosted experienced disappointing results.

Two risks were apparent. First, the sport was soccer, which had yet to achieve significance in the U.S. sport marketplace. Second, it was a women's sport, often considered outside the mainstream for appealing to typical sport fans. Yet, prepared with research suggesting that an enormous untapped market was available for those willing to sign on, event organizers managed to secure sufficient sponsorship dollars. This premier women's soccer event achieved unprecedented results including record crowds, unparalleled television ratings, and considerable media exposure. For the potential sponsors who neglected to sign on, a once-in-a-lifetime opportunity was missed.

Sport Failure & Sponsorship

The Women's United Soccer Association was launched as a direct result of the phenomenal success of the Women's World Cup. Corporate backers saw potential and committed to building a league that would capitalize on the interest realized during the 1999 World Cup. Organizers created the league with a solid vision and financial base of support. Yet, the long term plan included increasing levels of corporate sponsorship as the years progressed. Concern mounted as time wore on, due to unfulfilled goals. In today's hypercompetitive sport marketplace, setting realistic, attainable goals is crucial. Missing an established target market often results in the need to return to the drawing board. As sponsors' needs went unmet, it became apparent that the WUSA was missing its mark.

Three primary concerns contributed to the defection of sponsors and ultimately dissolution of the league:

1. Diminished television ratings,

2. Decreased on-site attendance, and

3. Pricing that did not equate to the market delivered.

Delivery of a realistic market estimate is vital to continued sponsorship. With teams competing in only eight markets, average attendance below 7,000, and television ratings of 0.1 (approximately 100,000 households), it was unrealistic to expect sponsors to contribute $2.5 million to sustain the league. As the WUSA works to answer the difficult questions and arrive at a new launching point, we can all learn valuable lessons from this promising sport property. Finding the fit between all the sport property has to offer and the image/goals of the corporate sponsor will lead to satisfaction and continued involvement for both parties.

Hot or not? X Games vs. Gravity Games

While sponsorship—through affiliation—can often establish a level of credibility for a sport, a lack of credibility in a sport product rarely can be altered, even with significant sponsors. For example, the X Games were created by ESPN to provide a venue for competition among the world's elite action or extreme sport athletes. Initially, the idea was considered a gamble or a fad, at best. Yet, as the success of the X Games became apparent, so too did the absence of any competitor in the same class. The Gravity Games were created to compete directly with the X Games for the action/extreme sport market. Multiple attempts have been made, yet the Gravity Games have not achieved the status of the original extreme sport competition, the X Games.

©Media Focus LLC

The image of Mountain Dew as a drink presumably chosen by extreme minded opinion leaders illustrates the magnitude of effectiveness the X Games has provided for its top tier sponsors. Without the X Games, Mountain Dew would have continued to struggle for a place in the soft drink market. The Gravity Games has not provided the same level of **image enhancement** for sponsors, largely due to the event's lack of credibility among the target audience. A surprising relationship to evolve from the success of the X Games was the U.S. Marine Corps sponsorship. The USMC became an associate-level sponsor of ESPN's X Games due to the fit between their target market for recruitment and this unique sport product. For the price of $600,000, males who enjoy a physical challenge and happen to have an age range of 17–24 years were exposed to the message and image crafted by the U.S. Marine Corps. Given the elite status of the USMC among all military branches, affiliation with the Gravity Games would not have provided the same level of credibility.

Creating "Buy In"

To create "buy in" for potential sponsors, the cost and value of a sponsorship deal must be equitable for both parties. The primary factor that contributes to the value for sponsors is the fit between the sport property and the corporate partner.

Fit is determined by the following criteria: a) the sport property's image should be compatible with the desired image of the brand, and b) a match needs to exist between the target market of the sport entity and the target market of the brand. The value of a sponsorship often is created by the sport entity's need for funding

or resources. However, problems can arise when the value associated with a sponsorship is lower than the associated cost.

In sport marketing, myopia is a common problem. In essence, marketing myopia is the result of sport personnel focusing solely on the sport product and not considering the needs and wants of consumers. In sponsorship relationships, sponsorship myopia occurs when sport representatives focus solely on the offerings associated through the sport sponsorship, yet neglect to consider the criteria that establishes the value or worth for the potential sponsor.

In a college town where an NCAA Division I program garners the majority of the sport media's attention, the concern for creating a fit between local sponsors and the athletic team or program is often neglected. The environment is one in which businesses commit to sponsorship deals more for the benefits associated with being perceived as a community leader or contributor to the university. Typically, sponsorships such as this lack the sophistication necessary in a more competitive marketplace and put the athletics marketing personnel in the dangerous position of becoming lulled into complacency. The creation of arbitrary sponsorship levels, which commonly occurs in these situations, results in a rigid menu of benefits available, with little room for focusing on the needs and wants of the sponsor. Thus, there is often a poor "fit," and, therefore, many of these types of sponsorships are ineffective at meeting the marketing needs of the sponsors. The only benefactor in this situation is the athletic program. Without a fair exchange of value and benefits, the sponsorship is at risk for non-renewal at any time.

Focus on Target Markets

When considering the aspect of buy in for sponsors that relates to their desired target market, a recognizable example can be seen in the relationship between Sears and the WNBA. Since the league's inception, Sears has experienced the benefits of communicating with a specific target market of active girls and their parents. From the Sears "Be Active" program, which traveled to multiple WNBA cities and utilized players to instruct and motivate girls on fitness, basketball skills, and healthy habits, to the cause-related promotions raising awareness and money for breast cancer research, Sears has exemplified the ideal fit between target markets for a company and the audience of a sport property. With a fit this clear, the effort needed to create buy in is reduced, therefore allowing more time to focus on enhancing communication platforms and promotional campaigns.

Beyond the cost and value factors, there remains the need to protect companies who commit to sport sponsorship. Increasing competition to get a promotional message across has resulted in diminished value in certain situations. The three primary concerns that arise from competition in the marketplace include clutter, noise, and ambush marketing. **Clutter** is the result of too many sponsors being associated with a sport entity. No single brand image stands out as the sponsor. Spectators are less able to distinguish competing brands in this instance, thereby diminishing the value for all. Clutter commonly occurs when no specific sponsorship categories are designated. Consider the typical 5K road race t-shirt. On the back is a conglomeration of company names and tag-lines. Yet, no single brand stands out or gains significantly from association with race participants.

Noise can be considered very similar to clutter. The average person is exposed to as many as 5,000 selling messages a day. Whether they are radio, television, Internet, billboards, or print advertisements, the noise from each begins to desensitize the consumer to all messages. This explains the yelling car salesman who is trying to break through the noise by being the loudest, or most annoying. Yet, the result is often a consumer who tunes out the message. Public address, or PA, announcements at stadiums and arenas come complete with sponsor mentions. Yet, very often these messages go unnoticed because of the noise factor.

Still the most challenging element of competition to handle in sponsorship is the deliberate attempts to ambush another sponsor's association with a sport entity. Take for example Coca Cola's decision to race eight cars complete with Coca Cola branding to launch their new "low carb" product, C2. The race chosen was the Pepsi 400. Obviously, Pepsi had paid a premium to be the title sponsor of the race. Coca Cola officials insisted there was no intent to ambush, yet this example exhibits the very definition of **ambush marketing**: a direct competing brand in the same product category, staging a presence to create confusion in the mind of the consumer regarding who is the official sponsor. Clearly, new or non-seasoned race fans may have confused the title sponsor of the race (who paid millions for the official rights) with the ambush company who bypassed the official payment to saturate the event with their own branded racecars. Increasingly, sponsors are requiring some assurance that ambush will be prevented by the sport property.

Emotion and Loyalty

Just as the Pepsi/Coke scenario points out, when creating buy in for potential corporate partners, nothing appeals quite as strongly as the example of NASCAR fans. It is not by accident that NASCAR has been one of the fastest growing sports in the industry. In this sport that incorporates sponsorship into every conceivable element, fans are famous for their degree of emotional commitment to each of their favorite driver's sponsors. Some fans have gone so far as to say that they will only buy the products from companies that sponsor "their" driver. This may seem logical if the sponsor happens to be involved in auto parts or a similarly linked product; however, products such as *Tide* laundry detergent have also been cited as chosen for purchase directly due to their sponsorship involvement with a race car driver. Few sports can claim this degree of emotional commitment and loyalty, yet it remains the ultimate goal of all who create sponsorship deals.

Sponsor Rationale

The most desirable strategies are those that create a win-win situation. A win for both the sponsor and the sport entity can best be achieved by meeting sponsors' objectives, including those that replace direct funding or dollar allocation with trade-outs or in-kind services. A familiar model in which this strategy is evident is the gift-in-kind of shoes and apparel to a collegiate sport team by a company such as adidas, Nike, or Reebok. The company in many instances provides little or no financial contribution to the athletic program. Instead, a trade is made in which the company agrees to provide their branded product for the right to be affiliated or directly associated with the team or program. The benefit for the shoe company is reaped when local fans become consumers and possibly develop loyalty to the brand as a result of the sponsorship for their favorite team. Additionally, if the team happens to receive significant media coverage, the brand then benefits from the university's success. When a university team appears on ESPN, March Madness on CBS, or a football bowl game on network television, then the return on investment is significantly increased. Recruits and the general public often judge coaches and teams as legitimate if they have a significant sponsorship deal.

Employee Motivation

While return on investment is arguably always a primary motivation, other motives can impact sponsorship decisions and lead to the accomplishment of many of the same objectives. Consider the sponsorship involvement of Safeway grocery stores and the LPGA. Safeway hosted a tournament at Superstition Mountain in Arizona, in which one of the primary benefits was the delivery of every tournament attendee directly to a tent, where product trials and samples for Safeway brands and partner brands who sell in Safeway stores were given out freely. The most direct path to the first tee box was through the Safeway tent, because very few sports fans will turn down free samples of food, drink, candy, and similar grocery store items. These fans were treated well and were aware of the sponsor before they had reached the actual tournament. Add to this the opportunity for Safeway employees to be a part of this premier professional sport event by performing the many volunteer duties, and one can see how value becomes more than monetary for both parties involved.

The final perk from this exemplary relationship was the participation of Michelle Wie, the then 14 year-old golf phenomenon. Due to Wie's decision to compete in the tournament during her high school spring break, the media attention included coverage by local and national newspapers, as well as television exposure. Based on this example, the assortment of benefits available to the sponsor and the ensuing rationale for involvement with the sport event/property becomes clear.

Awareness

Most often companies engage in sport sponsorship to create brand awareness and enhance their brand image.

The Lance Armstrong/Subaru sponsorship has been most effective in illustrating aspects such as lifestyle and affinity marketing. In **lifestyle marketing**, the company is attempting to cut through all the other selling messages by appealing to consumers who have or desire the lifestyle depicted in the sport sponsorship relationship. Lance Armstrong represents many facets of the active adult lifestyle considered to be attractive to a large target market. Lifestyle marketing often cuts across demographic lines, appealing to people who already have an affinity for the activity or lifestyle represented by the sport sponsorship. This is not to say that those who comprise this target market have an ambition to ride or win the Tour de France. However, the appeal of a winner who has overcome great odds and survived, and who competes in a sport that more people can participate in recreationally, certainly speaks to the value in creating brand awareness for the sponsoring company. Throw in a recognizable link such as the tag-line "Driven by what's inside," and this becomes an exceptional example of a win-win relationship.

Photo by Andy Gillentine

Image

There can be a negative side to sponsorship relationships, however, when ethical concerns are not addressed. Phillip Morris's Virginia Slims brand was the title sponsor of the women's professional tennis tour for nearly 20 years. The positive image of active, healthy elite women tennis players effectively transferred to the Virginia Slims brand. "There is a link between the word 'slim' and the activity of tennis as a means of becoming slim. Tennis champions are in peak physical condition, and since endurance is important, their hearts and lungs are particularly strong and healthy. The obvious implications of the linkage are that sport and smoking are desirable for women" (Howard & Crompton, 2004, p. 483). This type of relationship illustrates the ethical challenge that can arise when companies want to provide significant funding for association with a sport product, with the intent of using the sport image to improve their company or product image.

Clearly, opportunities arise in which the sport entity would be wise to back away from sponsorships that create ethical dilemmas. An example that better illustrates a positive link of brand image with a sport that has a lifestyle all its own, would be Roxy and surfing. The brand Roxy was created by Quicksilver to appeal to the women's surf market. Roxy has been so successful in associating with top women surfers and surf competitions that Roxy is synonymous with the surfing lifestyle among women.

Sales Objectives

Perhaps the most clear, rational, and measurable benefit in a sport sponsorship is meeting sales objectives. The case of the FIFA World Cup in South Korea illustrates this rationale well. Product purchase intentions are most often considered a key sales objective that can be measured. When consumer purchase intentions were examined, as influenced by the 2002 FIFA World Cup in Korea/Japan, a significant relationship was found. Consumers felt more positively about the image of the companies that sponsored the event, they were more accurate at recognizing the actual sponsors, and they indicated that they would be more likely to buy the products of the sponsors (Shin, 2002). To the companies involved, this indicates a successful sponsorship relationship due to the likely return on investment.

Selling Sponsorships

One of the most important factors to recognize relative to sponsorship in sport is that those who can sell well advance quickly. With this in mind, a focus on a few of the methods that enhance success in sales is provided. There are seven rules for effective personal selling according to Mullin, Hardy, and Sutton (2000).

1) The utilization of a marketing database generates leads who are likely to have a greater interest and/or ability to become consumers.

2) Communicate with consumers based on a shared interest in the sport product. Consider the potential consumer as a potential friend.

3) The LIBK rule needs to be adhered to. This means to "let it be known" that you are proud and enthusiastic to be selling a product you believe in.

4) Be prepared for the most common objections used. Be flexible in your approach and capable of providing examples that show how current consumers once had similar objections.

5) Be an effective listener. Then be prepared to react with points that address the consumer's concerns.

6) Take the consultant approach. Approach the consumer as though you are proposing possible solutions to the consumer's needs and wants, not just trying to make a sale.

7) Just as fit is critical to success in sponsorship, fit is key to success in sales. Match the consumer to a product that is appropriate for his or her budget and lifestyle.

When selling sponsorship, the most desirable measure from a sponsor's perspective is a return on investment (ROI). The impact that a sponsorship investment has on sales is the best indicator that the sponsorship was a success. Sales objectives are most often expressed in three ways:

- Increase in traffic at retail points of purchase

- Resulting number of new sales leads

- Actual increase in sales connected with a sponsorship

Actual sales can be measured by tracking coupon redemptions or ticket discounts given with a proof of purchase of the sponsor's product. Similarly, a comparison of sales during a three-month period corresponding with the event and the sales for a comparable period can be calculated to measure actual increases.

The AIDA concept for promotions was previously discussed relative to meeting sponsor's objectives. Yet, this concept can be extended to assist in the enhancement of sales. The **product adoption process** is an extension of the AIDA concept that awareness builds interest and knowledge of a brand's associated benefits, which in effect, creates an image in the mind of the consumer. When the image is congruent with an image the consumer desires, then a product trial is likely. Evaluation is being conducted in the mind of the consumer both before and after the product purchase. The goal is to move the consumer to purchase the product. Following the consumer's experience with the product, the option exists to repeat the purchase, re-evaluate and consider alternate brands, or discontinue the process.

If the consumer chooses to repeat their purchase, then product adoption has been attained. At this point, the levels of branding suggest that consumers have progressed from **brand recognition** to **brand preference**. Once brand preference has been achieved, loyalty builds as the consumer refuses to purchase any other company's product in that category. Ultimately, the consumer then moves into **brand insistence**, which is the creation of **brand loyalty**. As we have seen from NASCAR and other similar examples, sponsorships are often sold because of the potential for brand loyalty as exemplified in sport.

Take, for example, the recent sponsorship between Lexus and the Atlanta Braves. One of the attributes of the Lexus sponsorship was the provision of parking spaces at Atlanta Braves games free of charge for Lexus owners. This approach was intended to reward Lexus owners and encourage their loyalty to the brand, while also creating an opportunity to expose Atlanta Braves fans to new Lexus models. This strategy illustrates another important concept in selling, which is the **consumer escalator**. With the consumer escalator model, the goal is to move consumers from non-aware/non-consumers onto the consumption escalator and ultimately up each level from light to medium to heavy users. Heavy users are known to be responsible for up to 80% of all purchases. This is significant, especially considering that heavy users may represent as few as 20% of all consumers. This **80/20 principle** suggests that a focus be made on moving consumers up the escalator while keeping the existing heavy user segment content.

In sales, finding new consumers or leads is far more difficult than assisting the existing consumers to increase their level of consumption. In addition, existing consumers provide invaluable promotion through word of mouth. Many consumers step onto the escala-

tor as a direct result of influence by a friend or colleague who happens to be a consumer.

Why Sponsors Defect

Sponsors defect or discontinue their relationship with a sport entity for two primary reasons: 1) Their goals and objectives were not met, and/or 2) they have chosen a new marketing approach that may focus on a new target market or a different direction altogether. Little can be done when the second rationale is given; however, failure to meet objectives or company marketing goals rests with the company as well as the sport entity. The key strategy that must be incorporated is a leveraging or activation plan. **Leveraging** involves developing an integrated plan that specifies the role promotional tools will play and the extent to which each will be used. Unless a company invests in these additional means to amplify the intended message, their initial sponsorship fee will likely be a wasted investment. Sponsorship offers a unifying theme that needs to be exploited to communicate with a specific target market through the use of a full array of promotional tools. **Sponsorship activation** means that for every dollar spent on a sponsorship fee, an equivalent dollar is typically spent in the promotion of the sponsorship. This 1:1 ratio was once considered an industry standard. Thus, one of the surest ways to see a sponsorship fail is to neglect allocating funding to activate the sponsorship. Today, many elite sponsors say the ratio is more likely to be 1:5 for a sponsorship that will be short term (1 year or less). When the contract includes multiple years, the ratio can be closer to 1:2 or 1:1, with an extended period of time to create a strong association between the sport entity and sponsor to build the message and enhance loyalty.

Take, for example, Subaru and Lance Armstrong. Subaru has spent significantly more money promoting its association with the 6-time Tour de France winner than it paid initially to become an official sponsor. The tag line "Driven by what's inside" has become synonymous with Lance and Subaru. His success is its success. Yet, waiting for media coverage to catch a glimpse of Lance with a Subaru support vehicle behind him in a competition would be foolish. Subaru has created television, print, and web campaigns that utilize the association to communicate the message consistently and effectively over time. In contrast, when Subaru was a sponsor of the LPGA, little to no actual promotion of the LPGA sponsorship was created. Instead, at the end of the single year contract, Subaru opted out of its relationship with the LPGA. This shows the need to build into the contract a clear understanding of activation, leveraging, and servicing of the sponsorship.

Sponsorship Evaluation and Measurement

Generally, the one aspect in which many sport entities fall short in regard to corporate sponsorship is in the area of measurement and evaluation. Commonly, the only means for communicating with sponsors following the event ends up being a quickly written thank you note with a picture of their sign or logo at the event. Seldom are sponsors informed of the *impact* of their sponsorship. For example, how many people were in attendance, and who were they? What was the extended audience reach? The profile of the audience reach incorporates the media outlets that covered the event and the amount of coverage/publicity given by each. Most media outlets have data on their audiences that can assist in determining if the target market was reached. Yet, as simple as this type of feedback may seem, many of the best means for providing information can be acquired with equally simple recognition and recall techniques.

Recognition has occurred when a spectator can correctly identify the brand of a sponsor from a list. **Recall** equates to a higher level of effectiveness. In recall, a spectator can remember and correctly identify a sponsor's brand without input or prompting. The downside to recognition measuring is that oftentimes consumers identify brands that were not official sponsors, indicating ambush has occurred. In the case of the 2002 FIFA World Cup, most spectators surveyed indicated that Nike (63.7%) was an official sponsor. In reality, the official partner was adidas. Nike had contracted to supply uniforms for the Korean team, in addition to Brazil, Portugal, Russia, and Nigeria. Nike also had several well-planned promotions that confused consumers as to who was the official sponsor. Nonetheless, on a similar measure, the sponsorship by adidas proved to be effective. Purchase intentions towards the sponsoring company's products increased 41.5% for adidas due to their sponsorship of the FIFA World Cup. Purchase intention has been found to have a significant relationship with corporate image, prior use experience, and sponsor recognition accuracy (Shin, 2002).

Given the common omission of feedback provided by sport entities, specialized companies have emerged for the sole purpose of evaluating sponsorship effectiveness. One such company, Joyce Julius and Associates, created a model in which each and every second that a sponsor's brand was recognizable during a television broadcast was counted. An accumulation of hours and seconds that the brand was visible then was utilized to calculate the equivalent dollar amount that such visibility would have cost if the corporate sponsor had chosen to simply buy advertising time on that station, at that time, on that day. Surprisingly to some, the accumulation of minutes often equated to hundreds of thousands of dollars. More often than not, the cost paid by the sponsor was significantly less than the equivalent "value" attributed by this evaluation technique. Similar measurements can be calculated in print media coverage by measuring column inches (size), number of company mentions, and location within the print publication (i.e., newspaper sports section). A photo with the brand of the sponsor prominently displayed often is attributed a higher value than being mentioned in the text of an article.

Overall, sponsorship evaluation should be designed to meet two primary purposes: 1) measuring the accomplishment of the sponsor's objectives and 2) generating information that can be utilized when selling future sponsorships.

Summary

There are five primary concerns that need to be addressed to create success when selling sport sponsorships:

1) Benefits sought by potential sponsors are framed as specific, measurable objectives;

2) A good fit equates to a shared image between the corporate sponsor and the sport property with target market access;

3) Integration with other communication vehicles around a unifying theme should be incorporated with promotional actions that reinforce the sponsor's desired message;

4) Protect clients from ambush, clutter, and noise (perceptual distortion); and

5) Time/longevity of a sponsorship relationship contributes to improved recall, recognition, and product purchase intentions among consumers, thereby improving sponsorship effectiveness.

6) Sponsorship is one of the most valuable tools sport managers have to work with. Future sport professionals will need to understand and be capable of utilizing this essential tool.

Discussion Activities

1. Consider for a moment the sport events you have attended or consumed through some form of media. Next consider recent purchases you have made. Did sponsors of the sports you consumed influence these purchases? If so, why?

2. Look through some recent issues of Street and Smith's Sports Business Journal. Based on what you've learned in this chapter, select a few sport properties and match them with potential corporate sponsors.

References

Gwinner, K. P., & Eaton, J. (1999). Building image through event sponsorship: The role of image transfer. *Journal of Advertising, 28*(4), 47-67.

Howard, D., & Crompton, J. (2004). *Financing sport* (2nd ed.). Morgantown, WV: Fitness Information Technology.

Keeping the Olympics ideal. (1997, April). *Sport Business*, 32-33.

Lee, J. (2003, September 22-28). Thin ratings, lack of sponsors trip WUSA. *Sports Business Journal*, 4-5.

Lough, N., & Irwin, R. (2001). A comparative analysis of sponsorship objectives for U.S. women's sport and traditional sport sponsorship. *Sport Marketing Quarterly, 10*(4), 202–211.

Mullin, B., Hardy, S., & Sutton, W.A. (2000). *Sport marketing* (2nd ed.). Champaign, IL: Human Kinetics.

Pope, N. (1998, January). Overview of current sponsorship thought. *The Cyber-Journal of Sport Marketing.* Retrieved July 21, 2004, from http://www.cad.gu.edu.au/cjsm/pope21.htm.

Shin, H. (2002). *The effects of sport sponsorship on consumer purchase intentions.* Unpublished master's thesis, Illinois State University, Normal, IL.

Stotlar, D. (2001). *Developing successful sport sponsorship plans.* Morgantown, WV: Fitness Information Technology.

Stotlar, D. (2002). Sport sponsorship: Lessons from the Sydney Olympic Games. *International Journal of Applied Sports Sciences, 14*(2), 27-45.

Ukman, K. (1995). *The IEG's complete guide to sponsorship: Everything you need to know about sports, arts, event, entertainment and cause marketing,* Chicago, IL: IEG.

Suggested Reading

Lagae, W. (2005). *Sport sponsorship & marketing communications: A European perspective.* London, UK: Financial Times Prentice Hall.

Martin, P. (2003). *Made possible by: Succeeding with sponsorship.* London, UK: Jossey-Bass Wiley.

Chapter Nine

Sport Facility and Event Management

Bernie Goldfine and Thomas H. Sawyer

"He's right. We screwed up."

Learning Objectives

Upon completion of this chapter, the reader should be able to

- ■ Discuss the skills necessary to event and facility management;

- ■ Identify models used in the management of facilities;

- ■ Understand the importance of operational philosophies and mission statements regarding the management of venues;

- ■ Address the elements of public and media relations;

- ■ Explain the risk management considerations in the management of venues;

- ■ Identify revenue streams in facility management;

- ■ List the elements of event planning;

- ■ Describe how events can be most effectively organized for success; and

- ■ Recognize the role of marketing and budgeting in event and facility management.

Introduction

Have you ever been a spectator at a sporting event or concert and left with the feeling that you had just experienced something that was incredibly special? Conversely, have you ever had a miserable experience at a highly anticipated event? Your experiences could very easily have been influenced by the manner in which the event and/or facility was managed. If you have ever wondered how you would plan an event differently, perhaps facility and event management might be a career path to consider.

"The oldest standing building in Rome is the Colosseum."

Red Smith

To embark upon such a career, you have to be someone who likes organization, order, advanced planning, leading others, and does not mind being assertive and aggressive (Solomon, 2002). Specifically, some of the attributes that successful facility and event planners must possess are (1) interpersonal and leadership skills (i.e., inspiring others to perform effectively and calmly under pressure); (2) proactive thinking, (i.e., anticipating problems and having contingency plans ready when obstacles present themselves) (Walker & Stotlar, 1997); (3) organizational skills (such as when and how to delegate tasks); and (4) the ability to think quickly on one's feet when crises emerge. Also, this field calls for individuals who do not mind working nontraditional and extended hours.

There are many opportunities for sport management graduates to use facility/venue and event management skills, including working for a large, prominent organization that specializes in event management, such as Jack Morton Worldwide (www.jackmorton.com). Or you could work for a worldwide venue management company like Ogden Entertainment, which oversees concessions, merchandising, ticketing, maintenance, security, sponsorships, and complete venue management in over 125 entertainment venues internationally. However, this skill set can also be used in smaller boutique event or venue management firms.

The skills required for event and venue management are also advantageous for individuals seeking employment in sport-related organizations that manage their own facilities or run their own events. For example, sport organizations that do not outsource their operations need individuals whose focus is game day operations or event management. In **participant-oriented organizations**, individuals with very specialized skill sets often manage municipal parks, YMCAs, recreation departments, collegiate recreation settings, and special events. The aforementioned organizations' facilities, in addition to some **public assembly facilities** that are often run by the municipalities themselves, require competent personnel to operate them in the most cost-effective and safe manner.

Facility management and event management often go hand-in-hand; certainly most events require a venue in which to be held. There are, however, distinct differences in each job that will be spelled out in the following sections.

Sport Facility/Venue Management

"Whatever you do, do it with all your might. Work at it, early and late, in season and out of season, not leaving a stone unturned, and never deferring for a single hour that which can be done just as well now."

P. T. Barnum

Facility/venue management is a coordinated and integrated process of utilizing an organization's resources to achieve specific goals and objectives through the managerial functions of planning, organizing, leading, and evaluating. Venue management also includes effective booking and scheduling, provision of security and safety for fans and participants, and maintenance of the venue. Examples of outdoor venues could include

• aquatic centers,

• baseball and softball parks,

- football and soccer stadiums,

- motor sport tracks,

- golf courses and practice facilities,

- tennis stadiums and complexes,

- recreational sport fields, and

- parks and playgrounds.

Indoor venues could include

- basketball arenas,

- bowling alleys,

- domed stadia,

- field houses,

- gymnastic venues,

- fitness centers,

- family centers,

- ice hockey and skating rinks, and

- natatoriums.

Venue Ownership and Management

Venues are either publicly or privately owned. Public ownership requires management to operate the venue within regulations and procedures established by the governing body. Recently, both publicly and privately owned venues have moved toward private management companies, yet their different objectives have a direct impact on a facility and event manager's decision making process.

Public Ownership

The local government and/or government entities operate publicly owned venues such as Shea Stadium in New York and Soldier Field in Chicago. The objective of these governmental agencies is to provide a service to the community while generating enough revenue to break even. All revenue beyond expenses goes back into operation of the venue.

Private Ownership

A number of individuals privately own venues (e.g., Forum Arena, Pro Players Stadium, Texas Stadium, Wrigley Field) others are owned by corporations (e.g.,

Green Bay Packers, Green Bay, WI). The primary objective of a privately owned facility is to deliver a profit for the owners and/or stockholders. The management focuses on maximum return on investment.

Sport Authorities

These are not-for-profit entities generally operated by a commission or board of directors appointed by a governmental body. Sport authorities control a number of venues, such as Bank One Ballpark (Arizona Diamondbacks), 3 Com Park (San Francisco Giants), Coors Field (Colorado Rockies), ThunderDome (Tampa Bay Devil Rays), Turner Field (Atlanta Braves), Philips Arena (Atlanta Hawks), U.S. Cellular Field (Chicago White Sox), Camden Yards (Baltimore Orioles), among others.

Private Management (Privatization or Outsourcing)

When venue operations are privatized or outsourced, the owners pay a private organization to manage the day-to-day operation of the facility. There are five major private venue management companies including Centre Management, Global Spectrum, Leisure Management International (LMI), Ogden Allied, and Spectator Management Group (SMG). These companies manage venues worldwide. The first venue to be privatized or outsourced was the Louisiana Superdome. This type of management enables the owner to maintain control over the venue and at the same time (1) reduce or eliminate an operating deficit, (2) improve services, (3) increase the quality and quantity of the events scheduled, (4) join a larger national and international network of venues, which will expand opportunities for future booking of events, (5) provide greater flexibility concerning policies, procedures, and overall operational structure, (6) improve concessionaire (food service and pouring rights) and full-service restaurant agreements, and (7) expand the sale of licensed merchandise (Mulrooney & Farmer, 2001; Sawyer, Hypes, & Hypes, 2004). According to the **International Association of Assembly Managers** (**IAAM**) and the International Facility Management Association (IFMA), there are six easy steps in selecting a private management company. The steps include (1) preparing a **request for proposal** (**RFP**), (2) distributing the RFP to all major management groups, (3) providing venue tours for all prospective bidders, (4) reviewing propos-

Types of Venues

A simple and effective way to classify facilities is by the types of events held within them. Table 1 describes the various venues based on events. Most of the facilities below include administrative and staff office, bars, ballrooms, concession and merchandising spaces, day care facilities, dressing, locker, and shower areas, lobby, lounge, and reception spaces, maintenance areas, parking, press and interview spaces, public restrooms, restaurants, spectator seating (e.g., general admissions, club seats, private license seats [PSLs], and luxury [VIP] boxes), and ticket sales spaces.

Arenas, centers, coliseums, field houses, pavilions, palaces, and domes are indoor facilities that can be utilized for a variety of activities and events including circuses, concerts, shows, graduations, political rallies, and sporting events. Other specialized facilities include adventure areas, fitness centers, ice arenas, nata-

als, selecting the top five, and interviewing the top five bidders, (5) selecting the finalist and negotiating the contract, and (6) gaining final approval from both sides (Mulrooney & Farmer, 2001).

Table 9.1 Events and Types of Facilities

Event	Venue
Adventure Activities	low ropes course, high ropes course, challenge (confidence) course, rock climbing, climbing walls
Arena Football	arena, coliseum, dome
Baseball	ballpark, coliseum, dome, field, park
Basketball	arena, center, fieldhouse, gymnasium
Concerts	arena, coliseum, dome, field house
Circuses	arena, coliseum, dome, field house
Cross Country	course
Fitness	center
Football	coliseum, dome, field, stadium
Golf	course
Gymnastics	arena, center, gymnasium
Ice Hockey	center, coliseum, palace, pavilion,
Motor Sports	speedway, track
Soccer	field, stadium
Softball	field, park
Swimming & Diving	aquatic center, natatorium
Track & Field	track

toriums, and skate parks. An adventure area might provide a ropes course (high and low), challenge (or confidence) course, and/or a rock climbing wall. A fitness center might include activity spaces for cardiovascular exercises, free weights, gymnastics, martial arts, walking or jogging, racquetball courts, strength training, tennis, swimming, and aerobics. Ice arenas have been constructed for figure skating competitions, ice hockey, curling, and instructional and recreational skating. A natatorium is an aquatic center constructed to provide for swimming and diving, synchronized swimming, and water polo competition, and for instructional and recreational swimming and diving. Finally, skate parks have been designed as safe areas for kids to practice and compete in skateboarding activities. The number of parks nationwide has grown dramatically over the past decade.

Venue Organization

All successful venues have an established organization model to guide operations. The model outlines the personnel required for operations, an organizational philosophy, a mission statement, and goals and objectives based on the organization's philosophy and mission statement.

The Management Team and Personnel

A venue director, general manager, chief executive officer, or executive director heads the management team for a venue. The head of the management team is ultimately responsible for venue planning and management. Further, he/she is responsible for negotiating major contracts pertaining to the venue, often including events being scheduled in the venue. Other mem-

Figure 9.1 Typical Venue Personnel

The number of personnel needed to manage a venue depends on the size of the venue and the number of events scheduled annually. Commonly, the following positions are present within a venue:

Venue Director/General Manager/Chief Executive Officer/Executive Director

    Director of Operations

             Concessionaires
             Parking Attendants
             Ticket Takers
             Ushers

        Coordinator of Maintenance
             Housekeepers
             Maintenance Workers

        Coordinator of Events

        Coordinator of Security (Emergency Management, Risk Management and Safety)
             Security Officers
             Emergency Medical Technicians

    Director of Marketing
        Coordinator for Advertising
        Coordinator for Sales
             Ticket Sellers
             Retail Sales Associates

    Director of Finance
        Accountants

    Director of Customer and Public Relations

bers of the management team oversee marketing, public relations, customer relations, advertising, sales, and operations (Mulrooney & Farmer, 2001).

The **director of operations** is the primary assistant to the head of the management team. This individual has a wide variety of departmental responsibilities, including event coordination, engineering, security, safety, medical services, maintenance, and housekeeping. The **director of marketing** is responsible for market planning, advertising, and sales (i.e., sponsorships, merchandise, and tickets). The **director of finance** is responsible for fiscal accountability, budgeting, cost control, contract negotiations, and financing.

Mission Statement

The **mission statement** provides guidelines that outline the parameters for operating the venue and is the basis for the development of goals and objectives for the venue. **Goals** are achievable statements provided by management, ideally developed through consultation with all stakeholders in the venue. The goals are based on the mission statement and are used to justify the fiscal resources requested in a budget document. **Objectives**, sometimes called action strategies, are the activities to be implemented to reach the overall goal. Each objective should be measurable using assessments to evaluate whether or not the outcome has been met. A mission statement should be purposefully broad and vague, with more specific goals and objectives in support of the mission. Following is the mission statement of the Sports and Exhibition Authority of Pittsburgh and Allegheny County:

> *"The Sports & Exhibition Authority (SEA), formerly known as the Public Auditorium Authority, of Pittsburgh and Allegheny County was incorporated on February 3, 1954 pursuant to the Public Auditorium Authorities Law Act of July 29, 1953. As a joint authority for the City of Pittsburgh and Allegheny County, the SEA's mission is to provide venues for sporting, entertainment, educational, cultural, civic, and social events for the benefit of the general public. The SEA currently owns and operates the Civic Arena, leases the Benedum Center to the Pittsburgh Cultural Trust, and is responsible for the management of the David L. Lawrence Convention Center."*

Source: http://www.pgh-sea.com/The_Authority/the_authority.html (Policies and Procedures)

Policies should be developed with the mission statement in mind. A policy, although formal in nature, should be designed with some flexibility. Policies are general statements that serve to guide decision making and prescribe parameters within which certain decisions are to be made. Policies set limits but are subject to interpretation because they are broad in nature (Sawyer & Smith, 1999).

Procedures are a series of related steps that are to be followed in an established order to achieve a given purpose. Procedures prescribe exactly what actions are to be taken in a specific situation. They are similar to policies, as both are intended to influence certain decisions, but differ in that they address a series of related decisions (Sawyer & Smith, 1999).

All policies and procedures should be written and compiled into a policy and procedures manual or operations manual. This manual should be revised regularly to reflect changes or current practices within the organization. Finally, the manual should be provided to all employees so that they may familiarize themselves with all aspects of the operation.

Venue Operations

Operating a sport facility is challenging, complex, and requires knowledge of all managerial functions. There are important operational areas critical to the successful functioning of the venue, including booking and scheduling; customer and public relations; security, safety, and medical services; maintenance and housekeeping; retail sales; financial management; and risk management.

Booking and Scheduling

Revenue generated from holding events is the main source of income at most venues. The mission of the venue will determine what types of events are booked and scheduled. Facilities that are home to an NFL franchise often utilize the facility for other events beyond the ten home football games per year. Each venue relies on shows, concerts, and events to shape its image. A public facility is obligated to provide for the scheduling of community events (e.g., charitable activities, home and garden shows, non-profit functions, or political rallies) whereas a private venue, depending upon its formation agreement, may limit charitable and non-profit activities. Ticketing activities often fall under the auspices of the booking and scheduling departments.

Booking is the act of engaging and contracting an event or attraction. The mechanics of booking include reserving a specific space, within a specific venue, for a specified date, at a specific time, for an agreed-upon amount of money. **Scheduling** is the reservation process and coordination of all events to the venue's available time. The reservation process involves scheduling a series of events and providing the best possible event mix to fit the venue's usage. Written contracts, with specific penalties for cancellation, revenue sharing, and other concerns are part of booking and scheduling.

Tickets are sold through the box office, one of the most important areas in the venue. It is the first contact the public has with the venue. Tickets account for a large amount of revenue for the facility. There are many ticketing variables, including venue capacity, types of seating (e.g., reserved and general admission), and type of ticket (e.g., computerized tickets or rolled tickets). Finally, there are specialized seating contracts, including luxury boxes, club seats, and **private seat licenses (PSLs)**.

Public and Media Relations

"PUBLIC SENTIMENT IS EVERYTHING. WITH PUBLIC SENTIMENT, NOTHING CAN FAIL; WITHOUT IT, NOTHING CAN SUCCEED."

ABRAHAM LINCOLN

A **public relations** program is designed to influence the opinions of people within a target market through responsible and acceptable performance, based on mutually satisfactory two-way communication. In order to gain public sentiment, sport venue managers must be in touch with a wide variety of constituents, including booking agents, promoters, sponsors, risk management experts, fans and patrons, employees, government officials, and the public in general. An effective public relations program will open communication lines with various publics and effectively utilize the media in a manner that competently presents the objectives of the organization to the public at large. Further, it will modify the attitudes and actions of the public through persuasion and integrate them with those of the organization.

In modern society, with its sophisticated communications media, citizens are virtually bombarded by thousands of messages per day. It is critical for the venue operator to make his or her message stand out among all the noise.

Security, Safety, and Medical Services

The security, safety, and medical services usually are under the jurisdiction of the department of operations. Larger venues generally have some full-time safety personnel, but generally hire part-time help— usually police officers and EMS personnel to assist with particular events. Often, private crowd management firms like Contemporary Services Corporation (CSC) are retained to help with crowd control at events. All employees should be trained in CPR and first aid. The venue should also have an emergency response plan. Examples of potential emergency situations are bad weather, fire, bomb threats, medical emergencies, terrorism, an airplane crash, loss of power, and hazardous material leakage.

The majority of patron problems involve excess consumption of alcohol. This problem can be minimized by enforcing strict guidelines pertaining to alcohol distribution during events (e.g., no beer sales after the seventh inning in baseball or the third quarter in football). The quantity of beer sold to any one patron at a time (e.g., no more than one beer per patron per sale) should be regulated. Finally, all beverage sellers and other staff should be taught to recognize signs of unacceptable intoxication and the steps to be followed to limit further abuse.

Maintenance and Housekeeping

Studies have shown that a well maintained venue encourages repeat patronage. Maintenance and housekeeping are functions designed to keep a venue clean,

An opportunity for you to learn more about facility management is also a great way to raise money for your sport management student organization. Sport management students at Slippery Rock University in Pennsylvania work for Contemporary Services Corporation (CSC) at Pittsburgh Steelers and University of Pittsburgh games to raise money for the Sport Management Alliance. These funds offset some of the costs associated with annual sport management trips to Ireland, Costa Rica, Italy, and other international sites.

safe, and appealing for patrons. The maintenance and housekeeping staff work together cooperatively to keep the venue clean and in good repair. The housekeeping crew is responsible for all seats, stairways, stairwells, restrooms, offices, tile, concrete, carpet floors, walls, ceilings, elevators, upholstered seats, and much more. The maintenance crew is responsible for setup and breakdown of events, replacing filters, maintaining the seating area, operation of equipment, restroom facilities, doors, HVAC, and much more.

Retail Sales

This area is responsible for food services, pouring rights, and merchandise sales. The food service is the business operation that prepares, delivers, and sells food to customers. A concessionaire provides the food service. Various teams manage their own food and beverage service, but often venues contract with a private vendor. The main concessionaires in the sport industry are Ozark Food and Beverage, Inc., Ovation Food Services, Aramark, Levy Restaurants, Sportservice (Delaware North Company), and Centerplate. Sport venues may have two concessionaires working the same event, including one servicing the fans in the general concourse areas and a premium concessionaire servicing the club level and luxury suites.

Revenue from concessions and pouring rights plays a vital role in the success of any venue. Coca-Cola and Pepsi regularly compete for the pouring rights in professional and collegiate sport venues. **Pouring rights** are the exclusive ability to sell soft drinks, bottled water, and beer in a facility. Pouring rights in multipurpose venues, with upwards of 250 event nights per year, can be very lucrative.

Merchandise sales are another vital revenue stream for any venue. Gift shops, team stores, and vendors sell novelties and licensed products including tee-shirts, jerseys, sweat shirts, caps, blankets, cups, pens, pins, player cards, autographed balls or bats, disposable cameras, and more to patrons. Concessions, pouring rights, and merchandise sales can generate at least 60 percent of a venue's operating revenue.

Parking

Fees generated from selling parking spaces can be another source of revenue. It is often shared with local parking vendors. Parking fees can range from $5 per vehicle for minor league stadiums to $35 per vehicle at downtown major league stadiums. Additional sources of parking revenue can be generated from selling preferred, personalized parking spaces, like the Atlanta Braves did in 2004 by creating Lexus-only parking spaces (sponsored, of course, by Atlanta-area Lexus dealers) for season ticket holders driving Lexus vehicles. Premium parking spots are often sold to season ticket holders at professional venues and major athletic donors at colleges and universities. Parking lots can also be rented for new or antique car shows, carnivals, food festivals, driver's safety school, and other events.

Financial Management

No venue can be without a finance department. Large venues have an in-house staff and smaller venues outsource fiscal duties. Financial managers are concerned with developing and monitoring the operational budget, ordering equipment and supplies, paying accounts payable, collecting accounts payable, developing a capital budget, seeking financing when necessary, managing all internal accounting, working with internal and external auditors, establishing and maintaining bank accounts, and payroll.

Risk Management

Risk management is a process to reduce or limit risk exposure in a venue. The goal of risk management is to reduce or eliminate all types of risk the venue could be exposed to during operation. Every venue, large or small, should have a risk management committee and a person on staff directly assigned to risk management. The risk management committee should establish policies and procedures for identifying and assessing foreseeable risks faced by the venue. The risks should be classified into (a) high, moderate, or low loss potential and (b) high, moderate, or low frequency of exposure. After the risks are classified, an action strategy should be developed for each risk ranging from avoidance to modification to transferring a portion of the risk to a third party (e.g., insurance company). Finally, the risk management committee and the risk management director or coordinator should annually conduct a risk audit to identify progress made and new risks that surface.

Crowd Management

Crowd management is an organizational tool that can assist venue directors and/or event coordinators in providing a safe and enjoyable environment for patrons. The crowd management plan is an integral part of the larger risk management plan and includes training programs for staff, drills and procedures to be used in an emergency, procedures to eject disruptive people, a proper signage system, an efficient communication network, a security response plan, and measurable performance objectives. The personnel are either in-house or outsourced by the venue. Smaller venues often utilize on- or off-duty police in uniform. Larger venues have an in-house security force composed of part- and full-time officers. A number of venues have outsourced the security function.

Medical Emergencies

The venue should have as part of the larger risk management plan an emergency management plan. Emergencies can range from localized medical emergencies (e.g., slips and falls, heart attacks, diabetic complications) to mass casualty situations (e.g., collapse of bleachers, roof, or walkway) and large disasters (e.g., hurricane, tornado, earthquake, or fire). The plan should include training programs for staff (e.g., CPR, first aid, AED), drills, and communication links with outside emergency agencies. Evacuation strategies, security procedures, and measurable performance objectives should also be included.

Figure 9.3 Common Traits of Sport Event Managers

- Preparing and managing a checklist of activities
- Projects a positive attitude
- Working independently or as a team member
- Accurate and quick at details
- Articulate on the telephone and in written and oral communication
- Creative, flexible
- Working under extreme pressures for long hours
- Working with all levels of people including volunteers
- Effective at balancing multiple projects simultaneously
- Excellent time manager
- Effective negotiator
- Finance and budget conscious
- Possesses good typing, word processing, and other office skills
- Leadership ability
- Quick problem solver
- Good motivator
- Desire to learn and grow

Event Management – The Process

Event management, like any other form of management, is directing, working with, and overseeing human resources and motivating professional spirit and cooperative efforts toward fulfillment of goals (Horine & Stotlar, 2003). Any event, regardless of scope, requires more than one person to be successful. Therefore, effective leadership is an essential element in the production of events. All individuals, whether volunteers, interns, or paid staff, need to be treated with respect and encouraged to do whatever is necessary to make the event a success.

The key ingredients for successful event management are the same whether you are planning a small-, medium-, or large-scale event. While creating and managing an event can be viewed as a linear process where exact steps are followed, the reality is that many issues occur simultaneously, requiring managers to handle multiple tasks proficiently (Solomon, 2002). Event managers must not only be able to anticipate problems and have contingency plans in place, they need to be able to think quickly on their feet when unforeseen crises arise. A student who pursues event management as a career option must also be flexible and able to adapt to setbacks or changes.

Planning: A Must

The primary issue in planning an event is determining its purpose (Walker& Stotlar, 1997). When the mission or goals of an event are clearly delineated, the event manager and his or her team have a framework within which to operate. Examples of common event goals are

1) profitability;

2) raising awareness, sensitivity, or money for a particular cause or charity; and

3) improving organizational image and visibility.

Another consideration is whether or not an event will be a regularly scheduled occurrence (e.g., an annual road race) or simply a one-time affair (e.g., a visit by a candidate for political office). Obviously an event which may be run on a regular basis will be managed quite differently (e.g., long-term sponsorship agreements may be sought).

Once a mission and goals have been established, a timetable must be established for an event. The **timetable** can also be seen as a countdown to an event that provides the schedule of tasks and when they need to be completed. It is more difficult to plan a timeline with first-time or one-time events, but this should not deter event managers from developing a basic schedule. In addition to a timetable, written operational guidelines and responsibilities should be created to clarify roles and expectations for the management team (Walker & Stotlar, 1997). Regardless of whether an event is annual or one-time, such documentation helps to avoid duplication of effort and increases the likelihood of intra-group cooperation and a more smoothly run event.

Personnel

As an event manager, you need to address recruitment, selection, training, motivation, and evaluation of both paid personnel and volunteers. Being able to get the right people placed in key roles is essential; when this is accomplished, you will feel more at ease in terms of delegating responsibility. Also, **job descriptions** need to be clearly stated so that people know their roles and responsibilities. Once you have an event management team and all other personnel in place, the real test of leadership presents itself. Can you, as Jerry Solomon—one of the leading sport event managers in the country—asks, "create a team atmosphere and a sense of camaraderie that energizes others to go any length in making the event a success" (Solomon, 2002)?

Media and community outlets can be used to advertise for volunteers; additionally, volunteers can be recruited from local community service organizations such as the Rotary Clubs or university groups. Volunteers must be treated well and shown appreciation, especially if an event is going to occur on a regular, annual, or semi-annual basis. Creative gifts of recognition such a mugs or T-shirts and good food (which can be garnered from a sponsor) can be very motivating. In fact, if volunteers enjoy their experience, they can become informal recruiters in persuading others to volunteer the next time the event is held. Organizers of large-scale events, such as the PGA's 84 Lumber Classic, utilize well over 1,000 volunteers to help manage their event.

Members of the event management team must possess leadership skills, knowledge of small-group dynamics, excellent communication skills, the ability to motivate, and a talent for organizing committees. Team leaders and their committees need to know their responsibilities and keep an updated timetable regarding completion of tasks that is in concert with the master calendar for the event.

Location, Facilities, and Equipment

"THE DOCTOR CAN BURY HIS MISTAKES, BUT AN ARCHITECT CAN ONLY ADVISE HIS CLIENT TO PLANT VINES."

FRANK LLOYD WRIGHT

In order to draw participants or spectators, get commitments from athletes and/or performers, solicit sponsors, or, in some cases, negotiate a television deal, you must be able to have a location/venue secured. However, it is important to consider all your choices based on predetermined criteria before committing. In the case of a golf tournament, you would have to ask yourself a number of questions:

1) Is the golf course willing to work with our tournament parameters (e.g., shotgun start)?

2) What is the cost?

3) Is parking sufficient?

4) Is the course considered to be attractive by members of the golfing community

5) Can you sell your own concession?

Certain venues may seem perfect at first glance but have major drawbacks when analyzed more thoroughly. For example, Manhattan Beach, California, may seem like the perfect venue for a pro beach volleyball tournament until you consider the number of tickets you can sell is restricted by the California Coastal Commission to 25% percent of the total of spectators attending. In other words, if you have 4,000 seats, 3,000 must be given away for free (Solomon, 2002). Contracts need to be carefully analyzed so you know the restrictions to which you must adhere.

After you have decided where to hold your event, the venue must be staged. One of the best ways to be certain a venue is ready to use is to develop facility and equipment checklists. Walker and Stotlar (1997) developed a comprehensive list of items to include in these checklists:

• Cleaning the facility

• Providing adequate parking and special areas for emergency vehicles

• Testing the public address system and lighting

• Assuring proper signage for pedestrian and vehicular traffic

• Providing adequate ticket sales areas

• Examining first aid facilities

• Addressing the needs of participants

• Making proper provisions for concessions and merchandise stands or vendors

• Making special arrangements for sponsors

• Inspecting the permanent and/or temporary seating

• Addressing the needs of the media

• Developing a system for on-site communications among personnel

An area that is often overlooked when planning an event is meeting the needs of individuals with disabilities. A common misconception is that disabled individuals are confined to wheelchairs; event managers need to consider disabilities in a broader sense to include individuals who are hearing, visually, or mentally impaired.

Marketing and Budgeting for an Event

Event marketing includes determining if the potential event matches customers' interests. Will the target market of spectators or participants be attracted to an event and be available during the timeframe you select? Budgeting, advertising, recruitment, and developing promotions to inform the public about the

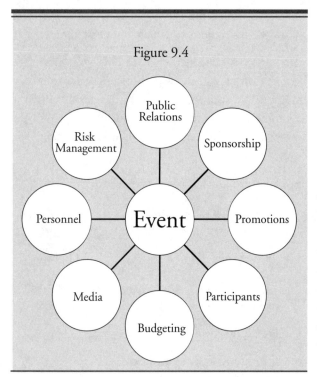

Figure 9.4

event are key components of event marketing. Figure 9.4 illustrates elements of event marketing.

Being able to attract customers requires research to determine if an event has appeal. Ideally, marketing research specialists can help determine an event's marketability; however, as a graduate from a sport management program, you will be able to collect your own data. Regardless of how this research is conducted, you ultimately need to be able to gain information that accurately portrays a picture of the potential customers' **sociodemographic** (i.e., age, income, gender, zip code) and **psychographic** (interests, attitudes, etc.) profile.

Most, but not all, events are set up to make a profit; therefore, it is of the utmost importance that the budgeting process be handled diligently. Someone on the event management team needs to oversee the accounting function so that the event's financial status can be determined at any given time. Also, it must be clear who is to pay the bills, authorize purchases, oversee petty cash, and handle contingency funds.

The Event and Post-Event Evaluation

On the day of the event, assuming everything has been staged properly, the focus of all personnel should be making sure that all spectators, participants, the media, and special guests have a wonderful experience.

The courtesy and friendliness of event staff cannot be overemphasized. Everyone from parking attendants, concession stand workers, ticket-takers, ushers, and bathroom attendants need to be as helpful, enthusiastic, and friendly as possible. In the area of risk management, when there are emergencies or problems that arise, there needs to be medical personnel and security in place and ready to act, as mentioned previously in the section on facility management.

A final evaluation plan for the event should be in place well before the event takes place and a timetable for completing the evaluation should be developed. This is especially critical for regularly occurring events. Establishing a baseline measurement for fan, participant, and media satisfaction is essential for continued improvement and success. The post-event evaluation process allows you to figure out what you did well and what you can improve upon the next time you stage the event.

Summary

The purpose of this chapter is to introduce the segment of the sport management field dealing with sport and facility management. The major concepts presented in this chapter include

- the skill set necessary for facility and event management;

- the differences in public and private ownership of public assembly facilities, in addition to approaches to management (in-house versus outsourcing);

- an overview of the wide array of participant-oriented facilities;

- the management and personnel required in facility management and execution of events;

- the concepts of planning, organizing, leading, and evaluating relative to facility and event management;

- the importance of risk management;

- the use of timetables in event management;

- marketing, budgeting, and public relations in facility and event management; and

- post-event evaluation.

Discussion Activities

1. If you had to initiate, organize, and oversee a four-person team co-ed volleyball tournament, what steps would you take to ensure its success?

2. As Director of Operations for women's basketball at Eagle University (a Division I program), you are charged with running the end-of-the-season conference tournament. The college does not outsource any of the facility functions. How will you manage this process? What considerations have to be made as far as preparing and managing the facility? What will you do to enhance the entertainment value, minimize the risk, and market the tournament?

References

Horine, L., & Stotlar, D. (2003). *Administration of physical education and sport programs* (5th ed). Boston, MA: McGraw-Hill

Mulrooney, A., & Farmer, P. (2001). Managing the facility. In B. Parkhouse (Ed.). *The management of sport: Its foundation and application* (3rd ed.). Boston, MA: McGraw-Hill.

Sawyer, T. H., Hypes, M.G., & Hypes, J. A. (2004). *Financing the sport enterprise*. Champaign, IL: Sagamore Publishing.

Sawyer, T. H., & Smith O. R. (1999). *The management of clubs, recreation, and sport: Concepts and applications*. Champaign, IL: Sagamore Publishing.

Solomon, J. (2002). *An insider's guide to managing sporting events*. Champaign, IL: Human Kinetics.

Walker, M. L., & Stotlar, D. K. (1997). *Sport facility management*. London, UK: Jones & Bartlett, Inc.

Suggested Reading

Howard, D. R., & Crompton, J. L. (1995). *Financing sport*. Morgantown, WV: Fitness Information Technology.

Chapter Ten

Sport Industry and the Law

Paul Batista

"What amazes me, Mr. Berquist, is not that you recorded the ball game without the express written consent of the commissioner. What amazes me is that you thought you wouldn't get caught."

Learning Objectives

Upon completion of this chapter, the reader should be able to

- Define "the Law" and "sport law;"

- Identify the three primary ways to resolve disputes;

- Discuss the philosophical basis for American law;

- List three general classifications of law;

- Explain the four main sources of law in the United States;

- Identify the eight content areas of sport law and the manner in which each affects the sport manager or organization; and

- Understand the obstacles facing students seeking to become an agent for professional athletes.

Introduction

A glance at the local newspaper or just a quick look at ESPN's SportsCenter demonstrates that sports and law are inextricably connected. We read and hear of athletes involved in criminal activities, illegal drug use, and domestic violence. There are free agents to sign and contracts to negotiate, collective bargaining agreements to finalize to avoid strikes by players, or lockouts by management. Amateur and professional athletes, as well as spectators, file personal injury lawsuits. Other athletes sue claiming they are victims of discrimination based on race, gender, religion, age, or disability.

"[I]N AMERICA THE LAW IS KING. FOR AS IN ABSOLUTE GOVERNMENTS THE KING IS LAW, SO IN FREE COUNTRIES THE LAW OUGHT TO BE KING; AND THERE OUGHT TO BE NO OTHER."

THOMAS PAYNE, *COMMON SENSE* (1776)

We look for the day's scores, but instead find that today's game takes second billing to the activities of judges, mediators, arbitrators, prosecutors, defense attorneys, investigators, and police officers. In 1986, R. K. Smith noted that "attorneys and judges are more than idle spectators at sporting events" (Appenzeller, 1998). Almost 20 years later, that observation has become even more accurate.

Most Americans became enamored with the pleasures of sports as youngsters, but as adults, we see that law permeates sports as much as it does other areas of society. As this book went to press, the media was reporting on

- performance-enhancing drugs in major league baseball and the Tour de France;

- the NCAA denying Jeremy Bloom's request to accept endorsement money for his freestyle skiing exploits while retaining his eligibility for Division I Football;

- an NHL hockey player going to prison for seeking a "hit man" to kill his agent;

- Kobe Bryant's sexual assault case;

- Nolan Richardson's unsuccessful racial discrimination suit against the University of Arkansas;

- the U.S. Justice Department's investigation of how ESPN acquires football and basketball programming;

- a trademark dispute between the University of Iowa and University of Southern Mississippi over athletic logo similarities; and

- passage of a Florida statute creating enhanced punishment for assault against sports officials.

But as the years progress, things really haven't changed. In a speech in 1987, Bart Giamatti, the late Commissioner of Major League Baseball, discussed the pervasive influence both law and sports have on American society: "The fact is, American culture, American daily life is soaked in the law, in legal and legalistic nuance, in mythology, anxiety, gossip, awe, resentment, impatience, admiration before, about and for the law. . .[i]t governs obtrusively and unobtrusively the culture's daily life" (Giamatti, 1988 p.2).

He continued by making an interesting analogy about law and sport: "Sport is about energy and action within rules, boundaries, codes; it has a vast body of internal law and regulation and officials to dispense judgment, if not justice, quickly and in public (p. 2)."

Clearly, despite internal rules such as the "chin music" delivered when a hitter digs in, or the unwritten rules enforced by the "goon" in hockey, law has permeated sport in the same manner that it has affected society as a whole. It is not surprising, then, that the sport management curriculum includes a study of the legal aspects of sport. You will note that the subject is called both "sport law" and "sports law," depending on the preference of the individual author. In this chapter, it will be referred to as "sport law," except when used in direct quotations.

What Is "the Law"?

While virtually every student will have an idea of what "the law" is, most likely the student's perception developed through the media—reading newspapers and magazines or watching television or movies. The study of any subject, and particularly law, should begin with a discussion of the basics.

Although there are hundreds of definitions of **law**, a reasonable description would be a body of enforceable rules, established by the lawmaking authorities of a society, governing the relationships among individuals and between individuals and their government. The New Jersey Legislature has defined law as "All the official rules and codes that govern citizens' actions, including the Constitution, statutory laws enacted by the Legislature, case laws established by court decisions, and administrative law as set forth by executive branch agencies" (Glossary, 2004).

Deciding on a definition, however, fails to answer the basic philosophical questions: What makes laws necessary, and why do we have laws?

What makes laws necessary?

The fundamental purpose of laws is to resolve (or avoid) conflicts. In ancient days, and indeed in parts of the world today, law was defined by the phrase "might makes right," where the strongest person/group made the laws and enforced them. As we have become more civilized, society has generally agreed that mortal combat is not the appropriate manner of resolving disputes. Therefore, laws have been established to resolve conflicts without the necessity of physical battle.

There are three primary methods of resolving conflicts. The first (and most widely used) is negotiation. While most people do not stop to think about how they resolve disputes, it is true that most disputes are resolved through negotiation. **Negotiation** is a process involving formal or informal discussions in order to reach an agreement.

Have you been involved in a negotiation lately? If you and your roommate wanted to watch different games on your shared television, you have a conflict. Rather than getting into a fight, your conflict is resolved by negotiation. Each presented his/her viewpoint, discussed the alternative solutions, then either jointly agreed which game to watch, or one party gave in to the other's desires. You resolved your conflict through negotiation. While one or both of you might not be completely satisfied, you have settled your differences. In its simplest form, this is negotiation.

The second way to resolve disputes is through **alternative dispute resolution (ADR)**. ADR may be defined as resolving a dispute through any means other than litigation or negotiation. The primary forms of ADR are mediation and arbitration.

Mediation is the submission of a dispute to a disinterested third person who intervenes between the parties in an attempt to settle their dispute without going to court. In mediation, the third party (**mediator**) communicates with all parties to the dispute, presents proposals from each party to the other, and facilitates resolution of the dispute, if possible. The mediator makes no ruling and has no authority to enforce his/her judgment on any party.

Arbitration is the submission of a dispute to a neutral third party (**arbitrator**) who listens to all parties, considers the legal position of each, and then renders a decision to resolve the dispute. The arbitrator acts much like a judge. The arbitrator's decision may not be binding on the parties, or may be binding if there is a prior agreement of the parties, or required by applicable law. Disputes in Major League Baseball are resolved by specially appointed arbitrators under the sport's Collective Bargaining Agreement.

The final manner of resolving disputes is **litigation**, which is the process of filing a lawsuit so that a court can resolve the disagreement. In the U.S., all citizens have access to the court system and have the right to petition courts to settle disputes.

Why do we have laws?

Although this question may seem to be the same as the first, the question of what makes laws necessary provides a practical answer. On the other hand, this question requires a philosophical answer. The founding fathers of the United States implemented several philosophical foundations when establishing our representative form of government.

The first reason we have laws is to enforce the will of the people, by electing fellow citizens to represent us in public office. The form of government in the United States is a constitutional republic, which is a government "of the people, for the people and by the people." We, the people, choose the laws to which we are subjected. As Thomas Jefferson wrote, "The will of the people is the only legitimate foundation of any government" (Jefferson, 1801).

The second reason we have laws is to maintain order. Imagine a football game without referees, or a baseball game without umpires. Eventually, the game would degenerate into complete chaos. Established laws create predictability, so that citizens are aware of the consequences of their decisions. We know that a batter hitting the ball off the "foul pole" has hit a home run and a batter hitting an "infield fly" is out, whether it happens in New York, Atlanta, Houston, or Los Angeles.

Finally, laws are created to ensure just treatment of all people. We would like for umpires and referees to get every call right, but it just doesn't happen. Likewise, we would like to see everyone get **justice**, but it would be naive to state that justice is always served. That is an aspiration that will never be met. Nonetheless, the founding fathers expressed the goal for which we strive, and the rights that we claim, in the **Declaration of Independence**.

The first of these rights is commonly referred to as our **natural rights**. The founding fathers concluded that these rights were not derived from any government, but were God-given rights inherent to all people (disregarding the truth that it applied only to white males at the time). They wrote:

> *We hold these truths to be self evident, that all men are created equal, that they are endowed by their Creator with certain unalienable rights, that among these are Life, Liberty and the pursuit of Happiness.*

The second set of rights is known as **civil rights**. These are personal rights that we as Americans have reserved for ourselves. They are set forth in the **U.S. Constitution** and the **Bill of Rights**, but trace their roots to the authority also set forth in the Declaration of Independence:

> *That to secure these rights governments are instituted among men, deriving their just powers from the consent of the governed. That whenever any Form of Government becomes destructive of these ends, it is the Right of the People to alter or abolish it, and to institute new Government, laying its foundation on such principles and organizing its powers in such form, as to them shall seem most likely to effect their Safety and Happiness.*

We have chosen, in laying the foundation of our government, to reserve to each of us these civil rights to affect our safety and happiness. Now that we understand the foundations of our law, let's get to the discussion of "sport law."

Does "Sport Law" Exist?

In his article in the Marquette Sports Law Review, Professor Timothy Davis uses the title to ask the pertinent question *"What is Sports Law?"* (Davis, 2001). Although students frequently have a preconceived idea that sport law primarily involves agents and the statues of player representation, the answer to the question is not so easily answered by lawyers and academicians.

Professor Davis presents the three prevailing views of sport law in order to allow the reader to form his/her personal answer to the question. He describes the first view as the traditional view, which holds that sport law does not exist, but "represents nothing more than an amalgamation of various substantive areas of the law that are relevant in the sports context," and that "sports law is a misnomer, given that sport represents a form of activity and entertainment that is governed by the legal system in its entirety" (Davis, 2001). The recent case involving Maurice Clarett's attempt to have the NFL's eligibility rules invalidated is a classic example. The court did not decide the case differently because it involved a sport setting, but followed traditional legal analysis, holding that "any remedies for [Clarett's] claim are the province of labor law" (*Clarett v. National Football League*, 2003).

The second alternative is called the moderate position, and presents a middle ground between the other two perspectives. This view argues that a body of law related to sport has not yet fully developed to the extent to be clearly recognized, but "factual peculiarities residing in sports . . . require the unique application of generally applicable legal doctrine(s) . . . [producing] results that would not occur in other contexts" (Davis, 2001). Therefore, according to the moderate position, the area of sport law is inevitably developing into a separate substantive area of law. This outlook points to the development of concepts such as the **limited duty** rule (baseball teams have a limited duty to protect spectators from foul balls, thus providing teams with protection from liability) and **assumed risk** by participants (participants injured by an inherent risk of the activity cannot recover for injuries).

Finally, the third alternative is the belief that the field of sport law already exists. This perspective emphasizes the "growing body of case and statutory law specific to the sports industry as evidence of the existence of a separately identifiable body of law" (Davis, 2001). This argument contends that most, if not all, identified areas of law are not entirely separate, but overlap with other areas. Therefore, according to this theory, cases emerging from sport settings create an "increasing body of judicial and legislative law specific to sports" (Davis, 2001). For example, professional athletes may need representation in various legal disciplines such as contract law (to negotiate contracts or endorsements), tort law (injury or death of player), constitutional law (drug testing or religious accommodation), intellectual property law (right to use player's name or likeness in advertising), international law (work visas for foreign-born athletes), probate (settling player's estate after death), labor and antitrust law (management and players' unions collectively bargain for terms and conditions of employment), tax law (to file tax returns), perhaps family law (divorce, paternity, or child support), and criminal law. Examples supporting this view are found in various statutes regulating athlete agents.

Regardless of the reader's viewpoint, Davis aptly notes that a lawyer practicing sport law is the "ultimate general practitioner," contradicting the idea of many "law students, novice practitioners and lay persons who equate the practice of sports law to the representation of players in their contract negotiations" (Davis, 2001).

Note: Professor Davis's article contains an outstanding bibliography of books, journals, law reviews, and other publications that contain a wealth of information and articles relating to virtually every aspect of the study of the legal aspects of sports.

The Study of Law

In most law schools in the U.S., the curriculum is based on the **case study method**, which is significantly different than how you have been taught in your undergraduate studies. The case study method presents students with the opportunity to read previous cases in order to learn how courts make legal decisions by applying relevant law to the facts of the case. In this manner, law students not only learn "the law," but also gain an understanding of the reasoning courts use in deciding disputes.

While you are not law students, this is still the best method to "learn" the law. It gives you the vicarious experience of being involved in the resolution of disputes arising out of actual situations involved in the real world. By acquiring the ability to understand courts' reasoning and to learn basic legal principles, you will gain at least a rudimentary basis for decision making.

As you progress through your career in sport management, you will undertake a more detailed study of the legal aspects of sport. Undoubtedly, you will be required to read court cases and thereby be exposed to this case study method of learning. The purpose of case study is to equip you with the knowledge you need to (hopefully) avoid situations that put your participants, your employer, or you at risk. Further, it will give you the vicarious experience of being involved in the dispute. Finally, it should alert you to the situations that need the intervention of your attorney. While you might not have an attorney whispering advice into your ear all the time, you will have basic legal principles that should create "red flags" when you are getting into dangerous legal territory.

©iStockphoto.com

Classifications of Law

Although law affects every person sitting in college classrooms, most students have a limited exposure to, and understanding of, how the legal system works. In an effort to simplify and distinguish the differences among various types of law, it is helpful to divide law into three general classifications and distinguish the characteristics within each of the three classifications.

Substantive v. Procedural

All court cases involve both of these types of law. **Substantive law** is the law that defines, describes, or creates legal rights and obligations—it is *what* the law is. In contrast, **procedural law** is the method of enforcing rights and obligations given to citizens by substantive law—it is the step-by-step mechanics concerning *how* the rights are enforced.

Example: The First Amendment to the U.S. Constitution states that "Congress shall make no law respecting an establishment of religion, or prohibiting the free exercise thereof." In *Santa Fe Independent School District (ISD) v. Doe* (2001), the U.S. Supreme Court held that Santa Fe ISD's policy authorizing prayers before high school football games violated this clause, but also acknowledged an individual student's right to engage in religious activities at public schools. Both the Constitutional provision and the Court's interpretation as it relates to the facts in *Santa Fe* are substantive law because they declare what the law is.

However, before the Supreme Court could hear and rule on the case, the plaintiffs were required to comply with the procedural prerequisites, such as filing the case in the proper court, giving notice of the suit to the school, completing discovery, engaging in alternative dispute resolution, trying the case before a judge and jury, properly appealing it to the appellate court, then ultimately asking the Supreme Court to resolve the dispute. In order to enforce rights given by substantive law, parties must comply with the rules of procedural law in the respective courts.

Public v. Private

Generally, **public law** governs the relationship between citizens and their government, while **private law** governs the relationship among private citizens. In many cases, these categories are not always easily distinguishable. Generally, public law includes areas such as criminal, tax, environmental, constitutional, and administrative, as well as protection of rights of the general public. Private law includes most other areas of law including contracts, property, personal injury, products liability, insurance, etc.

Example: There is a federal statute governing workplace safety that is enforced by the Occupational Safety and Health Administration (OSHA), a regulatory agency established by the U.S. Congress. The workers in professional sport stadiums are provided certain protections by this law and have the right to file claims with OSHA for violations. Enforcement of this statute would be considered in the "public" domain. On the other hand, although the professional athletes are also workers, they are represented by unions who collectively bargain terms and conditions of players' work with the owners and ultimately enter into a contract called a **Collective Bargaining Agreement** (CBA). In the event that either party violates this agreement, the parties have the "private" right to enforce its provisions, without government intervention.

Criminal v. Civil

Criminal law deals with unlawful acts committed against the public as a whole, in which a defendant is accused of violating a statute defining a criminal act, thereby committing a **crime**. Congress and the individual state legislatures create these criminal statutes, which authorize the government to punish the violator by either a fine or incarceration. It is the government seeking to impose the penalty that defines the violation as a criminal act. **Civil law** includes everything that is not criminal law. It should be noted, however, that a single situation could include both criminal and civil cases, such as in the Kobe Bryant case, where the government sought to send him to prison for sexual assault, and the alleged victim sued him for monetary damages based on the same set of facts.

Although these categories seem to create a clear distinction among the classifications, it is important to note that the divisions are not always as simple as they may appear. It is also important to note that most cases have one of the characteristics from each cate-

Example: As this book goes to press, the U.S. government is investigating allegations that employees of BALCO laboratories provided performance-enhancing drugs to various athletes in violation of federal statutes prohibiting possession and sale of illegal drugs. If the evidence warrants, the government will file criminal charges against the defendants, seeking to send them to prison for violating the criminal statute. An example of a civil case is the family of a collegiate football player, who died several weeks after surgery to repair a knee injury, suing the University, coaches, trainers, and team doctors, alleging their negligence in performing their duties was responsible for the player's death.

gory. For example, the case involving the deceased football player includes not only substantive and procedural law, but also represents a civil case involving private law.

Sources of Law in the United States

All law in the U.S. comes from one of four sources: 1) Constitutions, 2) statutes, 3) administrative rules and regulations, and 4) court cases. If you will review the definition of law by the New Jersey legislature cited above, you will see that it includes all these sources in the definition.

Constitutions

The "**Supreme Law of the Land**" is the United States Constitution. It takes precedence over any other law. Each state also has a constitution, but it is subordinate to the U.S. Constitution. If the terms of a state constitution violate a provision in the U.S. Constitution, the state provision will be declared unconstitutional. Constitutional questions raised in sport settings include issues relating to religion, criminal search and seizures, due process, equal protection, drug testing, persons with disabilities, etc.

Statutes

Statutes are particular laws passed by the U.S. **Congress**, or a state **legislature**, which declare, command, or prohibit some conduct or require citizens to act in a certain manner. Violation of these statues normally creates various kinds of penalties for acting in a manner contrary to the law, such as going to jail for driving while under the influence of drugs or alcohol. Legislatures can essentially institute whatever statutes they desire, so long as they do not violate provisions of an applicable constitution. Examples of statutory enactments include Title IX, Americans with Disabilities Act, the Sherman and Clayton Antitrust Acts, Bankruptcy Act, and state Athlete Agent Acts.

Administrative Rules and Regulations

When Congress or state legislatures pass statutes regulating some industry or activity, frequently they will also establish administrative agencies to oversee enforcement of the legislation. These agencies are granted authority to establish directives in order to carry out the legislative body's intent in passing the statute. These directives are known as **administrative rules and regulations**. They generally carry the force of law as if they were passed by Congress or the state legislature, and violators of the rules and regulations are subject to the penalties provided in them. Examples of administrative agencies that establish such rules and regulations include the Federal Communications Commission (FCC), which regulates television and radio, the Occupational Safety and Health Administration (OSHA), which regulates workplace safety, and the Office of Civil Rights (OCR), which administers Title IX.

Case Law

The final source is law established within the court system. The U.S. adopted the **common law** system from England, which allows courts to create rules of law. Under this system, appellate courts announce a rule of law that applies to the facts of a particular case. The rules established in this manner are called **case law**. Once case law is established, other courts will usually adhere to the opinion of the original court and follow its holding, citing the original case as a **precedent**.

Courts are not required to follow precedent unless it is announced from a higher court within the same court system. For example, a California intermediate appellate state court must follow a precedent established by the California Supreme Court, but is not required to follow a precedent of the Florida Supreme Court. Further, appellate courts on the same level may have different opinions on the same issue, with the issue remaining unresolved until a higher court establishes the precedent for all inferior courts.

Courts may also change their precedent and issue a new opinion changing the previous rule, although this is not a routine occurrence. An example of this is the 1954 U.S. Supreme Court decision in *Brown v. Board of Education*, which desegregated public schools. The existing educational system was based on a Supreme Court decision in an 1896 case which established the principle that a "separate but equal" system segregating races was constitutional. In *Brown*, the Court changed its precedent and held that such systems violated the Equal Protection clause of the 14th Amendment.

Each of these areas supplies various laws affecting sport. Let's take a look at some specific examples of the legal aspects of sport.

Practice Areas in Sport Law

As the study of sport management has exploded during the last 20 years, with sport management programs being established in hundreds of colleges and universities, there has been concern among sport management professionals that there were no standards in place to assure that all students were being taught the essential subject matter of the discipline. Too often, a sport management program was created within another department, when an interested faculty member decided it was time to offer sport management to students at the institution. Unfortunately, this led to programs that provided degrees modeled after the curriculum of the original department. Programs in business departments were business based, while programs in kinesiology or exercise science were primarily science based.

To ensure that all sport management students are receiving training in the appropriate educational subjects, two professional organizations, the National Association for Sport and Physical Education (NASPE) and the North American Society for Sport Management (NASSM), have designed specific curriculum standards for each of ten content areas identified in sport management (see Chapter 1). The legal aspects of sport is one of the ten content areas.

Although a discussion of all legal subjects related to sport law would be appropriate, the sheer volume of such a discussion makes it unrealistic. Therefore, discussion of content areas within the legal aspects of sport will be limited to the eight listed in the NASPE/NASSM Standards for Undergraduate Degree Programs in Sport Management.

Legal System

Although the legal system encompasses law from all four sources discussed earlier in this chapter, this portion will be limited to the court system and litigation. You will remember that one of the ways to resolve disputes is through litigation, or filing a lawsuit. Court systems have been established to handle these lawsuits.

There are two court systems in the United States—one federal system and 50 independent state systems. The U.S. Constitution established the federal system, and the state systems are created by the respective state constitutions or statutes.

1. **State Court Systems**. State court systems generally hear matters that occur within the boundaries of the state and involve disputes that involve state (as opposed to federal) law. Examples of cases normally heard in state courts are cases involving personal injury and other negligence claims, contracts, family disputes, defamation (libel and slander), products liability, workers' compensation, and state criminal matters.

Most state court systems have three levels. The first level where the case is initially filed is the **trial court**. This is the court where the parties actually "try" the case, presenting evidence to a jury and legal arguments to a judge. This is the type of court that is shown in most movies and television shows. The jury will render a **verdict**, then the judge will enter a ruling, or **judgment**, in favor of one party or the other.

If one of the parties thinks the judge made a mistake in the way he/she tried the case (such as applying the wrong law), that party can **appeal** to the next court level, the **intermediate appeals court**. Most of these courts are called "**Courts of Appeals**," although they have different names in various states. Litigants are not required to seek permission of these courts to process the appeal to the intermediate appellate level. The function of these courts is to determine if the judge followed the law (both substantive and procedural) when trying the case.

Appellate courts normally enter one of three results in a case:

- *Affirmed* – The trial court made no significant mistakes, and the ruling stands.

- *Reverse and remand* – The trial court made a significant mistake and the case should be tried again, but correctly this time. If the court allowed testimony that should not have been heard, the appellate court will order the case tried again, this time without the improper testimony.

- *Reverse and render* – The trial court made a significant mistake, but there is no need for another trial because when the correct law is applied, the winning party cannot prevail. If a court entered a judgment holding a state university liable for negligence, even though that state's sovereign immunity law protects the state from liability in negligence cases, the appellate court will reverse and "render" the judgment that should have been entered (that the plaintiff cannot recover from the university).

After the Court of Appeals has rendered its judgment, any of the parties—but usually the losing party—may take an appeal to the highest appellate court in the state, usually called the **Supreme Court**. In order to have a case heard, the litigant must file an application with the court asking that the case be heard. In most states, the Supreme Court can hear or refuse to hear any case it chooses, at its sole discretion. If the court refuses the application, the case is finished, with the result in the intermediate court being the final ruling in the case. If the Supreme Court accepts and decides the case, it will enter one of the same rulings as the intermediate appellate court.

2. **Federal Court System**. The federal system is established in Article III, Section 1, of the U.S. Constitution, which states, "The judicial power of the United States shall be vested in one Supreme Court and in such inferior Courts as the Congress may from time to time ordain and establish." Congress has established a court system similar to the state systems.

In order to file a case in a federal court, the litigant must establish that a law specifically allows for such a case to be filed in federal court. The four categories primarily used to establish that cases should be heard in federal court are 1) when a litigant is seeking to enforce rights created under the U.S. Constitution or a federal statute (this is called a **federal question**), 2) when the dispute is between two states, 3) when the United States is a party to the lawsuit, and 4) when there is **diversity of citizenship**, meaning that the parties are citizens of different states and the amount in controversy is above $100,000.

The **federal trial courts** are called **U.S. District Courts**, followed by a geographical description of the location of the court (e.g., United States District Court for the Western District of Pennsylvania). There are 94 throughout the country, with at least one located in every state. These courts operate essentially the same as state trial courts, providing a trial of the case before a judge and jury. When a judgment has been entered, either party has the right to pursue an appeal to the federal intermediate courts, called Courts of Appeals.

The Courts of Appeals are divided into 11 regional groups, called **circuits**, as well as a circuit for the District of Columbia and a specialized federal Court of Appeals. These courts are normally referred to by their circuit number, so that cases from Louisiana, Mississippi, and Texas are heard in the 5th Circuit, while cases from Alabama, Florida, and Georgia are decided in the 11th Circuit, etc.

In the event that a litigant wants to appeal a decision of a Circuit Court, the appeal would be taken to the United States Supreme Court by filing an application for a **writ of certiorari.** If the Court grants the application, the Supreme Court will issue a writ of certiorari, ordering the lower court to forward the case to the Supreme Court for its consideration. It takes a vote of four justices to issue the writ and hear a case.

The Supreme Court is not required to hear any case and may refuse to hear a case for any reason. A refusal to hear the case is not considered a decision by the Supreme Court. Therefore, the ruling of the Circuit Court becomes final. Further, a refusal by the Supreme Court to hear a case is not considered a comment on the Circuit Court's opinion.

In the most recent Supreme Court reporting period, the 2002-2003 Term of Court, 8,255 cases were filed, 88 cases were argued before the Court, and 79 cases were disposed of in 71 written opinions (U.S. Supreme Court Year End Report, 2003). If a litigant is dissatisfied with the result in the Supreme Court, there is no other avenue of appeal in the court system.

©iStockphoto.com

Contract Law

Of all the elements of sport law, the most publicized subject deals with issues related to player contracts. Think of the regularity with which sportscasters talk about free agency, trades, contract extensions, bonuses, suspensions, options, and other contractual matters. When you discuss sport law with your friends, most will immediately think of these contractual issues. With the amount of money involved in professional and amateur sports, contracts are common in every facet of sport.

Simply stated, a **contract** is an agreement, or exchange of promises, that creates legally enforceable duties and obligations for all parties to the contract. Except under certain circumstances, contracts are not required to be in writing to be enforceable. However, it is wise to remember the words of movie producer Samuel Goldwyn: "A verbal contract isn't worth the paper it's written on." Reducing a contract to writing not only establishes proof of an agreement, it also provides reliable evidence of the terms of the contract.

Four elements are required to form a valid contract: 1) legal capacity, 2) agreement, 3) consideration, and 4) legality.

1. **Legal Capacity**. Each party to a contract must be legally competent to enter into the contract. The courts are concerned with the relative strength of bargaining power, and if there is a great discrepancy among the parties, the courts will protect the party with much lower mental capacity. In this manner, contracts with **minors** (persons under age 18) and people with significant mental disabilities are normally not enforceable against them, and courts will allow those parties to avoid the terms of the contract. Recognizing the proliferation of world-class athletes under 18 (such as Freddy Adu in soccer and Michelle Wie in golf), sport managers should be especially vigilant when seeking to enter into contracts with minors. An experienced lawyer is essential in negotiating the terms of such contracts.

2. **Agreement**. The very essence of a contract is the agreement among the parties, and there can be no contract without an agreement. Normally, an agreement is reached through a process called **offer and acceptance**, which involves the parties making a series of proposals to the other until the negotiations culminate with an agreement. The normal pattern for negotiating player contracts is a classic example of the offer and acceptance scenario. The team will make a contract proposal to a player, who then presents a **counteroffer** to the team, and this process continues until the parties reach agreement on the terms of the contract. The final component of agreement is that all of the essential terms of the contract must be agreed upon, so that the parties have a "meeting of the minds" on all aspects of the contract.

3. **Consideration**. Once the parties have agreed to the terms of the contract, there must be an exchange of something of value for the contract to be valid. The purpose of consideration is to provide some agreed benefit to both parties of the contract. Each party must get and give consideration. In most instances, **consideration** is the payment of money by one party to the other, who in turn provides something of value. However, promises to perform an act or service, or even refrain from performing acts or services, will be sufficient to establish consideration. When a baseball player signs a contract with a team, the team promises to pay the player for performing, and the player promises to perform, follow team and league rules, refrain from dangerous activities, etc.

4. Legality. Courts will not enforce contracts that require performance of an illegal act. If the contract is the subject of an illegal act, the contract is void. If a person supplies an athlete with an illegal controlled substance (steroids, cocaine, etc.), then sues the player for not paying for the substance, the courts will not require the athlete to honor the contract.

Constitutional Law

Many provisions contained in the U.S. Constitution (and to a lesser degree, state constitutions) have become the focus of litigation in sports. Among the constitutional issues that have been raised are

- establishment or expression of religion in public schools (locker room or pregame prayer),

- free speech (wearing items of clothing as a political protest),

- search and seizure (drug testing),

- due process (right to notice and a hearing prior to suspension),

- equal protection (discrimination based on race, ethnicity, gender, religion, age, etc.), and

- freedom of association (discrimination by private clubs or societies).

This list could continue indefinitely, but the examples listed above are representative of the issues sport managers and participants have dealt with in the past.

The first topic to consider in constitutional issues is to determine if the plaintiff has been deprived of his/her rights by **state action**. The U.S. Supreme Court has said state action means that "the State [federal or state government] is *responsible* for the specific conduct of which the plaintiff complains" (*Brentwood Academy v. Tennessee Secondary School Athletic Association*, 2001), meaning that the state has caused the harm suffered by the plaintiff. Virtually all of the rights established in the U.S. Constitution are designed to protect citizens from actions by the government. Under most circumstances, if the state is not involved, there is no violation of the constitution.

Clearly, statutes passed by Congress or state legislatures, ordinances passed by city governments, or policies of public schools are state action, and subject to the provisions of the Constitution. In *Santa Fe ISD v.*

Doe (2001), the public school district established a policy that enabled a student chosen by the student body to say a prayer over the public address system before a high school football game. The Supreme Court held that the school was a state actor, and that the school's policy violated the **Establishment Clause** of the First Amendment.

However, it may be difficult to determine if some other entities are state actors, since they may be receiving money directly or indirectly from governmental entities or be performing a public function. Both the NCAA, which receives funds from public universities (*NCAA v. Tarkanian*, 1988), and the United States Olympic Committee (USOC), which was chartered by the federal government and given "exclusive jurisdiction" over participation by U.S. athletes in the Olympic Games (*DeFrantz v. USOC*, 1980), have been held to be private entities against which constitutional prohibitions do not apply. On the other hand, state high school athletic associations have been held to be state actors (*Brentwood Academy*, 2001).

Administrative and Statutory Law

As discussed in the sources of law section, Congress and state legislatures create law by passing statutes. Frequently, these laws establish agencies to enforce the laws that have been passed. Many agencies are more commonly known by their acronyms. Some of the agencies that sport managers are most likely to encounter during their careers, and the matters they regulate, are listed below.

- Equal Employment Opportunity Commission (EEOC) – workplace discrimination issues

- Occupational Safety and Health Administration (OSHA) – workplace safety

- Office of Civil Rights (OCR) – Title IX

- National Labor Relations Board (NLRB) – labor laws

- Internal Revenue Service (IRS) – tax

- Social Security Administration (SSA) – retirement

This is a representative list of federal agencies, but there are hundreds more. Additionally, sport managers should be familiar with state agencies in the state in which they are employed.

As previously stated, statutory laws are generated from both Congress and state legislatures. As sport management students, you will complete a more thorough examination of many of the applicable statutes later in your studies. However, a cursory exposure to some of these statutes is appropriate in an introductory course. (Note: The descriptions are for general informational purposes only and are not an exhaustive coverage of the particular statute. Detailed study will come in later courses.) Federal statutes dealing with sport include, in no particular order, the following:

1. **Title IX of the Education Amendments of 1972 ("Title IX").** (20 U.S.C. § 1681 et. seq.) Probably the most discussed statute relating to sport is Title IX. When it was passed in 1972, it was a one sentence law that stated, "No person in the Unites States shall, on the basis of sex, be excluded from participation in, be denied the benefits of, or be subjected to discrimination under any education program or activity receiving Federal financial assistance." The intent of Congress was to prohibit **gender discrimination** in educational activities. There was no mention of sport or recreation in Title IX. However, this is a good example of Congress authorizing an administrative agency to enforce the laws it has passed. The **Office of Civil Rights** (OCR) division of the **Department of Education** has been charged with enforcing Title IX. OCR has passed administrative regulations governing the implementation of Title IX and has determined that both interscholastic and intercollegiate athletics is an educational activity subject to Title IX.

2. **Title VII of the Civil Rights Act of 1964 ("Title VII").** (42 U.S.C. § 2000e, et. seq.) The Civil Rights Act of 1964 is a comprehensive set of laws that address discrimination issues in a wide range of circumstances. Title VII of the Act protects employees (and prospective employees) from discrimination by making it unlawful for an employer to discriminate against a person in employment activities (i.e., hiring, firing, compensation, promotion, classification), based on "race, color, religion, sex, or national origin." Courts are given wide-ranging powers to address and remedy violations of this Act.

3. **Americans with Disabilities Act of 1990 ("ADA").** (42 U.S.C. § 12101, et. seq.) The purpose of the ADA is "to provide a clear and comprehensive national mandate for the elimination of discrimination against individuals with disabilities." The ADA not only encompasses issues of accessibility to facilities, but also prohibits discrimination against disabled persons in employment, subject to some specific exceptions. The overriding feature of this law requires "reasonable accommodation" of disabled persons.

4. **Sherman Antitrust Act.** (15 U.S.C. § 1, et. seq.) As American business developed during the Industrial Revolution, the advances in manufacturing, transportation, and communication created a model of business operation that effectively created monopolies. This was accomplished by consolidating all existing companies in an industry into a single business entity called a **monopoly** and allowing all former companies to have an ownership interest in the new, single entity. The effect of removing all competition was deemed detrimental to American citizens. In response, Congress passed the Sherman Antitrust Act, which declared any contract, combination, or conspiracy "in restraint of trade or commerce" to be illegal. Although the U.S. Supreme Court, in *Federal Baseball Club v. National League*, has held that Major League Baseball was not involved in commerce and was not an interstate business enterprise, and, therefore, was not subject to this Act, all other major sports are subject to antitrust laws. In your later studies, you will find out that this Act (coupled with later legislation called the **Clayton Antitrust Act**) ultimately caused a change in the relationships between management and players, resulting in familiar scenarios such as unions, free agency, strikes, lockouts, and collective bargaining agreements.

5. **Copyright Act of 1976.** (17 U.S.C. § 101, et. seq.) Article I, section 8 of the U.S. Constitution authorized Congress to pass laws providing "Authors and Inventors the exclusive Right to their respective Writings and Discoveries" for a limited period of time. In response,

Congress has passed laws protecting "original works of authorship fixed in any tangible medium of expression," which means that no one may use the work in any manner without the author's permission. Things protected include books, music, pictures, print articles, cartoons, and broadcast of games. In order to copy, distribute, or use such works, the author must give his/her permission. This is why announcers in every game transmission say, "This telecast is the property of major league baseball (or NFL, NBA, etc.) . . . any rebroadcast, retransmission, or other use of the words, descriptions and accounts of this game are expressly prohibited without the express written consent of . . ."

6. **The Federal Trademark Act of 1946**. (15 U.S.C. § 1051, et. seq.) Also known as the **Lanham Act**, this statute authorizes owners of trademarks to register them with the U.S. government and provides protection against others who seek to use the trademark without permission. *Black's Law Dictionary* defines a **trademark** as a "word, phrase, logo or other graphic symbol used by a manufacturer to distinguish its product . . . from those of others . . . In effect, the trademark is the commercial substitute for one's signature." In the event that another attempts to use the registered trademark, the Lanham Act empowers the trademark holder to sue the violator for **infringement**, and protect its interest in the symbol. Team logos are examples of trademarks.

7. **Equal Access Act**. (20 U.S.C. §§ 4071-4074) The Equal Access Act was "intended to address perceived widespread discrimination against religious speech in public schools." The Act prohibits any school receiving federal funds from denying equal access to, or discriminating against, any student desiring to conduct a meeting on school premises, when the meeting deals with religious, political, or philosophical subjects.

Individual states have passed legislation that affects sport managers. It is impractical to list all, or even a small percentage, of state statutes. However, there are a few subjects that are appropriate to mention.

1. **Athlete Agent statutes.** Beginning in 1981, when California adopted the first statute attempting to regulate athlete agents, at least 32 states have adopted laws seeking to protect prospective professional athletes (Wolohan, 2003). Due to the differences in the various state statutes, there was no consistency among the acts in those states that attempted to regulate ath-

lete agents. The NCAA and other organizations sought to standardize the various state provisions, ultimately culminating in the passage of the **Uniform Athlete Agents Act** on November 30, 2000, by the National Conference of Commissioners on Uniform State Laws. It should be noted that this is not a federal statute, but merely a model for states to use in passing legislation.

As of July 30, 2004, the Act has been passed by 32 states or territories and has been introduced as legislation in several other states. The Uniform Law Commissioners have stated the purpose of the Act:

This act provides for the uniform registration, certification, and background check of sports agents seeking to represent student athletes who are or may be eligible to participate in intercollegiate sports. The act also imposes specified contract terms on these agreements to the benefit of student athletes, and provides educations [sic] institutions with a right to notice along with a civil cause of action for damages resulting from a breach of specified duties.

The provisions of the suggested uniform Act are available on the Internet at http://www.law.upenn.edu/bll/ulc/uaaa/aaa1130.htm.

2. **Sovereign Immunity**. The theory of **sovereign immunity** has existed for thousands of years and can best be summed up by the maxim that "the king can do no wrong." Under this theory, the state cannot be held liable for any act, unless it agrees to accept liability. While some states retain this protection, other states have **waived** or given up the right to be immune from liability. Most of these statutes are referred to as **tort claims acts**, indicating that the state has agreed to accept liability for certain tort claims. The state laws vary widely, from states that have waived liability in all cases to those that have waived liability only under limited circumstances.

3. **Recreational Use statutes**. Acknowledging the social benefits of recreational activities, state legislatures became concerned by the upsurge in lawsuits against owners of recreational facilities by injured participants. Reacting to the threat that lawsuits would cause these facilities to close, state legislatures passed laws that provide liability protection to the owners and operators. The statutes protect them by placing responsi-

bility for injury on the participant who voluntarily assumed the risk. Generally, as long as the assumed risk is inherent to the activity, the injured party cannot sue for damages. Legislation of this type has been passed in virtually every state and covers activities such as equestrian activities, snow skiing, roller skating, whitewater rafting, snowmobiling, amusement rides, and, in a few cases, provides protection for "any sport or recreational opportunity" (Spengler & Burket, 2001). Since these are state laws, each state protects different activities, so be aware of your state's protections.

4. **Charitable Immunity**. In addition to the benefits of recreational activities, legislatures have recognized the value of charitable organizations, such as youth sport programs that provide services and activities to citizens. Many states (and the federal government) have passed statutes that provide liability protection for **charitable organizations** that operate sports or recreational activities. For states that do not have such statutes, the federal **Volunteer Protection Act** (42 U.S.C. § 14501, et. seq.) provides protection (for individuals, only, not organizations) unless the state has specifically chosen not to be covered by the Act. Most of these statutes provide protection to volunteers, employees, and the organization, so long as the organization has insurance in the amount required by the statute to cover losses sustained by injured participants.

Tort Law

A **tort** is a civil wrong—other than a breach of contract—for which an injured party can recover damages. The basic premise of tort law is that a person who is damaged by the unlawful acts of another is entitled to recover his/her losses (**damages**) from the person causing the harm. In other words, the person responsible for the harm bears the financial loss. There are three categories of torts: intentional torts, negligence, and strict liability.

Intentional torts occur when the party acting wrongfully (called the "**tortfeasor**") intends to cause the harm by committing the act that causes the injury. For example, a group of experienced players engage in hazing activities to initiate their new teammates. A team member who sustains an injury has grounds to file a lawsuit against those who caused his/her injury. (Incidentally, not only is **hazing** an intentional tort, but

most states have enacted statutes making hazing a criminal offense.) Other intentional torts include assault, battery, defamation (i.e., libel and slander), invasion of privacy, etc.

Negligence is described as the failure to exercise ordinary care, or the degree of care that the law requires, by acting differently than a person of ordinary care would have acted under the same or similar circumstances. Negligence is an unintentional tort, where the responsible party acted without the intent to commit the act, or to cause harm or injury to the plaintiff. Most tort lawsuits are prosecuted under this theory, by alleging that the defendant has acted negligently, thus causing harm or injury to the plaintiff.

To decide whether the defendant has acted with ordinary care, the court will apply the **standard** known as the "**reasonably prudent person**" standard. The court will determine if the defendant acted as a reasonably prudent person would have acted under the same or similar circumstances. If so, then there is no negligence. If not, then the defendant acted negligently (assuming the other elements of negligence are present). For example, when a player is injured by lightening when a coach fails to end soccer practice after several nearby lightening strikes, the coach has not acted as a reasonably prudent coach would have acted under those circumstances. Even though being struck by lightening is normally considered an "Act of God," the coach is negligent and is liable for the injuries the plaintiff sustained.

In addition to negligence, you will study gross negligence, which falls somewhere between the standards of intentional torts and negligence. **Gross negligence** is acting in such a reckless manner that the court will consider that the defendant exhibited a conscious indifference toward the safety of the plaintiff, even though the defendant did not intend to injure the plaintiff. Driving while under the influence of alcohol or drugs is the classic example of gross negligence.

Strict liability is the tort theory of liability without fault. This theory is usually associated with products liability discussed below.

You will also study various defenses to tort liability, including the concepts of assumption of risk, waivers and agreements to participate, indemnification agreements, procedural noncompliance, sovereign immunity, charitable immunity, and recreation and Good Samaritan statutes protections.

Risk Management Procedures

Although this book contains a more detailed discussion of Risk Management in the facility and event management chapter, risk management entails more than providing a safe setting for participants and spectators. As Cotten and Wolohan state in their book *Law for Recreation and Sport Managers*, "Risk management is much more than just safety or preventing accidents—it is an organized plan by which a recreation or sport business can manage or control both the programmatic risks and the financial risks facing the organization" (Cotton & Wolohan, 2003).

Therefore, risk management not only includes identifying and reducing potential risks, but developing, implementing, and managing a written **risk management plan**. Successful organizations incorporate various concerns into risk management plans, such as employment and personnel practices, supervision, security, emergency care, crisis management, insurance, transportation, and legal issues involved in the operation and administration of the organization.

Crowd Control and Security

Although crowd control and security is a separate content area in the NASPE/NASSM standards, it is covered sufficiently in the facility and event management chapter.

Products Liability

A person who is injured by an object may be allowed to recover for his/her injuries under the concept of **products liability**. The theory is that a person who places a defective product into use is liable for the harm it causes. Virtually everyone involved in the design, manufacture, distribution, or sale of the product might be held liable.

Products liability encompasses three distinct concepts: negligence, breach of warranty, and strict liability. The first theory asserts negligence in the manufacture or design of the product or negligence for failure to warn purchasers of the dangers associated with the product. One case held the manufacturer liable for injuries sustained by a baseball player when his sunglasses were hit by a ball and shattered, causing loss of his eye, because the lenses were designed and manufactured to be too thin (*Filer v. Rayex Corp.,* 1970).

The second concept involves a **breach of warranty** by the defendant. A **warranty** is a promise or guarantee that products will comply with a certain standard. In such a case, the plaintiff alleges that the goods do not comply with the guaranteed standards. The "Golfing Gizmo" (a golf ball attached to an elasticized string) included in the instructions the statement, "completely safe ball will not hit player." While hitting the ball, a 13 year old suffered head injuries. The court held that the plaintiff should recover because the manufacturer/seller was liable for breaching its warranty that the gizmo was completely safe (*Hauter v. Zogarts*, 1975).

The Supreme Court of New Mexico has described the purpose of strict liability "to allow an injured consumer to recover against a seller or manufacturer without the requirement of proving ordinary negligence. Its goal is to protect the injured consumer" (*Aalco Manufacturing Co. v. City of Espanola*, 1980). In this case, the plaintiff was injured by a falling volleyball net standard, and the court held that the manufacturer was liable even though it did not negligently cause the injury. The strict liability theory also applies to the manufacture and sale of items that are unreasonably dangerous to the user of the product.

Summary

There is no area of sport management that is not impacted by "the law." For every category within the discipline, there is a special set of rules and regulations that impact virtually every decision you will make. This chapter is designed to introduce you to general principles of law involved in sport management, including

- a basic understanding of the law and how it works,

- the sources of law in the United States,

- the different methods of resolving disputes, and

- the body of law that applies to sport in America.

Neither this chapter nor your further study of the legal aspects of sport will make you a lawyer. The purpose of this chapter is to make you aware of legal issues when (or before) they arise, not to teach you to make legal decisions. Each fact situation is unique and may involve many rules of law or exceptions to the general rules you will learn. If in doubt, get a legal opinion from your lawyer. The best money you will ever spend is the cost to avoid problems before they arise.

Post Script – Representing Professional Athletes

"Show me the money!" has become the mantra of agents, and those who dream of representing professional athletes in negotiating their contracts, coordinating their business and financial dealings, and basically acting as a clearinghouse of information for the player. An **agent** is a person who is authorized to transact business or manage some affair for another person. The perceived glamour, prestige, and financial reward of being an agent attract many students, who envision themselves as a real-life Jerry Maguire.

When asked their career goal, a substantial percentage of sport management students express an interest in being an agent or working for an agency. These students have seen the cinematic *Jerry Maguire* and have read the exploits of agents in newspapers, books, and magazines. As an introduction to sport management, this book is designed to assist students in making appropriate career choices. Accordingly, it is appropriate to discuss the challenges and realities involved in becoming a player agent.

In *The Agent Game*, one of the earliest books examining the agent business, author Ed Garvey highlighted the criteria to become an agent: "How does someone become an agent? The answer is simple: find a client. If you have an athlete as a client who wants to play professional football, basketball, soccer, tennis, baseball, or hockey, *you are an agent*. Congratulations" (Garvey, 1984). Unfortunately, while a student may eventually become certified as an agent, successfully recruiting a client or securing employment with a player representation firm is extremely unlikely.

As the Executive Director of the National Football League Players Association at the time, Garvey wrote his book in an effort to educate prospective professional athletes about the perils of dealing with agents. He outlines some of the realities of dealing with agents ("each agent has to out promise the competition") and some of the unethical tricks-of-the-trade used to sign players, then reaches the conclusion that for agents, "recruitment, not performance, is the key" (Garvey, 1984).

In the 20+ years since Garvey's book was published, all of the professional players' associations have adopted strict rules regulating the actions of agents representing players, but recruitment of clients remains the most important aspect of being an agent. It is unrealistic to expect that a recent college graduate would be able to out-recruit established agents, with their impressive client lists, previous experience, and financial investments in the recruiting process.

The opportunity to secure employment with an established firm is also rare for newly graduated students. One well-known agent, who represents dozens of clients in various sports, has said that he and his partner received an average of more than 200 letters a month from students—including undergraduate, graduate, and law students—seeking a job or internship with his firm. In over 20 years, this two-man firm had hired only secretarial employees and not a single prospective agent.

Taking into account the perils of seeking employment as an agent, students should proceed at their own risk, acknowledging that the odds against them are monumental. One Internet source asserts that there are over 25,000 individuals who act as sport agents in the U.S., and about 3,500 of those agents are certified (Sports Agency Directory, 2004). As Garvey said, "The number of agents is astounding. . . How can so many agents make a living in this business? The answer is, they can't."

Follow your dreams, but understand the challenges ahead. The purpose of this section is not to discourage you, but to present relevant information so that you can make educated choices.

References

A few facts about the uniform athlete agent act. Retrieved October 13, 2004, from http://www.nccusl.org/Update/uniformact_factsheets/uniformacts-fs-aaa.asp.

Appenzeller, H. (1998). *Risk management in sport*. Durham, NC: Carolina Academic Press.

Black's law dictionary (8ᵗʰ ed.) (2004). St. Paul, MN: West Group.

Carpenter, L. J. (2003). Gender equity: opportunities to participate. In D. Cotton & J. Wolohan (Eds.), *Law for recreation and sport managers* (3ʳᵈ ed., pp. 548-558). Dubuque, IA: Kendall/Hunt Publishing Company.

Cotton, D. J., & Wolohan, J. T. (2003). *Law for Recreation and Sport Managers* (3rd ed.). Dubuque, IA: Kendall/Hunt Publishing Company.

Davis, T. (2001). What is sports law? 11 Marq. Sports L. Rev. 211, 214.

Garvey, E. The Agent Game 13, (Washington, DC: Federation of Professional Athletes, AFL-CIO 1984).

Giamatti, A. B. (1988). Morality strikes out, address before the justinian society, Chicago. *The Sports Lawyer, 6,* 1-3.

Glossary of Terms, Retrieved on October 13, 2004, from http://www.njleg.state.nj.us/legislativepub/glossary.asp.

Letter to Benjamin Waring, 1801.

Year end report of the federal judiciary (2003). Retrieved September 19, 2004, from, http://www.supremecourtus.gov/publicinfo/year-end/2003year-endreport.html.

Spengler, J. O., & Burket, B. P. (2001). Sport Safety Statutes and Inherent Risk: A Comparison Study of Sport Specific Legislation, *J. Legal Aspects of Sport 11,* 135.

Sports Agency Directory, Retrieved on October 13, 2004, from http://www.prosportsgroup.com/SportsAgentDirectory/features.htm.

Wolohan, J. T. (2003). Sport agent legislation. In D. Cotton & J. Wolohan (Eds.), *Law for recreation and sport managers* (3rd ed.). Dubuque, IA: Kendall/Hunt Publishing Company.

530 U.S. 290 (2000).

42 U.S.C. § 2000e-2.

42 U.S.C. § 12101(b)(1).

15 U.S.C. § 1.

U. S. Const. art. I, § 8, cl. 8.

17 U.S.C. 102(a).

Aalco Manufacturing Co. v. City of Espanola, 618 P.2D 1230 (NM 1980).

Brentwood Academy v. Tennessee Secondary School Athletic Assoc., 531 U.S 288, 295 (2001).

Brentwood, 531 U.S. at 298

Clarett v. National Football League, 369 F.3d 124, 143 (2ⁿᵈ Cir. 2004).

DeFrantz v. United States Olympic Committee, 492 F. Supp. 1181 (D.D.C. 1980), affirmed without opinion in 701 F. 2d 221 (Table) (D.C. Circuit 1980).

Filer v. Rayex Corp., 435 F.2d 336 (7ᵗʰ Cir. 1970).

Hauter v. Zogarts, 534 P.2d 377 (CA 1975).

NCAA v. Tarkanian, 488 U.S. 179 (1988).

Wong, G. (2002). *Essentials of sports law* (3ʳᵈ ed.). Westport, CT: Praeger Publishers.

Weiler, P., & Roberts, G. (2004). *Sports and the law: Text, cases and problems* (3ʳᵈ ed.). St. Paul, MN: West Group.

Suggested Readings

Champion, W. (2000). *Sports law in a nutshell.* St Paul, MN: West Group.

Cotten, D., & Wolohan, J. (2003). *Law for recreation and sport managers* (3ʳᵈ ed.). Dubuque, IA: Kendall/Hunt Pub Co.

Dougherty, N., Goldberger, A., & Carpenter, J. (2002). *Sport, physical activity, and the law* (2ⁿᵈ ed.). Champaign, IL: Sagamore Publishing.

Suggs, W. (2005). *A place on the team : The triumph and tragedy of Title IX.* Princeton, NJ: Princeton University Press.

Chapter Eleven

Sport Governance
Dennis Phillips

"Come with us, Clem. You know the rules:
No celebrating in the end zone after a touchdown."

Learning Objectives

Upon completion of this chapter, the reader should be able to

■ Discuss the origin and purpose of governing bodies;

■ Identify the differences between governing bodies;

■ Explain the benefits of membership in a governing body;

■ Understand the governance legislative process in sport;

■ Outline the principles and bylaws of the NCAA; and

■ Discuss the legal issues associated with governing bodies.

Introduction

As you race to the cafeteria to grab a quick bite of breakfast before your morning class, you notice the headline in the local newspaper stating that an Olympic athlete lost his medal because of a positive drug test for a banned performance-enhancing substance. Between classes, you hear two athletes discussing a new financial aid rule passed by the NCAA. Walking across campus you see a bulletin board flyer announcing an organizational rules meeting for all teams interested in participating in the intramural flag football league. After classes you go to the swimming pool for a workout and see signs on the wall from the Red Cross explaining mandatory safety procedures and CPR techniques. At dinner you flip the channel to ESPN's SportsCenter and hear about a new NFL disciplinary rule governing touchdown celebrations. In one day you have seen several indications of governance and policy development at work within the sport industry.

> "SPORT IS BEST GOVERNED AUTONOMOUSLY. LIKE UNIVERSITIES AND THEATRES, SPORTS ARE INTERMEDIATE SOCIAL INSTITUTIONS WHICH NEED PROTECTION FROM DAY-TO-DAY PARTISAN POLITICAL PRESSURES—BUT THEIR AUTONOMY IS ONLY VALUABLE IN SO FAR AS IT HELPS THEM TO PROMOTE AND PROTECT THE PUBLIC GOOD WHICH THEY GOVERN."
>
> SUNDER KATWALA

It is difficult to imagine the world of sport without organization or rules. What would sport be like without referees, league officials, commissioners, event managers, sport medicine personnel, scoreboard operators, or timekeepers making policy, enforcing rules, or following guidelines? Even children playing wiffle ball in a back yard establish an agreed-upon set of rules and boundaries to enjoy play. The sport continuum runs from relatively unstructured recreational play, through the various levels of club and youth sport leagues, to the more highly controlled contests of interscholastic and intercollegiate competition, and finally to the elite level of amateur and professional athletic achievement. As different as the participants and goals may be, they all share at least one thing in common: their actions are governed by someone or a group with authority, control, and power.

Importance of Sport Governance

A practice used by some sports reporters when writing a game summary is known as the "5 Ws and an H." A report of "Who," "What," "When," "Where," "Why," and "How" will "cover all the bases" of content needed to explain the story. That same technique may be used to explore the importance of governance in sport.

The "What"

Let's first start with the "*What*." What do we mean by the term "governance"? The Merriam-Webster Dictionary (2004) definition of governance is "to control and direct the making and administration of policy" (p. 313). Other descriptors could include "direct," "influence," "determine," "regulate," and "restrain." Authors Hums and MacLean (2004) operationally defined sport governance:

> Sport governance is the exercise of power and authority in sport organizations, including policy making, to determine organizational mission, membership, eligibility, and regulatory power, within the organization's appropriate local, national, or international scope. (p. 5)

Governance is usually recognized in terms of the power and authority vested in amateur and professional sport organizations at the municipal, state, national, and international levels. Local sport groups such as the Hattiesburg, Mississippi, Youth Soccer Association (HYSA), and Oak Grove, Mississippi, Dixie Youth Baseball Association, administer youth sport programs in the local community. The Pennsylvania Interscholastic Athletic Association Inc. (PIAA) is an example of a state level organization that develops policy and enforces rules governing athletic competition among nearly 350,000 athletes at approximately 1,420 public and private schools.

At the national level, amateur sport agencies such as the Amateur Athletic Union (AAU), the National Federation of State High School Associations (NFHS),

USA Track and Field (USATF), and the National Intramural-Recreational Sports Association (NIRSA) regulate sport and recreational activities. Examples of professional sport organizations include Major League Baseball (MLB), the Professional Golf Association (PGA), the Women's National Basketball Association (WNBA), and the National Association for Stock Car Auto Racing (NASCAR). International governing organizations include the International Olympic Committee (IOC), the Federation Internationale de Football Association (FIFA), which governs soccer (football), and the Federation Internationale de Gymnastique (FIG), the organization for international gymnastics competitions.

The "Why"

It is apparent then, that governing agencies are a common and extremely important part of the sport industry, but "*Why*" study it? For those who wish to engage in sport as their vocational pursuit, there are many reasons why knowledge of organizational governance will prove beneficial. A sport manager at the community level will need knowledge of local government structures and politics in order to effectively achieve budgetary approval for community recreational programs. An athletic administrator involved in intercollegiate athletics will need to know the legislative process of the NCAA in order to enact new rules and regulations. Detailed knowledge of the rules and regulations regarding eligibility, financial aid, and recruiting will enable the organization to act ethically in the pursuit of competitive excellence and avoid costly and embarrassing rule violations.

Awareness of governing principles of organizations will promote a smooth working relationship with your superiors and an understanding and appreciation of the functions of various committees and departments within your company. You will also appreciate the "big picture" of how various agencies within and outside of your industry segment relate and effectively interact with one another.

The "Who"

The "*Who*" of sport governance focuses on the leadership positions within an organization. Sport governing agencies, like all businesses, rely heavily on top-level management leadership to strategically plan for the fu-

ture, formulate and implement policy, and communicate the mission and goals of the organization. The leadership methods used by governing bodies of sport come in a variety of packages; however, there are some common practices familiar to most sport organizations. All organizations have membership requirements with specific dues, application documents, regulations, and minimal qualifications for acceptance in good standing with the group. When the large group of members gathers together for meetings, conventions, or special events such as conference tournaments, The Final Four, College World Series, etc., the body is frequently called a General Assembly, General Business Meeting, or Congress. Organizational business is conducted and policies developed and voted upon by the membership after a "quorum," or majority, of available attendees has been established.

The membership representatives are selected according to the bylaws and constitution guidelines of the organization, and the sessions are conducted under a set of established procedures common to most "official" business meetings called **Robert's Rules of Order**. These procedures assure legislative fairness, maximum participation, and an orderly process by participants, while protecting individuals from domination by certain vocal sub-groups. Membership can revise the bylaws or constitution by an overwhelming 2/3 vote of the assembly.

©iStockphoto.com

While most General Assemblies are composed of volunteer members of the organization, there is often a need for permanent, paid staff to conduct the business of the organization in between convention and business meetings. These full-time staff members are often referred to as the Executive Staff. The Executive Staff is frequently led by a person with a title such as Executive Director, Chairman of the Board, President, Chief Executive Officer (CEO), or Chief Operating Officer (COO). The staff assisting the leader usually consists of functional managers in charge of such areas as membership services, eligibility, marketing and sponsorship, finance and budgeting, publications and printing, media and public relations, administration, conference and special event planning, legislative advocacy, and educational services. These individuals are paid employees, located at a centralized headquarters to perform the tasks of the daily organizational business. Generally they work through committees comprised of selected membership with specific expertise and responsibilities, who gather together periodically to conduct particular tasks.

Annual or continuous tasks are completed by permanent *standing* committees. Finance, budget, championship, enforcement, legislative action, and appeals committees usually fall under the *standing* category. Single use, temporary committees assigned with a specific responsibility are frequently called "*ad hoc*," or *single-use planning* or *task force* committees. Tasks that require special problem-solving for non-programmed events—such as dealing with recruiting scandals, internet gambling abuse, penalties for distribution and use of an illegal performance-enhancing substance, or security plans for a sport venue following terrorist threats—are examples of directives assigned to a task force. Upon completion of the assigned responsibility, the committee will permanently disband.

The "How"

About now, the question of "*How*" may be surfacing in your thought patterns. How do sport groups get things done? How are they structured in order to be effective and efficient? We may have leaders and staff who guide the organization and membership who participate and financially support it, but how is it all organized? Are there management principles that help organize a sport unit in the process of delegating, coordinating tasks, and distributing human, financial, and informational resources to achieve objectives? The answer, of course, is yes. These principles guide the governance of a sport body by establishing the scope of authority, clarifying an individual's responsibility, coordination in task completion, and supervising employees. The principle of **Unity of Command** states that an employee should only have one boss to which he or she reports. The **Scalar Principle** refers to the Chain of Command that denotes a clear line of authority from the top to the bottom of the organiza-

tion. This principle shows who your immediate boss is, as well as those whom you supervise. Another principle is the **Division of Labor**, a directive that shows the separation of departments by function or specialization, such as marketing, finance, accounting, event management, media relations, or athletic training. The **Span of Management** principle refers to the number of employees reporting to a specific manager. Factors that affect this principle include the complexity and safety of the task, the experience and competence of the employees, the experience and competence of the manager, and the size of the organization. The greater the span of management, the broader the organizational chart. Lower level managers tend to supervise a larger number of employees; with a narrower span of management, the higher one ascends (Lussier & Kimball, 2004).

An organizational chart is generally used to represent a business structure. Lussier and Kimball (2004) defined an organizational chart as "a graphic illustration of the organization's management hierarchy and departments and their working relationships" (p. 152). See Chapter 4 for more discussion of organizational structure.

How can organizational charts help sport management graduates entering their first job or starting a new job in the sport industry? Organizational charts can provide great insight into the kind of organization environment in which you are employed. For example, if the chart appears to be very steep, with many levels of management, then it is probably a "tall" organization with a bureaucracy that involves many levels of managers or committees and decision making centralized at the top levels of leadership. If, however, the chart appears to be shallow and broad, it is probably a "flat" structure, characterized by few levels of management and decentralized decision making. Immediate and effective response to customer service is critical in today's sport industry, and "flat" organizations are often able to respond more quickly to the needs of their sport customers.

A recent example of this occurred during a "mystery shopper" adventure conducted by a consulting firm at a National Football League game. The mystery shopper played the role of a fan claiming to have lost his ticket and needing help from the guest services personnel to find a seat for the game. The NFL team customer service employee had the authority to make rapid decisions without going through many management channels in order to best serve the customer. The shopper was pleased at the rapid resolution to his problem and gave a positive report to executives of the team (R. B. Crow, personal communication, September 2, 2004).

Sport governing bodies can be organized in a variety of ways, the most common of which are by

1) function,

2) geographic location,

3) product line, and

4) customer segment.

The "When"

The question of "*When*" governance began in American sport can only be answered by going back to the historical foundations of organized amateur sport in the U.S. Organizations like the Young Men's Christian Association (YMCA), the Amateur Athletic Union (AAU), the National Collegiate Athletic Association (NCAA), and the National Federation of State High School Associations (NFHS) were extremely influential in the development of amateur sport in the United States. Each association faced challenges in developing rules, regulations, and policies during the early stages of its organizational life. Eligibility, amateurism, financial support, administrative and coaching leadership, equipment conformity and safety, and legislative control were just a few of the issues these early governing bodies had to face during their infancy. It became apparent that each organization needed a statement of its core values and operating philosophy in order to provide a compass for the direction the group would take.

For many sport associations, a mission or vision statement helped provide that direction. A mission statement, according to Bridges and Roquemore (2000), "is the broadest of objectives and defines the purpose

and uniqueness of the organization regarding its products, services, markets, and revenues" (p. 124). Every governing body of sport has a purpose for its existence and a unique quality that makes it unique. A brief summary of a few of the early governing bodies of sport and their origins, mission, growth and present day influence will help us discover "*When*" sport governance began.

The Young Men's Christian Association (YMCA)

George Williams founded the YMCA in London, England, in 1844, in response to declining moral, social, and cultural changes in English society following the Industrial Revolution. The organization, which mixed an emphasis on spiritual principles with athletic fitness and competition, rapidly grew and opened in the U.S. in 1851. The YMCA began to develop a fourfold purpose: "The improvement of the spiritual, mental, social, and physical condition of young men" (YMCA, 2004, p. 1). The successful formula of combining "inspiration and perspiration" led to a growth in fitness and sport programs as swimming pools and gymnasiums were built. By the 1890s, the mission had been narrowed to include the present day symbol of the inverted triangle representing the unification of mind, body, and spirit. The organization was blessed with gifted young leaders and inventors like James Naismith (basketball – 1891), William Morgan (volleyball – 1895), and Joe Sobek (racquetball – 1950). The network of national and international YMCAs provided an easy vehicle for the spread of such sports and activities to a worldwide audience. Today, the 2,500 YMCAs make it one of the largest not-for-profit community service organizations in America, working to meet the health and social service needs of 18.9 million men, women, and children in 10,000 communities in the United States. YMCAs stretch beyond the United States and are located in more than 120 countries around the world (YMCA, 2004).

Mission Statement

The YMCA mission is "to put Christian principles into practice through programs that build healthy spirit, mind, and body for all" (YMCA, p. 1).

The Amateur Athletic Union (AAU)

The Amateur Athletic Union is one of the oldest and largest multi-sport governing bodies in the United States. Formed in 1888, its original purpose was to bring uniformity and standards to amateur sport. The AAU quickly became the dominant sport organization in America and the driving force in representing our country in all international sport competitions, including the Olympic Games. The role of the AAU changed, however, following the enactment of the Amateur Sports Act of 1988 that established an official governing body for international sport, the United States Olympic Committee (USOC). The AAU then focused on the programming of the largest grass roots venture for sport competition, with over 50,000 volunteers helping administer over 250 national championships for over 500,000 participants. In 1996, the Disney Corporation and the AAU formed a strategic alliance to further the goals of each organization. The outgrowth of their partnership was *Disney's Wide World of Sports* complex, which is home to more than 40 national AAU events each year (AAU, 2004).

Mission Statement

The AAU mission is "to offer amateur sports programs through a volunteer base for all people to have the physical, mental, and moral development of amateur athletes and to promote good sportsmanship and good citizenship" (AAU, 2004).

National Federation of State High School Associations (NFHS)

The National Federation is a prime example of an organization formed to meet the needs of a growing program of interscholastic athletic competition. Interscholastic sport developed quickly in America during the late 1800s. Football became a very popular spectator and participant sport in the 1890s but suffered from some of the same ills as its intercollegiate counterparts. Problems such as increasing violence and injury, the overemphasis of winning, the use of ineligible players, and financial mismanagement were rampant (Rader, 1999). The need for adult supervision and a centralized organization with the authority to set minimum, consistent standards was apparent to many state association leaders. In 1902, the Fifteenth Conference on Academies and High Schools met and issued basic recommendations to initiate faculty and state association control of interscholastic sports. Upper Midwest states such as Illinois, Wisconsin, and Michigan had already organized state associations by the first decade of the 1900s, and rules governing minimum course loads, satisfactory progress, participation standards, and even basic rules controlling play were enacted to ensure fair and equitable competitions (Covell, 1998).

In 1920, the Midwest Federation of State High School Athletic Associations was formed when representatives of Illinois, Indiana, Iowa, Michigan, and Wisconsin met to discuss high school athletic competitions. Student-athlete welfare issues were discussed, as well as consistent rules for competitions across state boundaries. By 1923, the organization changed its name to accommodate new state associations, and the group became known as the National Federation of State High School Athletic Associations. The name remained unchanged until fine arts were added during the 1970s and the word "athletics" was dropped from the organizational title. (NFHS, 2004a).

Today, the organization represents 50 state associations and the District of Columbia. The NFHS works with over 17,346 high schools and almost 10 million students. The organization promotes educational programs in areas such as sportsmanship, citizenship, gender equity, sexual harassment, hazing prevention, drug and alcohol prevention, academic eligibility and participation standards, and eating disorders. The NFHS also publishes sports and rules books for over 16 interscholastic sports (NFHS, 2004a).

The governance power of high school sports, according to Wong (1994), rests in state and local agencies. School Boards, State Education Associations, State Legislatures, and Coaching Associations wield regulatory power over the conduct of sport programs. The NFHS is a service provider that assists state associations with programs, rather than a sanctioning body with enforcement personnel and penalty provisions. High school extracurricular programs are voluntary, and therefore participation is legally and financially viewed as a privilege rather than a right.

The NFSHA organizational chart consists of several committees that determine the direction of the governing body. At the top is the membership represented by each state association. The *National Council* is the equivalent to a Senate legislative governing body, as it consists of one member from each state association, meeting twice each year to enact legislation and consider bylaw and constitution revisions. The *Board of Directors* is composed of one member from each one of the eight geographic sections of the country and four additional at-large members for a total of twelve members. The Board conducts the business and financial affairs of the organization, approves committees, and oversees the annual budget. The *Executive Director* and *Executive Staff* support the daily activities of the Indianapolis headquarters including marketing, publications, information and member services, convention planning, certifications, educational training, and financial services. The rest of the organizational structure consists of the standing and special committees that administer the various programs and professional organizations of the NFHS.

Mission Statement

"The mission of the National Federation of State High School Associations (NFHS) is to serve its members and its related professional groups by providing leadership and national coordination for the administration of interscholastic activities which will enhance the educational experiences of high school students and reduce risks of their participation.

"The NFHS will promote participation and sportsmanship to develop good citizens through interscholastic activities which provide equitable opportunities, positive recognition and learning experiences to students while maximizing the achievement of educational goals" (NFHS, 2004b).

National Collegiate Athletic Association (NCAA)

One of the most powerful sport governing agencies in the United States is the NCAA. Prompted by the numerous injuries and deaths occurring in football dur-

ing the early 1900s, President Theodore Roosevelt called 13 college presidents and athletic leaders to the White House in 1905 to discuss needed reforms in the game. The outgrowth of that and subsequent meetings was rule reform and the formation of a group to organize college athletics. The Intercollegiate Athletic Association of the United States (IAAUS) was founded in 1906 with 62 members. Four years later, the association changed its name to the present day name of the National Collegiate Athletic Association (NCAA, 2004).

The organization evolved over time from a service-oriented, facilitative group based on the philosophy of "*Home Rule*," or local college control of all aspects of the athletic program, to a sanctioning body with enforcement and policy-making authority and responsibility. Factors that prompted the philosophical change in governance included eligibility and academic fraud, recruiting scandals, financial aid abuse, and amateurism violations. Following World War II, a "*Sanity Code*" was adopted to try to regulate and prevent further abuse in those areas. By 1973, the organization split into three divisions of competition in order to promote unity of likeminded institutions in athletic contests. The NCAA began to administer championships and programs for women in 1981-82, and the organization grew dramatically (NCAA, 2004).

©stock.xchng iv

The organization took a major step forward in 1997, when it reorganized the governance structure. Upon recommendations by the *Knight Foundation Commission on Intercollegiate Athletics*, more autonomy was given to each division for specific division-only matters, and presidential authority was required at all levels of policy making. The new Division I chart includes a Board of Directors composed of 18 college or university presidents charged with the responsibility of dealing with all legislative proposals (NCAA, 2004).

The Division I Management Council is made up of 49 members, most of whom are Athletic Directors. They are a recommending body for the Board of Directors, based on reports received from various committees. The Academic, Eligibility, Compliance, and Championships/Competition Cabinets serve the purpose of giving specific recommendations to the Management Council for reforms.

Mission Statement

"The NCAA is devoted to the expert administration of intercollegiate athletics for its membership. The purpose of the NCAA is to provide programming and deliver national championships for intercollegiate athletes" (NCAA, 2004).

The United States Olympic Committee (USOC)

One of the most visible sport competitions in the world is the Olympic Games. What is the governing body that administers the team and individual programs that compete for the United States in major international events?

The International Olympic Committee (IOC), headquartered in Lausanne, Switzerland, was founded in 1894 and is the umbrella organization that organizes the summer and winter Olympic Games. The IOC is comprised of National Olympic Committees (NOC) from each country that sends athletes to the Games. The NOC of the United States is the *United States Olympic Committee* (USOC).

The USOC was formed in 1978 when the U.S. Congress passed the Amateur Sports Act (now called the Ted Stevens Olympic and Amateur Sports Act) and gave the USOC overall authority to manage and promote the Olympic, Pan American, and Paralympic Games. The USOC is composed of over 78 member

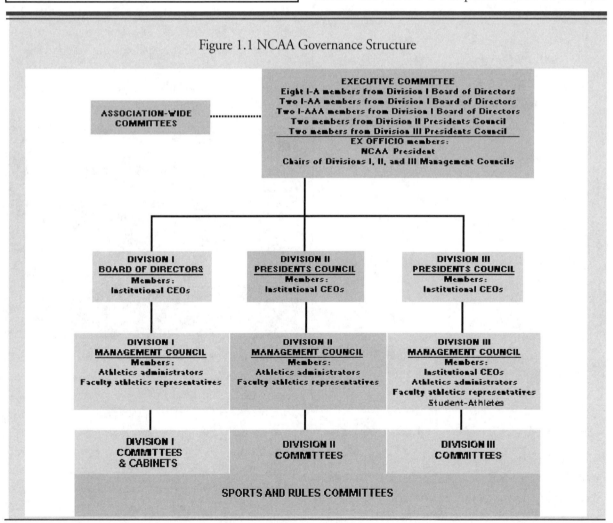

Figure 1.1 NCAA Governance Structure

organizations categorized by Olympic Sport, Pan American Sport, Affiliated Sport, Community-Based Multisport, Education-Based Multisport, and the Armed Forces. Headquartered in Colorado Springs, the USOC employs more than 500 staff, but it also relies heavily upon additional volunteers to run its extensive activities (USOC, 2004).

The USOC has recently undergone the most sweeping changes in its history because of allegations of code of ethics violations, infighting within the organizational leadership, the forced resignation of the President due to resume misstatements, and scandals involving illegal payments to IOC members. An independent commission was appointed by the U.S. Congress, as well as an internal Governance and Ethics Task Force created to investigate actions that had tarnished the image of the USOC.

The process began in 2003, as Bill Martin was named acting president and charged with leading the organization through a difficult time of reform, and culminated in recommendations to develop a more efficient governance structure. Peter Ueberroth, former President of the Los Angeles Olympic Organizing Committee (LAOOC) for the 1984 Olympic Games, will chair the new Board of Directors for the USOC. Ueberroth developed the financial and organizational model currently used by the USOC by managing the first privately financed games in Los Angeles that netted over $238 million profit. He later became commissioner of Major League Baseball.

He will preside over a new structure that will accomplish the following: (1) Reduce the size of the Board of Directors from an unwieldy 125 to 11; (2) Reduce the number of standing committees from 23 to 4; (3) Eliminate an Executive Committee from the governance structure; (4) Refine the mission statement to emphasize support for the U.S. athletes; and (5) Create an Olympic Assembly (USOCa, 2004). According to acting Secretary General Jim Scherr, "The new governance structure will enable the USOC to better fulfill its mission while reaffirming for the American public that its confidence and trust in our organization is well-placed" (2004b, p. 5).

Mission Statement

"Help U.S. and Paralympic athletes achieve sustained competitive excellence and thereby inspire all Americans, and preserve the Olympic ideals" (USOC, 2004b).

Professional Sport Organizations

Professional sport in America has a long and varied history beyond this chapter's discussion. The governance structure of the four major professional organizations, Major League Baseball (MLB), the National Football League (NHL), the National Basketball Association (NBA), and the National Hockey League (NHL) have many similarities. All four have a storied history, with MLB's National League the earliest to form in 1876 (Scully, 1989).

The first professional football league was the American Professional Football Association, created in 1920, which later became the National Football League (NFL) in 1922. The American Basketball League (ABL) was the first pro basketball league and was founded in 1924. After the ABL went out of business, two rival leagues, the Basketball Association of America (BAA) and the National Basketball League (NBL) came into existence, only to join together to become the NBA in 1949. The NHL began in 1917 with four Canadian teams. It expanded to the United States in 1924 (Quirk & Fort, 1992). All of the established leagues have withstood challenges by rival leagues, such as the Players and Federal Leagues in Baseball, American Basketball League, the American Football League and XFL, and the World Hockey League.

The "Big 4" professional leagues all have a number of teams divided into conferences and divisions of competition, usually based on geographical location. MLB has 30 teams divided into the National and American Leagues, each with East, Central, and West Divisions. The NFL has 32 teams divided into the American Football Conference (AFC) and the National Football Conference (NFC). The teams are further divided into North, South, East, and West Divisions. The NBA has 29 teams in an Eastern and Western Conference that is further divided into Atlantic, Central, Midwest, and Pacific Divisions. The NHL has 30 teams in the Eastern and Western Conferences. Northeast, Southeast, Atlantic, Central, Northwest, and Pacific Divisions provide competitions based on proximity (Hums & MacLean, 2004). Further similarities abound in the central governance of these leagues. All of the leagues have a league commissioner, a Board of Governors made up of team owners, a central office to administer daily business, a player's association, and individual teams—each with their own unique structure. All four leagues are headquartered in New York City.

Centralized league functions include security, marketing, policy development, dispute resolution, rule making, disciplinary actions, licensing, public relations, officiating, media coordination and production, and international business operations. Decentralized team functions cover some of the same areas, but with a local orientation. Teams usually have departmental units that focus on individual and group sales, facility security and management, marketing and promotions, concessions and merchandise sales, player development, finance and business operations, community outreach, and legal services.

The "Where"

The "*Where*" can be answered in two ways: *location* and *future*. Where is the location of the governance of sport? Put simply, it is everywhere! It is impossible to imagine organized sport without "organization." Governance gives us consistency with the past and guiding principles for the future. However, where does that future lead us?

Each level of governance has current and future challenges to overcome. Local, state, and national levels of amateur sport face issues of increasing costs of participant health care, increased insurance and product costs involved with the demands of a litigious society, unethical behavior by management, spectators and players, and the safety of athletes. In interscholastic sport, fundraising and sponsorship issues, hazing, funding for extracurricular activities, facility renovation and improvement, home school athlete eligibility, sportsmanship and character development, and a shortage of qualified coaches and officials present hurdles to overcome.

In intercollegiate athletics, issues include

1) maintaining (and in some cases establishing) academic integrity;

2) reducing operational costs;

3) complying with Title IX;

4) meeting the increased demands of television;

5) justifying runaway coaching salaries;

6) combating the use of illegal performance-enhancing substances;

7) dealing with financial aid and amateurism issues;

8) curtailing athlete involvement with agents;

9) increasing awareness about gambling and point-shaving scandals; and

10) reducing early entrance into professional leagues by student-athletes.

Summary

Sport as we know it today would not exist without the formal organizational structure under which teams, leagues, conferences, and governing bodies operate. There are many career opportunities within governing bodies in sport, all of which can be both financially and personally rewarding. As you've read elsewhere in the text, the best way to prepare yourself for these jobs is through volunteering and performing internships. Developing an understanding of the complexities of these various governing bodies will assist you as you prepare for a career in the industry.

Discussion Activities

1. Why do we need governance in Sport? Review the 5 Ws and an H and add a new reason in each area.

2. Locate the mission statement from your local university, and compare it with the mission statement of the athletic department at that school. What are the similarities? What are the differences? Are they in agreeance with each other?

3. Visit the NCAA web site (www.ncaa.org) and examine the organizational diagrams. Who is located at the top of the chart? Why is it structured in this manner?

4. Is the need for governance greater or less in professional sport organizations? Defend your answer.

References

AAU. (2004). *About the AAU*. Retrieved October 30, 2004, from http://www.aausports.org/.

Bridges, F., & Roquemore, L. (2004). *Management for athletic/sport administration: Theory and Practice* (4th ed.). Decatur, GA: ESM Books.

Covell, D. (1998). High school and youth sport. In L. P. Masteralexis, C. A. Barr, & M. A. Hums (Eds.). *Principles and practice of sport management*. Gaithersburg, MD: Aspen Publishing.

Crow, R. B. (September 2, 2004). Personal Communication.

Hums. M., & MacLean, J. (2004). *Governance and policy in sport organizations.* Scottsdale, AZ: Holcomb Hathaway Publishing.

Lussier, R., & Kimball, D. (2004). *Sport management: principles, applications, skill development*. Mason, OH: Thomson Learning South-Western Publishing.

The Merriam-Webster Dictionary (11th ed.). (2004). Springfield, MA: Merriam-Webster Inc.

MPSSAA. (2004). *MPSSAA Organization*. Retrieved October 30, 2004, from http://www.mpssaa.org/intro/organization.

NFHS. (2004a). *About the NFHS*. Retrieved October 30, 2004, from http://www.nfshsa.org/about/htm.

NFHS. (2004b). *National Federation of State High School Associations 2004-2005 Handbook*. Indianapolis, IN: NFHS.

NCAA. (2004). *About the NCAA. Purposes and Goals*. Retrieved October 30, 2004, from http://www.ncaa.org.

Quirk, J. & Fort, R. (1992). Pay Dirt: The Business of Professional Team Sports. Princeton, NJ. Princeton University Press.

Rader, B. C. (1999). *American sports: From the age of folk games to the age of televised sports* (4th ed.). Upper Saddle River, NJ: Prentice Hall.

Russell Athletic Corp. (2004). *About Russell Athletic*. Retrieved October 30, 2004, from http://www.russellathletic.com.

Scully, G.W. (1989). The Business of Major League Baseball. Chicago, Ill. The University of Chicago Press.

USOC. (2004a). *United States Olympic Committee*. Retrieved October 30, 2004, from http:// www.usolympicteam.com.

USOC. (2004b, June 14, 2004). *USOC Pressbox*. Retrieved October 30, 2004, from http:// www.usolympicteam.com.

YMCA. (2004). *YMCA History*. Retrieved October 30, 2004, from http://www.ymca.net/index.jsp.

Suggested Reading

Juico, P. (2000). *Sports & governance: Pole-vaulting into the 21st century*. Malate, Manila: De La Salle University Press.

Kluka, D., Stier, W., Schilling, G., & Smyth, A. (Eds.) (2003). *Perspectives: Sport governance*. Berlin, GM: Meyer & Meyer.

Quirk, R., & Fort, R. (1999). *Hard ball*. Princeton, NJ: Princeton University Press.

Wong, G. M. (1994). *Essentials of sport law*. Westport, CT: Praeger.

Chapter Twelve

Ethics in the Sport Industry
Lynn Ridinger and T. Christopher Greenwell

"Pound for pound, Louie's the best hockey player in the world."

Learning Objectives

Upon completion of this chapter, the reader should be able to

- ■ Define and understand key terms associated with ethics;

- ■ Demonstrate basic knowledge of ethical theories;

- ■ Examine his or her personal value system;

- ■ Appreciate the role that personal values and professional ethics play in the management of sport organizations;

- ■ Identify the progressive stages of moral development and reasoning;

- ■ Apply the steps of ethical decision making to help resolve ethical dilemmas;

- ■ Understand the role of codes of ethics and understand how codes of ethics are formulated; and

- ■ Discuss the impact socially responsible organizations have on key stakeholder groups.

Introduction

In 1999, Ben Christensen, a pitcher for Wichita State University, purposely threw a pitch at the head of Evansville's Anthony Molina. Actions such as this are common in baseball; however, this case was different. Molina was not in the batter's box, but in the on-deck circle, 24 feet from home plate. Christensen, apparently upset that Molina was timing his warm-up pitches, decided to throw at Molina, striking him in the head. His actions caused major injuries to Molina's left eye, requiring surgery to partially restore his sight. Unfortunately, the story gets worse. Christensen claimed he was doing what he was taught to do. His pitching coach acknowledged teaching him to do this and supported his actions. Further, his head coach was quoted as saying Wichita State was the team actually harmed in the incident because its player was ejected and suspended for the rest of the season (Kindred, 1999). Undeterred by the incident, the Chicago Cubs selected Christensen in the first round of the 1999 draft.

> "SOCRATES STATED, 'THE UNEXAMINED LIFE IS NOT WORTH LIVING . . . ,' PERHAPS WE SHOULD ADAPT IT FOR SPORT AND SUGGEST, 'THE UNEXAMINED SPORT IS NOT WORTH PLAYING . . .'"
>
> ANDY GILLENTINE

This case represents what happens when winning trumps the difference between right and wrong. Christensen, feeling that Molina was benefiting from timing his warm-up pitches, threw at him to keep his competitive advantage. Coaches taught him to react this way because they felt it would help them win. The Cubs drafted him based on his outstanding collegiate pitching record.

The Christensen case is not an isolated occurrence, as we see violence in other sports such as hockey, where, in 2004, Todd Bertuzzi of the Vancouver Canucks blindsided Colorado Avalanche forward Steve Moore with a punch, and then rode him to the ice, fracturing his neck and inflicting facial injuries (Dater, 2004). Incidents do not have to be violent to cause harm to others. Teams using ineligible players, players using performance-enhancing drugs, hiring discrimination against women and minorities by sport organizations, coaches cheating to gain a competitive advantage, professional teams circumventing salary caps, and academic fraud in college athletics are all common examples of unethical behavior in sport. This is problematic, as the sport industry prides itself on providing wholesome entertainment, promoting positive values, building character, and creating good role models. Unethical behavior threatens all of the positive benefits.

Ethics and Morals

The terms ethics and morals are sometimes used interchangeably, but they are different. Ethics deals with theories or principles, whereas morals have a more practical base and take into account social values, motives, and attitudes (DeSensi & Rosenberg, 2003). **Ethics** can be defined as a set of principles or values that are used to determine right and wrong. **Morals** are the fundamental baseline values that dictate appropriate behavior within a culture or society (Solomon, 1992). For example, most societies have the moral value that murder is wrong. Other types of conduct, however, may not be as clear. Providing a token of appreciation as a means to gain favor may be viewed simply as a gift in some societies, whereas that same token might be considered a bribe in another culture.

Billington (1988) identified six characteristics of ethical or moral questions:

1) **Dealing with questions of ethics and morals is unavoidable.** As long as one lives among and interacts with others, moral issues will arise and ethical decisions will need to be made.

2) **Moral decisions involve other people.** There is no such thing as a private ethics.

3) **Not all decisions have ethical implications.** Moral decisions are reserved for those ideals that matter most to a society, such as honesty, fairness, respect, and integrity.

4) **Ethical decisions offer no final answers.** Philosophers usually do not provide definitive right or wrong answers. Some ethical theories and actions may be shown to be more reasonable and correct than others, but rarely can a completely satisfactory solution be achieved.

5) **A central element of morality is choice.** Ethical dilemmas are associated with a variety of options or actions that can be taken.

6) **The aim of moral reasoning is to discover the right or correct form of behavior.** Because there are a variety of competing ethical theories and none without some weakness, no action can be declared as absolutely correct or incorrect. Nevertheless, through moral analysis, an appeal to ethical principles can be made and certain decisions may be deemed more justifiable than others.

Ethical Theories

The most widely accepted ethical theories are either teleological, deontological, or some combination of the two (Branvold, 2001). Theories based on **teleology** (from the Greek meaning "end") focus on the consequences of an action and weigh the benefits against the costs. A popular teleological theory is **utilitarianism**, whereby morality is assessed by whether or not the action creates the greatest good for the greatest number of people. In applying utilitarian decision making, the good of the group supersedes the good of the individual. For example, a coach may decide to play a star athlete to increase the chance of victory for the team despite the fact that the player is not fully recovered from an ankle injury.

Deontology (derived from the Greek for "duty") is based on the idea of absolute rules of moral behavior. Immanuel Kant provided the foundation for this approach with his categorical imperative statements. According to Kant, moral action 1) is universal and understandable to everyone in a similar situation, 2) demonstrates respect for the individual, and 3) is acceptable to all rational beings. Critics feel that this theory is too vague and that it does not address the issue of conflicting individual rights. In the previous example, would the action be considered moral under Kant's theory? Would all coaches in a similar situation keep the injured star in the game? Was respect shown for the individual? Would all rational beings agree that this was the appropriate action? For a more detailed discussion of ethical theories, refer to DeSensi and Rosenberg (2003).

Values

It is often said that sports builds character, provides positive role models, and teaches valuable lessons in teamwork, discipline, and sportsmanship, but there is little evidence to support this belief. Participation in sports does not automatically produce better or worse people (Weinberg & Gould, 2003). Character development is a learned process that involves the adoption and application of various virtues such as compassion, fairness, sportsmanship, and integrity (Shields & Bredemeier, 1995). These virtues are based on values that are instilled by socializing agents such as parents, teachers, coaches, and friends. Societal influences such as culture, religion, educational institutions, and the media also contribute to the formation of values, character, and moral development.

Values provide the foundation of ethics. A description of a person's ethics would revolve around his or her set of values (Hitt, 1990). According to Rokeach (1973), values are enduring beliefs that provide guidance for personal goals and behavior. He classified values into two categories: 1) **terminal values** that relate to end-states of existence (goals), and 2) **instrumental values** that relate to one's mode of conduct (behavior). Terminal values can be viewed as the ends toward which one is striving, whereas instrumental values are the means that one will use to achieve the ends. The ends and the means would be consistent and mutually reinforcing in a unified value system (Hitt, 1990).

Values Clarification Exercise

Listed below are a set of terminal values and a set of instrumental values from *The Nature of Human Values* by Milton Rokeach. To help clarify your own values, analyze the lists in terms of *their relative importance to you.* Choose the five most important values and the five least important values from each list.

Figure 12.1
Values Clarification Exercise

Terminal values

1. A comfortable life – a prosperous life
2. An exciting life – a stimulating, active life
3. A sense of accomplishment – lasting contribution
4. A world at peace – free of war and conflict
5. A world of beauty – beauty of nature and the arts
6. Equality – brotherhood, equal opportunity for all
7. Family security – taking care of loved ones
8. Freedom – independence, free choice
9. Happiness – contentedness
10. Inner harmony – freedom from inner conflict
11. Mature love – sexual and spiritual intimacy
12. National security – protection from attack
13. Pleasure – an enjoyable, leisurely life
14. Salvation – saved, eternal life
15. Self-respect – self-esteem
16. Social recognition – respect, admiration
17. True friendship – close companionship
18. Wisdom – a mature understanding of life

Instrumental values

1. Ambitious – hard-working, aspiring
2. Broadminded – open-minded
3. Capable – competent, effective
4. Cheerful – lighthearted, joyful
5. Clean – neat, tidy
6. Courageous – standing up for your beliefs
7. Forgiving – willing to pardon others
8. Helpful – working for the welfare of others
9. Honest – sincere, truthful
10. Imaginative – daring, creative
11. Independent – self-reliant, self-sufficient
12. Intellectual – intelligent, reflective
13. Logical – consistent, rational
14. Loving – affectionate, tender
15. Obedient – dutiful, respectful
16. Polite – courteous, well-mannered
17. Responsible – dependable, reliable
18. Self-controlled – restrained, self-disciplined

Discussion Questions

- Do you have a unified value system? In other words, do your instrumental values support your terminal values?

- Do you have a good understanding of your own value system? Was it easy for you to determine which values are most and least important? Why or why not?

- Compare your value selection with one or two of your classmates. Do you agree on which values are most and least important? Why or why not?

Values in Sport

There has been a growing concern that the value system of some sport participants, managers, and spectators is in decay. In an effort to combat moral transgressions and emphasize the important role that sports can play in contributing to positive societal values, nearly 50 influential sport leaders gathered for a conference in May of 1999 and issued the **Arizona Sports Summit Accord**. The Accord encourages greater emphasis on the ethical and character-building aspects of athletic competition. The goal of formulating this document was to establish a framework of principles and values that would be adopted and practiced widely by those involved with sport organizations. According to the Accord, "the essential elements of character building and ethics in sports are embodied in the concept of sportsmanship and six core principles: trustworthiness, respect, responsibility, fairness, caring, and good citizenship" (Arizona Sports, 1999, p. 2). A sample of the declarations of the Accord are listed below:

- It is the duty of sports leadership, including coaches, athletic administrators, and officials, to promote sportsmanship and foster good character.

- Sports programs must be conducted in a manner that enhances the mental, social, and moral development of athletes.

- Participation in sports is a privilege, not a right. Athletes and coaches have a duty to conduct themselves as role models on and off the field.

- The academic, emotional, and moral well-being of athletes must be placed above desires and pressures to win.

- Coaches and athletes must refrain from disrespectful conduct, such as verbal abuse, taunting, profane trash-talking, and unseemly celebrations.

- Sports programs should adopt codes of conduct for coaches, athletes, parents, spectators and other groups that impact the quality of athletic programs.

- Relationships with corporate sponsors should be continually monitored to ensure against inappropriate exploitation of the sport organization's name or reputation and undue influence of commercial interests.

Discussion Questions

- Do these ideals apply only to youth sports, or are they applicable to all levels of sport?

- What strategies could sport managers implement to promote these ideals?

Go to www.charactercounts.org/sports/strategies.htm and see how your answers compare to the strategies suggested on the website.

Personal and Professional Ethics

Personal values and professional standards of right and wrong do not exist in a social vacuum, nor are they mutually exclusive (Beauchamp, 1988). All organizations, including sport organizations, are guided by beliefs or values that communicate what is important to the organization. A healthy organizational culture is characterized by congruence between the organization's statement of values and the daily behavior of its members (Hitt, 1990). Sound professional ethics begins with good moral behavior of the people associated with an organization. An individual's personal values of honesty, fairness, and integrity will have a social effect through the decisions that he or she makes as a member of an organization. It is important for leaders within sport organizations to clarify the parameters of professional conduct and to set the tone for

merging personal and professional ethics through their own words and actions. Sport managers should express expectations about ethical and moral conduct in the workplace and define for members what is considered acceptable and unacceptable behavior (DeSensi & Rosenberg, 2003).

Moral Development and Reasoning

Even when guidelines for ethical behavior have been established, real-life ethical dilemmas are often complex and require some degree of moral reasoning. The capacity for moral reasoning is dependent upon an individual's level of moral development. **Moral development** refers to a process of growth in which a person's capacity to reason morally is developed through cognitive maturation and experiences. **Moral reasoning** is the decision process in which an individual determines whether a course of action is right or wrong. **Moral behavior** is the execution of an act deemed right or wrong (Weinburg & Gould, 2003).

According to Kohlberg (1987), a leading scholar on moral development, children and adolescents progress through distinct stages of moral reasoning. Kohlberg's model, comprising three levels, each with two stages, is based on the relationship between the individual and the rules and expectations of the society. Level I, **preconventional**, is characterized by a separation between conventions and the individual. This is the moral level of most children under age nine and many adolescent and adult criminals. Level II, **conventional**, is based on a person's conformance to society's rules and is the level of most adolescents and adults in societies. In Level III, **postconventional**, the individual's values are formed independently of social norms. This final level is reached by a minority of adults and is usually attained only after age 20 (Kohlberg, 1987).

Level I: Preconventional

- **Stage 1 – Heteronomous Morality.** At this stage, what is right is to avoid breaking rules that will lead to punishments. Individuals at this stage have a very egocentric point of view and do not consider the interests or intentions of others.

- **Stage 2 – Individualism, Instrumental Purpose, and Exchange.** What is right is to follow rules only as a means to achieve one's own interests and let others do the same. At this stage, the person is aware that others may have different interests, so sometimes a deal or agreement must be reached. What is right in this case is a fair or equal exchange.

Level II: Conventional

- **Stage 3 – Mutual Interpersonal Expectations, Relationships, and Interpersonal Conformity.** What is right is to be good, to have others recognize this goodness, to show concern for others, and to abide by the Golden Rule. An individual at this stage moves beyond self-interest to recognize the feelings and expectations of others.

- **Stage 4 – Social System and Conscience.** What is right is to perform duties, adhere to laws, and contribute to groups, institutions, and society. Someone at this stage views individual relations in terms of their place in the social system.

Level III: Postconventional or Principled

- **Stage 5 – Social Contract or Utility and Individual Rights.** What is right is being aware that others may hold different values, accepting those differences, and upholding basic fundamental rights like life and liberty in all societies.

- **Stage 6 – Universal Ethical Principles.** Right is based on self-chosen ethical principles such as justice, equality, and respect for the dignity of individuals. These principles are universal; they are comprehensive, consistent, and can be justified to any moral, rational individual. A person at this stage believes that most laws and social agreements are valid because they rest on such principles; however, when laws violate these principles, one acts in accordance with the principles.

In her work on teaching sportsmanship and values, Weiss (1987) outlined five levels of moral development that progress in a fashion similar to Kohlberg's model. Keep in mind that not everyone reaches the highest level of moral reasoning, and oftentimes adults operate at lower levels of moral reasoning despite their cognitive capacity to think at higher levels. *Level 1*, the lowest level of moral reasoning, is based on external control. In other words, one might say, "It's okay as long as I don't

get caught." At this stage, a child determines whether an action is right or wrong based on self-interest and the outcome of his action. If Billy is penalized for tripping his opponent, then the action must be wrong. On the other hand, if the official does not see the intentional trip, then the action is deemed okay.

In *Level 2*, one will compromise and rationalize to maximize self-interest. This "eye for an eye" orientation is often used in defending questionable actions. For example, Billy may feel justified in tripping his opponent because the opponent had previously tripped him. This type of moral reasoning is evident when athletes think that it is okay to use performance-enhancing drugs because everyone else is using them.

In *Level 3*, the child begins to take a more altruistic view and treats others like they would like to be treated. Billy may choose to not intentionally trip his opponent because he does not want to be tripped. A coach may insist that his players not taunt the other team because he wants his team treated with respect.

Level 4 of moral reasoning involves following external rules and regulations. At this stage, a child realizes that rules were made for the common good because not everyone can be trusted to do the right thing. Self-interest is no longer the driving force because the child can now understand the bigger picture and the importance of everyone playing by the same rules. In this case, Billy would not trip his opponent because it is against the rules.

Level 5 focuses on doing what is best for everyone involved, whether or not it is in accordance with the official rules and regulations. This is considered the most mature level of moral reasoning because a person seeks to maximize the interests of the group by taking action that does not violate anyone's fundamental rights as a human being. Thus, Billy would reason that he should refrain from tripping his opponent not just because it is against the rules, but because it would create an unsafe playing environment and could cause harm.

Ethical Dilemmas

An **ethical dilemma** occurs in situations where the course of action is not clear due to the presence of 1) significant value conflicts among differing interests, 2) real alternatives that are equally justifiable, and 3) significant consequences on stakeholders in the situation (McNamara, 1999). Sport managers face ethical dilemmas on a regular basis. Examples of situations associated with ethical dilemmas are reported in the sports media every day. For each of the following situations, decide if an ethical dilemma exists and discuss what, if any, action should be taken by sport managers.

- An athlete is under investigation for the use of performance-enhancing drugs and has just qualified for the Olympic team.

- You are interested in joining a private golf club, but you learn that club policies ban women from becoming members and restrict their tee times on the course.

- Sales of luxury suites in a new ballpark are slow, so the owner attempts to create incentive by falsely advertising that there are only a few suites left to purchase and that they are selling fast.

- A star player is accused of sexual assault just prior to the playoffs.

- A college basketball coach has been very successful in leading her team to the NCAA tournament for the past several seasons, but the graduation rate of her players is 0%.

- A NASCAR driver intentionally spins out to bring out a caution flag.

- In searching for a new coach, qualified minority candidates are excluded from the interview pool.

- The parents of players in a youth soccer league have become increasingly verbally abusive toward officials and opponents.

- A baseball pitcher intentionally hits a batter in retaliation for his teammate being struck by a pitch in the previous inning.

- The highest bid for naming rights for a new sports facility at a university is a beer company.

- During the last few seconds of a high school football game, there is confusion and the home team ends up winning on 5th down. The mistake is not detected at its occurrence, but becomes apparent the next day while reviewing the game film.

- The team mascot, an Indian Chief, has caused controversy. Some people are offended by this

symbol, but most of the alumni and financial donors associate the symbol with school pride and do not want the mascot changed.

©iStockphoto.com

Ethical Decision Making

Trying to decide on the best alternative to resolve an ethical dilemma can be a challenging task for sport managers who often deal with various stakeholders, all of whom have different interests. Ethical analysis and decision making should incorporate a systematic process of reasoning. McNamara (1999) recommends that organizations develop and document a procedure for handling ethical issues. He suggests that organizations form an ethics committee comprised of top leaders, board members, and staff to resolve ethical dilemmas. There are various models for ethical analysis that are built on the foundations of basic ethical theories. They are not designed to provide absolute answers, but do provide guidelines for assessing ethical issues and evaluating alternatives.

An adaptation of a model suggested by Zinn (1993) and presented by Crosset and Hums (1998, p. 129) outlines the following steps in the ethical decision making process:

1. Identify the correct problem to be solved.

2. Gather all the pertinent information.

3. Explore codes of conduct relevant to your profession or to this particular dilemma.

4. Examine your own personal values and beliefs.

5. Consult with your peers or other individuals in the industry who may have experience in similar situations.

6. List your options.

7. Look for a "win-win" situation if at all possible.

8. Ask the question, "How would my family feel if my decision—and how and why I arrived at my decision—were printed in the newspaper tomorrow?"

9. Sleep on it. Do not rush to a decision.

10. Make your best decision, knowing it may not be perfect.

11. Evaluate your decision.

While this may seem like a tedious process, keep in mind that ethical dilemmas and ethical decisions involve complicated problems. The decisions of sport managers are often publicly scrutinized and may receive more media attention than other types of businesses. It is therefore important to have a logical approach to deal with ethical issues and to develop a sound game plan for managing ethics in the workplace.

Managing Ethics

"THE INTEGRITY OF COLLEGE SPORTS HAS ALWAYS BEEN FIRST PRIORITY. IF IT WEREN'T FOR THE INTEGRITY OF THE SPORT, NO ONE WOULD BE INTERESTED—PLAYERS, FANS, MEDIA."

NCAA PRESIDENT MYLES BRAND (AS CITED IN BARNHOUSE, 2004, P. 1D)

Considering the importance of protecting the integrity of their respective sports, many sport organizations and governing bodies have developed **codes of ethics** to guide the actions of their constituents. By providing guidelines, organizations hope to both encourage ethical behavior and discourage unethical behavior by assisting individuals in making the right ethical choices.

Sport organizations and governing bodies incorporate codes of ethics to meet a variety of needs. Therefore, the content and purposes of these codes of ethics will vary from organization to organization. For example, the purpose of the International Olympic Committee (IOC) Code of Ethics is to stress commitment to the fundamental principles of the Olympics and the Olympic ideal (IOC, 2004). Its code focuses on four key themes: dignity, integrity, use of resources, and relations with states. The National Association of Sport Officials (NASO) publishes a code of ethics for the purpose of guiding the professional conduct of its members. Its code covers themes such as impartiality, conflict of interest, professional courtesy, and other themes that are important to sports officials. The USA Gymnastics Code of Ethics is written with the intent to "guide and to affirm the will of all of USA Gymnastics' members to safeguard the best interests of the sport by acting ethically at all times" (USA Gymnastics, 1996, p. 1).

Codes of ethics will target different stakeholder groups depending on the organization or governing body. For example, the New Jersey Sports and Exposition Authority is a state agency operating sports and convention venues. Therefore, its code of ethics has been written to define acceptable behavior for their members and employees. The National Youth Sports Coaches Association has a much different mission. Therefore, it publishes three codes of ethics: one for coaches, one for players, and one for parents. Some organizations take their codes a step further and address their fans. This is the case at the University of Florida where they produce the Gator Fans' Code of Conduct designed to prohibit inconsiderate or dangerous behavior from their fans.

Ideally, these codes are developed in advance to promote positive behavior and prevent problems. However, sometimes codes of ethics are developed in response to growing controversies. Recently, members of the National Association of Basketball Coaches (NABC) agreed to adopt codes of ethics for their basketball programs. This movement stemmed from unethical incidents involving basketball coaches at St. Bonaventure, Georgia, Baylor, Temple, and Iowa State that tarnished the image of the coaching profession (See Table 12.1)(Moran, 2003). Similarly, the International Skating Union (ISU) adopted a code of ethics in 2003 in response to the judging scandal at the 2002

Olympics where French judge Marie-Reine Le Gougne voted in favor of Russian skaters under suspicious circumstances ("ISU adopts," 2003).

Table 12.1

St. Bonaventure – Scandal began with admission of recruit, who never graduated from junior college and should neither have been allowed entry into the school nor declared athletically eligible to play. School was forced to forfeit several games and become ineligible for conference tournament. Incident forced the removal of University President, basketball coaching staff, and athletic director.

Georgia - Georgia announced findings of academic fraud involving assistant basketball coach, who granted credit hours to several players who did not attend the class in basketball strategy he was teaching.

Baylor - Basketball Coach told players to lie to investigators investigating the murder of team member by indicating he was dealing drugs.

Temple – Basketball coach is suspended for his decision to insert a player into the game to get physical with the opposing team, who coach thought was setting illegal screens. The player fouled out in just four minutes of action and broke the arm of opposing player with an excessive force foul.

Iowa State - Pictures of head basketball coach partying with college kids after a road game appear on Internet site. Stories of similar incidents the year prior shortly surfaced.

Criteria for Good Codes of Ethics

Considering the importance of encouraging good conduct, it is important to take care in developing a code of ethics to ensure the code will be effective in meeting its stated purpose. Mahony, Geist, Jordan, Greenwell, and Pastore (1999) identified several factors related to constructing an effective code of ethics.

- **Codes of ethics should avoid being too vague or too specific.** When codes are too vague, individuals are provided little guidance as to how to make ethical decisions. However, codes that are too specific are limited in that they may not apply to a wide variety of situations. For example, think of what happens when a new performance-enhancing drug is introduced that is not expressly prohibited by a governing body's code of ethics. Athletes may be tempted to use it because it is not expressly prohibited, even though it gives the athlete an unfair advantage.

- **Effective codes of ethics are founded on a few themes that can be used to guide individuals' decisions in a variety of situations.** These themes represent the organization's values and will vary from organization to organization. In a study of intercollegiate conference codes of ethics, several important themes emerged. **Sportsmanship, welfare** of participants, **compliance** with institutional and conference rules, **equitable treatment,** and professional **conduct** of employees were themes commonly found in codes of ethics (Greenwell, Geist, Mahony, Jordan, & Pastore, 2001).

- **Organizations developing codes of ethics should communicate what is in the code of ethics to those individuals addressed in the code.** The NCAA realizes this as they call for each member institution to continuously educate their stakeholders about policies related to sportsmanship and ethical conduct (NCAA, 2003). The NBA and NFL do this by hosting orientation events for rookies that focus in part on ethical behavior (Broussard, 2003).

- **Codes should be clear as to whom they apply.** This can be especially challenging in sport contexts due to the large number of stakeholder groups affected. The behavior of coaches, administrators, athletes, and fans can all impact the organization.

- **Consequences for violating ethical standards should be established** (DeSensi & Rosenberg, 2003; Lere & Gaumnitz, 2004). Without some sort of penalty, the code is simply a suggestion and is not likely to influence behavior. These penalties should be clear, identify who is in charge of enforcing penalties, and establish methods of appeal. In terms of common penalties, Greenwell, et al. (2001) found intercollegiate conferences included penalties ranging from reprimands and probation to player and team suspensions. For the most serious violations, penalties included institutional fines and institutional expulsion.

- **Finally, in order for codes to be effective, codes must be relevant to the stakeholders addressed in the code** (Wood & Rimmer, 2003). In order to encourage increased acceptance, codes should be developed with input from those who will be impacted by the standards (DeSensi & Rosenberg, 2003; Stead, Worrell, & Stead, 1990). This type of participatory approach to developing codes of ethics should lead to better understanding of what coaches and athletes desire from each other, which should ultimately lead to effective codes of ethics.

Discussion Questions

1. Select a sport organization. Who should be addressed in its code of ethics? What values should be highlighted in its code? How should those addressed be encouraged to follow what is in the code?

Social Responsibility

"THE PUBLIC IS FOCUSED NOW MORE THAN EVER ON WHAT FIRMS ARE SAYING ABOUT THEIR CORPORATE SOCIAL RESPONSIBILITY" (SNIDER, HILL, & MARTIN, 2004).

Sport organizations often impact multiple stakeholder groups, including employees, coaches, athletes, spectators, the business community, and the local community in general. Further, sport organizations often rely on these stakeholder groups for the resources they need to operate successfully. For example, organizations may utilize government money to fund programs like city recreation leagues or tax revenue to build stadiums and arenas. They may require other re-

©iStockphoto.com

sources from the community such as volunteers to staff an event or local media to promote events. Similarly, the actions of sport organizations impact the community in many ways, both positively and negatively. On the positive side, sport organizations contribute to the local economy and citizens are provided opportunities to participate in activities or enjoy sports performances. Negatively, unethical acts by an organization can harm the reputation of the community, and poor behavior by athletes can leave the youth of the community with inadequate or no role models. These points illustrate an inextricable relationship between the organization and its stakeholders; therefore, sport organizations' responsibilities toward their stakeholders is an important issue.

Corporate Social Responsibility

Corporate social responsibility is the term most often used to refer to the role an organization has within the community. According to Carroll (1999), socially responsible businesses have four main responsibilities: economic, legal, ethical, and philanthropic. Responsible organizations will seek to achieve each.

Economic responsibilities require organizations to produce goods and services and sell them at a profit because that is how a capitalist society operates (Carroll, 1999). At first this definition seems to imply that organizations should act in their self-interest without regard for other stakeholder groups, but Carroll (1999) argues that economic viability also influences other parts of society. For example, professional sports teams have a responsibility to make wise fiscal decisions, since the local economy may benefit from jobs, tourist dollars, and tax revenue generated by the existence of a team. In intercollegiate athletics, administrators are entrusted with funds from the university, donors, and corporate sponsors. These administrators have a responsibility to use these funds efficiently to maximize the experience of the student-athletes and contribute to the university.

Under this definition, socially responsible professional teams should strive to produce the best product. This would seem to be the goal of every team, but it is not always the case. After the Florida Marlins won the World Series in 1997, team owner Wayne Huizenga, frustrated by a lack of profits, dismantled the team by trading away many of the team's star players and not re-signing others in order to cut costs (Useem, 1998). This resulted in the Marlins becoming the first team to win the World Series and then lose over 100 games the following year, and attendance dropped dramatically over the next six years. Considering how much the community had invested—both economically and psychologically—into the team, was Huizenga justified in his actions?

Legal responsibilities require organizations to reach goals within legal constraints. Sport organizations are often under the scrutiny of contract laws, labor laws, criminal laws, etc., and socially responsible sport managers are expected to adhere to these laws. Further, legal responsibility also applies to organizational rules and procedures. For example, Olympic athletes have numerous eligibility and anti-doping rules to adhere to, and colleges are expected to adhere to rules in the NCAA manual.

The competitive nature of sport often provides challenges to organizations, coaches, and athletes who are tempted to "bend the rules" to their advantage. For example, bidding to host the Olympic Games is extremely competitive, and organizers of the Salt Lake City Games may have ignored bribery laws in order to win the bid (Hughes, 2002). We also see this in college sports when coaches break recruiting rules to land top athletes. These coaches may feel that winning is what is important, and that they should win at all costs. Socially responsible coaches also want to win, but they see more value in "winning within the rules."

Ethical responsibilities require organizations to operate by established norms defining suitable behavior. In other words, ethical responsibilities represent what organizations are expected to do above the rule of law. A good example of acting within the law but breaking ethical standards comes from the University of Colorado. The Buffaloes' football program admitted to hiring exotic dancers to entertain prospective recruits.

Although this activity was not prohibited by law or by NCAA rules at the time, it shocked many who felt it deviated from suitable behavior (Kluger, 2004). In professional sport, the Chicago Cubs have been accused of scalping their own tickets. The Cubs, in an effort to capitalize on high demand for tickets, set up its own brokerage service where it sells its own tickets at dramatically inflated prices. Whereas many Cubs fans have claimed it is unethical to "scalp" its own tickets, the team argues it is acting within the law (Ciokajlo, 2002). These two examples illustrate that even though an organization is working within the law, it may not necessarily be acting responsibly.

Philanthropic responsibilities require organizations to give back to their communities. Bill Veeck, who owned the Cleveland Indians Baseball team in the 1950s, exemplified philanthropic responsibilities. Contrary to most baseball owners at the time, who perhaps felt that the city owed them something, Veeck surmised that his team was dependent on the facilities of the city and the good will of the citizens (Veeck & Linn, 1962). Due to this belief, the Indians were active in philanthropy, inviting community groups to attend for free and contributing gate receipts to community charities and youth sports programs. This trend continues today, as many professional sports teams have established charitable foundations to contribute to their communities. In addition to financial contributions, many sport organizations contribute other resources to their community. Many universities create programs like the University of Louisville's Cards Care program. The Cards Care program organizes activities for student-athletes to donate their time to various community projects such as pen pal programs with local schools, visits to children's hospitals, shifts serving food at soup kitchens, etc.

Individual Social Responsibility

Social responsibility applies to individuals as well as organizations. Individual athletes, coaches, and administrators have a responsibility to their communities and to their peers. Administrators bear the weight of knowing their decisions affect many stakeholder groups ranging from owners, employees, athletes, and fans. Coaches are often responsible for teaching values in addition to skills, and these coaches often have a high public profile in the community. St. Louis Cardinals manager Tony La Russa actively uses his stature in the community to make a positive impact. La Russa is involved in promoting the arts and education, and his Animal Rescue Foundation has helped many unwanted animals find homes. Conversely, negative incidents involving coaches can send entirely different messages to their athletes and the people who follow their teams. Two recent examples involved high profile college basketball coaches. Former Iowa State head basketball coach Larry Eustacy was photographed drinking at a campus party, and University of Cincinnati head basketball coach Bob Huggins was arrested on drunk driving charges. In both cases, the coaches' actions were starkly opposed to the values they tried to communicate to their athletes and fans.

In addition to coaches, athletes impact their communities in many ways. Like it or not, athletes serve as role models for young kids who often emulate their heroes. This is why brands such as Nike and Sprite are willing to pay NBA star LeBron James millions of dollars in endorsement deals. They do this knowing kids will want to wear what LeBron wears and drink what LeBron drinks. This influence can be both positive and negative. On one hand, role models such as Mia Hamm and Lisa Leslie have encouraged girls to get involved in sports and to lead healthier lives. Many kids have taken up golf to be like Tiger Woods. On the other hand, much of the boorish behavior seen in youth sports can be attributed to kids emulating professional athletes such as Roger Clemens throwing at a batter, Manny Ramirez charging the mound, or Ron Artest charging into the stands to attack a fan. Think of the message sent to kids when an athlete like Shaquille O'Neal uses profanity in a live televised interview. Although many athletes may want to shun this responsibility, high profile athletes have to realize they are always being watched and emulated.

Athletes have the power to create positive change in their communities. Since his playing career ended, Magic Johnson has been actively investing in local businesses that have helped revitalize many neighborhoods. A large part of his policy is to invest in businesses in ethnically diverse and underserved neighborhoods (Pate, 2003). Major League Baseball recognizes the power athletes have in their communities and encourages athletes to be active by handing out the Roberto Clemente award each year to recognize devotion to work in the community. The 2003 winner, Jamie Moyer of the Seattle Mariners, contributed time and money through the Moyer Foundation, which provides support to children and families in distress. Over the years, The Moyer Foundation has raised nearly $3 million to support various community organizations (Stone, 2003).

Benefits of Being a Good Corporate Citizen

Just as socially responsible organizations deliver benefits to their stakeholders, they may also reap benefits, as organizations contributing to the **public good** often enjoy business success as customers reward organizations for their roles in the community (Besser, 1999). There is some evidence to suggest that socially responsible activities can boost an organization's image, generate increased business, and keep organizations out of trouble. Specifically, customers are more likely to buy from organizations that are socially responsible and less likely to purchase products from companies whose practices are viewed as being less socially responsible (Creyer, 1997; Sen & Bhattacharya, 2001). Perceptions of social responsibility also influence the prices customers are willing to pay for products. Customers reward ethical behavior by being willing to pay higher prices. Customers may buy from unethical organizations but do so at lower prices (Creyer, 1997).

Socially irresponsible organizations can suffer negative effects. A good example of how irresponsible activities can have damaging effects on the organization comes from the Salt Lake City Olympics scandal. In 1999, while Olympic officials involved in the Salt Lake City bid process were being investigated on bribery charges, John Hancock Financial Services, a major Olympic sponsor, decided to significantly scale back advertising for the Sydney Olympics (Bell, 1999) and a major donor withdrew a $10 million donation (Blevins, 2003).

Summary

- Morality and ethics in the workplace should be key components of all industries, including the sport industry.

- Sport managers routinely face ethical situations, and the decisions they make impact a variety of stakeholders, such as athletes, coaches, staff, corporate sponsors, and fans.

- Sport managers will be better equipped to deal with the daily dose of dilemmas if they have a sound grasp of their personal values, a commitment to professional ethics, a basic understanding of ethical theories, and the ability to apply moral reasoning and ethical decision making to resolve problems.

- It is important for sport managers to develop and enforce codes of ethics to ensure appropriate actions of constituents.

- Social responsibility should be strongly encouraged by our sport leaders at both the organizational and individual levels.

- Reflection upon the ethical choices currently being made in the world of sports, coupled with the knowledge and appreciation of ethical principles and moral behavior, can help guide future sport managers toward making the "right" decisions.

Discussion Activities

1. Answer the following two questions:

   a. Do sport organizations have a responsibility to their communities? Is the level of responsibility different for professional teams? College teams? Youth teams?

   b. Do athletes have a higher standard for behavior than non-athletes? Should more be expected of professional athletes? Should college athletes be expected to behave better than other college students?

2. Your minor league baseball team has regularly sold out each game, and you expect to sell out again this season. Despite the sellouts, your organization is experiencing a budget crunch, and you are under pressure to deliver as much revenue as possible. You feel you could sell all of your seats, but the local Drug Abuse Resistance Education (D.A.R.E.) program has asked you to set aside 250 tickets for each game to be used as rewards for school children who agree not to use drugs. Do you sell the tickets to the public or do you donate them to the D.A.R.E. program?

3. Your men's basketball coach, who has coached for 15 successful years, has been arrested for drunk driving and has admitted to the crime. You have to formulate some sort of disciplinary action. How severe should the penalty be for this type of offense? Should the coach be treated like any other university employee in a similar situation?

4. You have a football player who has been accused of a crime. The local police claim he signed for a package containing steroids and other illegal drugs. The athlete claims he did not know what was in the package. Should the athlete be able to continue to play? Will you support the player or take disciplinary action? What type of disciplinary action would be appropriate?

5. You are operating a youth baseball league. Throughout the season, the parents have gotten more vocal about criticizing coaches, umpires, and league officials. It has gotten to the point that the kids are becoming distracted on the field. What policies can you put into place to avoid this type of behavior? What could happen if this behavior is not controlled?

6. The day before the championship game you find out your star player may be ineligible due to a minor paperwork error. It appears that the player lives one block outside the district and should be playing for another team. The player has been on your team all season and you have received no complaints. The league office is not aware of the oversight, and it is possible that no one will ever notice. Should you report this to the league office? What is the right thing to do?

References

The Arizona Sports Summit Accord (1999). *Pursuing victory with honor.* Retrieved July 2, 2004, from http://www.character-counts.org/sports/accord.htm.

Barnhouse, W. (2004, February 13). Brand says ethics tops the NCAA's agenda. *Fort Worth Star-Telegram*, D1.

Bauchamp, T. L. (1988). Ethical theory and its application to business. In T. L. Beauchamp & N. E. Bowie (Eds.), *Ethical theory and business* (3rd ed., pp. 1-55). Englewood Cliffs, NJ: Prentice-Hall.

Bell, A. (1999, June 7). John Hancock fights to clean up Olympics. *National Underwriter, 103*(23), 3.

Besser, T. L. (1999). Community involvement and the perception of success among small business operators in small towns. *Journal of Small Business Management, 37*, 16-29.

Billington, R. (1988). *Living philosophy: An introduction to moral thought*. London, UK: Routledge.

Blevins, J. (2003, January 23). Major sponsors stand by U.S. Olympics despite ethical scandal. *Knight Ridder Tribune Business News*, p. 1.

Branvold, S. (2001). Ethics. In B. L. Parkhouse (Ed.), *The management of sport: Its foundation and application* (3rd ed., pp. 162-176). New York: McGraw-Hill.

Broussard, C. (2003, September 26). NBA rookies get lessons in life skills. *The New York Times*, p. D7.

Carroll, A. B. (1999). Corporate social responsibility: Evolution of a definitional construct. *Business and Society, 38*, 268-295.

Ciokajlo, M. (2002, October, 10). Chicago Cubs face ticket-fraud lawsuit. *Knight Ridder Tribune Business News*, p. 1.

Creyer, E. H. (1997). The influence of firm behavior on purchase intention: Do consumers really care about business ethics? *Journal of Consumer Marketing, 14*, 421-32.

Crosset, T. W., & Hums, M. A. (1998). Ethical principles applied to sport management. In L. P. Masteralexis, C. A. Barr, & M. A. Hums (Eds.), *Principles and practice of sport management* (pp. 117-136). Gaithersburg, MD: Aspen Publishers, Inc.

Dater, A. (2004, March 12). Canucks star out for season for hit on Av NHL also fines Vancouver for failure to control team. *Denver Post*, p. A01.

DeSensi, J. T., & Rosenberg, D. (2003). *Ethics and morality in sport management*. Morgantown, WV: Fitness Information Technology.

Greenwell, T. C., Geist, A. L., Mahony, D. F., Jordan, J. S., & Pastore, D. L. (2001). Characteristics of NCAA conference codes of ethics. *International Journal of Sport Management, 2*, 108-124.

Hitt, W. D. (1990). *Ethics and Leadership: Putting theory into practice*. Columbus, OH: Battelle Press.

Hughes, J. (2002, September 29). Olympics bribery case argued in Denver court. *Denver Post*, p. C1.

International Olympic Committee. (2004). *IOC Code of Ethics*. Lausanne, Switzerland: Author.

ISU adopts ethics code after Salt Lake scandal. (2003, August 12). *The Toronto Star*, p. E05.

Kindred, D. (1999, July 5). Blind ambition—baseball player hit in face with a pitch. *Sporting News*, 63.

Kluger, J. (2004, March 1). Entirely out of bounds. *Time, 163*(9), 59.

Kohlberg, L. (1987). *Child psychology and childhood education: A cognitive-developmental view*. New York: Longman.

Lere, J. C., & Guarnitz, B. R. (2003). The impact of codes of ethics on decision making: Some insights from information economics. *Journal of Business Ethics, 48*, 365-379.

Mahony, D. F., Geist, A. L., Jordan, J., Greenwell, T. C., & Pastore, D. (1999). Codes of ethics used by sport governing bodies: Problems in intercollegiate athletics. *Proceedings of the Congress of the European Association for Sport Management, 7*, 206-208.

McNamara, C. (1999). *Complete guide to ethics management: An ethics toolkit for managers*. Retrieved July 2, 2004, from http://www.mapnp.org.library/ethics/ethxgde.htm.

Moran, M. (2003, October 16). Coaches, NCAA agree to chart new course. *USA Today*, p. 7C.

Pate, K. (2003, April 3). New Starbucks location in Denver part of Magic Johnson's business strategy. *Knight Ridder Tribune Business News*, p. 1.

Rokeach, M. (1973). *The nature of human values*. New York: The Free Press.

Sen, S., & Bhattacharya, C. B. (2001). Does doing good always lead to doing better? Consumer reactions to corporate social responsibility. *Journal of Marketing Research, 38*, 225-243.

Shields, D. L. L., & Bredemeier, B. J. L. (1995). *Character development and physical activity*. Champaign, IL: Human Kinetics.

Solomon, R. C. (1992). *Above the bottom line: An introduction to business ethics*. Fort Worth, TX: Harcourt Brace.

Snider, J. Hill, R. P., & Martin, D. (2003). Corporate social responsibility in the 21st century: A view from the world's most successful firms. *Journal of Business Ethics, 48*, 175-187.

Stead, W. E., Worrell, D. L., & Stead, J. G. (1990). An integrative model for understanding and managing ethical behavior in business organizations. *Journal of Business Ethics, 30*, 185-195.

Stone, L. (2003, October 22). Clemente Award caps career year for Moyer. *The Seattle Times*, p. D1.

Useem, J. (1998, May 19). Ball club of the new economy. *Inc., 20*(7), 31-32.

USA Gymnastics. (1996). *USA Gymnastics Code of Ethics*. Indianapolis, IN: Author.

Weinberg, R. S., & Gould, D. (2003). *Foundations of sport & exercise psychology*. Champaign, IL: Human Kinetics.

Weiss, M. R. (1987). Teaching sportsmanship and values. In V. Seefeldt (Ed.). *Handbook for youth sports coaches* (pp. 137-151). Reston, VA: AAHPERD.

Wood, G., & Rimmer, M. (2003). Codes of ethics: What are they really and what should they be? *International Journal of Value-Based Management, 16*(2), 181-195.

Veeck, B., & Linn, E. (1962). *Veeck as in wreck*. New York: Putnam.

Zinn, L. M. (1993). Do the right thing: Ethical decision making in professional and business practice. *Adult Learning*, 5, 7-8, 27.

Suggested Readings

Badaracco, J. (2003). *Harvard business review on corporate ethics*. Cambridge, MA: Harvard Business School Press.

Bowie, N. E., & Duska, R. R. (1990). *Business ethics* (2nd ed.) Englewood Cliffs, NJ: Prentice Hall.

Boxill, J. (2002). *Sports ethics: An anthology*. Oxford, UK: Blackwell Publishers.

NCAA Division I Manual (2003-2004 ed.). (2003). Indianapolis, IN: National Collegiate Athletic Association.

Simon, R. (2003). *Fair play: The ethics of sport* (2nd ed.). Boulder, CO: Westview Press.

Seglin, J. (2003). *The right thing: Conscience, profit and personal responsibility*. Rollinsford, NH: Spiro Press.

Chapter Thirteen

Global Sport Industry

Artemisia Apostolopoulou and
Dimitra Papadimitriou

Learning Objectives

Upon completion of this chapter, the reader should be able to

- Discuss globalization trends occurring in the sport industry;

- Identify challenges facing organizations considering international expansion;

- Describe the Olympic Movement, its member associations, and its main functions;

- Understand U.S. professional leagues' efforts to expand internationally;

- Discuss the structure of the European sport industry; and

- Identify opportunities for a career in international sport management and skills needed.

Introduction

During the 2003-04 NBA season, American Express aired an advertisement tag-lined "Global Village." The ad featured Don Nelson, coach of the Dallas Mavericks, shopping for international dictionaries, then using his newly-acquired vocabulary to communicate during practice with his international players: Tariq Abdul-Wahad from France, Dirk Nowitzki from Germany, Eduardo Najera from Mexico, and even Steve Nash from Canada!

"SPORT IS PART OF EVERY MAN AND WOMAN'S HERITAGE AND ITS ABSENCE CAN NEVER BE COMPENSATED FOR."

PIERRE DE COUBERTIN

The message is simple: long gone are the days when U.S. born players monopolized NBA rosters. During the 2003-04 NBA season, 67 international players from 33 countries competed in the world's top basketball league ("International players," 2004), a dramatic increase from the number of international players in the NBA 10 years ago. An examination of Major League Baseball and the National Hockey League rosters reveals similar diversification trends. According to a *Sports Illustrated* (*SI*) special report on globalization published in 2004, the percentage of U.S.-born players in MLB in the 2003 season was 72.7 (compared to 83.4% in 1993), while the number of North American players in the NHL dropped to 67.7% in 2003-04 (from 81.3% in 1993-94) (Wertheim, 2004a).

The influx of international players into professional sport leagues is not the only indication that sport is increasingly becoming a global product. To further fuel international interest, the NBA is conducting basketball clinics in Africa, while MLB opened their 2004 season in Japan. Other indicators that point to this trend are the estimated 28.8 billion viewers that tuned in to the 2002 World Cup Soccer matches, the record 202 countries that participated in the Athens 2004 Olympic Games, Nike Park being created in Beijing, and IMG's 47 international offices. It is obvious that sport products and services are now being consumed by a greater number of nations than ever before. Welcome to the era of globalization in sport.

Globalization has been defined as "the process by which the experience of everyday life, marked by the diffusion of commodities and ideas, is becoming standardized around the world" ("Globalization," 2004). The key concept is "*the diffusion of commodities and ideas,*" which is illustrated by the sharing of information, products and services, labor, culture, and, of course, sport. In their book *Sport Business in the Global Marketplace*, Westerbeek and Smith (2003) identify seven driving forces of globalization: 1) economy, 2) technology, 3) social science, resources and natural environment, 4) demography, 5) governance, 6) conflict and war, and 7) religion and cultural identity. The authors point to the release of trade barriers and the increase of trade agreements between nations, the high-speed flow of information through new and improved communication vehicles (e.g., the Internet), and privatization as conditions that have facilitated the globalization of sport (Westerbeek & Smith, 2003).

Given these trends, it is imperative for sport managers to understand the **international environment** in which they operate. Sport professionals must be aware of the opportunities that are available on a global scale, as well as the challenges that arise from conducting business in this new, global market. For sport managers focused on selling their U.S.-based product globally, as well as those looking to capitalize on international imports, an understanding of the global sport industry is paramount.

The purpose of this chapter is to provide students preparing for a career in the sport industry insight into the global marketplace. The Olympic Games are considered to be the original international sport product and provide an excellent starting point for the examination of the international sport environment. Analysis of the Olympic Movement—more specifically, its member organizations and main revenue sources—will provide valuable insight into the international sport industry. We will also examine the impact of sport globalization in the U.S. and discuss the international expansion of the four major professional sport leagues: NFL, MLB, NBA, and NHL. The next section of this chapter addresses the European sport industry, particularly aspects of the football (soccer, for American readers) sector. The chapter concludes with a discussion of career opportunities for sport managers as well as skills necessary to become a successful international sport manager.

So, grab your passport (maybe your visa, too), dictionaries, and travel pack and get ready to embark on a tour of the global sport marketplace!

©iStockphoto.com

The Olympic Movement

There is little doubt that the modern **Olympic Games**, revived in 1896 by Pierre de Coubertin, represent one of the strongest examples of globalization in sport. Every four years the Games bring together a great number of nations to showcase a variety of athletic events and participants. Over the years, the world's most prestigious sporting event has grown to the point of incomparable international exposure, worldwide audience appeal, and multicultural activities that draw the attention of virtually every demographic. The **Olympic Movement** is a global phenomenon that transcends the boundaries of sport and culture and extends to education, politics, economy, and technology. This is clearly manifested in the current IOC global promotional campaign titled "Celebrate Humanity," which highlights the Olympic values of hope, dreams and inspirations, friendship, and fair play ("International Olympic Committee: News," 2004).

The Olympic Movement includes the International Olympic Committee, National Olympic Committees, the Organizing Committees of the Olympic Games, International Federations, National Governing Bodies, and the athletes. These member organizations work closely to promote the fundamental principles of Olympism and to effectively operate business functions vital to the continuity of the Movement.

The **International Olympic Committee** (IOC), an international, non-governmental, nonprofit organization, has its offices in Lausanne, Switzerland. This organization, whose main responsibility is to organize the Olympic Games, owns the rights to the Olympic properties, including the Olympic symbol, flag, motto, emblem, anthem, flame, and torch ("International Olympic Committee: Organisation," 2004). The IOC is represented in individual countries by **National Olympic Committees** (NOCs), which are responsible for promoting the Olympic Movement nationally, developing athletes, and sending delegations to the Games. Currently, there are 202 NOCs recognized by the IOC ("National Olympic Committees," 2004). **International Federations** (IFs) are responsible for developing their sport(s) worldwide and for staging world championships. Some of the largest IFs include FIFA (football), FIBA (basketball), IAAF (athletics), and FIG (gymnastics). On a national level, each sport is developed through respective **National Governing Bodies** (NGBs), such as USA Track and Field.

The **Organizing Committee of the Olympic Games** (OCOG) is formed once a city is awarded the honor and responsibility of hosting the Olympic and Paralympic Games. The role of the OCOG is to handle all operational aspects of the Games and to ultimately put on the events. Each OCOG is disbanded about two years following the Games. In addition to the aforementioned organizations, the promotion of the Olympic ideals is supported by a number of **IOC commissions** (e.g., marketing, medical, ethics, nominations, press, TV and Internet rights, Olympic solidarity) and **foundations** or **agencies**, including the International Olympic Truce Foundation (IOTF), the World Anti-Doping Agency (WADA), and a few IOC-owned or partly owned companies (Olympic Broadcast Services [OBS], Meridian Management, and the Olympic Games Knowledge Services [OGKS]) ("International Olympic Committee: Organisation," 2004).

The most significant driving force for the financial stability of the Olympic Movement is the IOC **Olympic Marketing Programme**. For the 2001-04 period, the program produced revenues of $4.26 billion. More than half of that money ($2.23 billion) came from broadcasting rights, 32% (or $1.33 billion) from sponsorship, 14% (or $680 million) from ticketing, and 2% (or $81 million) from licensing and other revenues ("International Olympic Committee: News," 2004). These significant resources support the entire family of the Olympic Movement as 92% of the revenues is distributed to the NOCs, IFs, and OCOGs and only 8% is used for the operation of the IOC ("International Olympic Committee: News," 2004).

As worldwide interest grows for the Olympic Games, so does the desire of multinational corporations and broadcasting agencies to share in the Olympic glory. The 2000 Olympic Games in Sydney were watched by more than 3.7 billion people from 220 countries, while it is estimated that more that 2.1 billion viewers from 160 countries watched the Salt Lake City 2002 Winter Olympic Games. Due to this increasing worldwide attention, the European Broadcasting Union (EBU) had to pay $746 million to obtain control over the IOC broadcast rights for Europe (excluding Italy). This agreement includes the 2010 Vancouver Winter Games and 2012 Summer Games (yet to be assigned) and represents a 40% increase from the previous contract ("International Olympic Committee: Organisation," 2004). For the United States, NBC spent $2.3 billion for the right to broadcast the 2004, 2006, and 2008 Olympic Games, and another $2 billion for the 2010 and 2012 Games ("The Authoritative," 2003).

Olympic sponsorship agreements are handled through **The Olympic Program** (TOP), which was introduced for the first time in the 1984 Los Angeles Olympic Games. This program, operated by the IOC, gives sponsors exclusive rights to associate with the Olympic Games and use all Olympic properties. Recognizing the tremendous effect that Olympic sponsorships can have on building a global brand, companies pay a lofty fee for the chance to be associated with the world's premiere sporting event. The total sponsorship revenue from the TOP III Program for the 1996 Centennial Olympic Games was $279 million, while the TOP IV Program generated $579 million for the 2000 Sydney Games ("International Olympic Committee: Documents," 2004). Current TOP sponsors include Coca-Cola, McDonald's, Atos Origin, General Electric, John Hancock, Kodak, VISA, Panasonic, Samsung, and Swatch ("International Olympic Com-

mittee: Documents," 2004). As part of becoming Olympic sponsors, companies also invest heavily in leveraging this partnership. For example, VISA recently extended its global sponsorship agreement for four consecutive Olympic Games and has spent more than $100 million worldwide to support Olympic athletes.

The Olympic Games are idiosyncratic in that they are as much a global phenomenon with worldwide reach as they are a local project. This contradictory reality demands that the Organizing Committees involved in bidding or hosting the Olympic Games address strategic issues that extend to many sectors in the society, including politics, the economy, technology, transportation, sporting infrastructure, communication and media, culture and national representation, tourism, and so on. Greece, a comparably small European country hosting the 2004 Olympic Games, has faced that challenge.

The Athens 2004 Olympic Games

For many cities and countries, worldwide exposure and financial gains are the two most important motivational factors for bidding to organize the Olympic Games. In Athens, the case was a bit different. The special attachment of Greece to the Olympic Movement—as it is the birthplace of the Games—remains the main driving force to "Welcome Home" the world. Many believed that the gigantic endeavor of hosting the Olympic Games seemed like perfect suicide for a small nation like Greece, at least in terms of finances and social policy. It is estimated that Greece spent over $2.7 billion (approximately $3.5 billion) from its public expenditure on the construction or upgrade of public transportation and medical facilities throughout the country. Furthermore, an additional $1.7 billion (approximately $2.2 billion) was invested for the development of the required sports infrastructure (20 new and five upgraded sports venues) (Manou, 2003).

As the opening ceremony lavishly introduced the new Olympic venues and athletes to the world, and with the hopes that the most expensive and sophisticated security systems in the world would adequately protect the world's largest athletic celebration, Athens was there, proudly fulfilling its obligation towards the Olympic Movement and its own history. The world's best athletes competed in authentic settings (e.g., the original marathon course for the marathon race, ancient Olympia for the shot put event, and a route through the historical sites of Athens for cycling) and the winners were crowned with olive wreaths. What remains to be seen is how the rich history of Greece and the intangible assets of the 2004 Olympic Games will affect the future of the Olympic Movement.

Challenges in the Olympic Movement

The Olympic Movement faces numerous challenges, not the least of which is doping control issues and over-commercialization. **Drug testing** at the Olympic Games has become a sophisticated and quite successful process, especially since the establishment of the WADA (World Anti-Doping Agency). However, there will always be incidents of cheating that go undetected. The IOC, in cooperation with its member nations, should maintain upgraded techniques and technologies, rigorous control, and strict measures in order to protect the integrity and spirit of the Games. The second issue, **over-commercialization**, is potentially as harmful for the IOC. Marketing studies have repeatedly documented the positive outcomes that multinational brands receive by associating with the Olympic ideals, but scarcely acknowledge the backlash that could result for the Olympic Movement. The Organizing Committee of the Athens Games claims that they faced this challenge by notably confining the number of sponsors affiliated with the Games to 36 (from 100 sponsors in the 2000 Olympics) and by taking out some of the needless show. A lot remains to be done, however, to balance sponsors' commercial interests with the Olympic image.

Another major issue that awaits future Organizing Committees of the Olympic Games is **gigantism**. The Olympic Games have progressively expanded through the years. The large number of participants (athletes, delegation members, media, and visitors) and the number of competitions creates immense pressure for host cities, especially in the areas of security and infrastructure. The IOC might have to impose new regulations in order to address this issue and secure manageable competitions. As Viviane Reding, a member of the European Commission responsible for Education and Culture, stated, the challenge lies in organizing "less high-flown games, smaller games closer to their Olympic roots" ("Europa," 2004).

Although the Olympic Movement has not yet fulfilled one of its most historical aims, to end war, it has experienced dramatic growth and attracted huge economic and political support from the private and public sector. Safeguarding its future and further development might not be as easy as it has been in the past.

International Expansion of U.S. Sport

As the U.S. sport industry continues to mature, professional sport leagues are investigating growth possibilities through expansion into foreign markets and developing new fans. International markets have become the source of substantial revenue for the leagues through the signing of broadcasting deals, the sale of licensed merchandise, and the acquisition of foreign-based sponsors.

The recent technological and communication advances allow U.S.-based sport organizations to reach new consumers almost anywhere in the world. Even though their choices for global expansion might vary, one thing is constant: U.S. professional leagues consider international expansion the cornerstone for their future growth. Evidence of that is the creation of league International Divisions to handle their business outside the borders.

The following sections provide some specific examples of initiatives that each of the four major leagues (MLB, NBA, NFL, and NHL) has taken to expand its reach in other countries. Sport management students interested in pursuing a career in the international sport setting must realize that U.S. leagues' efforts worldwide provide avenues for employment, as the leagues depend on qualified professionals with an understanding of the sport industry as well as the global market in order to successfully execute their international programs.

Major League Baseball (MLB)

For baseball fans in the United States and in many countries around the world, October means one thing: the World Series. But are these games between the two best teams in Major League Baseball a true *World* Series? After all, the competition involves teams from North America only. Nevertheless, the games could be considered a *World* Series if one takes into account the widespread interest in the league's main attraction. In 2002, sports fans from 224 countries were able to follow the World Series on television (King, 2003). The league has also been very active in making games available to its international fans through the Internet (King, 2003).

Major League Baseball has had an international presence for many decades, mainly with exhibition games and tours, as well as preseason and regular season games held outside the U.S. The league has held games in Japan, Mexico, Puerto Rico, even Cuba (Schaaf, 2004), while an off-season All-Star Tour has visited Japan since 1986 (Graczyk, 2003). March 2004 marked the return of Hideki Matsui to his homeland, where his New York Yankees and the Tampa Bay Devil Rays opened their season. Matsui's success with the Yankees, as well as All-Star performances of his countrymen Ichiro Suzuki and Hideo Nomo, have helped increase the popularity of MLB in Japan, making the country the source of half of MLB International's revenue (Adams, 2004). The league has also sponsored grassroots programs such as the *Envoy Program*, which sends baseball coaches to non-traditional baseball countries around the globe in order to teach the game to native players, coaches, and umpires ("Major League Baseball International," 2004).

With offices in Sydney, London, and, more recently, Tokyo, Major League Baseball is looking for ways to grow their global business even further. Allowing MLB players in the Olympic Games, a strategy that has provided a stage for other professional leagues to showcase their stars, might not be MLB's best bet, given scheduling conflicts between the Games and the MLB sea-

son. However, baseball could benefit from an international competition. In 2004, Bud Selig, the Commissioner of MLB, announced plans for a **Baseball World Cup Tournament**. The initial plans call for a 16-team tournament held during spring training in warm-weather cities across the U.S. (Bloom, 2004). Selig's proposal has the first Baseball World Cup tournament scheduled for March 2005 and held every four years thereafter. Should the deal come through, this tournament could bring worldwide attention to the game of baseball and the league itself, as it will include high-caliber players from all over the world competing in one true world championship. Also, it will provide an opportunity for many of the international players currently in MLB rosters (approximately 23% of MLB players are not U.S.-born, according to the *SI* 2004 report) to compete for their national teams.

National Basketball Association (NBA)

Basketball is an Olympic sport that is played worldwide in structured leagues and prestigious tournaments (e.g., Euroleague). In the 1992 Summer Olympic Games held in Barcelona, Spain, millions of basketball fans around the world were mesmerized by the stars of the first ever "Dream Team." Seen by many as a landmark in the league's international expansion, the participation of professional players in the Olympics provided the NBA with a vehicle to showcase to the world the talent available in the basketball Mecca. League officials have focused greatly on reaching additional markets and creating new and more loyal fans. Currently the league operates 13 international NBA offices worldwide (controlled by the International Division of the league) that handle local TV and sponsorship deals and promote the NBA brand in the respective markets ("NBA announces international," 2003).

The NBA has been able to generate global interest by using exhibition and preseason games, regular season games, and grassroots programs to promote its brand. In 2003, the league held preseason games in Mexico City, San Juan, Paris, and Barcelona, and opening season games in Saitama, Japan ("NBA announces international," 2003), and plans to expand with games in China and Russia in 2004 (Crowe, 2004). Conveniently, the selection of teams and locations reflects an effort to match the international players on the teams' rosters with their native countries, bringing Tony

Parker (San Antonio Spurs) back to Paris, Pau Gasol (Memphis Grizzlies) back to Barcelona, and Yao Ming (Houston Rockets) back to Shanghai. The NBA looks to capitalize on the fact that international NBA players are considered heroes in their countries.

Basketball tournaments and clinics are two other effective tools used by the league to develop fans around the globe. The NBA provides information about specific initiatives on the global section of their web site. For instance, in the 2003-04 season, the NBA's *Jam Session* was held in China for the first time. Also, in 2004, through its *Basketball Without Borders* community outreach program, the NBA took a number of its stars to Italy and South Africa. Those stars held basketball clinics and interacted with young fans in those emerging markets.

So, where does the NBA stand today? Is the league's investment in global initiatives providing a return? The answer is yes. There are many indications that the league's international efforts are returning a profit: NBA games and shows are televised in more than 200 countries around the globe, accounting for 20% of the league's annual broadcasting revenues; 20% of the league's merchandise sales come from overseas; and more than 40% of the visitors on nba.com live outside the U.S.–which is facilitated by the fact that nba.com is available in nine different languages besides English (Crowe, 2004; Lombardo, 2003a).

There has been an ongoing discussion regarding expansion of the NBA to countries outside North America by placing an NBA team or an NBA division in Europe. Currently the league has refrained from acting on these discussions. The lack of adequate facility infrastructure in Europe, other financial considerations, and increased security concerns following the incidents of 9/11 has the league reviewing the feasibility of international expansion at this time (Lombardo, 2003a). Additionally, established European leagues and franchises could pose a significant challenge should the NBA decide to introduce a European division.

One market that is rapidly developing for the NBA is China. In June 2002, audiences witnessed what may be considered by many to be the one most important development for the further global expansion of the NBA: the first ever selection of an international player, Yao Ming of China, as the No.1 draft pick of the NBA. Yao's move to the United States and the Hous-

ton Rockets created a chain of positive outcomes both for his franchise and the league as a whole: a lucrative naming rights deal for the Rockets' new Toyota Center, thousands of Chinese Rockets' fans, and more national and regional television deals in the country that holds 1.3 billion of the world's population. In an effort to strengthen its merchandise sales in the region, the NBA signed a 5-year deal with Reebok, making the manufacturer the exclusive league licensee in China (Lombardo, 2003b). China is opening up to the world, and there is no question that the NBA has front row seats.

Many are looking to see what the NBA will do next. Although an international division might not be in the league's near-future, be on the lookout for NBA teams holding their training camps in Europe, an NBDL All-Star team touring overseas, and NBA stores opening up in European and Asian cities.

National Football League (NFL)

Images of tailgating, Thanksgiving Day games, and Super Bowl Sunday are enough to get any American sports fan excited. However, these words have limited meaning outside the U.S. borders. Being a specifically American sport—and not an Olympic sport, for that matter—with more than 95% of its players born in the U.S. (Wertheim, 2004a), the NFL is presented with a greater challenge when considering international expansion. Any effort to become popular in other countries would have to include the education of audiences first.

Nevertheless, that has not stopped the league from spreading the word about the sport that captivates an entire nation from August to January every year. The NFL has held preseason games in other countries (Japan, England, Germany, Canada) since 1986, when the first American Bowl was played in Tokyo ("NFL history," 2004). For the 2003 season, the National Football League broadcast games and shows in 223 countries and territories worldwide ("NFL coverage," 2003). Though the NFL has not stumbled across the football equivalent of Yao Ming, the league is looking to develop fans in the world's most populated country with community programs such as the *NFL Flag Football Clinic* held in Shanghai in 2003 ("China holds," 2003).

However, the most aggressive international move came in 1991 when the NFL launched the **World League of American Football** (WLAF), which marked the first time a U.S. based professional sport league expanded to Europe. According to NFL Commissioner Paul Tagliabue, this extension league provided a platform for the NFL to showcase the game of American Football to those outside the U.S. (Madkour & Kaplan, 2003). In its original structure, the WLAF consisted of 11 teams from North America and Europe and involved weekly intercontinental play. The extension league ceased operations after two seasons and was reintroduced in 1995 in European cities only. In 1998, the league changed its name to **NFL Europe**. In its current form, NFL Europe consists of six teams in the Netherlands, Germany, and Scotland. Following the 2003 season, NFL owners voted to continue the operations of NFL Europe for at least another two years, despite the fact that the extension league has imposed financial burdens on the owners (Wahl, 2004).

National Hockey League (NHL)

Ice hockey is played all over the world, with established and internationally recognized championships held in the Czech Republic, Finland, Russia, and Sweden, among other countries. Although it has been an Olympic sport since 1924, it wasn't until 1994 that the NHL and the International Ice Hockey Federation (IIHF) agreed to allow NHL players to participate in the 1998 Winter Olympic Games ("NHL," 2004).

Of the four U.S. major professional sport leagues, the NHL has the highest percentage of players born outside North America. *SI* reported that in 2003-04 only 67.7% of NHL players came from North America, compared to 81.3% ten years ago (Wertheim, 2004a). To reflect that transformation, in 1998 the NHL changed its All-Star Game format and introduced a North America vs. The World All-Stars competition ("NHL," 2004). The international flavor of its rosters has also provided a unique opportunity for the NHL to promote its product in the native countries of its stars. In 2003, NHL programming was distributed to 217 countries, while the league's revenue from international television deals has reportedly tripled since 1998 (Wertheim, 2004b; Wertheim, 2004a).

As early as 1938, NHL teams played exhibition games in Europe ("NHL," 2004). Building on ice hockey's global appeal, in 1989 the Calgary Flames and Washington Capitals held part of their training camp in the (former) Soviet Union, while in 1997 the league opened its regular season in Tokyo, Japan ("NHL," 2004). In 2004, four European cities and three North American cities held the **World Cup of Hockey**, an international tournament including eight of the world's ice hockey powerhouses. This tournament, which is a joint effort of the NHL and NHLPA, is only the second of its kind (the first World Cup of Hockey was held in 1996) (Bernstein, 2004). Besides the Olympics and IIHF-sanctioned world championships, other international ice hockey competitions over the years have included the Summit Series (1972), the Challenge Cup (1979), Rendez-Vous (1987), and Canada Cup (1976, 1981, 1984, 1987, and 1991) ("World Cup," 2004).

The examples described indicate that the potential for growth in foreign markets is immense. However, this growth does not come without risks. In his overview of the global sport industry, Schaaf (2004) points to five considerations that sport organizations need to keep in mind when looking to become global brands: 1) Geography; 2) Competition from existing events; 3) Perception; 4) Patience; and 5) Talent. Schaaf suggests that international expansion could be hindered by geographical and time constraints, as well as the challenge of creating meaningful competitions for fans that are already loyal to existing events. He also stresses the importance of having business relationships that will give the perception of legitimacy to a new international initiative, patience from owners and/or other investors, and, finally, the cooperation from the actual players in securing a successful venture.

Challenges in the International Expansion of U.S. Sport

Even though international expansion is a promising avenue for future growth, there are some inherent challenges for U.S. sport organizations to consider when planning their international initiatives, not the smallest of which is *competition* from existing leagues and events in the markets where they are expanding. This becomes especially relevant when the leagues are considering the creation of international divisions.

Along with this come **financial considerations**. Given its financial losses, it is questionable whether NFL Europe would still be in business without the backing of the National Football League. The challenge lies in balancing the need for growth with the financial stability of the leagues' operations. Finally, another major concern for the global expansion of U.S. sport that should not be overlooked is the possible *resistance* from foreign nations. The events of 9/11 were a clear indication that sentiments about the "American way" can vary greatly throughout the world. As LaFeber (1999) points out, U.S.-driven efforts for global expansion might be viewed not as a form of globalization but rather as Americanization. Being sensitive to local cultures and taking into account national idiosyncrasies could make for a more successful international expansion.

The European Sport Industry

The year 2004 was significant for sport in Europe, as two major events took place within the European Union (EU): the Olympic and Paralympic Games in Greece and Euro 2004 in Portugal. The rapid growth evident throughout the continent has given the European sport industry a distinctive position within the international sport industry. It has also encouraged the **European Union** to include sport as a key element in its newly formulated Constitution discussed during 2004 ("International Olympic Committee: News," 2004). Following a European year dedicated to the concept of "Education through Sport," the EU recognized the need to take an active role in European sport policy and related sporting issues. This role, yet ambiguous, concerns "promoting fairness and openness in sporting competitions and cooperation between bodies responsible for sports, and by protecting the physical and moral integrity of sportsmen and sportswomen, especially young sportsmen and sportswomen" ("International Olympic Committee: News," 2004).

The organization of sport in Europe is based in a broad network of European sport governing bodies (e.g., UEFA, FIBA Europe) and umbrella sport organizations (e.g., European Olympic Committees [EOC], European University Sports Association [EUSA]) that aim to promote sports across the continent. These organizations are rights holders of a huge number of major sporting events held regularly in Eu-

ropean countries, including European championships in all recognized sports and various categories (e.g., Euroleague). In addition, National Governing Bodies of the various sports (e.g., Hellenic Basketball Federation) operate in each country and, along with the National Olympic Committees and state or non-governmental umbrella organizations, make up the sporting structure at a state level. Historically, however, it has been the sport clubs (e.g., Real Madrid) that have formed the backbone of the European sport system. Most often, these are voluntary associations, trying to satisfy the needs and interests of their members (Rubingh & Broeke, 1998).

The continuously expanding European Union (currently consisting of 25 countries) has provided a platform for the exchange of goods, players, and capital in relation to sport. For example, the 1995 **Bosman ruling** by the European Court of Justice, which established free agency for out-of-contract players, has been considered a landmark decision with significant impact on the structure, development, and economics of professional football (soccer) clubs throughout Europe (Dobson & Gerrard, 1999). The freedom of contract significantly enhanced the transfer opportunities of professional football players in Europe and created millionaires who have more control than ever over their sporting career (Szymanski & Kuypers, 1999).

As the European Union expands, issues of cultural integration and state equality are becoming more prevalent. Sport can serve as a stabilizer in this process. It can be used as the platform to pursue social objectives by encouraging European cultures to come close to each other in this joint European effort.

Football in Europe

Over the last 15 years there have been dramatic developments in the European football (soccer) industry. The 2003 Deloitte and Touche annual review estimated the total European football market to be around 10 billion (approximately $13.2 billion) for 2001-02, with **English Premiership** (the Division I Football League in England) accounting for 25% of this market. Furthermore, data indicates that gate attendance revenues have gone up, TV revenues have increased significantly, and huge investments have been made in football's infrastructure over the last ten years (Deloitte & Touche, 2003; Dobson & Gerrard,

1999). This provides strong evidence that European football is growing in commercial terms and, consistent with the U.S model, clubs are becoming profit-maximizing corporations (Drewes, 2003).

Professional football clubs in Europe vary significantly in terms of their legal structure and ownership. For example, the typical German club is a nonprofit entity with a large number of supporters sharing part of its ownership; whereas a few Italian clubs are often controlled by major companies (e.g., Juventus, AC Milan) (Hoehn & Szymanski, 1999). In Spain, the professional clubs are private companies, often with a single owner who works together with local and regional authorities to overcome financial problems. This is because most clubs, like Barcelona and Real Madrid, are associations with political power resulting from the large number of their members who are also fans (Garcia & Rodriguez, 2003). In France, clubs can vary from associations to corporations, while in Greece clubs are treated as commercial corporations.

In spite of the complexity in the legal structure of European football, many clubs have increasingly looked to the financial markets to supply investment capital. For more than 13 years, Manchester United, a club that stands as a striking case of a business-like operation, represents one of the most attractive stock market investments, generating significant profits. Another good example of a club with global appeal is Real Madrid. By acquiring some of the world's greatest players (Beckham, Zidane, Raul, Figo, and Ronaldo), Real Madrid has achieved vast international exposure and created new fans around the globe, making the team's president, Florentino Perez, proclaim that expected revenues from marketing alone in 2004 could reach $138 million (approximately $182 million), which is equal to the total team income from 2000.

Another clear indicator of the growth of European football is the **Euro 2004** competition, which is a tournament that scored record TV audiences. It was estimated that 2.5 billion individuals, or about 80 million per match, watched the quadrennial soccer tournament, even though perennial favorites England, France, Germany, and Italy were knocked out before the semi-final round and Greece was crowned champion after defeating the host country, Portugal. Furthermore, the event was also considered a unique opportunity to communicate with tens of millions of viewers, as eight main sponsors, including fast-food chain McDonald's Corp. and soft drink seller Coca-Cola, paid more than $15 million each to be associated with the Euro 2004 tournament.

The European football model differs significantly from the American model in that it is based on a league hierarchy and the relegation rule, which allows changes in the clubs that are eligible to compete at various levels (Drewes, 2003). The right to play in the **UEFA Champions League** and the **UEFA Cup** is linked to the clubs' sporting performance in their national competitions, which again involve a relegation system. However, the most contemporary challenge for the European football industry is to come closer to the American model by introducing and making viable the newly organized **Super League**, which is called **G14** and includes football giants like Ajax Amsterdam, Manchester United, AC Milan, and Real Madrid. It has been suggested that forming a closed European super league with granted franchise rights can be successful in terms of profitability, though at the expense of abolishing the very concept of open market and its advantages (Drewes, 2003).

©iStockphoto.com

Challenges in the European Sport Industry

As the European Union expands in geographical and political terms, so do the challenges related to the continent's sport industry. As described earlier, the European sport industry has special characteristics in terms of how sport is structured, developed, and governed in different countries. This raises major concerns over the role of the European Union, and its ability to intervene and promote pan-European rules and regulations in issues such as club licensing, broadcasting rights, professional players' transfer and salaries, anti-doping, youth sportsmanship, and others.

Other challenges involving especially the most powerful professional football clubs in Europe include the leadership and management of these organizations, as well as their global growth. With the Middle East (Qatar, United Arab Emirates, Saudi Arabia, Bahrain) and Asia (e.g., China) entering the global sport industry through big investments in infrastructure and bids for major sporting events (e.g., Formula One Grand Prix in the Bahrain International Circuit, 2008 Olympic Games in Beijing, etc.), the competition becomes tighter for everybody (including the U.S.). The primary aim of the expansion plan of any professional club is to build not only a global but also a profitable brand. This creates additional challenges in terms of the management of European clubs, which need to develop their marketing operations even further in order to be competitive and take advantage of growth opportunities.

Career Opportunities in International Sport

The globalization trends evident in today's sport world—including the increasing expansion of U.S. sport organizations internationally—provide numerous career opportunities for sport management professionals. Job titles such as Director of International Sports Marketing, VP of Global Sponsorships, Senior VP of International Division, VP of International Television and Media, and Director of Global Market Development are common among those involved in international sport.

However, some of these career lines might not be obvious choices. This section outlines some areas that students interested in a career in international sport should examine.

1) **The Olympic Movement.** Many opportunities for a career in the international sport setting are related to the Olympic Movement and its organizations. In the U.S., this means becoming involved with the National Olympic Committee, the USOC, or any one of the National Governing Bodies (e.g., USA Basketball, USA Gymnastics, USA Track & Field, etc.). Another avenue is to pursue an internship or job with the International Olympic Committee (IOC) or the International Paralympic Committee (IPC), the International Federations (e.g., FIFA), or even any of the Olympic Games Organizing Committees nationally or internationally (e.g., ATHOC, BOCOG). A majority of NGBs place their job announcements on www.teamworkonline.com.

2) **U.S. Professional Leagues.** Each of the four major professional sport leagues are very active in global initiatives and even have international divisions to handle that part of their business. Whether it is in licensing, television, the Internet, events, or any one of their international offices, there are a number of opportunities through the leagues for someone interested in a career in international sport.

3) **U.S. Professional Teams.** With the increasing number of international players on the rosters of U.S. professional teams, franchises require people who can assist those international players (e.g., interpreters), or can help the organization capitalize on the opportunities that are presented. For example, the signing of Yao Ming in Houston has created a unique opportunity to reach out to the Asian population in the area and also deal with Chinese organizations (e.g., sponsors, television stations) interested in forming business relationships with the franchise.

4) **Sport Management Agencies.** U.S.-based sport marketing and management agencies have long conducted business on a global scale. Companies such as the International Management Group (IMG) and Octagon each have international divisions as well as more than 50 offices worldwide. Becoming involved in one of those offices could be the avenue to an international career in sport.

5) **Athletic Apparel and Footwear Companies.** For those interested in entering the apparel and footwear side of the industry, there are opportunities for an international career. U.S.-based companies Nike and Reebok do business worldwide, from production and distribution to product promotion and sponsoring of international events. Furthermore, foreign-based companies like adidas and Puma have offices in the U.S and actively promote their products in North America. Working for one of those companies can provide the opportunity to be stationed overseas and pursue a career internationally. Take, for example, Puma.

On its web site (http://www.puma.com), the company advertises positions available not only in the United States but also in Hong Kong, Belgium, Austria, France, Germany, and Switzerland.

6) **U.S. Companies with International Sponsorships.** In 2002, Sports Business Journal published a special report on international sport. In that issue, it was reported that at the time there were 30 U.S. companies with overseas sports sponsorships and 65 overseas companies with U.S. sports sponsorships ("U.S. companies," 2002; "Overseas companies," 2002). Companies such as Coca-Cola, MasterCard, and Xerox have for years sponsored international sport organizations and events (e.g., Olympic Games). Consequently, they require personnel to handle those relationships. Although not always an obvious choice, this could be a great way to become involved in international aspects of the sport industry.

So, how does one prepare for such a career? What are those skills that will make you an attractive candidate for such a position? Here are some of the qualifications that employers will be looking for when hiring for a position in the international sector of the sport marketplace:

- **Educational background in international sport management.** Even if the program in which the student is enrolled does not offer an international sport management-type course, the student could take general business or international studies courses covering international business affairs.

- **Practical experience in international sport.** Especially if one is in the beginning of his or her career, the most appropriate way to obtain some experience in international sport might be through internships with an international sport organization or a U.S. organization doing business in other countries (Masteralexis & McDonald, 1997).

- **Foreign language skills.** The knowledge of a second (and even third) language enhances the appeal of a candidate when being considered for a position that involves dealing with people who speak another language. Even though one would be advised to avoid doing business in a foreign language unless they are fluent, a basic knowledge

of a foreign language could help form a warm relationship with international business partners (Gillentine, Goldfine & Orejan, 2004; Gillentine, A. and Orejan, J., 2003; Masteralexis & McDonald, 1997).

- **Knowledge and proficiency in new media.** As sport becomes more global, advances in technology, such as the Internet, web TV, and international cell phones become more commonplace. A student preparing for a career in international sport should be knowledgeable about such devices and able to incorporate them into their business operations.

- **Cultural sensitivity and the ability to adapt to other cultures.** An international sport manager should be able to effectively communicate and work with partners from different parts of the world and also adapt to various working environments. Openness and sensitivity to other cultures are essential skills. The best way to obtain those skills of course would be to live in another country. But since that is not always possible, participating in a study abroad or exchange program could provide one with an understanding of cultural nuances and with a tolerance for differences in cultures. Other ways to obtain cultural training would be through university courses (e.g., history, geography, world politics), or through interaction with people from other cultures.

- **Willingness to travel and/or relocate to another country.** Flexibility is important when working in the sport industry. It becomes even more important when one is involved in the international sector, since spending a great deal of time overseas might be a large component of one's job description.

Summary

- Over the past decade we have witnessed significant movement and expansion in our industry; sport is becoming a more global business. This globalization is facilitated by technological advances (e.g., the Internet) as well as administrative, political, and social developments across the globe.

- The Olympic Movement—which consists of the

International Olympic Committee (IOC), National Olympic Committees (NOCs), Organizing Committees of the Olympic Games (OCOGs), International Federations (IFs), and National Governing Bodies (NGBs) and is responsible for organizing the Summer and Winter Olympic Games—has experienced tremendous growth not only in participation and attendance figures, but also in broadcasting and sponsorship revenue.

- U.S. professional leagues (MLB, NBA, NFL, and NHL) are reaching consumers in new markets by holding games, tours, and clinics internationally. In addition, the increasing number of foreign players participating in U.S.-based leagues has created inroads for expansion in those players' native countries through lucrative broadcasting, sponsorship, and licensing agreements.

- The structure of European sport is based on European sport governing bodies (e.g., UEFA) and umbrella organizations (e.g., EOC) that promote the growth of sport throughout the continent. European sport differs from the league-based organization of U.S. sport; sport clubs (e.g., Manchester United) operate within a league hierarchy and relegation rules.

- Opportunities for a career in international sport exist with the Olympic Movement associations (e.g., IOC, USOC), with U.S. professional leagues and teams, sport management agencies (e.g., IMG), athletic apparel and footwear companies, and with corporations involved in international sponsorships.

- For those considering a career in the global sport industry, an educational background in international business, practical experience internationally, foreign language skills, proficiency in new media, cultural sensitivity, an ability to adapt to other cultures, and a willingness to travel or relocate to another country are some of the skills needed to be successful.

Discussion Activities

1. Have you had any indications in your everyday involvement in sport and study of sport management of the globalization process occurring in the sport industry? If so, please identify five specific examples of this process.

2. Identify two National Governing Bodies (NGBs) that operate in the United States. What are the functions of those organizations? What is their relationship with their respective International Federations and with the Olympic Movement?

3. This chapter provided examples of the international expansion of U.S. sport (particularly the four major leagues). What do you think are the positive consequences of their global expansion? What, if any, are the negative consequences?

4. What are the major differences between the structure of the U.S. and European professional leagues? Based on your understanding of the European sport industry, would an expansion U.S. league be successful in Europe? Please provide justification for your response.

5. What do you think is the best way for one to develop the suggested skills necessary for a career in the international sport industry? In addition to those characteristics discussed in this chapter, are there any other skills that could also be useful?

References

Adams, R. (2004, March 8-14). Road trip to Japan carries MLB international hopes. *Street & Smith's SportsBusiness Journal, 6*(45), 8.

Bernstein, A. (2004, January 26-February 1). NHL, union team up to fill World Cup roster. *Street & Smith's SportsBusiness Journal, 6*(39), 4.

Bloom, B. M. (2004, July 5). Tournament on track for 2005. *Major League Baseball: News.* Retrieved July 13, 2004, from http://mlb.mlb.com/NASApp/mlb/mlb/news/mlb_news.jsp.

China holds first NFL flag football clinic. (2003, October 13). *NFL.com – International.* Retrieved July 16, 2004, from http://www.nfl.com/international/story/6718422.

Crowe, J. (2004, June 15). Outside influence. *Los Angeles Times,* p. 7. Retrieved June 15, 2004, from Lexis Nexis database.

Deloitte & Touche. (July 2003). The annual review of football finance.

Dobson, S., & Gerrard, B. (1999). The determination of player transfer fees in English professional soccer. *Journal of Sport Management, 13*(4), 259-279.

Drewes, M. (2003). Competition and efficiency in professional sports leagues. *European Sport Management Quarterly, 3*(4), 240-252.

Europa: European Commission, Sport. (2004). *Europa: European Commission, sport-press releases.* Retrieved July 20, 2004, from http://europa.eu.int/comm/sport/action_sports/aees/aees_overview_en.html.

Garcia, J., & Rodriguez, P. (2003). From sports clubs to stock companies: The financial structure of football in Spain, 1992-2001. *European Sport Management Quarterly, 3*(4), 253-268.

Gillentine, A., Goldfine, B., & Orejan, J. (2004). *An examination of the need for international education and second language acquisition in the sport industry.* Paper presented at North American Society for Sport Management Conference, Atlanta, GA.

Gillentine, A., & Orejan, J. (2003). *An examination of second language requirements and international sport education at selected sport administration/management academic programs.* Paper presented at the North American Society of Sport Management Proceedings, Ithaca, NY.

Globalization. *Britannica Concise Encyclopedia.* Retrieved July 25, 2004, from Encyclopædia Britannica Premium Service. http://www.britannica.com/ebc/article?eu=390996.

Graczyk, W. (2003). Major League Baseball opens Tokyo office Aug. 1. *Tokyo Weekender –Sports News – Sports.* Retrieved July 26, 2004, from http://www.weekender.co.jp/new/030801/sports_news-030801.html.

Hoehn, T., & Szymanski, S. (1999). The Americanization of European football. *Economic Policy,* 203-204.

International Olympic Committee: Documents. (2004). *International Olympic Committee Document – Olympic Marketing.* Retrieved August 4, 2004, from http://multimedia.olympic.org/pdf/en_report_845.pdf.

International Olympic Committee: News (2004). *International Olympic Committee – New – Olympic News.* Retrieved July 15, 2004, from http://www.olympic.org/uk/news/olympic_news/week_uk.asp.

International Olympic Committee: News. (2004). *International Olympic Committee – News – Olympic News.* Retrieved July 5, 2004, from http://www.olympic.org/uk/news/olympic news/full_story_uk.asp?id=899.

International Olympic Committee: News. (2004). *International Olympic Committee – News – Olympic News.* Retrieved July 6, 2004, from http://www.olympic.org/uk/news/olympic_news/full_story_uk.asp?id=917.

International Olympic Committee: Organisation. (2004). *International Olympic Committee –Organisation – Olympic Marketing.* Retrieved August 4, 2004, from http://www.olympic.org/uk/organisation/facts/introduction/index_uk.asp.

International Olympic Committee: Organisation. (2004). *International Olympic Committee –Organisation – Olympic Movement.* Retrieved August 4, 2004, from http://www.olympic.org/uk/organisation/movement/index_uk.asp.

International Olympic Committee: Organisation. (2004). *International Olympic Committe –Organisation – Structures.* Retrieved August 6, 2004, from http://www.olympic.org/uk/organisation/ioc/index_uk.asp.

International players in the NBA. (2004, March 15). *NBA.com: International players in the NBA.* Retrieved July 26, 2004, from http://www.nba.com/players/international_player_directory.html.

King, B. (2003, October 13-19). League strengthens efforts to reach a worldwide audience. *Street & Smith's SportsBusiness Journal, 6*(25), 22.

LaFeber, W. (1999). *Michael Jordan and the new global capitalism.* New York: W. W. Norton & Company, Inc.

Lombardo, J. (2003a, October 27-November 2). Game plan calls for growth overseas. *Street & Smith's SportsBusiness Journal, 6*(27), 25.

Lombardo, J. (2003b, October 27-November 2). League scores big with merchandise sales. *Street & Smith's SportsBusiness Journal, 6*(27), 26.

Major League Baseball International Envoy Program visits 27 countries in 2004. (2004, July 9). *Major League Baseball News.* Retrieved July 26, 2004, from http://mlb.mlb.com/NASApp/mlb/mlb/news/mlb_int_press_release.jsp?ymd=20040709&content_id=793637&vkey=pr_mlb_int&fext=.jsp.

Masteralexis, L. P., & McDonald, M. A. (1997). Enhancing sport management education with international dimensions including language and cultural training. *Journal of Sport Management, 11,* 97-110.

Madkour, A., & Kaplan, D. (2003, September 1-7). Tagliabue keeps his focus on the future. *Street & Smith's SportsBusiness Journal, 6*(19), 1, 26-27.

Manou, N. (2003). Greece faces the challenge of growth. *Trade with Greece, the official magazine of the Athens Chamber of Commerce and Industry, 23,* 6-9.

NBA announces international preseason schedule (2003, June 2). *NBA.com: NBA Announces International Preseason Schedule.* Retrieved July 16, 2004, from http://www.nba.com/global/intl_preseason_030602.html.

National Olympic Committees: Missions of the NOCs. (2004). *International Olympic Committee – Organisation – Structures.* Retrieved August 6, 2004, from http://www.olympic.org/uk/organisation/noc/index_uk.asp.

NFL coverage spans the globe – agreements bring football to Japan, China. (2003, September 11). *NFL.com – International.* Retrieved July 16, 2004, from http://www.nfl.com/international/story/6633757.

NFL history. (2004). *NFL.com – NFL History.* Retrieved July 28, 2004, from http://www.nfl.com/history/chronology/1981-1990.

NHL – International timeline. (2004). *WCH2004.com Official site of World Cup of Hockey 2004.* Retrieved July 29, 2004, from http://wch2004.com/history/timeline.html.

Overseas companies and their U.S. sports sponsorships. (2002, April 22-28). *Street & Smith's SportsBusiness Journal, 4*(53), 23-24.

Rubingh, B., & Broeke, A. (1998). The European sports club system. In L. P. Masteralexis, C. A. Barr, & M. A. Hums (Eds.), *Principles and practice of sport management.* Gaithersburg, MD: Aspen Publishers, Inc.

Schaaf, P. (2004). *Sports, Inc.: 100 years of sports business.* Amherst, NY: Prometheus Books.

Szymanski, S., & Kuypers, T. (1999). *Winners and losers.* Harmondsworth, UK: Viking.

The Authoritative Annual Research Guide & Fact Book. (2003, December 29). Broadcast rights to major sports properties. *Sports Business Journal, 6*(36), 82.

U.S. companies and their overseas sports sponsorships. (2002, April 22-28). *Street & Smith's SportsBusiness Journal, 4*(53), 22.

Wahl, G. (2004, July 5). Football vs. Futbol. *Sports Illustrated,* 68-72.

Wertheim, L. J. (2004a, June 14). The whole world is watching. *Sports Illustrated,* 70-86.

Wertheim, L. J. (2004b, June 21). Hot prospects in cold places. *Sports Illustrated*, 62-66.

Westerbeek, H., & Smith, A. (2003). *Sport business in the global marketplace*. New York, NY: Palgrave Macmillan.

World Cup of Hockey 2004 to feature eight national teams. (2004). *WCH2004.com Official site of World Cup of Hockey 2004*. Retrieved July 29, 2004, from http://wch2004.com/news/ release.html.

Suggested Reading

Fay, T. G. (2003). International sport. In J. B. Parks & J. Quarterman (Eds.), *Contemporary sport management*. Champaign, IL: Human Kinetics.

Gladden, J. M., & Lizandra, M. (1998). International sport. In L. P. Masteralexis, C. A. Barr, & M. A. Hums (Eds.), *Principles and practices of sport management*. Gaithersburg, MD: Aspen Publishers, Inc.

Hums, M. A., & MacLean, J. C. (2004). *Governance and policy in sport organizations*. Scottsdale, AZ: Holcomb Hathaway, Publishers, Inc.

LaFeber, W. (1999). *Michael Jordan and the new global capitalism*. New York, NY: W. W. Norton & Company, Inc.

Maguire, J. (1999). *Global sport: Identities, societies, civilizations*. Cambridge, UK: Polity Press.

Riordan, J., & Krüger, A. (1999). *The international politics of sport in the 20th century*. New York: Routledge.

Rubingh, B., & Broeke, A. (1998). The European sports club system. In L. P. Masteralexis, C. A. Barr, & M. A. Hums (Eds.), *Principles and practices of sport management*. Gaithersburg, MD: Aspen Publishers, Inc.

Schaaf, P. (2004). *Sports, Inc.: 100 Years of Sports Business*. Amherst, NY: Prometheus Books.

Senn, A. E. (1999). *Power, politics, and the Olympic Games*. Champaign, IL: Human Kinetics.

Thoma, J. E., & Chalip, L. (1996). *Sport governance in the global community*. Morgantown, WV: Fitness Information Technology.

Westerbeek, H., & Smith, A. (2003). *Sport business in the global marketplace*. New York, NY: Palgrave Macmillan.

Chapter Fourteen

Sport Management Internships
John Miller

© 2003 Universal Press Syndicate   www.ucomics.com   2-1

"Get in here, Markman. I wanna bounce
some ideas off you, too."

Learning Objectives

Upon completion of this chapter, the reader should be able to

■ Explain how an internship increases the likelihood of attaining employment in the sport industry;

■ Describe the abilities a competent sport management professional should exhibit and how to better develop them;

■ Recognize the policy areas an intern should be familiar with prior to applying for an internship;

■ Discuss the different ways an intern can investigate a potential organization and why it is important in providing a successful experience;

■ Identify the legal concerns that an intern should address while investigating a potential organization; and

■ Understand how the evaluation processes assists the intern in making the experience a truly academic learning experience.

Introduction

Selecting a career path is among the most important proactive decisions a young person can make. Future sport management professionals can "stack" the odds in their favor or empower themselves by obtaining a specific internship in sport management. In fact, the internship experience has been identified as *the most critical element* of professional preparation for future

---

"IT IS FROM EXPERIENCES THAT WE GET OUR EDUCATION OF LIFE."

MARK TWAIN

---

sport managers (Coco, 2000; Cuneen & Sidwell, 1993; Li, Cobb, & Sawyer, 1994; Mason, Higgins, & Wilkinson, 1981; Stier, 2002; Sutton, 1989). According to Coco (2000), whereas only 1 out of 36 students had completed an internship prior to graduation in 1980, 75% of graduates had fulfilled an internship experience in 2000. A prime reason for this increase may be due to students viewing internships as a way to improve their likelihood of obtaining employment (Cook, Parker & Pettijohn, 2004).

Scott (1992) revealed that placement directors, graduates, and current students thought that internships were the single most effective strategy for gaining employment. Cannon and Arnold (1998) also reported that internships are often used by students as a way to improve their job searches. Additionally, Pianko (1996) reported that some organizations hired as many as 70% of the individuals who had participated in their company's internship program. A 2001 survey of graduates conducted by the National Association of Colleges and Employers (NACE) revealed that 57% of interns were offered full-time positions by the organization that had previously sponsored them (Altschuler, 2002). Concerning wages, the new hires who had taken part in the organization's internship program earned as much as $2000 more in terms of starting salary (Pianko, 1996). Gault, Redington, and Schlager (2000) supported this finding by indicating that students who successfully completed internships found employment faster at higher starting salaries and

higher levels of job satisfaction than those that did not participate.

While they can help the future sport manager obtain a professional position at a higher salary, it is important to understand "how" to have a successful internship experience. Internships, when designed and implemented effectively, can help future sport managers learn to navigate the sport business world as well as gain insight from mistakes that would likely be damaging under other conditions. Internships are an effective way to "test the waters" before taking a permanent position, and they are an invaluable resource for recruiting candidates, directing career paths, and enlarging the number of individuals that maintain their career path (Leach, 1998). This type of experience can give the sport management intern an opportunity to reevaluate and readjust their specific professional expectancies.

Linking Theoretical to Practical

"HOW EMPTY IS THEORY IN THE PRESENCE OF FACT."

MARK TWAIN

According to Stark and Lowther (1988), a competent professional should exhibit conceptual, technical, and integrative capabilities. Thus, competent professionals are often depicted as possessing the ability to link theoretical knowledge with suitable values and attitudes when making multifaceted judgments within vague parameters (Stark & Lowther, 1988). However, Paranto and Champagne (1996) reported that while employers were satisfied with graduates' professional attitudes and their technical abilities, they were not content with the interns' skills or their ability to apply conceptual theories to real-world situations. Skills that the intern should understand as being particularly important in a management-oriented setting are 1) willingness to learn, 2) reading and writing, 3) oral communication and listening, 4) creative and critical thinking and problem solving, 5) personal management, 6) group effectiveness, and 7) organizational effectiveness and leadership (Carnevale, Gainer, & Meltzer, 1990; McCormick, 1993).

Jones (1997) reported that employers thought college graduates often did not possess the ability to solve complex, ill-structured problems. According to Jones (1997), the employees frequently tried to develop a single "right" answer while infrequently suggesting alternatives, even when they were requested to develop more than one strategy. In fact, Useem (1995) questioned whether students will "be prepared to acquire knowledge later in a work environment that stresses personal initiative and collaborative work" if they "acquire knowledge by passively listening to authoritative figures at the lectern and experience no dialogue with them or with themselves" (p. 23).

The Business Higher Education Forum (1995) revealed that corporate leaders, nationwide, believed that graduates did not possess "leadership and communication skills; quantification skills; interpersonal relations; the ability to work in teams; the understanding to work with a diverse work force at home and abroad; and the capacity to adapt to rapid change" (p. 3). As such, it is not surprising that Van Horn (1995) found that over two-thirds of corporate employers felt that college graduates were incompetent. Thus, it appears that a significant amount of research indicates that potential interns, while not lacking conceptual or technical competencies, are sorely deficient in the integrative competency.

Examination of Sport Management Internship Policies

"SUPPOSING IS GOOD, BUT FINDING OUT IS BETTER."

MARK TWAIN

While standards established through the joint efforts of the National Association for Sport and Physical Education and the North American Society for Sport Management (NASPE/NASSM) (2000) endorse the internship experience, they provide little support for any specific, consistent standards and/or practices

within a sport management internship program. Therefore, a student must develop an understanding for the university's required standards for internship application. To accomplish this, the student should identify the **internship policies** required by the department. The following are some potential policy areas that the student intern should investigate:

1) **Credit requirements** – General requirements may include being a sport management major, successfully completing at least 50% of the total credit hours required at the institution, and possessing an overall grade point average of 3.0.

2) **Grade point average** – Many sport management departments may specify that students must hold a cumulative 3.0 GPA to qualify for internships. Possessing a high overall GPA makes sense, since an individual who has shown to be better educationally prepared may attain better internship opportunities (Beard 1997; Maynard, 1999).

3) **Deadlines for application** – Often students who desire to apply for an internship may be required to submit an application (along with a resume) by a specific deadline. The deadline should be during the time period prior to the term that the internship is to take place, so that there is sufficient time to help the student find appropriate placement (Verner, 2004).

4) **Identification of organizations** – Sport management departments often list organizations in which a previous student(s) had a successful experience. The potential student intern may consider asking if any policies regarding internship sites exist. These policies may outline the responsibility of the organization to willingly provide students with appropriate supervision and with an opportunity to perform professional quality work. These policies can also identify the characteristics of the person who is knowledgeable about the professional quality work that the student is supposed to perform. For example, if a facility management supervisor fails to communicate or delegate job responsibilities to the intern, it will give the intern a "non-learning" experience.

5) **Number of hours required to complete the internship** – NASPE/NASSM internship guidelines specify the standard number of hours an

intern should complete for a sport management internship is 40 hours per week (NASPE/NASSM, 2000). The student should inquire whether the internship must be completed in one semester or if it can be taken over continuous semesters. This is especially critical for students initiating an internship during the university's summer session.

6) **Evaluation of internship** – Henry, Razzouk, and Hooverland (1988) indicated that the internship should be graded according to a pass/fail system for evaluating the performance of the intern; however, the evaluation process is totally at the discretion of the university. Additional concerns regarding evaluation and assessment of the internship experience will be addressed later in this chapter.

The potential intern may also investigate policies that address a) the anticipation that the intern will work his or her agreed-upon hours and present excellent professional work; b) professional attitude, dress, and appearance requirements of the student during the internship; c) potential for unethical or illegal requests; d) need for confidentiality; and/or e) what to do if an organization with which the student has an internship goes out of business or relocates (Somerick, 2001).

©iStockphoto.com

Screening and Selecting the Sport Management Site

"HALF OUR LIFE IS SPENT TRYING TO FIND SOMETHING TO DO WITH THE TIME WE HAVE RUSHED THROUGH LIFE TRYING TO SAVE."

WILL ROGERS

Once the potential intern has adequately addressed policies that impact the internship, consideration should be given to ensuring that time is not wasted, since an internship program should satisfy both the industry reality and student expectation. Hite and Bellizzi (1986) indicated that if the internship site is not carefully investigated the intern may have an unsatisfactory experience due to three key points: a) unclear standards; b) misinterpretation or misrepresentation by students regarding the expectancies of the position; and c) misrepresentation by the firm concerning the required responsibilities. To prevent any of these from occurring, the student intern must identify, screen, and monitor potential sport management sites well in advance of the commencement of the internship. Suggested ways for students to gain this knowledge are to review literature related to their specific strengths and desires in sport management, visit the web site of the potential internship location, attend professional conferences/conventions, and/or volunteer for activities within their field(s) of interest.

The student should also be very wary of agencies that may place them with mentors who use them only as clerical staff. A general rule of thumb for the potential intern to consider regarding whether the experience will be meaningful is: if the assignment may be carried out by the intern's on-site supervisor or by a person of equal status in the organization, the internship has potential to be a meaningful experience (Verner, 2004). By thoroughly investigating the organization offering the internship, students can assess their strengths and desires as they relate to the organization, thereby providing them with a positive experience. These assessments can provide students with an opportunity to further understand and apply their theoretical and technical competencies while developing their skills.

An additional consideration when **screening** for an appropriate sport management internship site concerns the recognition and competency of the organization as it applies to the area of student interest. What would appear to be a career "fit" that looks good on paper may be tested through the internship experience. Therefore, the sport management intern should not look at the experience as important simply because it helps one obtain a professional position, but also because it helps identify a specific sport management career path. Sometimes students searching for an internship site apply to organizations that may have an availability that is close to, but not specifically, the area in which the student desires to work. For example, should the student wish to learn about facility management, it may not be beneficial for the student to apply for an internship in sport marketing. While these areas are within the confines of sport management, the integration of principles for each of these sub-areas is totally different, potentially depriving the student of an appropriate learning opportunity. Whereas the students may successfully pass the internship class in the immediate future, the actual impact may prevent them from being adequately prepared for a professional sport management position.

The potential organization should also provide the intern opportunities to *observe* and *participate* in management related issues. To make certain these opportunities take place, the intern, in conjunction with the on-site supervisor and faculty member, should compose a written list of responsibilities expected of the student. At the start of the semester in which the internship will be conducted, it is generally a good idea for the students to meet with their on-site mentors to talk about how they will be evaluated. The intern and mentor then sign an internship evaluation agreement that outlines specific evaluation criteria. Although the evaluations may vary slightly due to differences in tasks across the organizational areas, normal criteria to be evaluated include quality of task performance, attendance and punctuality, attitude and enthusiasm, communication skills, creativity, honesty, and initiative.

Interns need to have a *clear picture of all the duties and responsibilities* that are expected of a sport manager. Questions that the sport management intern may ask when screening organizations may include the following:

1. Will the organization allow the intern to be actively involved and receive ongoing feedback?

2. Will the intern be put into a position that will allow him or her to apply theoretical knowledge to longstanding and new real-world open-ended issues and problems?

3. Will the intern be put into a position that will allow him or her to integrate discipline-based knowledge with process skills, including problem solving, information literacy, critical thinking, analysis, communications, and teamwork?

4. Will the intern be put into a position that will allow him or her to improve existing abilities and skills?

5. Will the intern be provided time for continuous evaluation and reflection?

The aforementioned questions should be asked by the students of themselves as well as to the on-site mentor. Failure to do so may result in the student not only finding him or herself in a non-academic environment, but also one in which he or she is not able to integrate classroom knowledge. This is especially true since the quality of task performance is generally regarded as having the most importance in the evaluation process in many internship experiences.

Legal Concerns of Internship Experiences

Research has indicated legal issues such as **paid internships, workmen's compensation, sexual harassment,** and **general liability** issues should be investigated when screening a potential organization (Brown-Foster & Moorman, 2001; Miller, Anderson, & Ayres, 2002; Swift & Russell, 1999). The following will describe specific areas that the student should take into consideration when searching for an internship site.

Paid Internships

Many, if not most, student interns work for free. It is commonly estimated that at least 50% of all internships are unpaid (Barry, 2001; Gilbertson, 1997). According to Cook, Parker, and Pettijohn (2004), payment was not found to be a primary issue regarding a student's involvement with the internship program. Under the Fair Labor Standards Act (FLSA), *employers are not required to pay interns who qualify as trainees.*

However, if the internship is paid, the organization may limit the hours of the internship, thus preventing him or her from being eligible for benefits. This allows the organization to categorize the intern as a temporary employee (Sturges, 1993). Should this situation arise, the intern should still expect the organization to pay at least minimum wage or comparable to the wages earned by others in the organization doing similar work (Sturges, 1993).

Workman's Compensation

An organization may not provide an intern with enough hours to be considered an employee, thus rendering him or her ineligible for certain benefits such as workman's compensation, a type of coverage in which the organization is held liable for medical benefits and wages if the intern is injured on the job (Kaplan, 1994). There are several reasons for this. First, many state workman's compensation laws do not distinguish between employees and trainees (Swift & Russell, 1999). Secondly, workman's compensation boards may determine that interns contribute enough to a company to qualify as employees and receive this benefit (*Evanson v. Univ. of Hawaii*, 1971). Thirdly, some courts have held that even though a student is not paid for an internship, he or she gains important training and valuable experience that is equivalent to wages. For example, in *Hallal v. RDV Sports, Inc.* (1996), the plaintiff was enrolled in a sports internship class that was required within the university's curriculum. Although he was only involved in the program for academic reasons, the court held that he was still considered an employee. Therefore, it would be wise for the student intern and faculty advisor to investigate whether the potential organization possesses an effective risk-management program to cover interns

under workman's compensation, even though it is not required to do so.

The student intern as well as the faculty advisor must also note that the workman's compensation statute may hold that an internship employer in a university-sponsored internship program is considered to be an employer of a student intern, unless that internship is not paid. If the internship is an unpaid experience, the responsibility for coverage reverts back to the university (Henry, Razzouk, & Hoverland, 1988; *Kinder v. Industrial Claim Appeals Office*, 1998).

Sexual Harrassment

An area that the student intern should be particularly aware of is sexual harassment. While researching a specific organization, the intern should consider whether the organization provides any orientation to company policies concerning sexual harassment. This is an especially critical step since interns may be more vulnerable to sexual harassment than students or full-time employees (Bowen & Laurion, 1994). Therefore, sexual harassment may be a chief consideration when the institution is sending students to an organization as interns. However, the intern must understand that it is the responsibility of the organization to protect all employees from harassment; thus, interns should be encouraged to follow the same procedures of reporting incidents of harassment as the regular, full-time employees (Kaplan, 1994).

General Liability

Though many may think it is unlikely, it is possible that during the internship experience the student may be injured or may injure someone else. While workman's compensation can protect the intern as well as the sponsoring organization, the organization may be generally liable for the negligent act of a regular employee resulting in an injury to another. It is imperative for interns to understand whether they will be categorized as a 'regular' or 'non-regular' employee.

Miller et al. (2002) reported factors that may affect the intern's classification as an employee include number of hours worked, wages earned, indirect benefits received, discretionary decision making power, and genuine benefit to the ongoing operations of the organization. Thus, it is recommended that individuals entering an internship experience review the internship agreement with the on-site and faculty supervisors to gain a better understanding of their position or designation within the organization. The agreement must include provisions that assign legal responsibility for potential injuries that may take place during the internship.

©stock.xchng iv

Evaluating the Student Intern

The National Society for Experiential Education identified two key strategies for the student and faculty member to consider in creating strong, academically related internships (Inkster & Ross, 1995). First, it is suggested that the student work closely with faculty and the on-site mentor to recognize and express acceptable educational objectives relating to what the student intends to learn and do in the internship. Duly (1982) emphasized the importance of this step for students and supervisors, as it helps them understand how the skills and knowledge can be demonstrated as end products of the experience, while also showing what kind of conditions are likely to help promote these types of skills. Secondly, while many internships concentrate on the attainment of specific techniques and skills related to appropriate professional practices, the internship can also aid in a students' intellectual development. Internships can help students to learn how to reflect while in action, develop new methods of reasoning, construct and test new categories of understanding, experiment with different action strategies, and try new ways of framing problems (Schön, 1987).

Despite the major differences between college and work environments, there are ways that student interns can involve themselves in the learning experiences to more effectively prepare them for the transition to the workplace. The primary objective of a student engaged in an academic internship should be to *integrate* classroom teaching with field-based application opportuni-

ties to develop their potential management skills. Clear objectives regarding the proposed learning outcomes provide the basis for internship evaluations. Therefore, the assessments of student learning in internships should provide a precise and comprehensible description of learning, and the methods and reporting strategies used should enhance learning (Guskey, 1994). A series of goals in communications, listening, writing, problem solving, critical thinking, and critical reading can help the intern identify priorities (Jones, 1997). Each objective may be based on a comprehensive review of the literature and may outline a comprehensive framework for each major skill, and then it may also define in greater specificity key dimensions associated with strong mastery. Thus, while true learning is multifaceted, appropriate evaluation should be also. With that in mind, interns should understand the importance of the following strategies that they may be required to complete.

Weekly Journals

McCormick (1993) suggested that journal essays are one of the best ways available for the intern to develop **reflective learning**. Research has found that interns that have incorporated weekly journal reports as an integrative activity demonstrated the ability to transfer classroom knowledge to the "real world" (Eyler, 1994). The journal essays may be beneficially used for interns to think critically about the aptitudes required for a particular sport management position (Young & Baker, 2004). The interns then can reflect on their particular strengths and weaknesses for the position and indicate how they plan to improve the future quality of their work. The internship journal can also provide interns with the opportunity to identify specific situations that may be encountered in the organization and think critically about how they might handle the situation if they were in a decision making position. Additionally, not only will these weekly reports give interns time to reflect upon their internship experience, but they will also help interns and the instructor maintain regular contact when class meetings are not possible. In some cases, the faculty supervisor cannot make regular visits. However, through reading the weekly essays, the faculty advisor can keep track of the students' progress and the quality of their experiences while recognizing potential problems.

On-site Supervisor Evaluations

The on-site supervisor may be asked to provide a midterm and a final grade for their interns based on the interns' performance in the organization. At the start of the semester, interns meet with their faculty and on-site supervisor to discuss how the intern will be assessed. The intern, faculty, and on-site supervisor all sign an internship grading agreement that outlines detailed evaluation criteria. Items that are often included within the internship grade agreement are the a) quality of task performance; b) attendance and punctuality; c) attitude and enthusiasm; d) communication skills; e) creativity, honesty, and initiative; and f) professionalism. On predetermined midterm and final due dates, the interns' on-site supervisor submits a grade as well as a detailed written evaluation of the intern to the faculty supervisor.

Internship Projects

Often the most significantly weighted item when grading an intern is the *quality* or professionalism of task performances. For example, after a careful mentoring and observation phase, the on-site supervisor may ask the intern to evaluate a marketing plan to increase the number of season ticket-holders. This would involve integrating academic knowledge with information acquired by the intern through his or her organizational experiences. Other projects in which a sport management intern may be included are the renovation of a sport facility, designing media guides, developing fundraising plans, or creating policy manuals (Cuneen & Sidwell, 1994). Therefore, interns should be given or—even better—*ask for* projects that allow them to integrate their conceptual competencies with the technical skills needed to develop novel solutions to a problem.

Mid-Semester Internship Evaluation

During the middle of the respective semester, interns may be required to meet with the faculty supervisor to present verbal reports, indicate any problems they are having, help provide solutions to other interns who might be having difficulties, and obtain information on policies, performance appraisal strategies, and portfolio preparation. If the intern cannot meet directly with the faculty supervisor, other options, such as phone conversations, can be supplemented by faxes, email, or regular mail. The intern should also meet with the on-site supervisor on a formal basis to receive an assessment during the middle and end of the semester. This assessment should address the strengths and weaknesses of the intern as well as offer suggestions concerning how the intern may improve on his or her responsibilities. The mid-semester evaluation conference is significant, as it provides an opportunity for well thought out feedback, from the faculty as well as the on-site supervisor, regarding the intern's performance up to that time. Additionally, it gives the student and respective supervisors a chance to reevaluate goals for the remainder of the internship. At no time should the intern become defensive when given appropriately constructive feedback by either the supervisor or faculty during the mid-semester evaluation.

Final Evaluation Report Portfolio

Most interns are required to complete **final portfolio reports** in order to assess their overall sport management experience as well as critique their own performance. To best critique the internship experience, the interns are given the opportunity to reflect on which learning outcomes they have fully achieved and how those outcomes were reached. Additionally, the intern reflects on areas of the internship that could be stronger or improved, what behaviors they engaged in most often, which courses best equipped them for their experiences, and whether these experiences had an effect on their career interests (Palomba & Banta, 1999).

Portfolios can also be used to measure interns' development and progress. Interns place in the portfolio a collection of the materials they have produced through the internship. Items such as colleague or supervisor evaluations and the intern's work (i.e., proposals, brochures, reports, workshop outlines, memos, or letters) may be included.

Conclusion

Significant differences exist between the cultures of college and the workplace (Holton, 1998). Usually, university students get regular feedback about their performance through grades and comments from faculty and peers. Feedback in the workplace is infrequent and less precise (Holton, 1998). Students usually participate in highly structured professional preparation programs that provide a great deal of direction. Employees usually work in highly unstructured environments and engage in tasks that have few directions, and they experience less personal support than in college and also encounter frequent and unexpected changes.

How can a sport management student productively make the transition to becoming a competently skilled professional as previously identified? Internships provide opportunities for students to learn about life in the "real world" without the commitment of a full-time position. Internships can present sport management students with an opportunity to evolve from learning career-related skills in the classroom to the application of these skills in a management-oriented environment. This can help the intern not only "get a leg up" on the competition, but also obtain a position at a higher salary.

To better prepare themselves for the internship experience and, ultimately, the workplace, sport management student interns should consider the following recommendations. First, the sport management intern should concentrate on investigating and selecting sport related organizations that will allow them to integrate their conceptual and technical competencies to further develop such skills as leadership, teamwork, problem solving, time management, communication, and analytical thinking within the classroom setting. Secondly, potential student interns should focus on developing such personal traits as ethics, adaptability, self-management, global consciousness, and a passion for lifelong learning. Finally, the potential student intern should take any opportunity to apply theoretical concepts of sport management to "real" learning experiences such as volunteer or summer work prior to the internship experience.

Summary

- The internship experience has been identified as the most critical element of professional preparation for future sport managers as a way to improve the likelihood of obtaining employment.

- Interns should be able to develop their integrative skills in addition to their technical and conceptual capabilities to become an effective sport manager.

Specific integrative competencies include 1) learning to learn; 2) reading and writing; 3) oral communication and listening; 4) creative and critical thinking and problem solving; 5) personal management; 6) group effectiveness; and 7) organizational effectiveness and leadership.

- The student must understand the university's required standards before applying for an internship.

- The student intern must identify, screen, and monitor potential sport management sites well in advance of the commencement of the internship to ensure that industry's and student's expectations are met.

- The student should investigate such legal issues as paid internships, workman's compensation, sexual harassment, and general liability issues when screening a potential organization.

- Since true learning is multi-faceted, an appropriate internship evaluation may include weekly journals, internship projects, and evaluation report portfolios.

Discussion Activities

1. Discuss the importance of an internship. Why are these experiences even more important in the sport industry?

2. Conduct a search for possible internships in the sport industry that interests you. What are the job skill requirements for the positions? Are they paid? Will you need to relocate to accept the position? How do you apply for this position?

3. As a form of self-evaluation, make a list of all your strengths and weaknesses. Once completed, discuss ways to maximize your strengths and minimize your weaknesses. Do you have the strengths needed for the internships you identified in question 2?

References

Altschuler, G. C. (2002, April 14). A tryout for the real world: Interning is good for the resume. Better yet, it may get you hired. *New York Times*, p. 4A.

Barry, G. (2000, February 11). Interns get head start at careers. *St. Petersburg Times*, p. 9B.

Beard, F. K. (1997, August). *Inside the advertising and public relations internship*. Paper presented to the Internships and Careers Interest Group of the Association for Education in Journalism and Mass Communication, Chicago, IL.

Bowen, M., & Laurion, S. (1994, August). *Incidence rates of sexual harassment in mass communications internship programs: An initial study comparing intern, student, and professional rates*. Available at WL ED374485.

Bridges, F. L., & Roquemore, L.L. (1992). *Management for athletic/sport administration: Theory and practice*. Decatur, GA.: ESM Books.

Brown-Foster, S., & Moorman, A. M. (2001). *Gross v. Family Services Agency, Inc.*: The internship as a special relationship in creating negligence liability. *Journal of Legal Aspects of Sport, 11*(3).

Business-Higher Education Forum. (1995). *Higher education and work readiness: The view from the corporation*. Washington, DC: Business-Higher Education Forum and the American Council on Education.

Cannon, A. J., & Arnold, M. J. (1998). Student expectations of collegiate internship programs in business: A 10-year update. *Journal of Education for Business, 73*(4), 202-205.

Carnevale, A. P., Gainer, L. J., & Meltzer, A. S. (1990). *Workplace basics: The essential skills employers want*. San Francisco: Jossey-Bass.

Coco, M. (2000). A try before you buy arrangement. *Advanced Management Journal, 65*(2), 41-43.

Cook, S. J., Parker, R. S., & Pettijohn, C. (2004, January/February). The perceptions of interns: A longitudinal case study. *Journal of Education for Business, 79*(3), 179-85.

Cuneen, J., & Sidwell, M. J. (1993). Sport management interns: Selection qualifications. *Journal of Physical Education, Recreation, and Dance, 64*(1), 91-95.

Cuneen, J., & Sidwell, M. J. (1994). *Sport management field experiences*. Morgantown, WV: Fitness Information Technology.

DeSensi, J. T., Kelley, D. R., Blanton, M. D., & Beitel, P. A. (1990). Sport management curricular evaluation and needs assessment: A multifaceted approach. *Journal of Sport Management, 4*(1), 31-58.

Duly, J. S. (1982). *Learning outcomes: The measurement and evaluation of experiential learning*. PANEL Resource Paper, no. 6. Raleigh, NC: National Society for Internships and Experiential Education.

Fair Labor Standards Act 29 U.S.C. § 206 (2000 & Supp. 2002).

Evanson v. University of Hawaii, 483 P.2d 187, 190 (Haw. 1971).

Eyler, J. (1994). Comparing the impact of two internship experiences on student learning. *Journal of Cooperative Education, 29*, 41-52.

Gault, J., Redington, J., & Schlager, T. (2000). Undergraduate business internships and career success: Are they related? *Journal of Marketing Education, 22*(1), 45-53.

Gilbertson, D. (1997, October 19). Glamorous internships with a catch: There's no pay, *New York Times*, p. C16.

Guskey, T. (1994). Making the grade: What benefits students? *Educational Leadership, 52*(2), 14-20.

Hallal v. RDV Sports, Inc., 682 So. 2d 1235 (Fla. Dist. Ct. App. 1996).

Henry, L. G., Razzouk, N. Y., & Hoverland, H. (1988). Accounting internships: A practical framework. *Journal of Education for Business, 64*(1), 28-31.

Hite, R., & Bellizzi, J. (1986). Student expectations regarding collegiate internship programs in marketing. *Journal of Marketing Education, 8*(3), 41-49.

Holton, E. F., III. (1998). Preparing students for life beyond the classroom. In J. N. Gardner & G. Van der Veer (Eds.), *The senior year experience: Facilitating integration, reflection, closure, and transition* (pp. 95-115). San Francisco: Jossey-Bass.

Inkster, R. P., & Ross, R. G. (1995). *The internship as partnership: A handbook for campus-based coordinators and advisors*. Raleigh, NC: The National Society for Experiential Education.

Jones, E. A. (1997). *Goals inventories: Writing, critical thinking, problem-solving, speech communications, listening, and critical reading*. University Park, PA: National Center on Postsecondary Teaching, Learning, and Assessment.

Kaplan, R. K. (1994). The legal side of internship programs. *CPC Journal, 19*(5), 47-49.

Kinder v. Industrial Claim Appeals Office, 976 P.2d 295 (Colo. Ct. App. 1998).

Klein, D. (1994). *Knowledge, technical skills, personal qualities, and related selection criteria for sport management interns*. Unpublished doctoral dissertation, University of New Mexico.

Leach, T. (May, 1998). College internship: An aid to recruitment. *Law and Order*, 57-59.

Li, M., Cobb, P., & Sawyer, L. (1994). Sport management graduate programs: Characteristics of effectiveness. *Journal of Physical Education, Recreation, and Dance, 65*(5), 57-61.

Maynard, M.L. (1999, Winter). Challenging the 3.0 GPA eligibility standard for public relations internships. *Public Relations Review, 25*(4), 495-507.

Mason, J. G., Higgins, C., & Wilkinson, O. (1981). Sports administration 15 years later. *Athletic Purchasing and Facilities, 5*, 44-45.

McCormick, D. W. (1993). Critical thinking, experiential learning and internships. *Journal of Management Education, 17*, 260-262.

Miller, L.K, Anderson, P.M, & Ayres, T.D. (2002). The internship agreement: Recommendations and realities. *Journal of Legal Aspects of Sport, 12*(1), 37-60.

National Association for Sport and Physical Education/North American Society for Sport Management. (2000). *Sport management program: Standards and review protocol*. Reston, VA: National Association for Sport and Physical Education.

Palomba, C. A., & Banta, T. W. (1999). *Assessment essentials: Planning, implementing, and improving assessment in higher education*. San Francisco: Jossey-Bass.

Paranto, S. R., & Champagne, L. N. (1996, April). Perceptions of the business community regarding program effectiveness at a selected university. Paper presented at the annual meeting at the American Educational Research Association, New York, NY. (ERIC, ED 395 551), 30-33.

Pianko, D. (1996). Power internships. *Management Review, 85*(12), 31-33.

Schön, D. A. (1987). *Educating the reflective practitioner: Toward a new design for teaching and learning in the professions*. San Francisco: Jossey-Bass.

Scott, M. E. (1992). Internships add value to college recruitments. *Personnel Journal, 71*(4), 59-62.

Somerick, N. M. (2001, Spring). Strategies for managing an intern's performance. *Public Relations Quarterly, 46*(1), 23-25.

Stark, J. S., & Lowther, M. A. (1988). *Strengthening the ties that bind: Integrating liberal and professional study.* Report of the Professional Preparation Network. Ann Arbor: University of Michigan.

Stier, W. F. (2002). Sport management internships: From theory to practice. *Strategies, 15*(4), 7-9.

Sturges, J. S. (1993, October). When is an employee truly an employee? *HR Magazine, 38*(10), 56-58.

Sutton, W. A. (1989). The role of internships in sport management curricula: A model for development. *Journal of Physical Education, Recreation, and Dance, 60*(7), 20-24.

Swift, C. O., & Russell, K. (1999). Business school internships: Legal concerns. *Journal of Education for Business, 75*(1), 23-26.

Useem, M. (1995). Corporate restructuring and liberal learning. *Liberal Education, 81*(1), 18-23.

Van Horn, C. E. (1995*). Enhancing the connection between higher education and the workplace: A survey of employers.* Denver: State Higher Education Executive Officers and the Education Commission of the States.

Verner, M. E. (2004). Internship search, selection, and solidification strategies. *Journal of Physical Education, Recreation, and Dance, 75*(1), 25-27.

Woodward, N. H. (1998). From the classroom to the office. *HR Magazine, 43*, F2-F6.

Young, D. S., & Baker, R. E. (2004). Linking classroom theory to professional practice: Internship as a practical learning experience worthy of academic credit. *Journal of Physical Education, Recreation, and Dance, 75*(1), 22-24.

Chapter Fifteen

Your Future in the Sport Industry

Debra Ann Pace and Dallas D. Branch, Jr.

© 2003 Universal Press Syndicate   www.ucomics.com 2-8

"We drafted him right out of preschool. He's a long-term project, but we're fairly certain he has a future in the NBA. ... Those are his parents over there."

Learning Objectives

Upon completion of this chapter, the reader should be able to

■ Recognize the structure of grassroots, amateur, and interscholastic organizations;

■ Develop a professionally-accepted resume;

■ Recognize career opportunities in various segments of the sport industry;

■ Appreciate the depth and breadth of the sport industry; and

■ Project future trends in the sport industry.

Introduction

If you've carefully read the previous chapters in the text, undoubtedly you are excited about the prospects for a rewarding career in the sport industry. The authors have familiarized you with the core competencies necessary to attain a successful position in sport. Now it is time to learn about specific opportunities currently available in the field and what the future holds for the sport industry.

> "WE SHOULD REGRET OUR MISTAKES AND LEARN FROM THEM, BUT NEVER CARRY THEM FORWARD INTO THE FUTURE WITH US."
>
> LUCY MAUD MONTGOMERY

One main question, however, that might remain unanswered by you (and your parents) is "In which segment of the sport industry will I work?" As a first- or second-year student, it may be too early to know the answer. Rest assured that the skills you acquire—through the classroom and practical experience—will be relevant to most, if not all, segments of the sport industry. Developing marketing strategies for a professional football team is a similar process to developing marketing strategies for a minor league hockey program. The skills required to manage an on-campus recreation center are similar to those required to operate a minor-league baseball stadium. In addition, experience you may have gained outside the sport industry—volunteering at your church or working for the city—can also benefit your long-term career goals.

Obviously, the best way to acquire and hone these skills is through practical experience. Chapter 14 describes the benefits and outcomes expected from an internship experience. But is one internship experience enough? Consider the following example of one sport management graduate. This student completed five internships during and after college before landing her first job in the sport industry. As a student, she interned one summer for StreetBall Partners in their Hoop-it-Up 3-on-3 basketball division. During this internship, she met the New York Knicks' public relations specialist at an event, and he invited her to apply for one of their intern positions. She stayed in touch, and the following summer was a public relations intern for the New York Knicks.

Realizing that summer internships, particularly with an NBA team, don't offer a full range of experiences, the student took the following fall semester off and completed a semester-long internship with the Women's Sports Foundation. That exposure also allowed her to work for the now-defunct American Basketball League that fall. After returning to school in the spring, she completed an internship with the WNBA Team Operations Department, which was later merged with the NBA Team Operations Department.

Following these experiences, she began a job search in earnest and was contacted by a person in Nike Human Resources about a position in Corporate Communications. She worked for Nike for 16 months prior to taking her current position as public relations manager for AND1. Five separate internship experiences . . . five opportunities to network . . . five opportunities to gain valuable and transferable skills. While five internships is not the norm, nor is it necessary, this example shows the perseverance required to achieve your employment goals in the sport industry.

Consider also the practical experience requirements in the sport management program at Slippery Rock University (see Figure 15.1, next page).

The sport industry is undergoing dramatic change. The size and scope of the industry today is far broader and deeper than the initial design put forward by Walter O'Malley and Dr. James Mason to train future "sport managers" for major league baseball teams (Chapter 1). From those humble beginnings, both ends of the basic economic equation—supply and demand—have undergone phenomenal growth (Chapter 5). Today, there are approximately 200 undergraduate and graduate programs nationally, each with 100-200 students enrolled; a supply side of between 20K to 40K individuals all trying to do the same thing. From the demand side, there are approximately 14,000 sport and sport-related businesses, all trying to claim a slice of the over quarter-trillion dollar pie (Gottlieb, 2004).

Nearly every Fortune 500 Company, as well as medium-sized regional and national businesses, has some vested interest in this industry. Companies become involved by supporting local universities or colleges, buying signage at minor- or major-league to register that this industry is more extensive than just 132 professional sport franchises.

Your Search

It is very important, when searching this industry for the right fit between what the industry needs and what qualified applicants offer, to gather pertinent information. It is somewhat amazing that the most often-used line by young people to explain why they want to work in this industry is they "just love sports" or that "sport has been a big part of my life" (Chapter 1). Miller Lite conducted a national survey on "American Attitudes on Sports" and discovered that 98% of Americans are affected by sport on a daily basis (Mullen, Hardy, & Sutton, 2000). Who doesn't love sport? Unless the sport industry has room for 98% of all Americans in their employ, then simply a love of sport is not enough. You, by virtue of your education and experience, have more than that to offer.

Thus, what is more important to qualify for a position "outside the white lines" is to understand the "rules of the game" and to play the game within those rules. Crucial in this exercise is to keep a sharp focus on the fit mentioned earlier. A homeless person in New York City, when asked by a tourist, "How do I get to Carnegie Hall?" responded, "Practice, practice, practice!" Like an athletic contest, if you don't practice, you will not be prepared to play. Similarly, "practice makes perfect" in this industry as well. If you wonders where to get some practice, consider this. All 977 NCAA member institutions (Division I-A, I-AA, I-AAA, II, III) have an intercollegiate athletic program associated with them. These are the "labs" where one can "experiment" with different parts of this industry—i.e., facility management and operations, ticketing, publicity, broadcasting, marketing, promotions,

---

Figure 15.1

SRU Practical Experience

Students are required to enroll in four 1-credit hour practicum experiences, ideally in the summer between each academic year. Once enrolled, students must contact a sport organization and arrange to work 50 hours assisting in some managerial function. These four experiences must be completed at four different sites, with a different supervisor and with unique duties and responsibilities.

In addition, each sport management student must complete 200 documented hours of volunteer service during their academic career. Some students have worked for the Pittsburgh Pirates, local YMCAs, sport marketing agencies, and other sites.

Finally, in the student's final semester and upon completion of all coursework with a satisfactory grade-point average, students must complete a 12-credit-hour internship. This may be performed anywhere in the world, as students have worked as far away as Australia and Ireland.

So, students graduating with an undergraduate degree in sport management at Slippery Rock University will have earned nearly 900 hours of practical experience in a sport-related setting.

Practicum

4 experiences	50 hours each	200 hours

Volunteer	200 hours
Internship	480 hours
Total	880 hours

---

baseball parks, arranging stadium and arena naming rights deals, and developing regional television contracts with conferences and regional broadcasting rights holders. In addition, the industry involves ticket printers, credit-card verification software providers, computerized ticketing companies (Paciolan, Ticketmaster, Tickets.com), sport marketing consulting firms (Muhleman Marketing, Turnkey Sports, Game-Day Consulting), sport executive search firms (Team-Work Consulting, WomenSportsJobs.com). It starts

sport communications, media relations, development (fundraising), and business operations (finance and budgeting). What are you waiting for? Get into those offices and start practicing!

Resume Development

Each of these experiences should be recorded on one's resume. As experience grows and the resume begins to build, students are confronted with two serious professional dilemmas. First, almost every Career Services office will promote and insist on one-page resumes. In addition, they demand that, at the bottom of one's resume, the phrase "References Available Upon Request" be inserted, again to maximize the potential to keep the resume to one page. Think about this for a moment. How can someone adhere to the one-page resume myth when the experiences gained through volunteer, practicum, or internship makes this impossible? There's just too much stuff to put on one page! The only solution is to make the font so small as to be unreadable by the reviewer. That's one sure strike against the applicant. A two-page resume is perfectly acceptable, especially if the experiences won't fit onto one page in a readable format. Secondly, if a potential employer wishes to check one's references and they are not listed, the only way to get the contact information is to first contact the applicant and have that information relayed verbally or by email. That's a second strike against the applicant—too much effort and work for the prospective employer may lead them to a decision that is all too familiar to many applicants trying to enter the industry today—NEXT! In summary, it is very important to make the job of selecting the successful candidate as easy as possible. Anything that creates a barrier to entry may be the difference in one candidates' success versus another's failure. (See Figure 15.3 for a sample resume).

Taking Your Temperature

For you to be successful, know what you want to do, what you don't want to do, what you're good at, and what you're not so good at. Then, and only then, can you rationally begin the process of understanding what fit would be right for you. One might equate this search for a good fit to a dance—you don't want your partner continually stepping on your toes. Like a dance with a great partner, the successful search ends in something mutually beneficial—for the one search-

Figure 15.2

List of Common Reasons That Resumes Don't Pass the Critique

- No objective statement, or statement is vague or unclear
- Use of personal pronouns such as I, me, and my
- Education and/or experience not listed in reverse chronological order
- Accomplishment statements don't provide enough information (use action words)
- Bullets NOT used in experience section (bullets aid in readability and the flow of the resume)
- Use of periods at the end of bullet statements
- Use of dates under "Honors" and/or "Activities" section (too much congestion)
- Lack of organization
- Format and/or style is not consistent
- Length is not appropriate for education and experience
- Spelling and grammatical errors
- Improper use of acronyms and abbreviations

Source: University of Miami Toppel Center

ing and the entity doing the search. It is important to "know thy self" in this regard.

Everyone puts together his or her resume to demonstrate educational and professional competencies and experiences as well as honors, abilities, and awards achieved along the way. Yet, nowhere on anyone's resume is there a personal statement indicating a preference for, and ability to demonstrate proficiency in, specific position requirements within the industry. In short, many begin this search process with a "wish list" of organizational types—baseball, pro sports, college athletics, recreation department—without a clue as to the specific position(s) they are qualified to assume. Can you make a strong case that you are qualified to do the job? Without a clear answer to that question, the dance may continue without satisfaction.

Taking stock of your attributes—what you can offer as a set of skills and abilities to a sport organization—is the other crucial part of this fit arrangement. Without a good fit, one of you will be tripping over the other and both will be looking for new dance partners. This personal assessment and evaluation process is as important as anything else in getting one's "foot in the door" and ensuring the rest of you is invited inside. It is one thing to "talk the talk," but sometimes quite another to "walk the walk." You must demonstrate to a potential employer that you have the "right stuff" to secure the opportunity you seek.

One can only be "invited" into the sport industry if they can contribute something *of substance* and be able to demonstrate that their contribution is *substantially different* from everyone else's. Therefore, it becomes important to build a "better mousetrap." What are you prepared to do better than anyone else? What can you positively and unquestionably prove you are able to do better than anyone else?

The Company You Keep

Fortunately for most internship/job seekers today, they are not alone in their search process. Most sport management program coordinators and advisors have established a network of industry experts to assist them in their search. All programs have an established network of graduates who are currently in the sport industry. Use this program's legacy of alumni and the networks developed by program faculty to get an edge in the search.

The second and most overlooked aspect of the search is to utilize school break time to conduct informational interviews with prospective employers. Too often, when asked what one is doing during their fall, holiday, or spring break, the response is, "I'm going to Daytona Beach." Unless those industry professionals who are going to hire you are also planning to be there, how productive can that choice be? Instead, to further differentiate you from others, why not spend your time meeting with those who could actually be helpful in your professional pursuits? It would surprise you how receptive professionals in this field are to a 15 minute informational interview for someone who will be in their area and wants to stop in and discuss their business for a few minutes. Make sure to contact them and set up an appointment before you go.

First impressions are important, so be sure to dress for success—this is an interview, regardless of how informal. Pay very close attention to those you meet with—you want to take from this experience some insight into how they act, how they speak, how they carry themselves, how they dress, and how they project confidence, enthusiasm, and professionalism. The point is, you must begin to model or imitate their persona. Individuals are more likely to hire those like themselves. Professionals in this industry are no different than those in other industries—they are interested in conformity and "team" players, not renegades and non-conformists. In the sport industry, you are clearly defined by the company you keep. It is important to surround yourself with successful people or those who share your desire to be successful.

Your "Risk Quotient"

With a 10K-20K supply of qualified candidates from all programs nationally, the odds of getting an opportunity with a major professional sport franchise are

1:151 to 1:303, assuming all have an opportunity. By adding all Division I, II, and III NCAA institutions, the odds become 1:134 to 1:268. Adding an additional 500 minor league sport franchises in baseball, arena football, and hockey, the odds become 1:12 to 1:25.

By adding some 10,000 sport businesses that directly or indirectly support this industry, the odds improve to 1:2 to 1:4. Decide your risk quotient and know your odds. How much of a gambler are you willing to be? The odds with the greatest chances for success should be the ones sought first.

Don't Give In or Give Up

In addition to knowing the odds from the industry examples provided above, try coupling your personal assessment and evaluation with these odds to get a truer read of your chances for success in this industry. By understanding your strengths and weakness, your personal preferences, your skills, abilities, and interests, a better fit will be more assured, and success will certainly be more likely. Whatever the odds, don't ever give up on your personal dream and desire to get into and stay in this exciting industry. Your passion and love for sport will help you get where you want to go, but your talent and ability to contribute something unique and special will help you stay.

This industry is harsh in some respects and is not for the timid. Long work hours, weekends, holidays, and additional responsibilities upon request all combine to make 60-70 hour weeks the norm. In addition, the remuneration for starting positions is LOW. Many first-time work experiences are either low paying (hourly, small monthly stipend, etc.) or non-paying. These are other barriers to entry. Some may couch these considerations into the "dues we pay" for the privilege of wearing the "jacket." If one is willing to sacrifice their ego and financial well-being and hang in there during this time of trial, good things are likely to present themselves at the other end. In the long run, many sport management professional practitioners have gone through the same period of paying their dues. They have survived the "due diligence" period and are now thriving in a career that finally rewards them personally and financially as expected.

The Sport Industry Today and Tomorrow

Economic Trends in Sport

Sport analysts have classified sport-related spending into distinct categories accounting for billions in annual consumer spending. These categories range from monies spent on advertising, endorsements, and sponsorships to monies spent on spectator sports, medical treatment, travel, and gambling. Amazingly, the fastest growing segment in sport-related spending is *non-organized recreational sports*, a category that was not even included as one of the original ones. However, *non-organized recreational sports* spending accounts for greater than $16 billion annually. To you, this means even more opportunity to work in this category of sports-related activities, an area you may have never even considered.

Participant Trends in Sport

Alternative sports are becoming the fastest growing segment of sport spending in America. These sports are characterized as being individualistic and free-spirited, and participants tend to adopt alternative sports lifestyles, leading to infinite sport product extensions. Examples of *alternative sports* include skateboarding, snowboarding, in-line skating, BMX biking, windsurfing, mountain biking, kayaking, wakeboarding, and even more adrenaline-inducing activities such as bungee jumping, street luge, and sky surfing.

While *alternative sports* began in the 1990s as extreme sports, by the year 2000 they joined the mainstream. Now, over 80 million Americans spend billions of dollars annually on alternative sports equipment and apparel. As an example, $251 million is spent annually on in-line skating alone. Moreover, alternative sports participants are predominantly males between the ages of 12 and 24 years old. The implications of increasing participation in alternative sports in the sport industry is that the spending power of this group of "Generation Y" will continue to grow from an estimated $91.5 billion annual spending power until it levels off in 2030.

Alternative sports give sport organizations the opportunity to penetrate an increasingly difficult to reach youth market. As alternative sports become more and more mainstream, opportunities to target and reach the youth market will continue to grow. Adding the spending from both organized and alternative sport participants to the annual consumer spending on sport-related industry brings the total sport spending up to over $250 billion annually, securing the sport industry's continued growth in America.

Other Factors Contributing to the Economic Trends of Sport

The economic trends discussed above have been a part of the longest period of economic growth in American history. Sport organizations and sport-related activity have been at the heart of this economic growth. The following trends from the 1990s were a major part of this prolific expansion.

Spending on sport facility construction neared $16 billion in an eight-year time span. In this period, over 160 new facilities were built in America and Canada (Howard, 1999). Additionally, over 180 new professional sports teams were introduced along with 13 new leagues, such as the XFL and the West Coast Hockey League. These additions have contributed to the over 800 professional teams now in existence at all levels. Two factors significantly contributing to these numbers are the development of minor league hockey and women's sport leagues.

Increases in corporate involvement in sport also play a major role in the economic growth of the sport industry. This is evidenced in the corporate sponsorships, naming rights, and premium seating options that are taking over both intercollegiate and professional arenas across the country. Finally, annual expenditures on sporting goods alone have almost reached $75 billion. This is nearly 50% more than annual reported spending from ten years ago.

Challenges to Overcome

Despite the encouraging economics of the sport industry from the 1990s through to today, numerous challenges still await the aspiring sport manager. Ironically, the growth that sport has seen over the last 15 years has also led to market saturation, emerging technology, and fewer resources to be distributed.

Various segments of the entertainment industry are fighting for the average American's expendable income. As entertainment options increase, the market-place becomes cluttered, and consumers have to make tougher decisions regarding where and how to spend their money. The sport industry is no longer fighting just an internal struggle; it is battling the entire entertainment industry. Even television and the Internet will pose a challenge for sport managers as they will continue to offer more, better, and cheaper services. Sport managers can be held partially accountable for this challenge, since they positioned sport as entertainment. However, it is not just the expendable dollar they are competing for; it is also a scarcity of time that forces consumers to be selective in their entertainment options. Additionally, fine niche markets have been developed which further separates and defines market segments, creating even more options for the consumer. The best way for sport managers to combat this challenge is to embrace technology that may help them overcome market saturation.

Advancing technology offers a plethora of opportunities and challenges for sport managers. The Internet alone has accounted for significant increases in revenue generation. Professional teams and leagues have had to think creatively to capitalize on the ever-changing world of technology. One opportunity technology provides is personalized marketing. Other technological advances include the convergence of television with Internet technology and interactive viewing based on consumer preferences. These changes allow sport fans to increase their consumption of the sport, leading to greater expenditures. Moreover, greater consumption of sport and more personalized marketing interactions moves consumers up the escalator, which is the ultimate goal in marketing. Additional sport spectator technological advances include fancards, "smart" seats, and virtual signage. Finally, technological development is leading to increased globalization of sport and more access to sport from all over the world. All of these technological advancements add up to increased opportunity for revenue generation. As an example, the NFL expects total league Internet revenue alone to reach $5 billion.

The future of sport management lies in the ability of aspiring managers to creatively seek funding. As a result of some of the trends that have already been explained in this chapter and the reality of intercollegiate athletics and professional leagues today, sport managers today and tomorrow will be faced with the challenge of declining traditional revenue sources. This means they will be expected to do more with less. In an era where we must "Keep up with the Joneses," managers must be innovative in both seeking and utilizing resources that are available to them. Resources that are acquired must produce optimal benefits for both the sport organization and the stakeholders. However, if we are able to learn from the past, there is great hope for the future of sport management and sport managers, as this is a challenge that has been overcome by the industry many times before and will likely be faced many times in the future.

Opportunities abound for individuals with interests in sports management careers. However, future sport in-

---

Figure 15.3

SEBASTIAN D. IBIS
sdibis@miami.edu

Permanent Address
1234 Anyplace Lane
Dallas, TX 59648

Local Address
1987 Collins Ave.
Miami, FL 33126

OBJECTIVE

To obtain a full-time position that affords a broad range of experiences in the field of sport finance.

EDUCATION

University of Miami, Coral Gables, FL
Bachelor of Science Sport Administration, May 2005
Major in Sport Administration, Minor in Business Administration, GPA 3.5

EXPERIENCE

Mucho Sport Properties, Miami, FL
Database and Marketing Team Lead, 2/04 to Present
- Research information about stocks and mutual funds for current and prospective clients
- Assist in the maintenance of a client base of over $100 million
- Design database to allow for client retention through the use of various ACT tools

Bobbleheads R Us, New York, NY
Financial Analyst Intern, 5/03 to 8/03
- Presented results on a project to reconcile $500,000 discrepancy between perpetual inventory levels and general ledger
- Developed weekly director labor reports in order to better align production efforts with business plan budgets
- Assisted in yearly inventory audit by designing an Access database

Beach Front Health and Fitness Center, Miami Beach, FL
Practicum Intern, 5/02 to 9/02
- Provided service training for a 43-member staff meeting including ice breaker, handouts, and Power Point presentations
- Updated 2400 member list into active monthly statistics using Microsoft Excel
- Calculated fiscal year Health and Fitness Center ratios that increased 9%
- Researched and collected data for PowerPoint presentation for the CEO to present at the ACSM conference

---

Department of Residence Halls, University of Miami, Coral Gables, FL
Resident Assistant, 8/01 to 5/02
- Responsible for the safety and well-being of 50 resident students
- Ensured resolution of all floor conflicts and disciplinary situations
- Planned educational programs to foster positive environment for learning and living

HONORS/ACTIVITIES

- Sport Professionals Organization of Research & Training (S.P.O.R.T.)
- Alpha Kappa Psi (President and Treasurer)
- Golden Key National Honor Society
- School of Business Peer Counselor
- Toppel Career Center Student Advisory Board

SKILLS

Microsoft Word, Excel, Access, PowerPoint, FrontPage, Bloomberg
Fluent in Spanish

REFERENCES

John Q. Citizen
President, Mucho Sports Properties
111 Calle Ocho
Miami, FL 33146
(O)305-212-8965
(F)305-212-4562
jqcitzen@mucho.net

I.M. Wobblen
Finance Director, Bobbleheads R Us
1357 Bobble Dr.
New York, NY 22156
(O)212-564-9137
(F)212-564-9515
imwobblin@bobbleheads.com

R. U. Fitt
Manager, Beach Front Health and Fitness Center
5792 Ocean Dr.
Miami Beach, FL 33142
(O)305-595-9874
(F)305-595-9632
rufitt@beachfront.net

dustry professionals may be better served by turning their efforts from the traditional intercollegiate and professional jobs towards grassroots and recreational positions. Many apprehensions of sport management college students revolve around their future as professionals and their ability to put the classroom information to use in a practical environment. At the highest levels of sport, job requirements are specialized, either as a marketer or public relations official. Many grassroots organizations are smaller in nature, either as a public recreation office or high school athletic department. Smaller offices require employees to wear numerous hats, working in any number of areas of sport, providing these individuals with invaluable experience.

As expendable income increases and the desire of parents to have physically-active children grows, so will opportunities for sport management in these fields. Furthermore, as active youth continue to mature into active adults, there will always be opportunities for managing programs that target individuals of all ages, genders, and backgrounds.

The future of the sport industry promises to be exciting and dynamic. Along with the changes and challenges mentioned in this chapter, sport managers will be challenged to be innovative in their methods of dealing with each. New methods to generate revenue will need to be developed to ensure a financially stable sport industry. Those sport managers that are able to adjust and find new ways to manage and lead our sport organizations will find themselves in enviable positions. The failure to adapt to changes as they occur can only lead to the eventual failure of the organization and the individual. Properly prepared sport managers will have the opportunity to provide leadership to the sport industry as it continues to mature as a consumer product.

The sport industry has some big shoes that need to be filled. Are you ready to fill them?

References

Gottlieb, R. (Ed.). (2004). *2004 sports market place directory.* Millerton, NY: Grey House.

Mullin, B, Hardy, S., & Sutton, W. A. (2000). *Sport marketing* (2nd ed.). Champaign, IL: Human Kinetics.

Glossary

Glossary

80/20 principle: a marketing principle suggesting that a focus be made on moving consumers up the consumer escalator while keeping the existing heavy user segment content, as heavy users are known to be responsible for up to 80% of all purchases, though they may represent as few as 20% of all consumers.

ad valorem taxes: a tax, duty, or fee which varies based on the value of the products, services, or property on which it is levied.

Administrative Rules and Regulations: directives enforced by administrative agencies that generally carry the force of law as if they were passed by Congress or the state legislature, and violators of the rules and regulations are subject to the penalties provided in them.

The Age Discrimination in Employment Act (ADEA) of 1967: U.S. law initially passed to protect workers age 40 and older from age discrimination. The ADEA was amended by the Older Workers Benefit Protection Act of 1990 (OWBPA) to include a focus on age discrimination and loss of workplace benefits.

agencies: businesses or services authorized to act for others.

AIDA: advertising concept that stands for Awareness, Interest, Desire, and Action, which is designed to move consumers along in the progression towards actual product purchase.

alternative dispute resolution (ADR): resolving a dispute through any means other than litigation or negotiation.

ambush marketing: a direct competing brand in the same product category staging a presence to create confusion in the mind of the consumer regarding who is the official sponsor.

The Americans with Disabilities Act (ADA) of 1990: U.S. law that protects individuals with disabilities from being discriminated against in the workplace.

appeal: the transfer of a case from a lower to a higher court for a new hearing.

arbitration: the submission of a dispute to a neutral third party (arbitrator) who listens to all parties, considers the legal position of each, then renders a decision to resolve the dispute.

arbitrator: neutral third party who acts much like a judge and listens to all parties in an arbitration, considers the legal position of each, then renders a decision to resolve the dispute.

Arizona Sports Summit Accord: edict issued in May of 1999 by a gathering of nearly 50 influential sport leaders that encourages greater emphasis on the ethical and character-building aspects of athletic competition. The goal of formulating this document was to establish a framework of principles and values that would be adopted and practiced widely by those involved with sport organizations.

assumed risk: the inherent danger within an activity.

Athlete Agent statues: laws that seek to protect prospective professional athletes and regulate athlete agents.

balance sheet: a snapshot of a business's financial condition at a specific moment in time, usually at the close of an accounting period, which comprises assets, liabilities, and owners' or stockholders' equity.

barriers to effective communication: variables that impede productive interaction and correspondence, the three most notable being linguistic, psychological, and environmental .

Baseball World Cup Tournament: plan announced in 2004 by Bud Selig, the Commissioner of MLB, which called for a 16-team tournament to be held during spring training in warm-weather cities across the U.S.

behavioral approach: in conceptualizing leadership, this approach emphasized what leaders and managers actually did on the job, as opposed to their personal characteristics; theorists focused not only on what leaders would do, but also on how often and at what intensity they would do certain things to distinguish themselves as leaders.

benefits: the distinct advantages gained from an investment.

Bill of Rights: the first ten amendments to the U.S. Constitution, added in 1791 to protect the essential rights and liberties of all citizens.

booking: the act of engaging and contracting an event or attraction.

Bosman ruling: 1995 ruling by the European Court of Justice, which established free agency for out-of-contract players; it has been considered a landmark decision with significant impact on the structure, development, and economics of professional football (soccer) clubs throughout Europe.

brand equity: all of the distinguishing qualities of a commercial brand that results in personal commitment to and demand for the brand.

brand insistence: behavior in which the consumer wants or is willing to buy or purchase a specific product only.

brand loyalty: a more intense form of brand insistence in which the consumer develops a passion about or loyalty to a specific product.

brand preference: the extent to which a customer prefers to use a certain product or service.

brand recognition: the extent to which a brand is recognized for its advertised attributes or communications.

breach of warranty: a breach by a seller of the terms of a warranty.

business (personal) financial management: directing and controlling the use of cash flow and monetary operations and funds.

buy in: the incentive for companies or potential sponsors to invest in a program, event, team, etc.

case law: law based on judicial decision and precedent rather than on statutes.

case study method: a curriculum that presents students with the opportunity to read previous cases in order to learn how courts make legal decisions by applying relevant law to the facts of the case.

cash budget: a forecast of estimated cash receipts and disbursements for a specified period of time.

cash flow: money entering and exiting an organization; cash inflows and outflows in your personal life and in various business enterprises.

casuals: types of visitors who were not drawn in by the event being studied.

Certificates of Participation (COPs): public financing instruments that require the governmental entity creating a corporation to buy/build a public assembly facility, such as an arena or convention and visitors' center; financing is obtained by buying a share of the lease revenues of an agreement made by a municipal or governmental entity, rather than the bond being secured by those revenues.

Charitable Immunity: immunity from civil liability, especially for negligent torts, that is granted to a charitable or nonprofit organization.

charitable organizations: institutions or organizations established to help the needy or for humanitarian or philanthropic purposes beneficial to the public.

circuits: the area or district under the jurisdiction of a judge in which periodic court sessions are held.

civil law: the body of laws dealing with the rights of private citizens; includes everything that is not criminal law.

civil rights: the rights belonging to an individual by virtue of citizenship, especially the fundamental freedoms and privileges guaranteed by the 13th and 14th Amendments to the U.S. Constitution and by subsequent acts of Congress, including civil liberties, due process, equal protection of the laws, and freedom from discrimination.

Clayton Antitrust Act: law passed by the U.S. Congress in 1914 as an amendment to clarify and supplement the Sherman Antitrust Act of 1890, which prohibited exclusive sales contracts, local price cutting to freeze out competitors, rebates, interlocking directorates in corporations capitalized at $1 million or more in the same field of business, and intercorporate stock holdings.

clutter: the result of too many sponsors being associated with a sport entity in which no single brand image stands out as the sponsor.

codes of ethics: a system of principles governing morality and acceptable conduct.

Collective Bargaining Agreement (CBA): a negotiation contract outlining the collective bargaining terms drawn up by the owners and union representatives, who are acting on the behalf of workers and employees.

commitment: in sport, the frequency, duration, and intensity of involvement, or the willingness to expend money, time, and energy in a pattern of sport involvement.

common law: the system of laws originated and developed in England and based on court decisions, on the doctrines implicit in those decisions, and on customs and usages rather than on codified written laws.

competitive balance: when conditions exist within competition that cause parity, or equality, in amount, status, or value.

competitive imbalance: when conditions exist within competition that cause a disparity in amount, status, or value.

compliance: observance of official requirements.

compound interest: interest which is calculated not only on the initial principal but also the accumulated interest of prior periods.

conceptual skills: in sport management terms, these skills involve the ability to conceptualize how all the different parts of the organization fit together so that established goals and objectives can be achieved.

conduct: the way a person acts, especially from the standpoint of morality and ethics.

consideration: the payment of money by one party to the other, who in turn provides something of value.

consumer escalator: a marketing model in which the goal is to move consumers from non-aware/non-consumers onto a consumption "escalator" and ultimately up each level from light to medium to heavy users.

contemporary theories: leadership theories, developed in the past two decades, that presented a broader perspective of the leader-follower relationship as they examined the changes in the followers that came as a result of leader influence, and characterized the leader as charismatic, inspirational, visionary, and/or transformational.

content: the subject matter or essential meaning of something.

contingency approaches: see definition for *situational approaches*

contract: an agreement, or exchange of promises, that creates legally enforceable duties and obligations for all parties to the contract.

conventional: the second of Kohlberg's three stages of moral reasoning, which is based on a person's conformance to society's rules and is the level of most adolescents and adults in societies.

Copyright Act of 1976: law that extended the length of protection for individual authors to the author's entire life plus fifty years and did the same for works for hire with seventy-five years.

core: the basic or most important part.

Corporate social responsibility: obligation of a corporate business to fulfill a role within the surrounding community, assuming economic, legal, ethical, and philanthropic responsibilities.

corporation: a company formed by an agreement between the state and the persons forming the company, with the state requiring legal documentation of the agreement.

counteroffer: an offer made in return by one who rejects an unsatisfactory offer.

Court of Appeals: a court to which appeals are made on points of law resulting from the judgment of a lower court.

credibility: the quality of being believable or trustworthy.

crime: an act committed or omitted in violation of a law forbidding or commanding it and for which punishment is imposed upon conviction.

criminal law: law that deals with unlawful acts committed against the public as a whole, in which a defendant is accused of violating a statute defining a criminal act, thereby committing a crime.

crowd management: organizational tool used to assist venue directors and/or event coordinators in providing a safe and enjoyable environment for patrons.

culture: the socially transmitted behavior patterns, arts, beliefs, institutions, and all other products of human work and thought.

damages: money ordered to be paid as compensation for injury or loss.

decision making: choosing a course of action based on the evaluation of necessary information.

Declaration of Independence: the declaration of the Congress of the Thirteen United States of America, on the 4th of July, 1776, by which they formally declared that these colonies were free and independent States, not subject to the government of Great Britain.

defection: to abandon a position or association; in sport sponsorships, to cause a company or sponsor not to renew.

demographics: the characteristics of human populations and population segments that are used to identify consumer markets, and those which describe their state of being, such as income level, education level, zip code, marital status, age, race, religious affiliation, occupation type, number of children in the home, and gender.

deontology: ethical theory concerned with duties and rights, based on the idea of absolute rules of moral behavior.

Department of Education: the United States federal department, created in 1979, that administers all federal programs dealing with education, including federal aid to educational institutions and students.

depreciation: the allocation of the cost of an asset over a period of time for accounting and tax purposes.

direct spending: dollars spent explicitly for a specific program or purpose.

director of finance: assistant to the head of the management team who is responsible for fiscal accountability, budgeting, cost control, contract negotiations, and financing.

director of marketing: assistant to the head of the management team who is responsible for market planning, advertising, and sales (i.e., sponsorships, merchandise, and tickets).

director of operations: the primary assistant to the head of the management team who has a wide variety of departmental responsibilities, including event coordination; engineering; security, safety, and medical services; and maintenance and housekeeping.

discretionary expense: a recurring or non-recurring expense for goods and services that are either non-essential or more expensive than necessary; examples include entertainment expenses, wellness program, and speakers; also referred to as step cost.

discrimination: treatment or consideration based on class or category rather than individual merit; partiality or prejudice.

disseminator: an informational role filled by the sport manager in which he or she screens information and passes it along to employees who otherwise would probably not have access to it.

disturbance handler: a decisional role filled by a sport manager in which the individual is responsible for reacting to changes affecting the organization that are unexpected and beyond his or her immediate control.

diversity: a range or variety; having difference among the assembled or included parts of a group.

diversity of citizenship: a condition in which the parties to an action are of diverse state or national citizenship.

Division of Labor: a directive that shows the separation of departments by function or specialization.

drug testing: testing administered to detect the presence of drugs, especially from a blood or urine sample and especially for illegal substances.

economic benefit: a measure of the economic gain in the local economy.

economic impact: the total economic gain or loss after accounting for an event's costs.

economic responsibilities: implicit requirement of organizations to produce goods and services and sell them at a profit, because that is how a capitalist society operates.

emotional content: the emotions or feelings inherent in a communication that often offers information other than that of the intended message.

English Premiership: the Division I Football (Soccer) League in England.

entrepreneur: a decisional role filled by a sport manager in which he or she looks for ways to improve his or her work group, adapt to internal and external changes, and direct the organization towards opportunities which initiate growth.

environment: the totality of circumstances or conditions surrounding an individual or group of individuals.

Equal Access Act: act that prohibits any school receiving federal funds from denying equal access to, or discriminating against, any student desiring to conduct a meeting on school premises, when the meeting deals with religious, political, or philosophical subjects.

equilibrium price: the point at which the supply curve and the demand curve overlap, where the amount of product demanded equals the amount of product supplied.

equitable treatment: handling or dealing with equally.

Establishment Clause: a clause in the U.S. Constitution forbidding Congress from establishing a state religion.

ethical challenge: moral conflict; an ethical situation that requires a choice between options that are or seem equally unfavorable or mutually exclusive; also called an ethical dilemma.

ethical dilemma: see *ethical challenge*

ethical responsibilities: requirement of organizations to operate by established norms defining suitable behavior.

ethics: a set of principles or values that are used to determine right and wrong.

Euro 2004: 2004 European soccer tournament which saw record TV audiences, topping those from the 2000 tournament by more than 15 percent; it was estimated that 2.5 billion individuals, or about 80 million per match, watched.

European Union: an economic and political union established in 1993 after the ratification of the Maastricht Treaty by members of the European Community, which forms its core. In establishing the European Union, the treaty expanded the political scope of the European Community, especially in the area of foreign and security policy, and provided for the creation of a central European bank and the adoption of a common currency by the end of the 20th century.

evaluation: the process of examining a system to determine whether or not certain criteria were met.

exclusivity: having the exclusive right or privilege.

expense: any cost of doing business resulting from revenue-generating activities.

expense budget: a calculation of projected future expenses analyzed in relationship to cash available, which is used to make planning and management decisions.

explicit expenditures: the cost of explicitly making one choice over another.

fad: a fashion that is taken up with great enthusiasm for a brief period of time; a craze.

federal court system: court system established by the federal government and having jurisdiction over questions of federal law.

federal question: a question that falls under the jurisdiction of a federal court because it requires a resolution of the construction or application of federal law.

The Federal Trademark Act of 1946: statute that authorizes owners of trademarks to register them with the U.S. government, and provides protection against others who seek to use the trademark without permission; also known as the Lanham Act.

federal trial courts: courts that operate essentially the same as state trial courts, providing a trial of the case before a judge and jury; also called U.S. District

Courts, followed by a geographical description of the location of the court (e.g., United States District Court for the Western District of Pennsylvania), of which there are 94 throughout the U.S., with at least one located in every state.

figurehead: the first of three interpersonal roles a sport manager must fulfill, which involves fulfilling certain ceremonial functions as the result of being in charge of a certain department or the organization as a whole.

final portfolio reports: formal assessments written at the conclusion of an internship by interns in order to assess their overall experience as well as critique their performance.

financial considerations: concerns about cost or funding.

fit: in sport marketing, the compatibility of the sport property's image with the desired image of the brand, as well as how well needs are matched between the target market of the sport entity and the target market of the brand.

fixed cost: a cost that does not vary depending on production or sales levels, such as rent, property, insurance, or interest expense; also referred to as non-variable cost.

foundations: institutions founded and supported by an endowment.

future value: the value at some point in the future of a present amount of money.

G14: a proposal, also referred to as Super League, offered by the European football (soccer) industry to come closer to the American model, which would include football giants like Ajax Amsterdam, Manchester United, AC Milan, and Real Madrid.

gender discrimination: discrimination based on sex.

general liability: liability for bodily injury, death, or damage to property owned by others to which an employer may be subject either directly or by reason of liability arising out of an act, error, or omission of its employee, agent, or officer in the course and scope of employment.

general obligation bonds: bonds typically used to finance traditional capital projects such as highways, roads, and sewers that will be paid back through the taxing power of the issuing authority. General obligation bonds are issued against the general full faith and credit of state and local governments.

Generally Accepted Accounting Principles (GAAP): a combination of authoritative standards, set by policy boards made up of the American Institute of Certified Public Accountants (AICPA) and Financial Accounting Standards Board (FASB), in addition to the Security Exchange Commission (SEC), an agency of the Federal Government, which establish the accepted ways of doing accounting.

gigantism: excessive growth of a body or any of its parts.

globalization: the process by which the experience of everyday life, marked by the diffusion of commodities and ideas, is becoming standardized around the world.

goals: in regard to a mission statement, the achievable statements provided by management, ideally developed through consultation with all stakeholders in the venue, usually based on the mission statement and used to justify the fiscal resources requested in a budget document.

grassroots programs: programs that focus on people or society at a local level rather than at the center of major political activity.

gross negligence: acting in such a reckless manner that the court will consider that the defendant exhibited a conscious indifference toward the safety of the plaintiff, even though the defendant did not intend to injure the plaintiff.

hazing: to persecute or harass with meaningless, difficult, or humiliating tasks.

human skills: in sport management terms, these skills involve aspects of leading, communicating, motivating, and, in general, dealing with all aspects of employee relations on a daily basis.

idealized influence: the position of role model that the transformational leader assumes in the eyes of his or her followers.

image: a distinctive but intangible quality that surrounds a product that is to make it appealing to the consumer.

image enhancement: the positive effects done to the image of a company or sponsor as part of being associated with a certain event, team, or fundraiser.

implicit expenditures: the intangible benefits lost by making one choice over another.

income statement: a business financial statement that lists revenues, expenses, and net income throughout a given period.

indirect spending: dollars spent as a secondary result of direct spending.

individualized consideration: the role of coach, or mentor, that the transformational leader assumes in the eyes of followers in an organization.

induced spending: dollars spent by wage earners as a result of increased money flow caused by direct and indirect spending.

induction: the act or process of inducing or bringing about.

infringement: encroachment of a right or privilege.

inspirational motivation: the idea that transformational leaders will inspire and motivate those around them, encouraging others to find challenge and personal meaning in their work, and will thereby foster enthusiasm throughout the organization.

instrumental values: in ethical theory, the means that one will use to achieve the ends.

intellectual stimulation: the component of transformational leadership theory that resides in the leader's ability to challenge followers to be more creative and innovative, and to be supportive of follower efforts even when in error.

intentional torts: civil wrongs that occur when the party acting wrongfully, called the tortfeasor, intends to cause the harm by committing the act that causes the injury.

intermediate appeals court: a court whose jurisdiction is to review decisions of lower courts or agencies.

International Association of Assembly Managers (IAAM): a group comprised of leaders who represent a diverse industry—entertainment, sports, conventions, trade, hospitality, and tourism—and manage, or provide products and services to, public assembly facilities like arenas, amphitheaters, auditoriums, convention centers/exhibit halls, performing arts venues, stadiums, and university complexes.

international environment: cultural or social conditions extending across or transcending national boundaries.

International Federations (IFs): federations that are responsible for developing their sport(s) worldwide and for staging world championships.

International Olympic Committee (IOC): an international, non-governmental, nonprofit organization whose main responsibility is to organize the Olympic Games, but also owns the rights to the Olympic properties, including the Olympic symbol, flag, motto, emblem, anthem, flame, and torch.

internship policies: the rules, guidelines, and specifications given by the department that is offering the internship.

interviews: a formal meeting in person in which questioning is used to gather data and opinions.

involvement: to occupy or engage the interest of; when referring to sport consumers, can be behavioral (the actual doing of a sport activity), cognitive (seeking out information and knowledge about a sport), and affective (the feelings and emotions a sport consumer has for a particular activity or team).

IOC commissions: groups whose duty is the promotion of Olympic ideals (e.g., marketing, medical, ethics, nominations, press, TV and internet rights, Olympic solidarity).

job description: a summary of all the roles and responsibilities of a particular job.

judgment: a determination of a court of law; a judicial decision.

justice: the upholding of what is just, especially fair treatment and due reward in accordance with honor, standards, or law.

kinesics: the appearance and physical mannerisms of a speaker.

Lanham Act: statute that authorizes owners of trademarks to register them with the U.S. government, and provides protection against others who seek to use the trademark without permission; also known as the Federal Trademark Act of 1946.

law: a body of enforceable rules, established by the lawmaking authorities of a society, governing the relationships among individuals, and between individuals and their government.

law of demand: the law that states that when the price of an item declines, the demand for that item increases.

leader: the second interpersonal role a sport manager must fulfill, which involves directing subordinates toward the achievement of assigned tasks and may require the manager to hire, train, supervise, motivate, and evaluate employees in the workplace.

legal capacity: a person's capability and power under law to engage in a particular undertaking or transaction or to maintain a particular status or relationship with another.

Legal responsibilities: requirements for organizations to reach goals within legal constraints.

legality: adherence to or observance of the law.

legislature: an officially elected or otherwise selected body of people vested with the responsibility and power to make laws for a political unit, such as a state or nation.

levels of branding: the levels used to assess consumer enthusiasm or intensity toward a specific brand, starting with brand recognition and brand preference, on through to brand insistence and brand loyalty.

leveraging: developing an integrated plan that specifies the role promotional tools will play and the extent to which each will be used.

liaison: the third interpersonal role a sport manager must fulfill, which involves developing and cultivating relationships with individuals and groups in other departments or from different organizations.

lifestyle marketing: type of marketing technique in which the company attempts to cut through all the other selling messages by appealing to consumers who have or desire the lifestyle depicted in the sport sponsorship relationship.

limited duty: the limited responsibility of management to protect those involved in an event who are at risk for injury, such as the obligation of baseball franchises to protect their fans from foul balls.

Limited Liability Company (LLC): a business entity formed upon filing articles of organization with the proper state authorities and paying all fees, which provide the limited liability to their members and are taxed like a partnership, preventing double taxation.

linguistics: the study of the nature, structure, and variation of language, including phonetics, phonology, morphology, syntax, semantics, sociolinguistics, and pragmatics.

litigation: the process of filing a lawsuit so that a court can resolve the disagreement.

marginal cost: how much more an individual has to spend to get more of what he or she wants, without worrying about what already has been spent.

marketing objectives: the reasons or goals behind a particular promotion or marketing campaign which clearly identify the desired results.

mediation: the submission of a dispute to a disinterested third person who intervenes between the parties in an attempt to settle their dispute without going to court.

mediator: the third party in a mediation who communicates with all parties to the dispute, presents proposals from each party to the other, and facilitates resolution of the dispute, if possible.

message credibility: believability or trustworthiness associated specifically with the source and content of a message.

minors: in legal terms, persons under the age of 18.

mission statement: guidelines that outline the parameters for operating a venue and provide the basis for the development of goals and objectives for the venue.

monitor: an informational role filled by the sport manager in which he or she must search the internal and external environment for information that could affect the organization.

monopoly: a company or group having exclusive control over a commercial activity.

moral behavior: the execution of an act deemed right or wrong.

moral development: a process of growth in which a person's capacity to reason morally is developed through cognitive maturation and experiences.

moral reasoning: the decision process in which an individual determines whether a course of action is right or wrong.

morals: the fundamental baseline values that dictate appropriate behavior within a culture or society.

municipal bonds, or **munis:** bonds in the capital market issued by state and local governments to finance their capital spending programs for building arenas, stadiums, parking lots, and infrastructure upgrades, including roads, water/sewer, utility right of way, and other utility needs.

The bonds are issued by municipalities, subdivisions of states; they are tax exempt because the interest investors receive is exempt from federal taxation.

myopia: in sport marketing, the result of sport personnel focusing solely on the sport product and not considering the needs and wants of consumers.

myths: a popular belief or story that has become associated with a person, institution, or occurrence, especially one considered to illustrate a cultural ideal, which may often seem like fact but is not always the case.

National Governing Bodies (NGBs): respective organizations that develop sport on a national level; e.g., USA Track and Field.

National Olympic Committees (NOCs): individual countries representing the IOC that are responsible for promoting the Olympic Movement nationally, developing athletes, and sending delegations to the Games.

natural rights: rights that are not derived from any government, but are God-given and inherent to all people.

negligence: the failure to exercise ordinary care, or the degree of care that the law requires, by acting differently than a person of ordinary care would have acted under the same or similar circumstances.

negotiation: a process involving formal or informal discussions in order to reach an agreement.

negotiator: a decisional role filled by the sport manager in which he or she is responsible for conferring with employees and work groups located within the organization, as well as those that are on the outside.

NFL Europe: extension league created after the WLAF disbanded after two seasons, which was reintroduced in 1995 in European cities only; currently consists of six teams in the Netherlands, Germany, and Scotland.

noise: the collective dissonance caused by radio, television, internet, billboards, print advertisements, etc. that helps desensitize the consumer to all messages.

non-price promotions: publicity other than price promotions that are designed to make the activity or event more attractive and enjoyable to consumers, such as giveaways, fireworks, autograph signing sessions, and concerts.

non-variable cost: a cost that does not vary depending on production or sales levels, such as rent, property, insurance, or interest expense; also referred to as fixed cost.

objectives: the activities to be implemented to reach the overall goal, sometimes called action strategies.

observational studies: a data-gathering procedure used primarily in the psychology and sociology fields in which information is obtained by observing and recording subjects' behavior without their knowledge.

offer and acceptance: a process that involves the involved parties making a series of proposals to the other until the negotiations culminate with an agreement.

Office of Civil Rights (OCR): the division of the Department of Education that has been charged with enforcing Title IX, which is the law that prohibits sex discrimination in education agencies that receive federal funding.

Older Workers Benefit Protection Act of 1990 (OWBPA): amendment to the Americans with Disabilities Act of 1990 meant to include a focus on age discrimination and loss of workplace benefits. The OWBPA also provided for older worker protection in the area of protocol establishment that must be followed when employers are asked to waive their rights when filing settlement claims regarding age discrimination.

Olympic Games: a group of modern international athletic contests, revived in 1896 by Pierre de Coubertin, held as separate winter and summer competitions every four years in a different city.

Olympic Marketing Programme: the driving force for the financial stability of the Olympic Movement, which produces revenues through broadcasting rights, sponsorship, ticketing, licensing, and other means.

The Olympic Movement: the term used to refer to the incomparable growth of international exposure, worldwide audience appeal, and multicultural activities that draw the attention of virtually every demographic of the Olympic Games.

The Olympic Program (TOP): introduced for the first time in the 1984 Los Angeles Olympic Games, this program, operated by the IOC, handles Olympic sponsorship agreements and gives sponsors exclusive rights to associate with the Olympic Games and use all Olympic properties.

operating expense: expense arising in the normal course of running a business, such as an office electricity bill.

opportunity cost: what one gives up in turn for obtaining what one wants.

Organizing Committee of the Olympic Games (OCOG): formed once a city is awarded the honor and responsibility of hosting the Olympic and Paralympic Games, its role is to handle all operational aspects of the Games and to ultimately put on the events.

over-commercialization: the overwhelming presence of commercial business, marketing, etc. that may be so saturated as to deter consumers.

paid internships: a paid appointment in which the individual undergoes supervised practical training for future employment.

participant-oriented organizations: organizations often managed by individuals with very specialized skill sets, such as municipal parks, YMCAs, recreation departments, collegiate recreation settings, and special events.

partnership: a company owned by two or more individuals who have entered into an agreement.

perception: recognition and interpretation of sensory stimuli based chiefly on memory.

personal credibility: believability or trustworthiness associated specifically with a person or organization's character or past actions.

philanthropic responsibilities: requirement for organizations to give back to their communities.

planning: formulating a scheme or program for the accomplishment or attainment of a specific goal.

postconventional: the third of Kohlberg's three stages of moral reasoning, in which the individual's values are formed independently of social norms.

pouring rights: the exclusive ability to sell soft drinks, bottled water, and beer in a facility.

precedent: a judicial decision that may be used as a standard in subsequent similar cases.

preconventional: the first of Kohlberg's three stages of moral reasoning, which is characterized by a separation between conventions and the individual.

The Pregnancy Discrimination Act: an amendment to Title VII of the Civil Rights Act of 1964, which provides protection against pregnancy-based discrimination including pregnancy, childbirth, and pregnancy-related medical conditions.

present value: the value of what a cash flow to be received in the future is worth in today's dollars.

price promotions: type of publicity in which the actual cost of consuming an event is manipulated or lowered to encourage people to attend.

primary skills: in sport management terms, these are the skills necessary to direct employees towards the achievement of established goals and objectives, without which a sport manager would be ineffective.

private law: law that governs the relationship among private citizens.

private seat licenses (PSLs): an amenity offered at certain venues in which the purchaser obtains exclusive use of his or her own private seat(s).

pro forma statements: statements based on hypothetical figures used as a means of assessing how assets might be managed under differing future scenarios.

procedural law: the method of enforcing rights and obligations given to citizens by substantive law.

product adoption process: an extension of the AIDA concept that awareness builds interest and knowledge of a brand's associated benefits, which in effect, creates an image in the mind of the consumer.

product purchase intentions: a key sales objective that is most often measured to assess consumers' tendencies and perceptions when buying certain products.

products liability: liability imposed on a manufacturer or seller for a defective and unreasonably dangerous product.

proxemics: the study of how an individual communicates through their use of space.

psychographics: the use of demographics to study and measure attitudes, values, lifestyles, and opinions, as for marketing purposes; often refer to consumers' state-of-mind, exploring the likes and dislikes of consumers and using the similarities to create the segments.

psychological: of, relating to, or arising from the mind or emotions.

public assembly facilities: assembly halls, conference centers, stadiums, arenas, etc. which are available to fulfill the needs of public meetings, conventions, and conferences, as well as host a number of different events such as athletic contests, concerts, conventions, and trade shows.

public good: the well-being of the general public.

public law: law that governs the relationship between citizens and their government.

public relations: a program designed to influence the opinions of people within a target market through responsible and acceptable performance, based on mutually satisfactory two-way communication.

racism: discrimination or prejudice based on race.

reasonably prudent person standard: standard applied by the court that will determine if the defendant acted as a reasonably prudent person would have acted under the same or similar circumstances.

recall: the ability of a spectator to remember and correctly identify a sponsor's brand without input or prompting.

recognition: the ability of a spectator to correctly identify the brand of a sponsor from a list.

Recreational Use statutes: legislation that provides liability protection to owners and operators of recreational facilities by placing responsibility for injury on the participant who voluntarily assumed the risk; the statues cover activities such as equestrian activities, snow skiing, roller skating, whitewater rafting, snowmobiling, amusement rides, and, in a few cases, provides protection for "any sport or recreational opportunity."

reflective learning: an educational philosophy meant to engage one's knowledge about the world and others critically and analytically, including self-assessment of teaching goals, responsibilities, and effectiveness.

regional multiplier: the value multiplied by direct spending to estimate total spending, or economic benefit, which is used to measure how many times money changes hands in the community before it leaves or leaks out of the region.

relational: of or arising from kinship; indicating or constituting relation.

renewal: the act of restoring or resuming a contract.

request for proposal (RFP): an invitation for providers of a product or service to bid on the right to supply that product or service to the individual or entity that issued the RFP.

resource allocator: a decisional role filled by a sport manager in which he or she distributes organizational resources to different employees or work groups.

return on investment: the income that an investment provides in a year.

revenue bonds: bond issued by a municipality to finance a specific public works project and supported by the revenues of that project.

revenue budget: a calculation of projected future revenue used to make planning and management decisions.

risk management: the process to reduce or limit risk exposure in a venue.

risk management plan: a document defining how reducing or limiting risk exposure will be implemented in the context of a particular project.

Robert's Rules of Order: procedures that assure legislative fairness, maximum participation, and an orderly process by participants, while protecting individuals from domination by certain vocal subgroups.

S Corporation: a C Corporation—also known as a standard business corporation—that files IRS form 2553 to elect a special tax status with the IRS.

Scalar Principle: principle referring to the Chain of Command that denotes a clear line of authority from the top to the bottom of the organization.

scheduling: the reservation process and coordination of all events to the venue's available time.

screening: to examine (a job applicant, for example) systematically in order to determine suitability.

segmentation: the process of dividing large, unlike groups of consumers into smaller, more defined groups of people who share similar characteristics.

semantics: the meaning or interpretation of a word and/or sentence.

semi-variable cost: a cost that has a fixed cost component and a variable expense component.

sexism: discrimination based on gender.

sexual harassment: employment discrimination consisting of unwelcome verbal or physical conduct directed at an employee because of his or her sex.

Sherman Antitrust Act: an 1890 federal antitrust law intended to control or prohibit monopolies by forbidding certain practices that restrain competition.

simple interest: the interest calculated on a principal sum, not compounded on earned interest.

situational approach: in the study of leadership (also referred to as 'contingency theories'), this approach resulted in an understanding that the traits and behaviors identified previously would only be successful to the degree to which any particular situation allowed; intervening, or moderating, factors were considered in this approach.

social institution: any place where there is a set of rules for behavior; examples include churches, colleges, and places of business.

sociodemographic: of or relating to characteristics of a particular group or demographic, such as certain age groups, people of the same income levels, gender, etc.

sociolinguistics: the impact that differing social and/or cultural groups have on the meaning and interpretation of language.

sociological analysis: thorough examination of a social institution or societal segment as a self-contained entity or in relation to society as a whole.

sole proprietorship: a company owned by one person.

sovereign immunity: an exemption that precludes bringing a suit against the sovereign state without the state's consent; often known by the maxim "the king can do no wrong."

Span of Management: principle that refers to the number of employees reporting to a specific manager.

spokesperson: an informational role filled by the sport manager in which he or she communicates information to groups that are outside the organization.

sponsorship: the provision of resources (e.g., money, people, equipment) by an organization (the sponsor) directly to an individual, authority or body (the sponsee), to enable the latter to pursue some activity in return for benefits contemplated in terms of the sponsor's promotion strategy, and which can be expressed in terms of corporate, marketing, or media objectives.

sponsorship activation: the idea that for every dollar spent on a sponsorship fee, an equivalent dollar is typically spent in the promotion of the sponsorship.

sport sociologist: one who studies human social behavior in sport, including the analysis of sport as an industry, the political and cultural implications of sport, sport and globalization, the relationship between gender, class and economics, deviance in sport, and the social organization of sport.

sport sociology: the method of analyzing sport from a cultural perspective that concerns itself mainly with how humans relate to each other in the sport context, how values affect these relationships, and how humans organize sport activities.

sportsmanship: conduct and attitude considered as befitting participants in sports, especially fair play, courtesy, striving spirit, and grace in losing.

standard: a requirement of moral conduct.

state action: an action in which the State federal or state government is responsible for the specific conduct of which the plaintiff complains.

state court system: court systems that generally hear matters that occur within the boundaries of the state, and involve disputes that involve state law.

statement of cash flow: a financial statement that shows the sources and uses of cash for a business over a certain period of time.

statutes: particular laws passed by the U.S. Congress, or a state legislature, which declare, command, or prohibit some conduct, or require citizens to act in a certain manner.

step cost: a recurring or non-recurring expense for goods and services that are either non-essential or more expensive than necessary; examples include entertainment expenses, wellness program, and speakers; also referred to as discretionary expense.

strict liability: liability that is imposed without a finding of fault.

substantive law: the law that defines, describes, or creates legal rights and obligations.

Super League: a proposal, also referred to as G-14, offered by the European football (soccer) industry to come closer to the American model, which would include football giants like Ajax Amsterdam, Manchester United, AC Milan, and Real Madrid.

supply: the quantity of a product that an owner is willing to offer or make available at a given price.

Supreme Court: the highest federal court in the United States, consisting of nine justices and having jurisdiction over all other courts in the nation.

surveys: paper forms used to gather a sample of data or opinions considered to be representative of a whole group, sometimes referred to as questionnaires.

symbiotic: a relationship of mutual benefit or dependence.

target market: the group of people at which all marketing efforts are aimed.

technical skills: in sport management terms, these skills involve a knowledge of operations, activities, and processes necessary to accomplish organizational goals and objectives.

teleology: a doctrine explaining phenomena by their ends or purposes; a focus on the consequences of an action.

terminal values: in ethical theory, the ends toward which one is striving.

time-switchers: people who plan to attend an event, but cancel or change time in order to attend to something else.

timetable: a chart used to provide the schedule of tasks and when they need to be completed; can be seen as a countdown to an event.

time value of money: the idea that a dollar now is worth more than dollar in the future, even after adjusting for inflation, because a dollar now can earn interest or other appreciation until the time the dollar in the future would be received.

Title VII: law passed in 1964 that protects employees and prospective employees from discrimination by making it unlawful for an employer to discriminate against a person in employment activities (i.e., hiring, firing, compensation, promotion, classification), based on race, color, religion, sex, or national origin; formally referred to as Title VII of the Civil Rights Act of 1964.

Title IX: law passed in 1972 as part of the Educational Amendments Act that prohibits sex discrimination in education agencies that receive federal funding; formally referred to Title IX of the Education Amendments of 1972.

TOP sponsors: companies that have been granted a four-year contract deal with The Olympic Partner Programme that includes both the Summer and Winter Games; they are granted the right to Olympic affiliation in every participating country with worldwide exclusivity in their product category.

tort: a civil wrong—other than a breach of contract—for which an injured party can recover damages.

tort claims acts: statues in which the state has agreed to accept liability for certain tort claims.

tortfeasor: a person who commits a tort.

trademark: word, phrase, logo, or other graphic symbol used by a manufacturer to distinguish its product from those of others.

trait theories: some of the earliest systematic attempts to conceptualize leadership, these approaches focused on the characteristics, or attributes, that distinguished leaders from non-leaders; traits under investigation included physical characteristics (e.g., height, appearance), personality traits (e.g., arrogance, self-esteem), and general ability traits (e.g., intelligence, insight, energy).

trial court: the court before which issues of fact and law are tried and first determined as distinguished from an appellate court.

UEFA Champions League: the Union of European Football Associations' football (soccer) league that is open to each national association's domestic champions, as well as clubs who finish just behind them in the domestic championship table.

UEFA Cup: championship title of the UEFA Champions League.

Uniform Athlete Agents Act: act that provides for the uniform registration, certification, and background check of sports agents seeking to represent student athletes who are or may be eligible to participate in intercollegiate sports; also imposes specified contract terms on these agreements to the benefit of student athletes, and provides education institutions with a right to notice along with a civil cause of action for damages resulting from a breach of specified duties.

Unity of Command: principle that states that an employee should only have one boss to which he or she reports.

U.S. Congress: the national legislative body of the United States, consisting of the Senate and the House of Representatives.

U.S. Constitution: the fundamental law of the United States, framed in 1787, ratified in 1789, and variously amended since then, which prescribes the nature, functions, and limits of the government.

U.S. District Courts: courts that operate essentially the same as state trial courts, providing a trial of the case before a judge and jury; also called federal trial courts. There are 94 throughout the U.S., with at least one located in every state.

utilitarianism: an ethical theory whereby morality is assessed by whether or not the action creates the greatest good for the greatest number of people.

variable expenses: unavoidable periodic cost that does not have a constant value, such as electric, gas, and water bills.

verdict: the finding of a jury in a trial.

vertical integration: the degree to which a firm owns its upstream suppliers and its downstream buyers.

Volunteer Protection Act: act that provides protection to volunteers, employees, and the volunteer organization itself, so long as the organization has insurance in the amount required by the statute to cover losses sustained by injured participants.

waived: given up; relinquished.

warranty: a promise or guarantee that products will comply with a certain standard.

welfare: health, happiness, and good fortune; well-being.

word of mouth: advertising through personal recommendations amongst consumers.

workmen's compensation: compensation for death or injury suffered by a worker in the course of his or her employment.

World Cup of Hockey: an international ice hockey tournament, introduced in 2004 in four European cities and three North American cities, which included eight of the world's ice hockey powerhouses.

World League of American Football (WLAF): extension league introduced in 1991 that provided a platform for the NFL to showcase the game of American Football to those outside the U.S., especially in Europe.

Writ of Certiorari: a common law writ issued by a superior court to one of inferior jurisdiction demanding the record of a particular case.

Index

Sampson, David, 1
"sanity code," 149
Santa Fe Independent School District v. Doe, 130, 135
Scalar Principle, 146, 218
Schaaf, Phil, 176
scheduling, 117, 218
Scherr, Jim, 151
Schlager, Tammy, 186
Schultz, Howard, 85
Scott, Mary E., 186
screening, 189, 218
segmentation, 91, 218
Selig, Bud, 174
semantics, 23, 218
semi-variable cost, 79, 218
sexism, 15, 218
sexual harrassment, 190, 218
Sherman Antitrust Act, 136, 218
simple interest, 79-80, 218
situational approach. *See* leadership
SLEEPE model, 43-44
SMARTS, 5
Smith, Aaron, 170
Smith, Red, 112
Smith, R. K., 126
SMPRC, 6
Sobek, Joe, 147
social institution, 12, 218
sociodemographic, 122, 218
sociolinguistics, 23, 218
sociological analysis, 12, 218
sole proprietorship, 70, 218
Solomon, Jerry, 120
sovereign immunity, 137, 218
span of management, 146, 218
spokesperson, 45, 218
sponsorship, 72-74, 100-101, 218
    activation, 107, 218
Sport Business in the Global Marketplace (Westerbeek & Smith), 170
sport facility and event management
    event management—the process, 120-121
    facility/venue management, 112-114
    location, facilities, and equipment, 121-122

public and media relations, 117-119
types of venues, 114-115
venue operations, 116-117
venue organization, 115-116
sport governance
    importance of, 144-152
        professional sport organizations, 151-152
        the "how," 146-147
        the "what," 144-145
        the "when," 147
        the "where," 152
        the "who," 145-146
        the "why," 145
sport industry, unique aspects of
    career paths, 7
    customer base (fans), 8
    finance, 7
    marketing, 7
    social influence of sport, 7-8
    sport venues, 8
sport law. *See* law
sport management
    problems with the name, 6-7
    why it matters, 11-18
Sport Management Arts and Sciences Society (SMARTS), 6
Sport Management Program Review Council (SMPRC), 6
sport marketing
    definition of, 84-85
    role of research, 91-92
    the four P's, 86-91
sport sociologists, 12, 218
    what areas they investigate, 14-15
sport sociology, 14, 218-219
sports information outputs, 29
sports journalism, 29-30
sportsmanship, 163, 219
standard, 138, 219
Stark, Joan S., 186
state action, 135, 219
state court system, 132-133, 219
statues, 131, 219
step cost, 79, 219
Stern, David, 85
Stotlar, David, 100, 121
strict liability, 138, 219
Super League. *See* G-14

supply and demand. *See* economics
Supreme Court, 133
"Supreme Law of the Land," 131
surveys, 17, 219
Sutton, William A., 84, 85, 106
Suzuki, Ichiro, 174
symbiotic, 100, 219

T

Tagliabue, Paul, 176
target market, 100, 219
technical skills, 41, 219
teleology, 157, 219
The Agent Game (Garvey), 140
"The Apprentice," 36
The Nature of Human Values (Rokeach), 157
ticket revenue, 71-72
time-switchers, 61, 219
timetable, 120, 219
time value of money, 79, 80, 219
Title VII, 136
    definition of, 15, 16, 219
    myths about it, 13
Title IX, 136
    definition of, 15, 219
    myths about it, 13
TiVo, 28
Tollefson, Jeff, 62
TOP sponsors, 101, 219
tort, 138, 220
    claims act, 137, 220
    intentional, 138, 213
tortfeasor, 138, 220
trademark, 137, 220
trait theories, 47, 220
trial court, 132, 220
Tribune Company, 68
Tschauner, Peggy R., 43
Twain, Mark, 186, 187

U

Ueberroth, Peter, 151
UEFA
    Championship League, 178, 220
    Cup, 178, 220
Uniform Athlete Agents Act, 137, 220
United States Olympic Committee (USOC), 150-151

unity of command, 146, 220
U.S. Constitution, 128, 220
U.S. District Courts, 133, 220
Useem, M., 187
utilitarianism, 157, 220

V

values
  instrumental, 157, 213
  terminal, 157, 219
  See also ethics
variable expenses, 79, 220
variable pricing, 71
Van Fleet, David D., 48
Van Horn, C. E., 187
Veeck, Bill, 164
verdict, 132, 220
vertical integration, 68, 220
Volunteer Protection Act, 138,
  220

W

waived, 137, 220
Walker, M. L., 121
Walt Disney Company, 68, 75,
  148
warranty, 139, 220
Wayne, John, 86
Weber, Max, 49
Weiss, Maureen R., 160
welfare, 163, 220
Westerbeek, Hans, 170
Wie, Michelle, 105
Williams, George, 147
Wolf, Eli A., 43-44
Wong, Glenn M., 148
Wooden, John, 13
Woods, Tiger, 166
word of mouth, 107, 220
workmen's compensation, 190,
  220
World Cup of Hockey, 176, 220
World League of American
  Football (WLAF), 176, 220
Wright, Frank Lloyd, 121
Writ of Certiorari, 133, 220

X

X-Games, 102-103

Y

Young Men's Christian Academy
  (YMCA), 147
Yukl, Gary A., 48, 50, 51

Z

Zimbalist, Andrew, 63
Zinn, Lorraine M., 161

About the Editors

Andy Gillentine is an associate professor and coordinator of the Sport Administration Program at the University of Miami. His research interests are sport marketing, professional development, and management issues in sport theory. He served as athletic director and coach for over 15 years and as Executive Director of MAHPERD. Dr. Gillentine is recognized for his expertise in sport management curriculum and program development. He served on the Sport Management Program Review Council Executive Board for three years and frequently serves as a consultant in this area. He also served as Chair of the National Sport Management Council (AAHPERD). He has conducted marketing research projects for the Ladies Professional Golf Association; the NASDAQ 100-Open; World Championship Wrestling, Inc.; and the Mississippi Coaches Association. Dr. Gillentine's work has resulted in forty publications and over 90 national and international presentations. His combination of practical and research experience provides students with a well-rounded academic and personal development for a career in the Sport Industry.

R. Brian Crow is currently in his 4th year as Associate Professor of Sport Management in the Department of Sport Management at Slippery Rock University, where he teaches Sport Marketing and Sport Communication at the undergraduate level and Sport Marketing and Sport Budget and Finance in the graduate program. He is presently the President of the North American Society for Sport Management (NASSM). Prior to this election, Crow was NASSM's Business Office Manager for two years and a Member-at-Large on the Executive Council. Crow recently ended his three-year tenure as Editor-in-Chief of the *Sport Marketing Quarterly*, a publication for which he presently serves as a member of the Editorial Review Board. As Editor of *SMQ*, Crow was a founding board member of the Sport Marketing Association. In 2005, Crow started a sport marketing and fan consultation company, *GameDay Consulting, LLC*, a firm specializing in the training, certification, and monitoring of gameday employees at sport venues.. Current clients include the Buffalo Bills. Dr. Crow currently is an educational consultant for Nike Grassroots Basketball and the Nike All-America basketball camp, and served as a strategy consultant for SOKOL USA. Crow has done research for the Nokia Sugar Bowl, the Black Sports Agents Association, and the Mississippi Sea Wolves (ECHL).

About the Authors

Artemisia Apostolopoulou is an assistant professor in the Sport Management Program at Bowling Green State University. She teaches sport marketing at the undergraduate and graduate level. Her area of research involves brand extension strategies implemented by sport organizations. Her secondary research interests include sponsorship and endorsement issues. She has presented work in numerous national and international conferences, and her publications have appeared in *Sport Marketing Quarterly* and the *International Journal of Sport Marketing and Sponsorship.*

Paul Batista is an assistant professor at Texas A & M University. He received his B.S. from Trinity University in 1973 and his J.D. from Baylor Law School in 1976. Professor Batista is licensed to practice law before the U.S. Supreme Court and all Texas courts, and previously served as County Judge of Burleson County, Texas. He has taught sport law at Texas A & M since 1991 and has received numerous teaching excellence awards. He is a member of the Sport and Recreation Law Association and serves on the Editorial Board of the *Journal of Legal Aspects of Sport.* His primary research interest is sports related liability issues in schools.

Matt Bernthal received his Ph.D. in marketing from the University of South Carolina, where he now serves as associate professor in the Sport and Entertainment Management Department. Bernthal teaches numerous courses related to sport and entertainment marketing and serves as Graduate Director for USC's Master's of Sport and Entertainment Management program. His research has appeared in the *Journal of Consumer Research, Sport Marketing Quarterly, Journal of Nonprofit and Public Sector Marketing, School Psychology International, Journal of Sport Behavior,* and other journals. He also consults with numerous firms in the sport and entertainment industry.

Cheri Bradish is entering her ninth year as an assistant professor of sport management at Brock University, responsible for the sport marketing and sponsorship course offerings. While at Brock, she has served as the Chair of the Department of Sport Management, and currently is a member of the University Board of Senate. Bradish earned both her Ph.D. and M.S. in Sport Management from Florida State University. She has presented and published at over thirty related international forums. She has also held positions in the Communications Department with the NBA's Vancouver Grizzlies and with the Sport Marketing Department at Nike Canada.

Dallas D. Branch, Jr., has been teaching for the past sixteen years in the graduate and undergraduate Sport Management Program at West Virginia University, where he served as the program's coordinator for eight of those years and, in 1992, developed the *Sport Marketing Quarterly (SMQ),* a professional sport marketing journal. In 1994, Dr. Branch was selected as one of 3 charter members of the NASSM/NASPE Sport Management Council (SMC), and was also selected to serve a 3-year appointment as a member of the Sport Management Program Review Council. He served nationally as the Sport Management Council's Program Planner for the 1996 AAHPERD National Convention in Atlanta, Georgia, and was selected in 1996 to become one of seven Resident Faculty Leaders (RFLs), part of the WVU President's Operation Jump-Start initiative in freshmen residence halls. Dr. Branch and his wife Jeannine have three stepchildren and three grandchildren.

Matthew T. Brown is an associate professor at the University of South Carolina. Previously he held positions as associate professor and undergraduate coordinator in the Division of Sports Administration at Ohio University. He received his B.A. in political science from Truman State University, his M.S. in sport management from Western Illinois University, and his Ed.D. from the University of Northern Colorado in sport administration. Prior to pursuing his doctorate, Dr. Brown worked in campus recreation, collegiate athletics, and tennis club management. At Ohio, he taught sport finance, quantitative analysis in sport, and research seminar. Dr. Brown currently is investigating financial management in professional sport.

John Clark is an assistant professor of Sport Management in the Marketing and Management Department of the Robert Morris University School of Business. He has conducted and published research in the areas of relationship marketing, sport sales, sociological implications of corporate marketing efforts, sponsorship sales and processes, cause related marketing programs, service quality in various industries, and customer loyalty/customer retention in professional sport franchises. John has conducted customer-oriented market research consulting projects for many major and minor league sport organizations, as well as other organizations in the leisure/sport entertainment industry.

Bernie Goldfine is a professor at Kennesaw State University. He has taught a variety of undergraduate and graduate courses throughout his ten years in higher education, including venue and event management. Additionally, Dr. Goldfine oversaw the operations and management of a wide variety of facilities and events in his 13 years as a high school athletic director. He has completed numerous presentations and articles for publication at the state, national, and international levels, as well as contributed to textbooks on facility and event management. Dr. Goldfine received his Bachelor of Arts from the University of California, Santa Barbara, and his Master of Arts and Ph.D. from the University of Southern California.

T. Christopher Greenwell is an assistant professor at the University of Louisville. He holds a Ph.D. in Sport Management from The Ohio State University, an M. S. in Sport Management from Georgia Southern University, and a B.B.A. from McKendree College. He teaches in the areas of sport marketing, sport publicity, and event management. He has had recent articles published in the *International Journal of Sport Management, Sport Management Review, Contemporary Athletics,* and *Sport Marketing Quarterly.*

Catriona Higgs is a professor in the Sport Management Department at Slippery Rock University. She is a sport sociologist who specializes in research on gender relations in sport. She has edited or co-edited over 90 national and international presentations, and written numerous publications on issues ranging from coverage of women in sport by the media, to a socio-

historical analyses of the All American Girls' Professional Baseball League, to gender equity issues at the elementary school level. Her latest publications have appeared in the *Women in Sport and Physical Activity Journal, The Canadian Journal of the History of Sport, The Journal of Sport and Social Issues, Nine: A Journal of Baseball Policy and Social Perspectives,* and the *Sport Sociology Journal.*

Jeremy S. Jordan is an assistant professor in the Sport Administration Program at the University of Miami. His research focuses on organizational behavior and human resource management issues within sport organizations. Specifically, examination of the influence of organizational justice on employee attitudes and behaviors demonstrated in the workplace. He teaches courses in management, organizational behavior, and legal issues in sport. Published manuscripts have appeared in the *International Journal of Sport Management, International Sports Journal, Physical Educator,* and the *Journal of Applied Research in Coaching and Athletics.*

Aubrey Kent is an associate professor in the Sport Management Program at Florida State University. His primary areas of interest are leadership and organizational behavior within sport organizations. He teaches courses in management and the current issues facing the sport industry. His published work includes articles in the *Journal of Sport Management, The European Journal of Sport Management, Sport Marketing Quarterly, The Journal of Park and Recreation Administration, The International Sports Journal,* and *The Journal of Applied Sport Psychology.* He currently lives in Tallahassee, Florida, with his wife Courtenay and their daughter Madeline.

Nancy Lough is an associate professor with the University of New Mexico Sport Administration Graduate Program. She has worked in sport extensively, with experience as a collegiate coach, athletic administrator, and consultant. Dr. Lough's research has focused on corporate sponsorship, marketing of women's sport and women's leadership in sport, as evidenced by numerous national presentations and publications. She has consulted with various sport organizations including the LPGA, NACWAA, and the Native American Sports Council. Similarly, Dr. Lough has contributed to the sport management field through involvement with NASSM, NACWAA, NAGWS, SMA, and the Sport Management Program Review Council.

Betsy McKinley, an associate professor, has been teaching PETE methods classes and supervising student teachers at Slippery Rock University since 1995. In addition to numerous state activities, Dr. McKinley serves as an educational consultant for the Pennsylvania Department of Education and school districts in numerous states. Her research interests focus on H/PE pedagogy, standards-based health and physical education teaching, and creating a socially responsive pedagogy in the H/PE classroom. Dr. McKinley has presented nationally and internationally at numerous conferences and publishes extensively.

John Miller is an associate professor at Texas Tech University. He coached at the intercollegiate level for 16 years and is recognized for his expertise in several sport management related issues including student internships. He has been instrumental in the development and implementation of the graduate internship experience at Texas Tech as well as teaching Legal Aspects of Sport, Sport Facility Design and Management, Sport Leadership, and Sport Marketing. His areas of research include legal aspects of sport and recreation, sport facility design and management, and sport management education.

Debra Ann Pace is a professor of Sport and Leisure Studies in the University of Nevada Las Vegas' William F. Harrah College of Hotel Administration, where she teaches courses in sport and recreation management in the Department of Tourism and Convention Administration. Debra formerly taught in the Division of Sport Administration at Ohio University. Dr. Pace is a graduate of Boston University (B.S. and M.Ed.), where she earned degrees in Human Movement, and The Ohio State University (Ph.D.), where she earned her doctorate in Sport and Exercise Management. Her research interests include youth sport and mentoring.

Dimitra Papadimitriou teaches in the Department of Business Management at the University of Patras, Greece. Her research interests include organizational performance of national sport governing bodies and local sports clubs, as well as nonprofit board effectiveness. In addition, she is involved in multi-disciplinary research in the areas of volunteer management, brand management, and Olympic sponsorship. She has published in *Sport Management Review, European Journal of Sport Management, Sport Marketing Quarterly,* the

International Journal of Sports Marketing & Sponsorship, and *Managing Leisure,* and has presented her work in numerous national and international conferences.

Dennis Phillips has been a college professor and administrator for 24 years, the past 13 at the University of Southern Mississippi. He is currently the Associate Director of the School of Human Performance and Recreation at USM. He has also been the Graduate Coordinator for the School of HP & R, a college assistant athletic director at Springfield College, and assistant director of marketing and special events for the Volleyball Hall of Fame. He has been the President of the Mississippi State AAHPERD organization, Chair of both the Athletic Council and Sport Management Councils of the Southern District of AAHPERD, and on the Executive Boards of the National Council on Accreditation of Coaching Education (NCACE) and The Sport Law and Recreation Association (SLRA). Dr. Phillips has been an active member and presenter at the North American Society of Sport Management (NASSM) and SLRA for many years, and has been a reviewer of both organizations' presentation proposals. He has written two chapters in *Law for Recreation and Sport* Managers, one chapter on *Legal Issues of Hazing in Sport,* and is co-author of the book *Profiles of Sport Industry Professionals.* He currently serves on the Governor's Commission on Physical Activity and Sport in Mississippi.

Tom Regan is the Chairman of the Department of Sport and Entertainment Management at the University of South Carolina. Research emphasis focuses on the economic impact of sport and entertainment events on regional economies and the financing and feasibility of live entertainment events. He has completed numerous studies on professional, collegiate, and touring sports. Publications have highlighted his work on the Denver Broncos Football Club, the University of South Carolina athletic department, NASCAR, golf in South Carolina, USTA and WTA professional tennis, and other studies involving live entertainment. He was invited to the Brookings Institute to discuss the impact of professional sport facilities on regional economies. He has consulted with many professional organizations concerning financing venues and determining the economic benefit of facilities, events and teams. Dr. Regan's education experience includes Bachelor and Master of Accounting degrees from the University of Wyoming and a Doctorate degree in Sports Administration at the University of Northern Colorado.

Lynn Ridinger is an assistant professor of sport management at Old Dominion University in Norfolk, Virginia. Her research interests include consumer behavior and involvement with women's sports. Dr. Ridinger teaches courses in sport marketing, sport administrative theory, event planning, sport psychology, and research methods. She is an alumna of The Ohio State University (Ph.D.), Kent State University (M.A.), and Central Michigan University (B.S.). Prior to pursuing her doctorate, Dr. Ridinger worked as a high school athletic director and coach.

Thomas H. Sawyer is a professor of physical education and recreation and sport management at Indiana State University. He has been in higher education since 1969 and has been a department head, department chair, director, and acting dean as well as a collegiate coach and associate athletic director. Dr. Sawyer has been engaged in scholarly work for his entire career. He has had published 116 peer reviewed articles, 29 articles for compensation, authored or co-authored four chapters in four textbooks, and authored, co-authored, or edited nine books. He has made over 175 professional presentations at state, regional, national, and international conferences. Dr. Sawyer was elected as a fellow to the North American Society for Health, Physical Education, Recreation, Sport, and Dance Professionals.

David Matthew Zuefle is on the Park and Recreation Management faculty at the University of Mississippi in Oxford. He earned his Ph.D. from Texas A & M University and his main scholarly interests include outdoor recreation and education, recreation and tourism development, and environmental attitudes. Dr. Zuefle is the Book Review Editor and an Associate Editor for the journal *Schole* and writes a semi-regular column for the weekly newspaper *Oxford Town*. He also has just finished work on a book of essays about Appalachia and the South.